Electronic Inspirations

THE NEW
CULTURAL
HISTORY
OF MUSIC

Electronic Inspirations

Technologies of the Cold War Musical Avant-Garde

JENNIFER
IVERSON

OXFORD
UNIVERSITY PRESS

UNIVERSITY PRESS

Oxford University Press is a department of the University of Oxford. It furthers
the University's objective of excellence in research, scholarship, and education
by publishing worldwide. Oxford is a registered trade mark of Oxford University
Press in the UK and certain other countries.

Published in the United States of America by Oxford University Press
198 Madison Avenue, New York, NY 10016, United States of America.

Library of Congress Cataloging-in-Publication Data
Names: Iverson, Jennifer, author.
Title: Electronic inspirations : technologies of the Cold War musical avant-garde / Jennifer Iverson.
Description: New York, NY : Oxford University Press, 2018. |
Series: New cultural history of music series | Includes bibliographical references and index.
Identifiers: LCCN 2018006765 | ISBN 9780190868192 (hardcover : alk. paper) |
ISBN 9780190868208 (pbk. : alk. paper)
Subjects: LCSH: Electronic music—20th century—History and criticism. |
Westdeutscher Rundfunk. Studio umlaut: Elektronische Musik.
Classification: LCC ML1380.I84 2018 | DDC 786.709/045—dc23
LC record available at https://lccn.loc.gov/2018006765

This volume is published with the generous support of the AMS 75 PAYS Endowment of the
American Musicological Society, funded in part by the National Endowment for the Humanities and the
Andrew W. Mellon Foundation.

For Della and Ian: dream it.

*Don't stop after beating the swords
into ploughshares, don't stop! Go on beating
and make musical instruments out of them.
Whoever wants to make war again
will have to turn them into ploughshares first.*

—Yehuda Amichai, *"An appendix to the vision of peace"*

CONTENTS

ACKNOWLEDGMENTS

Once I articulated "invisible collaboration" as a central theme of this book, I began to see it everywhere. My own work is deeply and immeasurably enriched by the collaborative encounters that define my scholarship. In researching this book, I have spent considerable time in European archives, foremost among them the Paul Sacher Foundation in Basel—the city I call my second home. While I am there and while I am not, I am grateful for the attentive guidance of Heidy Zimmermann, Matthias Kassel, Angela Ida de Benedictis, Michèle Noirjean-Linder, Evelyne Diendorf, and Isolde Degen. At the WDR Historical Archive in Cologne, I benefited from the help of Jutta Lambrecht, Petra Witting-Noethen, and Maria Lutze. At the Stockhausen Foundation in Kürten, I am grateful for the significant assistance of Maria Lukas, Suzanne Stephens-Janning, and the always responsive Kathinka Pasveer. Several copyright holders have generously given permission to publish archival materials, including the Amichai family, the Nono family, the Xenakis family, the Pousseur family, and the Berio family. I have benefited much from sustained interactions with European interlocutors who know midcentury electronic music inside and out, including Kees Tazelaar, Pascal Decroupet, and Elena Ungeheuer. I have especially enjoyed many conversations with Gottfried Michael Koenig, who generously shared his insider experience and deepened my understanding of everything from the techniques to the politics of the studio.

I began working on this project in fits and starts at the University of Iowa, where the support of David Gier (now at University of Michigan) and the mentoring of Christine Getz and Jennifer Sessions helped me toward a crystalized idea. I learned so much in conversations and continuing study with my then-junior colleagues, including Matthew Arndt, Nicole Biamonte (now at McGill), Bob Cook, Trevor Harvey, and Nathan Platte. I remain so grateful for the way they each helped me grow as a scholar and as a person.

Writing the manuscript at the Stanford Humanities Center was a dream come true. It was a privilege to work in the company of a generous, welcoming staff and so many brilliant scholars, who were unfailingly warm, supportive, and encouraging. We shared lunches and happy hours, unfolding our scholarship and our lives. Several Stanford faculty members, including Charles Kronengold, Carol Vernallis, Anna Schultz (now at University of Chicago), Jesse Rodin, and Fred Turner remain fantastic interlocutors and treasured friends.

The University of Chicago is an enormously enriching intellectual home, and I could not be more grateful to have landed here. I have benefited from conversations with brilliant graduate students; from the advice, ideas, and encouragement of *all* of my colleagues; and from immersion in a milieu where the humanities still matter. Several of my colleagues, including Seth Brodsky, Philip Bohlman, Berthold Hoeckner, Steven Rings, and Lawrence Zbikowski, have read my work carefully and improved it with crucial questions and penetrating insights. I am fortunate to have the camaraderie of a new faculty cohort, which includes Sam Pluta, Catherine Kearns, Tom Pashby, and Emily Austin; Jessica Swanston Baker's sage friendship has been a saving grace on more than one occasion.

I have enjoyed presenting portions of this work—and receiving engaged feedback—in colloquia at several institutions, including University of Wisconsin, the Stanford Humanities Center, the Stanford Music Department, CCRMA, Mills College, University of California Santa Barbara, Stony Brook University, Northwestern University, and Harvard University. Likewise, I am very grateful for the comments and improvements suggested by those who read all or part of the manuscript: Amy Beal, William Cheng, Eric Drott, Jane Fulcher, James Gardner, Peter Gillette, Jonathan Goldman, Katherine Kaiser, Mara Mills, Benjamin Piekut, Trevor Pinch, Alexander Rehding, Kay Kaufman Shelemay, Jonathan Sterne, and several colleagues previously mentioned. I am ever grateful for the continuing support and guidance of my mentors, who include James Buhler, Eric Drott, David Neumeyer, and Joseph Straus.

When it came to producing the book, Ulrike Carlson advised me on idiomatic German translations. Elena Musz, an undergraduate at Stanford, revised the bibliography and notes. George Adams, a graduate student at University of Chicago, expertly produced the figures and edited the bibliography. Along with John Lawrence, George remained at my beck and call during last-minute edits and near-panics. I was fortunate to have connected so easily with Josh Rutner, whose masterful editing and indexing improved my voice. Suzanne Ryan, my editor at Oxford University Press, is a master of insight, equanimity, and encouragement; I've loved working with her and the production team. Maybe you see what I mean about a collaborative effort.

Throughout these years of work, I have been surrounded by a network of strong women. My University of Texas girls, including Rachel Mitchell, Christine Boone, and Kim Schafer, inspire me. My friends in Iowa City—many connected with the yoga community—offer grounding and growth. I am filled up again whenever I see Stephanie Jensen-Moulton, Fannie Hungerford, Hannah Rapson, Betsy Rippentrop, Monica Brasile, Melissa Moreton, Brinda Shetty, and Rachel Young. The move to Chicago brought difficult changes, though I remain grateful for the support Darren offered over many years. I delight in new friendships, including those with my yoga teacher Adam Grossi, with Jon and Alana Beadell, whose daughter Aelwen adopted me as a third mama, and with Todd Wells and Virginia Pace, whose backyard is a respite. I will never tire of analyzing every last detail of life with Jenny Beavers, my beloved best friend, who knows me better than anyone.

My sister and parents have always supported me in whatever way possible, including financial infusions, child care, patient listening, and endless cheerleading. I am especially grateful that they set their course to grow with me. I am astonished by the love I share with Steve, who has provided wise encouragement, close reading, and extraordinary insight. Walking with someone I respect so very much is pure joy. I am inspired, challenged, and loved every day by Ian and Della, my wonderful children. Thank you for believing in me and for sharing this life with me.

Electronic Inspirations

| Introduction

Imagine you are a young composer, just out of university, in mid-1950s West Germany.[1] Having survived the war, you are eager to offer your creative work as part of the country's massive rebuilding campaign. In the immediate postwar years, you eked out your existence day by day in a destroyed city amid food shortages, unemployment, and skyrocketing inflation. Watching the uneven denazification proceedings unfold only added to the tangle of grief. The economic situation has stabilized now, and you are poised to take advantage of the government's plentiful funding for cultural reconstruction, much of it channeled through the infrastructure of regional radio stations. In July 1951, you heard a presentation about electronic music—made with sine tone and white-noise generators, magnetic tape, and loudspeakers—at the *Internationale Ferienkurse für neue Musik* [International Summer Courses for New Music] in Darmstadt. You were absolutely invigorated by these exciting developments, these incredible sounds, these promising new technical avenues, so you contacted Herbert Eimert at the newly opened *Westdeutscher Rundfunk* (WDR [West German Radio]) studio in Cologne and accepted his stipend offer to work there for several months as a visiting composer.

When you arrive at the radio station, you are greeted by Gottfried Michael Koenig, a fellow composer and technician, who offers you a tour of the facilities.[2] He first takes you up to the third floor—to the studio affectionately known as *die Hexenküche* [the Witch's Kitchen]—where Karlheinz Stockhausen is montaging together tape fragments with a technician named Heinz Schütz. Koenig then takes you two levels belowground, where you will be working with him. This basement space, outfitted with a speaker's booth, a control room, and an editing room, is referred to as the "emergency studio." The radio station hopes to be able to safely produce broadcasts here in the case of nuclear Armageddon, but, until the bomb hits, this studio is producing avant-garde electronic music.

It was in this uneasy Cold War climate that electronic music burgeoned in France and West Germany in the early 1950s, and, soon after, elsewhere in Europe, the United States, Latin America, and Japan.[3] Electronic music was emblematic of a Janus-faced Cold War attitude toward technologies.[4] Looking forward, gadgets were imbued with charismatic promises of an exciting, smooth, peaceful, middle-class future. Proponents of electronic music sketched optimistic visions of a timbral utopia, animated by ever-new sonic innovations. Looking backward though, technologies cast a shadow of despair, as memories of wartime trauma and the threat of nuclear annihilation loomed over both the Continent and the United States. Technophobic audiences and critics in the 1950s frequently rejected electronic music's disembodied, austere bleeps and bloops, yet it remained a core obsession of avant-garde composers. These conflicted dynamics raise significant questions. Was avant-garde electronic music a marginal cultural experiment or a revolutionary new paradigm? How did the electronic studio connect in the cultural sphere? In short, why did this difficult, avant-garde electronic music matter?

By means of close analysis of the WDR studio in Cologne—the premiere electronic music studio of the 1950s—this book traces three main themes. First, the WDR studio was absolutely central to the evolving Cold War musical ecosystem. With its mixture of formalist aesthetics, scientific concepts, and new technologies, the WDR electronic studio opened up entirely new avenues for sonic and conceptual exploration. Composers and their collaborators working together in Cologne marshaled the intellectual climate and technologies of the Cold War, creating new sounds and new techniques. This book illustrates how these ideas permeated the entire avant-garde scene, such that the WDR studio's innovations and failures quickly became the driving forces behind both electronic and acoustic music.

Second, the WDR studio engendered a heterogeneous, laboratory-like working culture. The studio's success was connected to its synthesis of many disparate resources: composers, engineers, technologies, scientific research, aesthetic discourse, political capital, financial capital, and institutional priorities. At the WDR, as well as in other electronic music studios, collaboration was essential for the creation of musical works. This book, by showcasing invisible collaborators and intellectual informants, shifts our attention from figure (great men and great works) to ground (a heterogeneous network of collaborators). The WDR studio is an ideal site to study how collaborations and technologies shaped artistic production.

Third, the WDR studio contributed to a cultural process of reclamation, which served to mitigate the Cold War's despairing, threatening shadows. The WDR studio technologies—many of which were created for wartime uses in the 1930s and 1940s—were reclaimed for aesthetic purposes in the 1950s. Although composers explicitly professed interest only in pure musical structure, they were well versed in contemporary intellectual and political discourses. The WDR studio (and others like it) created new aesthetic applications for wartime technologies, new sounds, and new possibilities for "progress," as defined under the terms of the cultural Cold War. To embrace midcentury electronic music was to implicitly reckon with past traumas and threats of future violence.

The book's main themes—the studio's centrality in the Cold War musical ecosystem, its heterogeneous invisible collaborations, and its wartime reclamations—are developed over the course of six chapters, plus introduction and epilogue. The analyses and discussions contained here are grounded in West Germany and span only a decade—the early 1950s through the early 1960s—but the implications can certainly be carried much further. Grasping the impact of electronic music more broadly means taking seriously the interpenetration between acoustic and electronic spheres. Studios invite us, furthermore, to pay close attention to invisible collaborations. To think carefully about the studio milieu means we must reevaluate the work-centric and composer-centric "autonomous genius" mythology still so prevalent in high-art music and in our histories of it. Finally, electronic music demands that we consider the dialogic impact of scientific research and military technologies on the cultural sphere. Electronic studios were heterogeneous, intensely collaborative environments, where wartime ideas were appropriated and technologies were repurposed. For these reasons electronic music carries incredible cultural salience in music history and far beyond. Before turning to the evidence, it will be helpful to situate the midcentury studio within the history of electronic music and more specifically within the cultural logic of Cold War West Germany.

The Cultural Logic of the *Stunde Null* and the Cold War

In broad strokes, postwar West Germany was characterized by a rationale in which aesthetic modernism signaled political progressiveness.[5] The Nazis had been aesthetically conservative, embracing the lush, late-romantic tonal music of Richard Strauss, Richard Wagner, and Carl Orff, while persecuting and expelling "degenerate" modernists such as Arnold Schoenberg, Anton Webern, and Paul Hindemith (with only a few exceptions).[6] If music had been a powerful propaganda tool during World War II, it continued to be such in the Cold War era.[7] In the 1950s West Germany defined itself not only against its own past, but also against Andrei Zhdanov's Socialist Realist doctrines. In East Germany and Soviet-controlled states, orchestras and radio stations played accessible, neotonal, folk-oriented art music by composers like Dmitri Shostakovich, Bedřich Smetana, Béla Bartók, Pyotr Ilyich Tchaikovsky, and

Leoš Janácek.[8] Waging a so-called cultural Cold War, governments on both sides propagated music, visual art, and literature believed to reinforce and nurture a particular political orientation: democracy and freedom (for the West) or Socialism and Communism (for the East).[9] As a result of the Nazi history and the Socialist Realist prescriptions, many young West German composers found it unthinkable to reengage with traditional musical forms and aesthetically conservative idioms. In such a climate, electronic music appeared to be a necessity. The only morally acceptable position was on the avant-garde.

This sketch of music's role in the cultural Cold War is accurate in its broad outlines but can be nuanced in its details. The Nazis' antimodernist policies were enforced only selectively, despite the still-tenacious myths that Adolf Hitler and Joseph Goebbels exercised totalitarian control over unified, coherent, cultural policy mandates.[10] Instead, National Socialist artistic and musical practices were negotiated in a complex, shifting relationship with racial discrimination, technological fascination, and German national identity. Likewise, Socialist Realist aesthetic prescriptions and cultural policies of the 1950s were anything but watertight. Plenty of official and unofficial modernist experimentation took place in the Eastern Bloc, amid the Soviet government's ever-changing investment in its artistic mandates. The Eastern Bloc, moreover, was hardly a block. Policies, practices, and enforcement varied among Poland, Hungary, East Germany, and the Soviet Union; cultural policies loosened during the "Thaw" after Joseph Stalin's death in 1953 but tightened intermittently in response to local conflicts and uprisings.[11]

Likewise, cultural Cold War discourses in France, Italy, West Germany, England, and the United States all took on a slightly different tenor, depending on the shifting alliances among national political aims, governmental agencies, funding streams, prestigious artists, and aesthetic protocols. Given these significant differences, it might be better to speak of various cultural Cold Wars.[12] West German conditions in the 1950s allowed for a strong articulation of the moral alliance between modernist aesthetics and political progressiveness, not least because of the Allied, American, and West German governmental funding that was consistently directed toward new music.

Further nuancing the West German situation means interrogating the multifaceted myth of the *Stunde Null* [Zero Hour].[13] Of course, one part of the Zero Hour required Germany to face up to its collapse. Screening the country's physical and moral destruction, "rubble films" grappled with the consequences of military occupation and new Cold War tensions growing within a divided nation.[14] Yet Germany and the rest of the world struggled to fully come to terms with the Holocaust. Despite the public visibility of the Nuremburg trials, the Allied military governments and, later, West Germany's Adenauer-led government failed to adequately pursue justice for Nazi war crimes.[15] In the immediate postwar era, military governments (American, French, British, Soviet) enacted discrepant denazi-fication processes—screening prospective politicians, cultural leaders, and government-paid workers with questionnaires in their respective zones but employing different policies for gray- and black-listing. As denazification dragged on, panels were increasingly amenable to overlooking unsavory Nazi affiliations if, for example, German scientists were willing to contribute to the American Cold War military effort or if impresarios were willing to be artistically progressive advocates in the cultural Cold War.[16] Precious few cultural events directly addressed the Holocaust trauma in either Eastern or Western Europe, though several performances of Schoenberg's *A Survivor From Warsaw* were a notable exception.[17] Public memorials—where they existed at all—sidestepped language that would directly name Jewish victims.[18]

Despite these lapses, the reconstruction [*Wiederaufbau*] that began at the *Stunde Null* promised lasting peace, economic stability, and moral prog-ress. Although musical life hardly ceased during the war, the immediate postwar period included an expansive cultural renaissance, in which military governments rebooted radio broadcasting, orchestras, opera houses, theaters, and newspapers as soon as they were able. The military occupiers maintained varied policies for broadcasts and concert performances in their respective zones, but broadly speaking, the Germans heard again—or perhaps for the first time—music that the Nazis had suppressed or banned, such as the atonal modernist music of the 1920s and 1930s and music by Jewish composers such as Felix Mendelssohn and Gustav Mahler.

Allied governments also poured money into commissioning new music, the fruits of which were showcased in international festivals, on regional con-cert stages, and on the radio. One of the most famous and enduring of these initiatives is the *Internationale Ferienkurse für Neue Musik,* a two-week-long summer course held since 1946 in the West German town of Darmstadt.[19] Here, pan-European musicians, composers, and impresarios gathered to play and listen intensively to new music, to participate in seminars, and to ana-lyze, discuss, and share their own works. Young composers and performers who attended the Summer Courses relished the chance not only to become acquainted with new repertoires, but also to expand their cultural horizons. As the Italian composer Luciano Berio remembered,

> As young people, we were in a hurry, wanting to get back the time lost with the war. I remember feeling lost and angry when I realized that war and fascism had stopped any contact with my European cul-tural roots, already compromised by my upbringing in a small provin-cial town. Culture and its dynamics, however, are also made of these privations.[20]

European composers, performers, and audiences were eager to catch up to the rest of the world. The Darmstadt Summer Courses, in part because of sustained and robust government funding, quickly became an important locus for this recovery project, yet we should not overinflate their importance. In the 1950s, diplomatic exchanges, concert series, and cultural reconstruction efforts proliferated year round in Italy, France, East Germany, and elsewhere. Furthermore, we should bear in mind the significance of day-to-day institutions.

Radio, in particular, was the key medium for cultural offerings in West Germany. As Alexander Badenoch explains, "Almost without interruption from the mid-1930s to the late 1950s, the radio was not only the primary source of information, but also one of the cheapest sources of entertainment and one of the wealthiest supporters of culture."[21] Beginning at the *Stunde Null* moment, Allied governments established their own military stations in addition to funding state-sponsored voices such as the British Broadcasting Corporation (BBC) and Voice of America (VOA). The American government was entangled with "independent" propaganda broadcasters such as Radio Free Europe (RFE) and Radio in the American Sector (RIAS), which aimed messages of freedom and democracy toward the Soviet-controlled zones of East Germany and Eastern Europe.[22] Simultaneously, also with the underwriting of Allied governments, the robust extant network of regional West German radio stations was immediately reinvigorated, with West German administrators taking full control of regional stations by 1949.[23]

In addition to broadcasting a wide range of information and entertainment programs, each regional station maintained symphony orchestras, chamber orchestras, and choirs, which performed in concert halls within their facilities.[24] These ensembles were reliable proponents of new music, as conductors and programming directors at regional radio stations were often screened (as a result of the denazification process) to support modernist programming in both the broadcast and live offerings. Given the starkly drawn lines of the cultural Cold War, West German support for new music was a deliberate reversal of the Nazis' previous policies against "degenerate" music, as well as an emphatic rebuke of the Soviets' current policies against "bourgeois decadence." As Otto Tomek, the director of the WDR new music division from 1957 to 1971 said, "[Radio's objective], with its difficult new sound-world, is to encourage a constantly developing character and gradually [nurture] more understanding in contemporary listeners."[25] Although this is a rather paternalistic position, West German radio administrators believed in a "take your medicine" approach, whereby new music offered a cure for domestic closed-mindedness as well as a counterweight to the culturally isolationist policies of the Soviet regime during the Cold War era.

The WDR was one of the most active of the regional radio stations in postwar West Germany, offering financial and institutional support for a wide range of artistic and musical initiatives, including experimental *Hörspiele* [radio plays], regular live concerts from the two in-residence orchestras, dedicated new-music-themed broadcasts (e.g., Herbert Eimert's *Musikalisches Nachtprogramm* [Musical Night Program]), a dedicated new music concert series (*Musik der Zeit* [Music of the Time]), and one of the first electronic music studios.[26] The studio was funded in 1951 and was ready for use by early 1953.[27]

Powerful figures like Herbert Eimert (1897–1972)—an administrator, composer, scholar, and advocate for modern and electronic music—channeled funding and other resources of the WDR in support of a rotating cast of young visiting composers that he, in many cases, hand-selected to apprentice in the studio. Eimert and other like-minded administrators also cultivated a robust European new music network, which connected publishers, conductors, and performers.[28] Impresarios, with the support of sympathetic publishers, founded new, specialist journals such as *Darmstädter Beiträge, Die Reihe, Incontri Musicali*, and *Gravesaner Blätter*, which published analytical, technical, and theoretical accounts of electronic and serial music. Composers had plenty of venues in which to premiere their new works, too. Radio stations and other institutions across Western (and even Eastern) Europe revived or inaugurated new music concert series, such as *Musik der Zeit* (Cologne), *Donaueschinger Musiktage* (Donaueschingen), *Incontri Musicali* (Venice, Naples, and Milan), *Domaine Musical* (Paris), and the Warsaw Autumn Festival (Poland). Such festivals and concert series, reflecting the regional variance in cultural policies, received varying levels of state support—for instance, the *Domaine Musical* concerts were not funded or broadcast by French state-funded radio until shortly before they folded.[29] Young avant-garde composers were drawn to West Germany in particular because they could leverage varied institutional and financial supports: They could write articles for the new journals, produce radio broadcasts, receive stipends to compose electronic works, premiere recent pieces at their local concert series, teach seminars at the Darmstadt Summer Courses and other new music conferences, and connect with new-music-friendly performers and publishers through colleagues.

Within this growing ecosystem of new music, the WDR studio was the main hub. Whereas the Darmstadt Summer Courses met for only two weeks annually—with uneven attendance—the Cologne studio hosted many of the same collaborators for several months at a time. Composers such as Karlheinz Stockhausen, Gottfried Michael Koenig, Henri Pousseur, Mauricio Kagel, György Ligeti, Luciano Berio, Bruno Maderna, John Cage, and numerous others met and mingled at the WDR studio, many of them regularly and repeatedly producing music there. When the composers were not in residence together, they wrote letters to each other, sharing new developments in electronic music, discussing their quandaries and frustrations, and developing solutions together.[30] This private correspondence offers a useful corrective to the strident tone of much of their published writings, in which the composers often argue a polemical position in opaque formalist terms, with little overt discussion of their formative experiences in the studio. By contrast, their personal exchanges from the 1950s show that electronic music studios pulsated with excitement but were also laced with musical and technical uncertainty. In no small part because of the centrality of the WDR studio, the avant-garde music scene coalesced in the 1950s into an increasingly tight-knit, self-referential network of collaborators who were interested in similar questions and problems.

There was more than a hint of Cold War competition folded into the WDR's willingness to fund an electronic music studio. Initially, the studio fell under the auspices of the *Nordwestdeutscher Rundfunk* (NWDR [Northwest German Radio]), which broadcast dually from Hamburg and Cologne. The name changed in 1956 when the station split into the NDR (*Norddeutscher Rundfunk*, or North German Radio, in Hamburg) and the WDR (*Westdeutscher Rundfunk,* or West German Radio, in Cologne).[31] The Cologne station had been marginalized within the NWDR scheme in the immediate postwar years. The new electronic music studio was one strategy the Cologne branch used to distinguish itself and cultivate its eventual independence from the Hamburg branch. The WDR studio founders were equally attentive to their visibility in national and international contexts: The West Germans were perpetually interested in catching up to the French, particularly Pierre Schaeffer, who had maintained an electronic music studio in Paris at *Radiodiffusion Française* since the mid-1940s.[32] They were also aware of developments in electronic music in the United States led by Otto Luening and Vladimir Ussachevsky, and with a new studio in Cologne, were seeking to outpace the Americans as well. Without minimizing the importance of the intermittent experimentation that took place in East Berlin, Poland, Moscow, and elsewhere, electronic music was neither embraced nor institutionally funded in the Socialist Realist East with the same sustained vigor as in Western Europe.[33] In sum, one important facet of West Germany's Cold War agenda was to revivify its worldwide reputation, not least by being among the first to advance technological and artistic progress by means of electronic music.

The Evolution of Electronic Music

When the WDR hosted a world premiere to showcase the first pieces of German electronic music at the *Neues Musikfest Köln* [Cologne New Music Festival] in May 1953, the concert received plenty of attention in the press. The sympathetic critic H. H. Stuckenschmidt wrote that, though the sounds of *musique concrète* and *elektronische Musik* were "ungraspable and abstract," they were also "compelling in effect."[34] According to Stuckenschmidt, the concert presented the audience with a precise idea of the problems facing the avant-garde: "While much is still in the stage of evolution and research, this art is here and it demands our active participation." He went so far as to say that the concerts demonstrated Germany's "commitment to Europe and to humanity," clearly placing him among the cadre of progressive Western Europeans who believed that musical innovation, especially that which embraced electronic technology, was both their birthright and their ethical obligation.

Several other critics and audiences received early electronic music with much more skepticism. The 1948 French radio broadcast premiere of Schaeffer's early *musique concrète* work *Concert de bruits* [Concert of Noises] scandalized listeners, who fiercely debated the controversial new sounds. The Schaeffer–Henry collaboration *Orphée 53* was shouted down at the Donaueschingen festival in 1953, though it is unclear whether the audience detested its sounds, its aesthetic incoherence, or both.[35] German audiences and critics dubbed the new electronic music *"unerhörte Musik"* ["shockingly unlistenable music"], complained that the sonic materials were extracted from the realms of both music and noise, and asked, "Is this really a concert? Wouldn't this be just as good on the radio?"[36]

Flirting with the technological shadow of despair, some critics questioned "whether the total dehumanization of art stands at the end of this development [. . .] One wonders whether these artistic concepts, infiltrated by the spirit of technology, will infect us with 'neurotic' anxiety."[37] Others complained that performers—and by extension, "real" musicians—would be made irrelevant: "between the work and the recorded playback, there is no room for the interpretive musician to slide in."[38] Critics wondered whether the essence of the work wouldn't have been just as well realized with acoustic, instrumental materials.[39] Thoroughly scandalized—especially by the reversed sound envelopes made possible by tape recording—one critic asked, "Brother, fellow listener, are you shuddering now?"[40] Audiences, critics, and composers may have wanted to embrace avant-garde electronic music for all the Cold War political cachet it carried, but the assaulting, grating sounds left many listeners baffled and bewildered.

The 1956 concert premiere of six pieces of WDR electronic music (pictured in Figure I.1) epitomized these conflicting dynamics. Although the concert drew a standing-room-only crowd and dozens of reviews, the young composers seemingly gained more notoriety than praise. As one critic raged about Stockhausen's *Gesang der Jünglinge* [Song of the Youths], "The boy's voice is 'manipulated.' A human voice, the highest gift from God to Man, is handled as if it were mud, according to the perverse possibilities of the machinery, including blurring, distortion, reduction, multiplication, which results in screeching, crying, groaning, howling, deforming, and shredding, all so it can be cooked into a hellish sonic pulp and poured over us."[41] Although such hostile reviews did little to threaten the WDR studio's funding (or, in this case, Stockhausen's position as charismatic leader of the West German avant-garde), the young composers nevertheless were irritated

FIGURE I.I. WDR large concert hall, set for the premiere of electronic works on a *Musik der Zeit* concert of May 30, 1956. WDR Bildarchiv.

at having to constantly confront such aesthetically conservative, retrograde opinions.

Contrary to common assumptions, most modernist composers *did* care about audience reception and made efforts to bridge the gap, especially by discussing their electronic music in preconcert lectures and radio broadcasts, as well as in middle-brow popular-audience music journals such as *Melos* and *La revue musicale*.[42] The thinking here was that if critics and listeners better understood the technologies and sound possibilities of the studio, they would be less hostile toward electronic music. In these public venues, composers often historicized the development of electronic music, tracing it back to instrumental and musical developments of the nineteenth century or earlier.[43] They portrayed electronic music as an inevitable stage in a consistent cultural progression, from harpsichord to piano to electronic Melochord. This lineage would—composers hoped—defuse the public's fear of technology. As Eimert soothed, "film does not replace the theatre, and the radio does not replace the concert hall."[44] In other words: electronic music does not strive to replace acoustic, orchestral music, but only to improve on it!

Ironically, even as composers historicized the project of electronic music, they usually minimized their aesthetic and creative debts to the historical avant-gardes of the 1910s and 1920s.[45] Postwar composers rarely discussed interwar figures such as Luigi Russolo and the Futurists or Kurt Schwitters and the Dadaists, though their works were certainly aesthetically and ideologically relevant.[46] Likewise, WDR studio founders mentioned "precursors" to the postwar project of electronic music only in passing. They treated the microtonal electronic organs by the esoteric inventor Jörg Mager (1880–1939), which were briefly popular in the late 1920s, as well as the better-known 1930s-era electronic instruments such as the Theremin and the Trautonium, as mere curiosities.

Why such postwar ambivalence toward the historical avant-gardes and early electronic instruments? As Karin Bijsterveld suggests, the sounds produced under the rubric of the Futurist and Bruitist movements were hotly debated and, in many cases, impoverished.[47] Moreover, electronic instruments of the 1920s and 1930s had aesthetic limitations, being capable of playing only single-line melodies or in experimental tuning systems.[48] Newly composed pieces for the curious new instruments were few, and so electronic organs were often used to demonstrate arrangements of middle-brow classical and romantic "hits"—think Ludwig van Beethoven's *Moonlight Sonata* and themes from Wagner's *Tristan*—to curry favor with domestic amateur performers and radio listeners. The very design of the instruments, which often included a keyboard or other gestural playing mechanism, limited the composers' creative possibilities and bound them to playing music of the past. According to the postwar avant-garde composers, then, the early electronic instruments were used unimaginatively and did not actually advance the modernist project.[49]

A more serious problem was that some instruments—the Trautonium in particular—had been embraced by the Nazis.[50] Friedrich Trautwein and his simple but effective electronic organ gained fame in the early 1930s, in part because of compositions written especially for the instrument by Paul Hindemith and performed by Oskar Sala and Harald Genzmer.[51] At the tail end of the Weimar Republic, the instrument was produced and distributed by the company Telefunken as the *Volkstrautonium* [people's Trautonium], a radio add-on that would use the wildly popular *Volksempfänger* [people's radio receiver] as an amplifier. Trautwein joined the National Socialist movement in 1933 concurrently with the Nazi seizure of power, and Goebbels found a place for the Trautonium under the motto of "steel romanticism"—a concept that, according to Thomas Patteson, "fused the soulful depths of the German artistic tradition with the tough and unsentimental attitude demanded by the challenges of modernity."[52] Sala and Genzmer continued to concertize on the Trautonium all over Germany in the late 1930s and early 1940s, receiving the lauds of the Nazi cultural ministry.[53] Mager and other experimental composers and inventors were not so fortunate: the Nazis persecuted them as Marxist, Communist, or degenerate, even as Trautwein's career flourished.[54]

The Nazis' surprising embrace of some early electronic instruments accords with Jeffrey Herf's analysis of the Nazis' "reactionary modernism."[55] Although they were aesthetically conservative and racially exclusionary, the Nazis also opportunistically encouraged technological innovation. Peter Fritzsche notes how unsettling it is to understand the Nazis as "modernists and tinkerers who built a racial utopia in accordance with a scientific spirit."[56] It seems that the Nazis always understood that their campaign for dominance would hinge on technological superiority, and they recruited the scientists, engineers, and inventors who would advance that agenda.

With this context in mind, it is much easier to understand the postwar composers' ambivalence toward the electronic developments of the 1920s and 1930s: Early electronic instruments and music were both aesthetically lacking and, in some cases, politically and ethically tainted. For these postwar composers, it was convenient to refute this complicated past and to signal their resistance against Socialist Realism in the present by positing a sharp break with precursors that were conservative, tainted, or both. The polemical essays of the 1950s are fraught with such "neither–nor" rhetoric, which sprang from the double bind of the postwar and the Cold War.[57] The midcentury modernists could neither take up the electronic music project exactly where it had been left, nor could they abandon their utopian dreams for a new, electronic sound world. The composers instead defaulted to an isolationist rhetoric that emphasized starting from scratch. In the WDR studio, this meant sidelining the historical avant-gardes; eschewing the Trautonium, Theremin, and other electronic instruments; and building sounds from the ground up using sine tone and noise generators, filters, and tape.

This book both recognizes and problematizes these polemics of isolation. The postwar explosion of electronic music, depending as it does on a convergence of people, spaces, funding, technologies, and ideologies, is deeply linked to the emerging Cold War dynamics. Nevertheless, I seek to situate the WDR studio within a longer trajectory. The younger generation of composers (born in the late 1920s) proffered brash, polemical expressions of ambivalence toward the past, and yet, the midcentury studio capitalized on several crucial technological and aesthetic projects from earlier in the century.[58] Composers of postwar electronic music took great pains to position their work as an outgrowth of the music that they believed worthy— nurturing, for example, a collective obsession with Anton Webern's music (perhaps as a way of deflecting their discomfort with more obvious electronic predecessors like Trautwein). In fact, the postwar studio composers greatly depended on the literary, technological, and aesthetic insights of the 1920s and 1930s. For instance, the literary playfulness of James Joyce's *Ulysses* and *Finnegans Wake*, as well as the 1930s–1940s speech synthesis research involving the Vocoder at Bell Labs, were at the core of the WDR studio's aesthetic project in the late 1950s and early 1960s.

It is more accurate, then, to say that postwar composers *selectively* incorporated and revised earlier twentieth-century ideas and sounds for their own ends. This process of selective reincorporation is likewise evident in postwar visual art and design.[59] Artists revisited the works formerly prohibited, denied, and denigrated, and, in so doing, layered new interpretations and meanings onto familiar structures. As Peter Galison has argued, the postwar *Aufbau* [construction] aimed to (re)build Germany's cultural, social, and political institutions with much more integrity and fortitude. Ironically, this process involved reappropriating a shared repertoire of words, images, and innovations that were rooted in the Nazi era, the Weimar era, and earlier.[60] Rebuilding necessarily involved some measure of reclaiming. The WDR studio eagerly participated in this process. The studio's music both staked clear political ground in the cultural Cold War, rebuilding West Germany's cultural hegemony, and offered an aesthetic rejoinder to contemporary technological and scientific questions.

The Cologne Studio as Heterogeneous Laboratory

The WDR studio, fed by the steady funding of the regional radio structure, was one of the first institutional electronic music studios established in either Europe or the United States. It quickly became a legendary destination. Perhaps the studio's biggest strength, however, was its heterogeneous working culture.[61] The studio provided a meeting point for scientists, instrument builders, impresarios, critics, technicians, architects, literary intellectuals, and performers.[62] Several of these figures at least dabbled in composition—not to mention the steady stream of conservatory- and university-educated young European avant-garde composers. In the WDR studio's early years, its founders played host to a number of foreign visitors, including Pierre Schaeffer, the Bell Labs scientist Homer Dudley, and the American electronic music pioneers Luening and Ussachevsky, who, in the early 1950s, were showcasing their own tape music experiments in New York City and building a studio at Columbia University. All of this illustrates the studio's extraordinarily rich, multidisciplinary environment, in which figures hailing from different backgrounds capitalized on a shared interest in electronic music.

The WDR studio was one of the first to exploit such a heterogeneous structure, but in fact, that structure would be a feature of many or most subsequent electronic studios, including RAI (*Radio Audizioni Italiane* in Milan), Philips (in the Netherlands), San Francisco Tape Music Center, BBC Radiophonic Workshop (British Broadcasting Corporation in London), IRCAM (*Institut de recherche et coordination acoustique/musique* in Paris), CCRMA (Center for Computer Research in Music and Acoustics at Stanford), and others.[63] Electronic studios—and even technologies like synthesizers—concentrated and distilled the overlapping concerns of industry, scientific research, and art.[64] At the WDR studio, composers' inspirations for electronic music often came directly from the reappropriation of scientific, performative, literary, or technological insights. Composers used these cognate areas of knowledge—often gained through direct personal contacts in the studio—to advance their own musical projects; those musical techniques in turn influenced the very scientists, linguists, and acousticians whose work the composers leaned on. As collaborators enacted this series of negotiations and translations in the WDR studio, they began to build up the relevance of electronic music and shape cultural discourses.

In addition to the heterogeneous structure, the working methodologies of the WDR studio mirrored experimental, technoscientific, laboratory research cultures.[65] Composers worked in concert with the studio's technologies in the manner of scientists in a lab, corralling knowledge of acoustics (the science of sound) and psychoacoustics (the science of hearing) in order to extend those insights to new aesthetic contexts. This laboratory culture was especially evident in timbral synthesis experiments—as analyzed in Chapters 2 and 3—that became codified as shared techniques only through collaborative experiments, trial-and-error adjustments, and translations that incorporated the work of an array of contributors. The translation of scientific knowledge is likewise evident in the composers' speech synthesis experiments detailed in Chapter 6, where the technologies and discoveries of experimental phonetics were repositioned as the raw material for new acoustic and electronic musical works. The WDR studio was a laboratory—a space that mimicked but stood outside of nature—where sounds could be isolated, deconstructed, manipulated, and reconstructed. The studio of course differs from a lab inasmuch as its experimental methodologies produce aesthetic works rather than revealing the "facts" or "truth" by means of hypotheses, experiments, and theories; nevertheless, like a laboratory, the WDR studio was characterized by contingency and conflict in moving from experiment to codified practice.

The aesthetic extension of scientific knowledge in the WDR studio, as in laboratories, depended on somewhat unstable analog technologies that worked imperfectly, or at least had to be coaxed into working properly. These negotiations are clearly evident in the technical shortcuts detailed in the information theory and statistical form compromises of Chapter 4, and likewise in the composers' embrace of machines' limitations as a proxy for their own choice-making, as in the aleatory compositions analyzed in Chapter 5. Andrew Pickering's "mangle of practice" may provide a framework for thinking through the consequences of human negotiations with technologies in electronic studios.[66] Analyzing laboratory practices as they unfold in time, Pickering shows that human behavior and technological affordances are tightly intertwined, that is, "interactively stabilized."[67] The functions of the humans and machines are "tuned" to one another in such a way that knowledge is co-constructed during their interaction. The pressing together of human and machinic agency is a simple definition of Pickering's mangle of practice. Its "dialectic of resistance and accommodation" will be familiar to artists, scientists, and engineers as a failure–revision cycle, in which the results of human–machine interactions are contingent and experimental.[68] Pickering emphasizes that a moment of "capture" or stability—a finished piece of electronic music, for instance—is an emergent synthesis of human and machinic agencies.

This perspective has a certain affinity with actor–network theorists like Michel Callon and Bruno Latour,[69] who famously proposed the still-hotly debated symmetry between humans and their technologies.[70] Machinic agency continues to draw strong and sustained critique, especially from those who argue that machines are not sentient and need to be animated by humans, but it may still be a useful provocation.[71] As Benjamin Piekut has argued, "Many different kinds of things represent, summarize, exhort, cajole, afford, implore, or persuade."[72] We need not believe that machines are sentient agents in exactly the same way as humans.[73] The actor–network theory (ANT) perspective instead suggests that we focus on making material entanglements and mediators visible. As Callon has argued, we must grapple with "the distance between the heterogeneous and 'impure' sociology of the engineers and the 'pure' and homogenous sociology of the sociologists."[74] Taking technologies seriously as agents sharpens our focus on the heterogeneity of the studio, in which technologies both afford and limit certain moves.[75] As Pickering suggests, "we need to recognize that material agency is irreducible to human agency if we are to understand scientific practice."[76]

Although I take technologies very seriously in this book, my aim is to avoid a deterministic attitude. Technologies of the studio should definitively not be left as "black boxes"—that is, opaque, unexplained shortcuts that mysteriously accomplish invisible work.[77] By trying to understand how human, technological, scientific, economic, and other (invisible) actors worked together, this book sheds more light on the electronic works, as well as on the processes by which they were produced. The machinery was initially unfamiliar, and at times unforgiving, but it was an inescapable part of the compositional process. The capabilities of the machines both expanded and limited what the composers could do and how they could do it. Technological breakdowns had an impact on the network, both in defining the scope and dimensions of the creative products and in the new collaborations they engendered.

Following this line of reasoning, this book exposes the role of the technician, whose knowledge is vital to the success of the project. As Susan Schmidt Horning has argued, the growth of commercial studio music has depended on the recording engineer, who brings tacit knowledge to tasks like microphone placement, mixing, and innovative solutions to unique technological problems. This knowledge is "unarticulated, implicit knowledge gained from experience," and yet this invisible collaborator's skills make him or her "the strongest link in the chain."[78] Steven Shapin, who has analyzed the culture of the seventeenth-century scientific laboratory, correctly points out that technicians remain invisible so long as machines and experiments are working well.[79] Technicians become visible only when there are breakdowns, failures, or mistakes—their knowledge being critical for repairing machines, constructing new machines, revising setups for new experiments, and drawing conclusions from experimental data (which were often collected by the technician).

I show WDR studio technicians to be pivotal collaborators from the studio's first moments in Chapter 1, where my analysis reveals that the earliest pieces credited to the composers Eimert and Robert Beyer were in fact *re*compositions of the technician Heinz Schütz's "piece zero." As Georgina Born's ethnography of IRCAM well demonstrates, visiting composers usually came to electronic music studios with little previous experience and as a result were often dependent on a host of technical collaborators—full-time studio employees who were able to explain the fundamental principles and handle the machines.[80] Likewise at the WDR, contributions of technicians—or technically knowledgeable composers, such as Gottfried Michael Koenig—often facilitated the creative work of more visible composers.[81] The physicist Werner Meyer-Eppler was an indispensable yet often-invisible collaborator, who introduced the scientific frameworks that structured, guided, and validated the WDR studio composers' experimentation. And though we colloquially think of tape music as excluding the human performer, virtuoso performers like David Tudor and Cathy Berberian made important contributions to electronic works at the WDR and RAI studios, and, more generally, to the intellectual and musical landscape that developed in those studios.

This actor–network perspective on laboratory culture also sheds new light on the midcentury avant-garde's fierce public disagreements and passive–aggressive polemics.[82] The basic question is whether the European avant-garde hangs together as a group at all, and under what conditions. Many scholars, responding to the contestation and controversy that frequently characterized the Darmstadt Summer Courses, have understood the midcentury avant-garde to be a collection of creative, strong-minded individuals—or, as Charles Wilson puts it, an "archipelago of composer-islands, some more tightly clustered than others, but each surrounded by its own ring of blue water."[83] Jonathan Goldman's recent scholarship on spatialization and stereophony points us in another direction: the midcentury composers had individualistic compositional methods and substantial disagreements, to be sure, but they were responding to a shared set of concerns.[84]

Building upon the arguments of Eric Drott, Benjamin Piekut, and others, this book shows that the WDR studio nurtured a dynamic, iterative grouping process, in which the avant-garde formed and re-formed.[85] The studio—and the discourses of electronic music more generally—opened a space in which avant-garde compositional practices grew from a repertoire of shared resources. Collaborators met in the studio to experiment with new technologies and ideas, to address breakdowns and mitigate failures, and to pursue promising new techniques and directions together. The composers were united by their collective engagement with the studio's technologies and discourses, not by a lock-step assent to an aesthetic dogma. Furthermore, that engagement with technologies and with each other often produced disagreements, controversies, frustrations, and hierarchies. As in scientific laboratories, power and hierarchy were created as individuals made truth claims, engaged collaborators, sidelined dissidents, promoted their works, and so on.

Although the WDR studio–laboratory was heterogeneous both in its array of professional collaborators and in its entanglement with technology and scientific discourses, it was homogeneous in terms of race, class, gender, and sexual orientation. The open romantic partnerships between Heinz-Klaus Metzger and Sylvano Bussotti, as well as between John Cage and Merce Cunningham, provide two exceptions to the overwhelming heteronormativity of the West German avant-garde scene, though these couples existed toward the margins of the WDR studio's network. The Darmstadt Courses displayed a nascent diversity, owing to the participation of Nam Jun Paik (a Korean-born experimental composer), Toshi Ichiyanagi and other Japanese avant-gardist composers, as well as Cathy Berberian and several female composers and performers; and yet the courses were populated in the majority by white European men.[86] The WDR studio milieu in the 1950s was even more of a boys' club (as music composition has long been), in contrast to the important roles that women played in many other war-time technoscientific scenarios such as cryptography, code-breaking, and computer programming.[87] Women composers and technicians *did* make enormous contributions in many other postwar electronic music studios, including the BBC, Columbia-Princeton, and the San Francisco Tape Music Center, as well as several of the second-generation studios that blossomed in US universities in the 1970s.[88] So we might ask why women appeared in such traditionally gendered roles in the WDR milieu, for instance as performers who helped advance the male composers' reputations, or as obedient wives (frequently greeted in composers' correspondence) who stayed home to raise the children.

There is no simple answer to explain the WDR studio's heteronormativity and gender asymmetry, but these demographics do resonate with a broader mentality in which rigid social roles were a psychological defense against the escalating Cold War.[89] Elaine Tyler May has shown that in the United States in the 1950s, white heteronormativity was enforced in workplaces and neighborhoods; people of color were excluded from suburban housing developments and gay and lesbian people were persecuted under sodomy laws as threats to social order.[90] In both the United States and Europe, women were encouraged to stay home and raise compliant children, and men were called to enliven and rebuild their families and societies through professional contributions.

In such a cultural climate, the function of spaces like the WDR "emergency studio" is to implicitly mitigate the ever-present danger of nuclear threats by offering a steady, heteronormatively male, institutional project. At the WDR, technologies were coded as charismatic, hopeful, and aesthetically valuable, not least because the public was told it could trust the men who were reclaiming and making good use of them. In the opinions of sympathetic critics and administrators, composers were innovators, who would bring much laud to West Germany. The WDR studio remasculinized West Germany's international reputation during the cultural Cold War, providing a positive foundation from which West Germany could reclaim its hegemony. This speculative project of cultural remasculinization resonated easily with the electronic studio project in Cologne, which was largely staffed by white, middle-class, college-educated males. In this way, the studio's remasculinization was both metaphorical and literal.

The coincidence between the WDR's actual demographics and its cultural work makes for a strong correlation between specific situations and general attitudes. Here is one place to witness the building of gendered, technoscientific tropes such as the heroic inventor, the esoteric tinkerer, and the autonomous genius composer.[91] As Tara Rodgers says,

> the figure of the composer or technological innovator who creates these worlds of sound is always already figured as a man, in the same ways that [. . .] the all-knowing subject of science is normatively white, western, and male. These deep-seated norms are at the root of the ongoing dissonance between the words *woman* and *composer*, or *woman* and *inventor*.[92]

The Cold War electronic studio, and the WDR in particular, is one site at which such broader social discourses are made visible.[93] In the cultural imagination and in our writing about electronic music, the studio's composers are figured as clever, independent, and visionary—these men embody ingenuity and integrity. They are innovators to whom we can collectively entrust our technological future. Such intransigent narratives leave little room for women to be appreciated on their own terms in histories of electronic music, for to be admitted into the pantheon of important electronic music pioneers, they can be figured only as "exceptions to the rule."[94]

These conflicted tropes emerge in the case of Cathy Berberian, who is doubly exceptional as a virtuosic performative force and as a female creator in a studio scene that was otherwise exclusively male. In Chapter 6, I explore Berberian's contributions against the backdrop of the gendered public presentations of speech technologies like the Vocoder, which used women's bodies as veneers of domesticity and safety. Furthermore, the hierarchical relationships between studio technicians and composers analyzed in Chapter 1 are examples of gendered dynamics, inasmuch as technicians freely offered skills and expertise behind the scenes, without expectation of recognition. Although it is impossible to counteract the racial, educational, class- and gender-based homogeneity of the WDR scene, we can destabilize several of these cultural tropes by turning our attention away from the framework of "great men and great works." By widening the scope of the network, as Lucie Vágnerová advocates, we see the complex ways in which women and "others" participate—such as technicians, consumers, tinkerers, self-taught inventors, educated composers, virtuosic performers, and laborers—and we also see the ways in which gender norms and women's bodies help to provide structure for social and artistic collaborations.[95]

Cultural Reclamations

Although it is a speculative argument, it is compelling to think about the ways the Cold War electronic studio reclaimed wartime "technologies," here figured broadly as both machines and discourses. When the Italians, wanting to build an electronic studio in the mid-1950s at their national radio station, found themselves short of funds, they sent their electrical engineer Alfredo Lietti down into the basement closet to rummage for usable parts among the discarded wartime communication equipment.[96] From this detritus, Lietti hand-built a set of nine oscillators and two unique filtering machines, which gave the RAI studio a distinctive technological signature. Likewise, the early analog synthesizers built from scratch by Americans Don Buchla and Robert Moog in the late 1950s and early 1960s repurposed capacitors, vacuum tubes, and oscillators, which were cheaply available in military surplus stores in the United States and London.[97]

As Friedrich Kittler claims, this kind of military repurposing also defined the technological resources of the WDR studio:

> When Karlheinz Stockhausen was mixing his first electronic composition, *Kontakte,* in the Cologne studio of the Westdeutscher Rundfunk between February 1958 and fall 1959, the pulse generator, indicating amplifier, band-pass filter, as well as the sine and square wave oscillators were made up of discarded U.S. Army equipment: an abuse that produced a distinctive sound.[98]

Kittler is wrong that *Kontakte* is Stockhausen's first electronic composition—it is actually his fifth—but he may be right that the studio's oscillators, amplifiers, and generators were sourced from discarded military broadcasting equipment. The provenance of the WDR studio's oscillators remains unknown—and

Cologne was in the British zone—but Kittler's claim is plausible insofar as re-building radio stations was a priority of the Allied occupiers in the immediate postwar era. Kittler's larger point, argued with slippage between concrete and metaphorical terms, is that numerous sonic technologies were first engineered for military applications.[99] Magnetic tape—the essential medium for storing and manipulating midcentury electronic music—was developed by engineers at BASF (*Badische Anilin und Soda Fabrik*) and AEG (*Allgemeine Elektricitäts-Gesellschaft*) to create secure, portable, and reproducible sound for the German military. Tape migrated to the United States and Soviet Union during denazifica-tion, "albeit forcibly," as Peter McMurray writes, "as a spoil of war."[100] Although McMurray traces several earlier, nascent inventions that gestured piecemeal toward the invention of magnetic tape, in Kittler's broad brushstrokes, "the world-war audiotape inaugurated the musical-acoustic present."[101]

In the midcentury electronic studio, the materiality of reel-to-reel tape revolutionized the serial thought of the musical avant-garde. Durations be-came translatable into physical objects—tape lengths—that could easily be proportioned according to the same compositional schemes as pitch. Whereas oscillators and noise generators provided new raw sonic materials that stood outside of the tempered tuning systems of acoustic instruments, magnetic tape provided a material medium in which sounds could be physically manipulated—captured, stored, revised, measured, cut, and montaged.[102] The studio's technologies—their affordances and their limitations—deeply shaped the paths of midcentury electronic music, as well as those of the acoustic music that was in dialogue with the studio's developments.

Even more than reclaiming spaces and machines, the WDR studio collaborators repurposed intellectual discourses such as information theory and experimental phonetics to produce their electronic music. Claude Shannon's information theory, which discussed noise and information density in commu-nication systems of any type, was initially developed at Bell Labs in the mid-to-late 1940s as a theoretical solution to wartime cryptography problems.[103] Information theory reemerged in the postwar WDR studio, as well as in psy-chology, genetics, and linguistics.[104] The WDR studio is less directly connected to the sister discourse of cybernetics, with its central tenets of feedback, pre-diction, and (self-)regulation, but cybernetics likewise grew from wartime research—in this case, Norbert Wiener's work on antiaircraft missile systems and prediction technologies designed to shoot down Nazi bombers.[105] In one demonstration of a cathartic reclamation, Wiener disavowed the militaristic applications of cybernetics in the postwar era, developing it instead into a hu-manistic social theory.[106] The interdisciplinary Macy Conferences contributed much to this domesticating, socializing project in the late 1940s and early 1950s, drawing together researchers in the hard sciences of math, physics, and neurobiology with intellectuals in the social sciences of anthropology, sociology, psychology, and psychiatry.[107] The WDR electronic composers accomplished a similar kind of domestication as they appropriated the concepts of experimental phonetics expounded by means of technologies like the Vocoder—a secret military speech synthesizer developed at Bell Labs in the 1930s and 1940s—for their electronic music.

Information theory, cybernetics, and experimental phonetics are distinct yet overlapping discourses. They are all characterized by an imbrication of evolving technologies, wartime military applications, wide-ranging scientific generalizations, and aesthetic applications. When it comes to the uptake of wide-ranging discourses like information theory in the WDR studio, it has been the habit of critics to more or less dismiss them as "scientistic"—as tangentially related to science, at best.[108] This dismissal follows the lead of the composers themselves: Koenig explicitly cautioned that information theory was never discussed in the WDR studio, while Stockhausen, Ligeti, and others persistently elided or effaced their connections to invisible collaborators like Meyer-Eppler as well as to contemporaneous scientific discourses.[109] Despite these disclaimers, I demonstrate that information theory and experimental phonetics were central to the aesthetic project of the WDR electronic studio, even if composers had varying degrees of conscious involvement with these discourses.

The close relationship between electronic music and wartime technology will not surprise sociologists and cultural historians, who have long recognized the substantial interpolation among military, industrial, and academic scenarios.[110] As Peter Galison explains, postwar physics reoriented around the "nodal points" of collaborative intersection:

> Among the war's consequences was a profound realignment of all relations between the academic, governmental, and corporate worlds, especially as physics began contemplating the funding necessary for the construction of atomic piles, larger accelerators, and new particle detectors. Further, the war forged many collaborations and working groups among scientists that continued smoothly into the postwar epoch. And finally, the war provided astonishing quantities of surplus equipment that fed the rapidly expanding needs of postwar "nucleonics."[111]

It has become a twenty-first-century cliché to complain that the military–industrial complex pervades everything, but the very idea of a "complex" originates in the attitudes, funding patterns, and institutional structures of the early Cold War years. We might begin to see the "complex" as including artistic scenarios such as electronic music studios, which played host to a heterogeneous array of collaborators, creating music from a synthesis of scientific, technological, and aesthetic principles.

The electronic studio, with its ability to aestheticize and redeploy technologies, performed indispensable cultural work in postwar healing. The military apparatus of World War II visited horrifying destruction upon

Europe and much of Asia. The Cold War electronic studio offered a chance to domesticate wartime technologies—communication technologies in particular—by putting them to good use in the service of making art. In the studio, the modernist striving toward the new was bound to the catharsis of aesthetic repurposing, though such calculated self-representation was also a prominent cultural strategy in Nazi Germany and Vichy France.[112] Even so, the postwar WDR studio claimed progress as it repurposed technological resources, institutional spaces, military research, and intellectual discourses. Electronic studios reprogrammed World War II legacies, their new sonic possibilities shaping the Cold War future.

1 | Origins

Creating a Laboratory

In the 1950s, electronic music was a necessity for rebuilding West Germany's cultural hegemony—at least, that is how the studio founders argued their case to administrators at the WDR in October 1951:

> It is advisable to tackle the issue in Cologne, since the scientific and technical conditions here [. . .] are particularly favorable, including the provision for suitable spaces in the new radio station building. If the questions that were raised are not moved toward realization this year in Germany, they will be brought forward by next year in the USA.[1]

For a trampled West Germany, a dedicated electronic music studio was a promise of better things to come.[2] At the WDR, Herbert Eimert (1897–1972) was at the forefront of the charge. A World War I veteran who later trained as a violinist, composer, and scholar, Eimert published the influential and controversial treatise *Atonale Musiklehre* in 1924.[3] By 1931, he had earned his PhD in musicology with a more conventional dissertation that addressed form in seventeenth- and eighteenth-century music. During the Weimar and Nazi eras, Eimert continued to compose, worked as a music critic for the *Köln Stadt-Anzieger*—a role that he would hold into the postwar era—and worked as an editor for the *Kölnische Zeitung*.[4] In the postwar era, Eimert found favor with Hans Hartmann, the director of the NWDR station, and began working at the Cologne branch as head of musical programming. Hartmann was a "man of letters" and was apparently sympathetic to Eimert's long-standing new music interests. In 1948, Eimert began producing his famed *Musikalisches Nachtprogramm*, a bimonthly broadcast aimed at educating listeners on the concepts and sounds of the "new" music that had been suppressed or unknown during the war. The electronic studio was funded in 1951 owing, in large part, to Eimert's well-placed connections with Hartmann and other WDR administrators, but the project would have been untenable without the expertise of certain collaborators.

One such collaborator, Werner Meyer-Eppler (1913–1960), was a scientist with wide-ranging expertise in acoustics, psychoacoustics, and experimental physics.[5] Meyer-Eppler completed his PhD in physics at the University of Bonn and continued to teach there in the Nazi and postwar eras. His first dissertation (1939) addressed photoelectric measurements for radio spectra; his *Habilitation,* which yielded a promotion from research assistant to professor in 1942, addressed channel width, distortion, and periodicity in broadcasting.

During World War II, Meyer-Eppler continued this research both at the University of Bonn and for a Nazi military research group within the *Kriegsmarine.*[6] Meyer-Eppler authored eight military research reports for the U-boat division between October 1943 and February 1945.[7] His interdisciplinary team produced "wave research," exploring topics such as electronic circuit design, frequency analysis, noise reduction, and sonic mapping, which advanced U-boat projects such as sonar and threat detection systems. The University of Bonn was destroyed by bombing and fire near the end of the war, and work stopped briefly. In the immediate postwar months, Meyer-Eppler was "collared"[8]—employed by the British Military Government to transmit his knowledge in six reports addressed to the Royal Air Force and delivered between October 1945 and January 1946.[9]

Despite his cooperation with the British, he struggled through an extensive denazification process that included accusation, testimony, decisions, and appeals, which dragged on between October 1945 and June 1949. Meyer-Eppler's initial judgment of *Kategorie III-IV* rendered in June 1948 was eventually downgraded in June 1949 to *Mitläufer,* or nominal party member whose participation is perfunctory and excusable. As part of this revised judgment, Meyer-Eppler made a professional pivot away from physics and toward research in experimental phonetics and information theory. Paul Menzerath endorsed him as a colleague who could help rebuild the Phonetics Institute at the University of Bonn, where he requalified for his faculty position in 1952 with a second *Habilitation* on voiced and unvoiced consonants.[10]

The extent of Meyer-Eppler's wartime activity has not yet come to light in print, and much more remains to be said about it.[11] His case is indicative of a broad network—in the United States, and Germany, and elsewhere—that connects military research and technology to civilian industry, science, and arts.[12] Crucial to Meyer-Eppler's successful pivot was his growing reputation as a leader in the field of electronic music. It was easy to transport his knowledge of circuits, waveforms, noise, and synthesis from military communications technologies to electronic music instruments in the nascent WDR studio, given the extensive technological overlap between them.[13] And it was certainly expedient and even necessary for him to do so.

Such recasting defined Meyer-Eppler's Cold War work, as seen for example in his 1948 exchange with the American company Bell Laboratories, the research division of AT&T. Meyer-Eppler's postwar research focused on the artificially synthesized speech of electronic larynges, the same technologies that engineers at Bell Labs developed for use in the Vocoder (short for Voice-Coder), a machine that encrypted and decrypted spoken messages. Rather than unpacking the military implications of speech synthesis, however, Meyer-Eppler's *Elektrische Klangerzeugung* [*Electric Sound Generation* (1949)], addressed phonetics in light of its applications in electronic music.[14] Meyer-Eppler's Cold War turn toward research that mingled electronic music, phonetics, and information theory recast his wartime immersion in military circles, in which broadcasting, wave research, speech synthesis, and encryption were primary concerns.

Meyer-Eppler's career trajectory is, then, a microcosm of the larger cultural project of reclaiming wartime technology. It furnishes vivid examples of how communications technologies and scientific discourses could be reappropriated for aesthetic uses. Meyer-Eppler was not a trained musician, but he was musically curious and endorsed the aesthetic use of electronic technologies. In the immediate postwar era, he cultivated relationships with instrument builders (such as Friedrich Trautwein and Harald Bode) and performers who used the new electronic instruments (such as Oskar Sala).[15] Because Meyer-Eppler's expertise in acoustics, phonetics, and information theory was unsurpassed in West Germany, and also because he lived and taught in very close proximity to Cologne, he played a major role in educating the younger generation of composers, including Stockhausen, Kagel, and others, until his early death in 1960.

As Meyer-Eppler began to move in electronic music circles, he seems to have met the third of the Cologne studio founders, Robert Beyer, at the 1949 meeting of the *Tonmeister Tagung* [Sound Engineer Conference] in Detmold, Germany. Beyer (1901–1989) was a composer, recording engineer, and new music impresario active in the development of electronic music in the Weimar years (1920s) as well as in the early postwar era. In the Weimar years (1928–1934), Beyer worked as a sound engineer for Tobis, a German film production company. It is not clear what he did during the war, but from 1946 to 1953 he worked as a sound engineer at the WDR in Cologne.[16] Eimert, Meyer-Eppler, and Beyer joined forces in 1950 for a seminar on electronic music at the Darmstadt Summer Courses, before making the successful funding proposal for the studio to WDR administrators in 1951.[17] Beyer's affiliation with the WDR studio ended in 1953, evidently because his rather low-brow aesthetic orientation toward film sound effects and popular genres like *Hörspiel* [radio play] was increasingly incompatible with Eimert's high-art proclivities.[18] Nevertheless, Beyer's writings, which exhibit remarkable continuity of thought between the 1920s and 1950s, are essential in establishing the conceptual foundations for the WDR electronic music studio.

Historicizing a Timbral Utopia

All three of the studio founders wrote and lectured about electronic music in the crucial period of 1950–1953, as the studio moved from dream to reality. Their topics and narratives overlapped considerably, forming an internally coherent discourse. One of their primary shared preoccupations was to historicize electronic music as the logical next step in a continuous lineage. As Beyer wrote in 1953,

> The history of electronic music is different from the history of the equipment and its technical development. There, we have an unbroken chain of inventions, the path from Cahill via Mager, from Theremin to Trautwein, Martenot, and Bode [. . . .] The actual history of electronic music begins at the moment that forward-thinking musicians discovered that the traditional acoustic media no longer met their musical needs, and out of this, began to discover technology with its superior possibilities of sound. This process becomes more relevant given the progressive dissolution of the tonal system, the default until now, and the liberation of new musical energies that is connected to this.[19]

In Beyer's view, then, the history of the technologies was only one branch of the larger tree of the continuous evolution of musical thought. Electronic music became a necessity at the moment that composers realized they were limited by tonality. Thus electronic music was a logical outgrowth of the "emancipation of dissonance," a process that unfolded from the late nineteenth century into the early twentieth century and continued with electronic music in the postwar era.

For the studio founders, the key figures in this music–historical trajectory were Ferruccio Busoni, Jörg Mager, and Arnold Schoenberg. Beyer idolized Busoni, the early twentieth-century progressive composer and pianist, owing to the perhaps apocryphal story that Busoni heard Thaddeus Cahill's Telharmonium (an electric organ ca. 1897) and thought of "the possibility for free compositional flight attempts."[20] Eimert repeated this story nearly verbatim in his Darmstadt lectures and his *Melos* and *Die Reihe* articles.[21] In a slightly more esoteric and technical turn, Beyer and Eimert also praised the work of the composer and inventor Jörg Mager, whose pioneering 1920s electronic instruments used non-equal-tempered tunings and microtonal intervals.[22] From these rather esoteric, early twentieth-century inventors, Beyer and Eimert predictably traced the genealogy to Schoenberg, who, according to them, encountered the limits of the tonal system and set sound free from the gravitational pull of the tonic. Schoenberg's work led to Anton Webern's, whose isolated, crystalline sound atoms taught them to "hear again" by isolating each aspect of the musical structure.

Eimert made it clear that he regarded Webern's music as the foundation of serial thought, and the electronic music studio as the epitome of serialism, a story that deftly folded together the younger composers' delight in Webern with the project of electronic music. It was in the studio that the composers could finally control every aspect of the sound. As Eimert said, "That way, the sound structure can become a part of the structure of the work for the first time—that is the great, indelible thought that Anton Webern brought to music."[23] Eimert's historical narrative remained consistent with Beyer's throughout the 1950s, but it also deepened. In its fullest elaboration, in his 1955 *Die Reihe* article, Eimert surrounded electronic music with a web of additional precursors, including fourteenth- and fifteenth-century polyphony, experimental nineteenth-century chromaticism, and Debussy's late works.[24]

The genealogy that Eimert elaborated in the 1950s was consistent with the narrative that Beyer began in the 1920s, wherein Beyer posited an immanent historical logic for electronic music linked specifically to the problem of timbre.[25] Historically, timbre (or sound-color) was too often a secondary consideration for composers; the melodic, harmonic, contrapuntal, and formal logic of the piece came first, the orchestration, last. In this narrative, timbre was reduced to mere window-dressing.[26] Of course, this is a rather selective telling of the history of orchestration and timbre—the nineteenth century witnessed many changes in instrument design and considerable growth in orchestrational and timbral possibilities.[27] Suffice it to say that the midcentury composers were obsessed with timbre and actively looked for techniques that could help them elevate the role of timbre in their compositions.

On this account, Schoenberg offered one of the most intriguing possibilities with his theory of *Klangfarbenmelodie*, or melody of timbres, which he introduced at the end of his 1911 treatise *Harmonielehre* but never fully explicated in either words or music. For Schoenberg, timbre or sound-color was perhaps even more salient than pitch. He dreamed of making a music that foregrounded and exploited timbres: "It must also be possible to make such progressions out of the tone colors [. . .] progressions whose relations with one another work with a kind of logic entirely equivalent to that logic which satisfies us in the melody of pitches."[28] According to Beyer, electronic music lay at the organic conclusion of this development. Schoenberg's dream could be realized in the studio: "Through electronic media it becomes possible to successfully realize the idea of *Klangfarbenmusik*."[29]

In concocting a narrative history of electronic music from aesthetic developments, Beyer, Meyer-Eppler, and Eimert elided and effaced Meyer-Eppler's military entanglements, as well as instruments such as the Nazi-tainted Trautonium, one of the more prominent developments of the 1920s and 1930s.[30] Although the history of electronic music was littered with military–musical imbrications, and concomitant moral quandaries, the studio founders did not abandon their historicizing project. Instead, they reclaimed the esoteric Busoni and the Marxist Mager, folding in the insights of acoustic avant-garde composers like Schoenberg and Webern. The studio founders furthermore signaled their independence by promising that the freestanding generators, filters, and magnetic tape of the Cold War studio offered an even more elegant solution to the problem of timbre than did early electronic instruments. As Meyer-Eppler said at Darmstadt in 1950, the way forward in timbral innovation would have to be beyond instruments to sound itself:

> with our musical instruments, there is a Gordian knot between the shape of the instrument and its timbre, which makes it impossible to connect one timbre to another. What lies, for example, sonically in the middle between clarinet and oboe? There is no continuous pathway. This can succeed only with the help of electricity. An analogy would be color in painting. Earlier, we had natural colors, few tones, choices committed not by artists, but given by chance. Now we have aniline [chemically formulated] colors, and free compositional possibilities.[31]

Meyer-Eppler's choice of metaphors was purposeful: sound-color was comparable to visual color, and scientific advances could be couched safely within the realm of aesthetic advances. Moreover, the studio's electronic technologies would liberate the composers' creativity. Instruments, whether orchestral or electronic, presented an impasse that was impossible to transcend without the WDR studio's configurable technologies.

Meyer-Eppler was particularly utopian when he claimed that the composer of electronic music would become something of a sound-sculptor, shaping the sound itself without the annoying interference of instruments and notation: "He can experiment with sounds and forge ahead into a completely unknown new land. [. . .] Since his work comes to life under his own hands, he can avoid all the mistakes that inhere in a written composition."[32] Whereas most traditional orchestral techniques favored existing timbres and instrumental combinations, fixed notation, and equal-tempered tuning systems, electronic music idealistically offered the ability to escape these traditional shackles. Beyer wrote, "The equipment, conceived in such a way, offers a completely new sonic world. It makes possible the *deliberate construction of timbres.* Technology unlocks an as-yet unexplored world, about whose construction and systems we know almost nothing."[33]

Laboratory Collaborations

A technological utopia seemed within grasp at Darmstadt in 1952, when Eimert issued a veritable call to arms:

> For the first time the sonic material shows itself in its true limitless-ness. [. . .] The idea of boundless sonic material is an age-old mu-sical dream. [. . .] This is not about fantasies of the future. Instead, this first task is as concrete as it is difficult. *Anfangen!* Let's begin![34]

But as the composers would soon find out, the studio's generators, oscillators, filters, and tape decks would prove to be limiting and unwieldy. Beyer was closer to the truth when he admitted, "The expectations for the realization of a new sound world remain, as yet, unfulfilled."[35] It is deeply ironic that the studio founders were uniformly excited to create a timbral utopia but were simultaneously ill-equipped to do so. Contrary to the promises of unshackled independence they proclaimed in their writings, their dream of controlling timbre now depended on multiple new instruments and technicians.

Beyer, probably owing to his background as a sound engineer for film, seems to have been the most knowledgeable about negotiating this gap be-tween dream and reality. He proposed a research-and-development structure, characterizing the not-yet-constructed studio as a laboratory:

> The equipment cannot be imagined as an instrument that is geared toward reproduction through playing, but rather as a free arrangement of electro-acoustic procedures, in the way that is common in research laboratories. In other words: *the technological, in its entirety, is implicated in the realization process.*[36]

Beyer understood that a secure understanding of the machinery—an ability to manipulate it effectively—would be essential for the artistic works. When the studio got off the ground in 1953—and even during the early experiments in 1952—Beyer's research laboratory did come to pass. A host of technical collaborators advanced the studio's research paradigm, helped the composers learn to use the new machines, and midwifed the composers' new artistic works.

Throughout this book, I focus on the invisible collaborators—the technicians, administrators, performers, and scientists—who make the cre-ative work of the composer possible. The analyses in this chapter decon-struct musical works that are ostensibly "by" Eimert and Beyer, showing that the composers leaned heavily on their technician Heinz Schütz. The sound engineers and technicians, who had moved into the studio from the radio-play division, threaten to disappear entirely from the historical record. As Susan Schmidt Horning has argued, technicians often remain invisible until unexpected results, mechanical failures, or breakdowns expose the technician as a skilled laborer, who creates a solution by making his tacit, practice-based knowledge explicit.[37] Steven Shapin's analysis of the seventeenth-century scientific laboratory reveals a profound asymmetry between the laboratory leader—the scientist possessed of knowledge and authority—and the technicians who carried out most of the experimental work.[38] A similar working culture characterized the midcentury electronic studio, though in both scientific and aesthetic scenarios, such asymmetries were often explained away as a pragmatic division of labor.[39] As Eimert wrote,

> It would be an error to suppose that it is merely necessary to construct apparatuses and machines in order to produce electronic music. People not machines are the prime requisite—technicians and musicians ceaselessly engaged in a cooperative effort to solve the problems of electronic music.[40]

The cooperative laboratory environment that Eimert described, with creative energy moving among machines, technicians, and composers, was the dominant working model for the studio.[41] Yet the asymmetries in power, recognition, and authorship raise the question: In what sense can the technicians (in a laboratory, in a studio, etc.) be understood as co-creators?

Shapin suggests that the seventeenth-century scientist was an author because he possessed authority in his laboratory, meaning it was he who determined the research program, enforced the boundaries between skill and knowledge, hired and fired, and determined the final form of the work.[42] A similar conclusion can be drawn for the electronic studio as well. Composers claim authorship and authority based on their artistic synthesis of various intellectual, technical, and aesthetic sources. Although we recognize the importance of collaboration in many artistic scenarios (film, record production, theater, etc.), in the existing paradigm of "great men and great works," we still fumble for a coherent vocabulary for analyzing the network of invisible collaborators behind a piece of high-art music.[43] It is essential to understand electronic music as a collaborative effort, as a complex negotiation between multiple humans and technological processes.

The collaborative paradigm was established at the WDR even before the studio had an actual space. In articulating the studio's guiding mythology, its founders drew heavily from electronic-music-themed Darmstadt sessions in 1950–1952, where critics, composers, musicologists, and instrument builders (such as Theodor Adorno, Pierre Boulez, Antoine Goléa, Ernst Grunert, Pierre Schaeffer, Friedrich Trautwein, and Edgard Varèse) all contributed ideas about the problems, promises, and paths for future electronic music research.[44] Likewise, in practice, a laboratory-like collaboration marked the very first West German experiments with electronic music. In March 1952, Eimert entertained the Italian composers Luigi Nono and Bruno Maderna at Meyer-Eppler's office in Bonn, where they undertook a first draft of the experimental piece *Musica su due dimensioni*.[45] As Eimert reported,

we (Nono, Maderna, Eimert) are together each day, travelling to Bonn and in [the village of] Siebengebirge. In Bonn I took them not only to the Beethoven house but also to Meyer-Eppler's Institute for Phonetics and Communications Research to demonstrate our electronic tapes, over which they almost flipped their lids [lit.: ran out of the cottage]. Maderna began at a station and with a job, electronics to compose and montage on to tape—three of the melodies produced by the Melochord layered on top of one another. For a short time Jelinek from Vienna was here, then I had arranged a discussion session with Professor Menzerath [director of the Institute] and Meyer-Eppler in Bonn. Ultimately, the discussion unfolded with true spirit and charming courtesy. It all appears to me that we are going the right way with these things.[46]

It was not quite so smooth for Maderna, who wrote to Nono in May, as he was having trouble integrating his serial schemes for the flute part with the electronics: "One cannot simultaneously use a new medium and seek a synthesis of all our thoughts and all our research."[47] Although *Musica su due dimensioni* was played at Darmstadt in July 1952, Maderna later withdrew it, recomposing the piece almost entirely in 1958.[48] With this first experience, Eimert aimed to create a rich and compelling introduction to electronic music, one that was creatively valuable for Maderna and Nono, but he depended on Meyer-Eppler's access and expertise to operate the Melochord, as well as on the scientist Menzerath to discuss the technical dimensions. Maderna is described as concentrating on the tape montage and synchronization, a job that composers seem to have been comfortable performing, as we will subsequently see. Nevertheless, for the composers' earliest experiments with electronic music, it is likely that Meyer-Eppler supplied the sounds.[49]

From Sound Catalogue to *Spiel*

In April 1952, just a month after hosting Maderna, Eimert reported on his own experiments in a letter to Stockhausen:

Meyer-Eppler compiled a catalog of sound types for me, 12, 24, or 48, which one should be able to compose with just as one does with 12 tones. Of course, one needs to have the sounds exactly in one's mind first; then one can apply the 12-tone technique. Composing is rhythmicizing, which in reality means a laborious process of tape tailoring. After long considerations, I believe that there is no other way out at our current level of technology.[50]

Surprisingly, Eimert's compositional imagination seems to extend little beyond *de rigueur* dodecaphonic techniques. Despite the studio founders' professed enthusiasm for manipulating timbre, actually doing so with the electronic instruments was an unfamiliar and difficult task. Instead, Eimert began his foray into electronic composition by "rhythmicizing" sound samples on tape with *Spiel für Melochord*, composed in 1952 but never premiered.

As Table 1.1 shows, the piece was constructed almost entirely from sounds that Meyer-Eppler supplied.[51] Eimert and Beyer used three examples that were produced for the NWDR *Nachtprogramm* on electronic music in October 1951. These sounds (C2, C8, and C9) were used in *Spiel* exactly as they are preserved in Meyer-Eppler's archive and most likely exactly as they were broadcast over the radio.[52] The sounds showcase the synthesized faux-voices of the Vocoder, pitch drones with octave filters, intervals with audible acoustic beats, and meandering chromatic melodies. Eimert and Beyer also used three samples from an undated tape of Meyer-Eppler's, titled only "Farben" (F2, F8, and F10). Because this tape does not appear to illustrate any of Meyer-Eppler's numerous lectures on electronic music, it was quite possibly made specifically for Eimert as part of a "sound catalogue." The materials from the "F tape" are a bit less melodic and more noise oriented, including a buzzy ostinato treated with a dramatic crescendo and a glitchy ostinato made of white-noise impulses layered over a repetitive minor-third melodic interval.

Meyer-Eppler's sounds were apparently created on the Vocoder (or another electronic larynx) and the Melochord, a keyboard instrument designed by Harald Bode and reportedly Meyer-Eppler's favorite of the early keyboard instruments at the time.[53] In fact, all of the 1952 experiments mentioned or analyzed in this chapter—including Maderna's *Musica*, Eimert's *Spiel*, and Eimert and Beyer's *Klangstudie II* and *Klang im unbegrenzten Raum*—were produced mainly using the Melochord. This instrument, shown in Figure 1.1, featured a dual-manual keyboard connected to a tone generator, which could produce sine tones as well as sounds with overtone-rich spectra.[54] One of the signature features of Bode's Melochord was its ability to vary the timbre of generated sounds by way of various dynamic or tunable filters, noise generators, and ring modulators installed on the instrument. These timbral variations understandably interested Meyer-Eppler, Eimert, and Beyer.

Despite the synthesized timbres, however, tonal references abound in both Meyer-Eppler's sound catalogue as well as in the attendant *Spiel*. It is as if the composers sat at the Melochord's keyboard and could remember only their

TABLE 1.1. Meyer-Eppler's sound catalogue materials, and their reuse in Eimert and Beyer's *Spiel für Melochord* (1952).

Meyer-Eppler Sound Catalogue Label	Description	Original Purpose	Location in *Spiel*	Comments
C2 "Vocoder & Melochord" (track 9, 0:00–1:14)	thin, synthesized meandering melody above faux-vocal drone. Vocoder performs vowel manipulation (yai) with occasionally intelligible phrases: "give me thy hand"	sound example for NWDR *Nachtprogramm* 18.10.1951	2:31– 3:44	exact
C8 "Klangfarbenostinato" (track 11, 1:49–2:08)	pitch with various ascending octave filters applied	sound example for NWDR *Nachtprogramm* 18.10.1951	2:13– 2:31	exact
C9 "1. Satz" (track 12, 1:07–1:51)	beating M3 narrows to a m3, then M2, then expands back to M3. Pitch with various octave filters is superimposed. Ends on unison drone.	sound example for NWDR *Nachtprogramm* 18.10.1951	3:44– 4:28	exact
F2 "Klangspiel Schlag" (track 24, 1:26–1:40)	buzzy single-pitched drone crescendos in volume to a minor triad, which then decrescendos	unknown; undated tape "Farben"	1:18– 1:32	exact
F8 "Rauschrhythmus und Töne" (track 26, 0:35–0:48)	"glitch" bursts of white-noise impulse above yawning melodic m3 ostinato	unknown; undated tape "Farben"	1:32– 2:13	looped; additional sounds added
F10 "Polyrhythmische Glockentraube" (track 27, 0:06–1:00)	tinny synthesized keyboard plays harmonic intervals: M7, tritone, M3; bass interjections; timbral changes	unknown; undated tape "Farben"	0:15– 0:17 and 0:24– 1:18	broken apart; looped; reverb and distortion added

counterpoint classes: the sound catalogues are rife with melodies that can be easily put to *solfège*, as well as minor triads, descending-fifth bass motions, and harmonic intervals like resolving tritones that suggest two-voice tonal counterpoint.

This tonal flavor is amplified in the only apparently newly composed sample in *Spiel*, the arpeggiated minor triad that opens the piece (see Figure 1.2). Although it is rather unimaginative, the arpeggiation forms a transparent thematic link between the various montaged samples. Both the F2 and F8 samples contain prominent minor thirds or minor triads; F8 is looped, manipulated, and layered together with the arpeggiated triad

FIGURE 1.1. Bode's Melochord. WDR Bildarchiv.

of the opening. The minor-third motive is also touched on during the
intervallic narrowing and widening of sample C9, which ends the piece.
In this way, variations on the minor-triad motive appear as the thematic
connective tissue in the beginning, middle, and end sections of the work.
Eimert and Beyer's newly composed material makes this thematic coherence obvious.

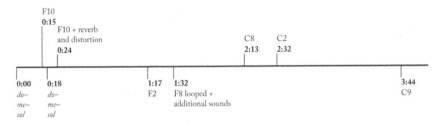

FIGURE 1.2. Timeline of Eimert and Beyer's *Spiel für Melochord* with source materials from Table 1.1.

Because *Spiel für Melochord* was never premiered (it was released on CD in 2008), we can safely assume it was a practice work for the composers, designed to improve their tape montage techniques.[55] For Eimert, there was no dissonance in the idea that "composing" was really just montaging Meyer-Eppler's sounds. As Eimert intimated, creating the sounds was not really the work of the composer, but was instead the work of the technician:

> The technique of electronic composition requires a good deal of knowledge of a kind not generally found among musicians. This includes familiarity with the operation of the apparatuses, as well as at least an elementary acquaintanceship with the field of acoustics (which in its modern form is essentially electroacoustics). But with the mastery of the "material" the work of composition is just begun. That is, given the methods of producing and processing electronic, musical material must grow logically and directly from the nature of these materials.[56]

This "mastery of the apparatuses"—the production of sound effects using the machines—was only the precursor to the work of the composer, who was then responsible for the logical aesthetic development and "mastery of the material." Eimert's orientation was deeply serial, with his insistence on a logical connection among the sounds' acoustic nature, technique, and musical form, but he also alluded to a hierarchical division of labor.[57] The technicians, whose labor and expertise were audible but invisible in fact played a crucial role in the important work of sound production. Moreover, although Eimert and Beyer assisted with the tape montage in *Spiel*, they must have derived only a little practice with "logically developing" the materials, as the majority of *Spiel*'s sounds were co-opted wholesale from Meyer-Eppler's catalogue.

Sound Effects Anxiety

In the 1954 photograph shown in Figure 1.3, the composers Gottfried Michael Koenig and Eimert are on the far left and far right, respectively.

FIGURE 1.3. In the WDR *Studio für elektronische Musik* ca. 1954. From left to right, Gottfried Michael Koenig, Erhard Hafner, Heinz Schütz, and Herbert Eimert. WDR Bildarchiv.

Between them are Erhard Hafner and Heinz Schütz, technicians who worked with Eimert, Beyer, and other visiting composers in the earliest years of the studio. Both had close ties to the *Hörspiel* division, producing sound effects for radio plays. As Koenig explained, when he began working as a technician at the WDR in 1954,

> Hafner then went to the radio play division. And I took his place, more or less. [. . .] There was always work to do [with the visiting composers]. Schütz alone was not always the right person, because he came from radio technique and was of little help to composers who wanted to discuss musical problems during the work.[58]

Although Hafner and Schütz's expertise was mainly technical, they nevertheless had quite inventive creative minds and liked finding new ways to make interesting sounds.[59] In fact, creative sound production fell well within the scope of their work in the radio-play division. *Hörspiel* is an art form for theatrical speaking voices with sound effects that illustrate the narrative.[60] Made explicitly for broadcast over the radio, *Hörspiel* has generic connections with film, theater, music, literature, and television, but is analogous to none of them.[61] A soundtrack for *Hörspiel* is usually sparse, involving some combination of music, sound effects, and noises.[62] Although it has been almost completely written out of the history, the sounds produced for radio plays in the 1940s and 1950s were the most direct precursors and inspirations for the electronic music of the early 1950s.

In Germany, the first radio plays were produced and broadcast in 1924. When the Nazis came to power in 1933, radio was quickly centralized and controlled by the Reich.[63] *Hörspiel* productions were curtailed, and those that were produced were propaganda for the Nazi regime. The genre flourished again in the postwar era, achieving wide influence and "classic" mainstream status.[64] The older generation—including studio founders Eimert (b. 1897), Beyer (b. 1901), and Meyer-Eppler (b. 1913)—would have been at prime ages to remember the birth of radio broadcasting and Weimar-era *Hörspiel*. When it came to the rebirth of *Hörspiel* in the postwar era, Eimert and the older composers would have known the genre much more intimately (and perhaps nostalgically) than the younger generation, most of whom were born in the mid-1920s and reared during the Nazi Reich. Many radio plays were produced and broadcast at the NWDR in Hamburg and Cologne in the early 1950s—three, on average, per week.[65] Eimert was involved with making the soundtrack for one of these in the mid-to-late 1940s, a production of Lord Byron's *Kain*, which was scored for large orchestra.[66] As one can imagine, soundtracks for *Hörspiel* were much less costly to produce with a single technician at the keyboard of an electronic instrument like the Melochord. Likewise, tape recording was a key technological advance for radio plays, inasmuch as it allowed for a catalogue of sounds—both electronic and orchestral sounds—to be maintained as a library and deployed according to the situation at hand.[67]

Hörspiel was essential to early electronic music not only on the technical level, but also when we consider the substantial overlap between the producers of radio-play sound effects and high-art electronic music. A number of composers had their first experiences making sound effects for radio plays, including Bruno Maderna, Luciano Berio, Mauricio Kagel, Dieter Schnebel, and John Cage. These high-art composers composed little-known music for *Hörspiel* to make a living or to gain hands-on, practical experience with electronic technologies and techniques.[68] For instance, in 1954 Berio and Maderna collaborated to produce the soundtrack for an Italian radio play at RAI ([*Radio Audizioni Italiane*], the Italian national radio).[69] Their soundtrack for *Ritratto di città* (1954), perhaps inspired by Dylan Thomas's famous radio play *Under Milk Wood* (1953–1954), is a rather experimental sonic and poetic portrait of daily life in Milan.[70] Berio and Maderna had been collaborating with RAI on these types of "functional music" projects since 1953; as Angela Ida de Benedictis points out, "in Italy, the only place that could guarantee an instrumental support to work with tapes, scissors, and tape recorders was the RAI."[71] The same was true at the BBC Radiophonic Workshop, where electronic music composers made advertising jingles, call signs, and sound effects by day, because it afforded them access to the electronic equipment at night, when they produced their creative works.[72]

Similarly, Pierre Schaeffer's *musique concrète* sound effects, produced since the mid-1940s at *Radiodiffusion Française* (RF, French national radio), were indebted to experimental British documentary film sound of the 1930s and intimately connected to postwar radio projects.[73] Boulez, Stockhausen, and many other composers, including Jean Barraqué, Karel Goeyvaerts, Olivier Messiaen, Darius Milhaud, and Hermann Scherchen, had their first experiences with electronic sound in Schaeffer's Paris studio.[74] By the early 1950s, West Germans were anxious to catch up to Schaeffer and the French with their own experimental electronic studio.[75] Writing from Paris, Stockhausen complained about the situation to Eimert:

I feel for them [German intellectuals], as they have to strain to make a studio possible for Meyer-Eppler or a chamber music concert series for young composers. And that is the sole place in all of Germany! In Paris they know very well that Cologne is the only place where something is actually done! Only you seem to think not, that it is different here! [. . .] But, in any case, the young ones stick together. Boulez and Barraqué have nearly managed to throw out that crazy Schaeffer and are gaining momentum. Boulez and Barraqué are almost in a position where they have at least some influence at the radio, and can make broadcasts about rhythmics, etc. and construct tape études, which bypass Schaeffer completely. Each year there is an event (public concert of the Schaeffer Group) in which all the young colleagues present the experiments that they have dared to make. This year, people will probably sense that *musique concrète* has no association with the nonsense that Schaeffer has fabricated until now—and that it [electronic music] should be anything else, except *musique concrète*.[76]

In a series of letters exchanged between Paris and Cologne in 1952, Stockhausen and Eimert commiserate over their inferiority complex, expressed on behalf of all Germans. Stockhausen's disdain for Schaeffer is apparent—he and the younger composers contemplate a mutiny. Schaeffer's personality was, reportedly, somewhat overbearing, and he seemingly directed the interns to work on his projects rather than experiment with their own.[77] But Stockhausen's and Eimert's objection to *musique concrète* went beyond interpersonal relations toward a deep aesthetic discord.

When Schaeffer began his experimentation leading to the *Concert de bruits* in 1948, he did so with materials he procured from the RF's sound effects department:

I find clappers, coconut shells, klaxons, bicycle horns. I imagine a scale of bicycle horns. There are gongs and birdcalls. [. . .] I take away doorbells, a set of bells, an alarm clock, two rattles, two childishly painted whirligigs. The clerk causes some difficulties. Usually he is asked for a particular item. There are no sound effects without a text in parallel, are there? But what about the person who wants noise without the text or context?[78]

Schaeffer's vivid description clarifies exactly how he got to the idea of *musique concrète*: by reappropriating the sound effects of the radio-play department. Schaeffer's work over the next two decades would decontextualize and aestheticize these previously familiar sonic objects, making them abstract by detaching them from a particular source.[79] Electronic technologies were absolutely essential to this process.[80] Using studio techniques such as montaging, looping, tape-reversal, and filtering, Schaeffer defamiliarized real-world sound samples. In addition, Schaeffer strove to develop a systematic way to describe the sounds' acoustical qualities and to classify and organize them accordingly.[81]

The German composers, however, never really believed that such sonic abstraction would be possible. As they saw it, the problem with both *Hörspiel* and *musique concrète* was this: sounds could never really be decoupled from their sources.[82] In their sales pitch to the WDR administrators, the studio founders pragmatically noted the ways that a new studio would complement and extend the station's already burgeoning *Hörspiel* productions.[83] But in their public lectures on electronic music at Darmstadt and elsewhere, the founders always extolled the idea of a high-art music that would stand apart from the sound effects of both *Hörspiel* and *musique concrète*. For the WDR studio founders and composers, sound effects were an insubstantial and impoverished use of the new technology. As Eimert said in 1952, the new electronic sound world should neither "emulate existing instruments" nor recreate the "sonic-decorative effects of dance bands."[84] Rather, the new sound world should be developed only out of the sound itself, from the internal potentialities of the material.

It was the critique of sound effects that led Eimert, Meyer-Eppler, and Beyer to posit an immanent historical logic for electronic music. Their mantra of aesthetic progress functioned as a salve for their anxiety, staving off the admission that "composing" electronic music to this point had mostly meant montaging technicians' sound effects. In the first pieces, Eimert and Beyer certainly made efforts to sanitize and elevate the appropriated sounds using the compositional logic of high-art music, but their efforts had uneven results. For example, the newly composed minor-triad opening theme of *Spiel* tries to fashion a motivic coherence among the inherited samples, but instead sounds anachronistic, hokey, and desperate. Not only was it challenging to logically connect and develop the sounds, it was difficult to decouple them from other associations, too. The Vocoder sounds in Eimert's *Spiel*, for instance, were strongly coded as the "robot voices" of 1950s science-fiction-themed radio plays and films.

In addition to the composers and technologies, the technicians were a third direct link between *Hörspiel* and the earliest pieces of electronic music. Heinz Schütz, the technician who worked with Eimert in 1952–1956, produced the electronic sounds for a 1955 science-fiction *Hörspiel* titled *Das Unternehmen der Wega* [The Adventure of Vega].[85] The Cold War–themed piece dramatized the establishment of a new society on the star Vega, during which the space travelers prepared for the last great battle with Russia. Amid subtle electronic whirring sounds, the *Hörspiel* opens with this phrase: "Hier Abteilung Morgenröte. Präsident bereit. Sendet Geheimbericht 'Unternehmen Wega'" ["This is Dawn Division. The president is ready. Please send the secret report 'Mission Vega'"]. In the end, the leader of the interplanetary free world declines to drop the atom bomb, giving Russia one last chance.

Schütz, whom we have now met as a studio technician and a composer of science-fiction *Hörspiel* scores, was also the composer of the WDR studio's "piece zero" produced in late 1952. Its title, *Morgenröte* [*Dawn*], is certainly suggestive of the founding ("dawning") of the new WDR studio, but it is also inextricably intertwined with the Cold War science-fiction rhetoric of the 1950s. Appropriately, this piece zero—and especially its subsequent iterations—stands as a vivid example of invisible collaboration and the elevation of sound effects toward high art.

Incarnations of *Morgenröte*

Morgenröte was not officially premiered as a coherent, self-contained work in the first West German concert of electronic music (see Figure 1.4). But nearly all of *Morgenröte*'s sounds were heard in May 1953, as they were the foundation of Eimert and Beyer's joint compositions premiered at that concert.[86] In the WDR archival sound library, *Morgenröte* is catalogued as piece zero, *Klangstudie II* as piece two, and *Klang im unbegrenzten Raum* (hereafter *KuR*) as piece four. These related pieces were apparently composed over a span of months in late 1952 using the Melochord. As Figure 1.5 shows, *Morgenröte* is most closely tied to *Klangstudie II* and the third movement of *KuR*. But as Table 1.2 and Figure 1.5 show, *Morgenröte* is also a significant part of the source material for the first and second movements of *KuR*.

Given the sonic evidence, it seems that Eimert and Beyer cannibalized *Morgenröte* to create *Klangstudie II*, which was then presented again in a new context, as the third movement of *KuR*. Some of the leftover sounds from

neues musikfest 1953

veranstaltet vom
centre de documentation
de musique internationale
in verbindung mit dem
nordwestdeutschen rundfunk

25. bis 28. mai
funkhaus köln

Dienstag, 26. Mai 1953, 11.00 Uhr

MUSIQUE CONCRÈTE

Pierre Schaeffer (Paris)   Einführung und Beispiele

ELEKTRONISCHE MUSIK

Werner Meyer-Eppler	„Die akustischen Grundlagen"
Fritz Enkel	„Die technischen Grundlagen"
Herbert Eimert	„Die kompositorischen Grundlagen"

Herbert Eimert
Robert Beyer
Vier Stücke
Klangstudie I
Klang im unbegrenzten Raum (drei Sätze)
Ostinate Figuren und Rhythmen
Klangstudie II

Technik: Fritz Enkel, Winfried Bierhals, Heinz Schütz

FIGURE 1.4. Program for *Neues Musikfest Köln*, May 26, 1953. The first public German concert of *elektronische Musik*. WDR Historisches Archiv.

Morgenröte, plus additional materials, were assembled to make movements one and two of *KuR*. It would not be surprising to find that the additional materials of *KuR* were reused in Eimert and Beyer's contemporaneous pieces. Because *Klangstudie III, Ostinate Figuren und Ryhthmen*, and *Struktur 8*—WDR studio pieces three, five, and seven, respectively—are available only archivally, it is difficult to establish with comparative close listening how extensively sonic materials were repurposed; but as the following analysis makes clear, *Morgenröte* provides the main sonic inspiration for *Klangstudie II* and the movements of *KuR*.

One of the most aurally recognizable gestures repurposed from *Morgenröte* is a siren-like major triad that slides from roughly B to B♭ and back in either the fourth or the fifth octave (motive C in Table 1.2). The pieces are also saturated with variations on motive D, a cascading series of sine tone or impulse "bubbles" that (1) ascend, descend, or both; that (2) are unfolded more slowly or more quickly, relatively speaking; that (3) are transposed to different octaves; and that (4) are treated with varying amounts of reverberation. The three pieces share a prominent melodic motive (E), which consists of an ascending third followed by a descending second. Drone elements (motives A and G) are used in opening and closing functions. As Table 1.2 shows, the high, violin-like drone (motive G), which was not original to *Morgenröte*, was introduced midway through the compositional trajectory in *Klangstudie II* and was carried forward into all movements of *KuR*. The gong-like descending fifth (motive B) is one of the more prominent *Morgenröte* materials not used in *Klangstudie II*, but it does

Piece 0: *Morgenröte*

A	B	C+D+E+F	B+additional elements (F, C)	C	E	A+distortion → A
0:00	0:10	0:18	0:48	1:55	2:44	3:07 3:22

Piece 2: *Klangstudie II*

C(3×)	E+D(4×)	C+D+E	E+D+distortion	C+D+E	A	G+additional elements	C → distortion
0:00	0:40	0:57	1:25	2:08	2:24	2:52	4:14

Piece 4: *Klang im unbegrenzten Raum*, mvt. I

D¹+G	D¹+addl. impulses	B¹	A	B	D¹+G	silence
0:00	0:31	1:28	1:55	2:10	2:25	2:56

Piece 4: *Klang im unbegrenzten Raum*, mvt. II

metallic melody +arpeggios	G+arpeggios+ shells tapping	metallic melody +arpeggios	G+arpeggios+ shells tapping	metallic melody	silence
3:01	3:34	4:30	4:53	5:51	6:04

Piece 4: *Klang im unbegrenzten Raum*, mvt. III

C(3×)	E+D(4×)	C+D+E	E+D+distortion	C+D+E	A	G+additional elements	C → distortion
6:13	6:52	7:10	7:39	8:04	8:21	8:49	10:10

FIGURE 1.5. Formal schemes for *Morgenröte* (Schütz); *Klangstudie II* (Eimert and Beyer); and *Klang im unbegrenzten Raum* (Eimert and Beyer). Motivic letters refer to Table 1.2.

appear in the first movement of *KuR*. Likewise, the first and second movements of *KuR* include motives that resemble similar motives from *Morgenröte*, but do not copy them entirely (B¹ and D¹). The only motive from *Morgenröte* that does not appear in *Klangstudie II* or any movement of *KuR* is the insistent ascending siren (motive F). Perhaps one siren (motive C) was enough.

TABLE 1.2. Sonic materials shared among *Morgenröte* (Schütz), *Klangstudie II* (Eimert and Beyer), and *Klang im unbegrenzten Raum* (Eimert and Beyer). Pitches are approximate.

Motive (cf. Fig. 1.5)	Description	Piece 0: *Morgenröte* (Schütz)	Piece 2: *Klangstudie II* (Eimert/ Beyer)	Piece 4: *Klang im untegrenzten Raum* (Eimert/ Beyer)	Graphic Score Notation (cf. Fig. 1.5)
A	drone; cello-like with harmonics or distorted	0:02	2:24	I, 1:55 III, 6:13	
B	metallic, gong-like descending 5th	0:10		I, 2:10	
B¹	metallic low bells descending 2nd			I, 1:28	
C	siren-like major triad slides B–B♭ in 4th or 5th octave	0:18	0:00	III, 7:11	
D	sine tone "bubbles"	2:44	0:40	III, 6:54	
D¹	impulse "bubbles"			I, 0:00	
E	melodic motive (asc. 3rd, desc. 2nd)	2:44		III, 6:52	
F	siren; insistent	0:55			
G	violin-like, high frequency, wind-like		2:52	I, 0:08 II, 3:39 III, 8:49	

Figure 1.5 shows the formal outlines of *Morgenröte, Klangstudie II*, and the three movements of *KuR*. The third movement of *KuR* is nearly identical to *Klangstudie II*, save for a truncation of about sixteen seconds during the highlighted section. The sound world of *KuR* is, on the whole, a bit more reserved, because *KuR* was either mixed at a lower volume or mastered in a way that minimized its dynamic and timbral contrasts. Despite this truncation and "veiling" of the sound in *KuR*, the order of events is exactly the same as in *Klangstudie II*.

The blatant repurposing revealed in Figure 1.5 is surprising. Why, one is left to wonder, would Eimert and Beyer present a nearly unchanged version of *Klangstudie II* as the third movement of *KuR*, given that the two pieces were premiered on the same concert? We might conjecture that Eimert and Beyer wanted to (subversively) offer the audience and critics repeated hearings, which would have given them a chance to become more familiar with, and therefore more receptive to, the new-sounding music. After all, Eimert had worked as a music critic and was attuned to issues of audience reception.[87] Eimert and his collaborators wrote as many lectures, broadcasts, and articles as they did because they believed they could educate the public into embracing electronic advances. Like the lecture–recital format, the repeated hearings built into the May 1953 concert could very well have been a strategy to foster familiarity and receptivity. If these speculations about repetition and reception are plausible, *Morgenröte*'s ambiguous status still leaves several questions open: Did Eimert and Beyer appropriate Schütz's creative work as their own? Are *Morgenröte*'s offspring merely a sonic demonstration of the collaborative process of composing early electronic music? Further analysis can clarify the extent of Eimert and Beyer's borrowing, as well as the relative coherence of *Morgenröte* as a stand-alone work.

Figures 1.6a and 1.6b show one thirty-second section that Eimert and Beyer borrowed nearly wholesale from *Morgenröte*. These graphic scores

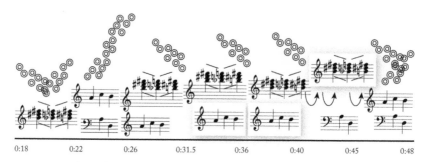

FIGURE 1.6A. Graphic score of *Morgenröte* (0:18–0:48).

FIGURE 1.6B. Graphic score of *Klangstudie II* (0:57–1:25).

seek to represent all of the sonic elements in the mixture and also attempt to render the chronological unfolding of events over the excerpts. The graphic score is an analytical representation of the sounds—no notation or sketch material exists for any of these pieces. Throughout, the shadow behind a motive signifies reverberation. The two excerpts share many similar events, which are often altered only by their ordering or their contours. Both excerpts begin with the hallmark siren motive (C) in the fourth octave. The siren disappears shortly, only to be reintroduced and pervasively repeated in the fifth octave, while it is moved into the background of the mix. Both pieces share the cascading sine tone bubbles (motive D) in various contours. The *Morgenröte* excerpt begins and ends with a u-contoured cascade that seems to superimpose an ascending contour over a descending contour—a gesture also used at 1:01 in *Klangstudie II*. *Morgenröte*'s sine tone bubbles at 0:22 form a longer ascending sequence that is treated with more reverberation. The same sequence occurs at 1:05 in *Klangstudie II*, though without the descending fifth (motive B), which is excised entirely from *Klangstudie II*. Whereas *Morgenröte*'s sine tone bubbles often descend, *Klangstudie II*'s sine tone bubbles often ascend—differences further distinguished by changes in register. These changes are probably the result of tape-editing techniques such as changing the speed of the tape (which induces complementary changes in pitch) or reversing the tape direction.[88] Both pieces pervasively feature the melodic motive E. In each work this motive appears after about four seconds, and it becomes—along with the sine tone bubbles—increasingly reverberant and foregrounded in the respective mixes.

The differences between Figures 1.6a and 1.6b are representative of the differences between Schütz's and Eimert and Beyer's rendering of the material on the whole. As both Figures 1.5 and 1.6 illustrate, *Morgenröte* generally introduces more material within a shorter amount of time, resulting in a denser listening experience. *Morgenröte*'s insistent ascending glide (motive F, at 0:40 and 0:45), which recalls a second siren, and the gong-like metallic motive of descending fifth (motive B, at 0:22, 0:45, and 0:48) are excised entirely from the parallel passage of *Klangstudie II*—in fact, these motives are excised from *Klangstudie II* altogether. Figure 1.5 shows that over the course of *Morgenröte*, Schütz increasingly isolated and developed sonic materials (such as motives B, C, and E) that were presented in tandem in early moments of the piece. In *Klangstudie II,* Eimert and Beyer went much further with this impulse to develop and transform motives. They did so primarily by presenting the gestures in three or four repetitions with timbral variations on each iteration, in keeping with the aims of a "sound study" (Figure 1.6b). Although Schütz also used varied repetitions, he gave up on the development of the motives sooner, instead complicating the sonic texture by introducing more new material.

If Eimert and Beyer exploited the compositional logic already inherent in Schütz's *Morgenröte*, they also capitalized on the technical strengths of the Melochord, the instrument on which the sounds were produced. The composers likely used the Melochord's sound filters to add reverberation [*Resonanzkreise*]; its vibrato generator or low-frequency oscillator [*Vibratogenerator*] to produce a frequency between 6 Hz and 8 Hz that could be combined with the generated tones; and its regulator [*Regelanordnung*] to deploy particular attack and decay characteristics. As we have already established, for the composer of electronic music, timbre was very much at the forefront of the imagination. Because the Melochord was particularly well suited to timbral variation, Eimert and Beyer prioritized varied repetitions in *Klangstudie II*.

Eimert and Beyer's extensive use of repetitions suggests that they may have understood Schütz's sounds as raw materials that could be detached, further processed, and recombined, just as they had understood Meyer-Eppler's sounds in *Spiel*. There is no evidence of hand-wringing over whether Schütz's creative voice was marginalized as *Morgenröte* was deconstructed, altered, and reconstructed again and again. As Schütz said, "Since I produced it, it is attributed to me—I do not see myself as a composer. Pure chance."[89] These comments suggest that *Morgenröte* was probably never imagined by Schütz, Eimert, or Beyer as a finished piece, but as a "mock-up," a provisional demonstration of the studio's existing technology and sound possibilities.[90] Yet, in examining the formal arcs in Figure 1.5, it is clear that *Morgenröte* can indeed be understood as a piece of music. *Morgenröte* displays an internal logic that transcends a simple catalogue of disconnected sounds. It has a beginning–middle–end structure with a brief return to the opening material, and motives that develop over the course of the piece. All of the sonic materials are presented in the first forty-seven seconds or so, at which point the piece begins to develop and dwell on motives individually (B, C, and E) for longer periods of time. The piece ends with a return to the drone motive (A), producing a formal rounding-off. All of these elements present evidence of compositional design, even if rather hastily construed.

Eimert and Beyer's early compositional methodology as revealed here—that is, montaging Schütz's sound effects—runs up against the commonplace assumption that *elektronische Musik* composers were using additive and subtractive synthesis to work directly with timbres from the start.[91] As my analyses reveal, Eimert and Beyer instead built their earliest pieces by montaging together sound excerpts from catalogues (Meyer-Eppler) and technician's pieces (Schütz). In *Spiel*, they selected samples from the catalogue that had harmonic or melodic correspondences and then composed new material that would tie them together with a motivic thread. In *Klangstudie II* and *KuR*, they amplified the compositional logic of *Morgenröte* by further exploiting the concept of timbral variation, making the formal logic of presentation–development–return even more transparent. These adaptations created a logic for sounds that were previously disconnected (as in Meyer-Eppler's catalogue) or ineffectively connected (as in Schütz's rapid-fire motivic presentation in *Morgenröte*). In so doing, Eimert and Beyer believed that they were creating high-art works, effectively sublimating their sound effects anxiety by rationalizing the new sounds into the formal paradigms of high-art classical music.

Conclusions

In October 1953, Stockhausen complained to his best friend, the French-Belgian composer Henri Pousseur:

> My situation [in the studio] is difficult. Eimert is "composing" again and has limited my time to three hours daily. I believe he hates me and my music. [. . .] I need music and this work and a technician who does not laugh at me, because he can easily sell radio play noises.[92]

The analyses of this chapter help to contextualize Stockhausen's complaints—whereas Eimert believed he was composing, Stockhausen looked skeptically on his montaging of Schütz's *Hörspiel* sounds. Although the creative collaborations between technicians and composers were evidently pragmatic and mutually agreeable, the studio's laboratory-like working scheme remained deeply hierarchical. Consider the bolded, foregrounded, and repeated name of Eimert in the concert poster shown in Figure 1.4, as compared with the veritable footnote listing the names of the "Technik." At the premiere, the people credited for the creative work were Eimert and Beyer. Eimert appeared prominently as the studio's advocate, its creative director, and its leading composer. Meanwhile, the creative contributions of Schütz and other technicians remained all but invisible, even if technicians were complicit in their own elision.[93] Reminiscent of a gendered division of labor, technicians created the studio's sonic palette but offered it up as common property, apparently expecting that the more visible or trained composers would freely use the materials. As Stockhausen's complaints suggest, Eimert publicly reaped the rewards—no doubt mostly in the form of cultural capital—of being a progressive, capable composer of electronic music, all the while his early works were underwritten by the extensive creative help of sonic engineers.

The collaborative working environment of the WDR studio was strongly conditioned by technical circumstances, as we will continue to see throughout this book: instruments and technologies were unfamiliar, so composers needed technical collaborators who could manipulate the machinery for them or with them. Practically speaking, two or more people were often needed to simultaneously turn knobs during the sound-production phase.[94] Invisible technicians like Schütz made further lasting contributions, such as reversing the order of tape heads so that superimposed layers could be efficiently created with a minimum of hiss from re-recording and tape loops.[95] In this way, the studio's technicians were indispensable in creating the conditions under which composers brought forward their aesthetic works. Technicians were important partners who used their knowledge to mitigate failures and breakdowns, to improve efficiency, and to translate composers' ideas into sounds.

Eimert and Beyer glossed over these technical dimensions as they posited a coherent, historical lineage for *elektronische Musik* based mostly on the evolution of timbre in avant-garde acoustic music. The studio founders sidelined all but the most obscure early electronic instruments in order to focus on the liberatory potential of composing "the sound itself." In fact, the studio founders oriented the WDR studio toward timbral innovation even before they had a handle on the sonic possibilities of the studio's freestanding machinery. This brings us to a notable revision of another common misapprehension, namely that the timbral preoccupations of the WDR studio "began" with Stockhausen's arrival in 1953.[96] It is true that Stockhausen and the younger composers better matched their compositional techniques to their timbral goals, as we will see in Chapter 3; however, we should credit Meyer-Eppler, Eimert, and Beyer with articulating the foundational logic for the studio. The rhetoric that Meyer-Eppler, Beyer, and Eimert propagated as early as 1950—even as early as 1928, in Beyer's case—already articulated the dream of a timbral utopia. With their writings (more than their music), these three studio founders opened the intellectual space in which Stockhausen and all of the younger generation would work.

Finally, the studio's invisible collaborations also reflect electronic music's uncomfortable transition from *Hörspiel* and *musique concrète* sound effects to the high-brow, avant-garde aspirations of *elektronische Musik*. Schütz and other technicians remained invisible not only because their skill set differed from that of the composers, but because their aesthetic orientation and expertise was connected to low-brow, mass-media genres. As long as the work of "the *Hörspiel* technician" Schütz remained safely behind the curtain, Eimert and the other composers could suppress their sound effects anxiety. The musical products of the WDR studio could be presented as high-art works, claiming a compositional logic disciplined by the trained composers. Promulgating dreams of timbral innovation, the studio founders established a model of collaborative production that began to distinguish the WDR studio in the Cold War landscape. In the next chapter, the story of collaboration continues, as we learn that the early composers of electronic music also looked to John Cage and David Tudor for inspiration in creating their timbral utopia.

2 | Kinship

Cage, Tudor, and the New Timbral Utopia

The oft-repeated story about the American experimental composer John Cage and the 1950s European avant-garde (led by Stockhausen and Boulez) goes something like this: Cage and the Europeans repelled each other like oil and water because Cage's interest in chance and indeterminacy was incompatible with the dogmatic European serialists, who were striving for total control of musical materials.[1] This familiar narrative of rivalry uses as its primary point of evidence John Cage's incendiary visit to the Darmstadt *Ferienkurse* in September 1958. Cage and pianist David Tudor (his "invisible" collaborator) presented a concert of two-piano works that was met with a mixture of genuine appreciation and heckling.[2] Cage then delivered three lectures, ostensibly on his own indeterminate compositional practices and philosophies, but peppered throughout with barbs against the compositional practices and attitudes of Stockhausen, Boulez, and others.[3] His critiques were made only more provocative by hasty, inelegant translations, which amplified their confrontational tone.[4] As Christopher Shultis writes, "No other event in Darmstadt's history ever generated more controversy than Cage's 1958 lectures."[5] This narrative places Darmstadt as the epicenter of the European avant-garde and concludes that the Europeans received Cage's work somewhere between ambivalence and antagonism.

In this chapter, I encourage an expanded focus—temporally, geographically, and interpersonally—in order to rethink the relationship among Cage, Tudor, and the European serialists. Although Darmstadt 1958 was a visible controversy, it was not Cage's first or most important encounter with the European avant-garde. Between 1949 and 1954, Cage enjoyed a warm courtship, lasting relationships, and significant celebrity among a small but powerful segment of the European avant-garde. This early embrace of Cage was especially apparent in the emerging WDR studio, where Cage's prepared-piano works were crucial to the development of electronic music. (A prepared piano is a piano in whose strings various objects or "preparations" like screws, bolts, and rubber have been placed). Moreover, after Cage's relationships with some of his European colleagues became more strained in the late 1950s, Tudor remained exceptionally important as a nodal figure, connecting American and European strands of the avant-garde well into the 1960s. Cage and Tudor's contributions, especially in the milieu of the WDR studio, were important facets of the emerging discourse of electronic music.

Past Tense

Cage's first encounter with the European avant-garde was in Paris in June and July 1949, when Cage and Merce Cunningham presented *Sonatas and Interludes* and *Three Dances* for prepared piano, among other works, in Olivier Messiaen's class, in Jean Hélión's salon, in Suzanne Tézenas's salon, and at the Théâtre du Vieux-Columbier.[6] Boulez, a close associate of the socialite and patron Tézenas, gave a spoken introduction to Cage's work at her salon; afterward, Cage and Boulez maintained a lively correspondence and a close friendship for several years. In 1951, when the two were exchanging warm letters frequently, their compositional techniques overlapped closely. Both composers used gameboards or other precompositional charts in part to minimize their own moment-to-moment choices. As Boulez wrote to Cage, "I've taken over your chess board system for my own purposes, by making it serve on dissociated, antagonistic, and parallel or anti-parallel levels."[7] Cage replied in solidarity, "By making moves on the charts I freed myself from what I thought to be freedom, and which actually was only the accretion of habits and tastes."[8]

As this exchange shows, Boulez and Cage shared a desire to move beyond their own inherited instincts. This is a well-understood aspect of Cage's poetics.[9] In his own words, throwing the dice allowed him "to make a composition the continuity of which is free of individual taste and memory (psychology) and also of the literature and 'traditions' of the art."[10] Achieving such aesthetic freedom was also a major preoccupation of the postwar European avant-garde. As Boulez said, "dodecaphonists and independents alike work to inculcate *liberty*. [. . .] Any musician who has not experienced—I do not say understood, but truly experienced—the necessity of dodecaphonic language is USELESS."[11] When Boulez and Cage argued the "necessity" of compositional systems based on their affordances of liberty and freedom, they revealed that their aesthetic choices were implicitly linked to historically conditioned, political–aesthetic circumstances.

In short, the appeal of such systems, whether serial or aleatoric, lay in their ability to neutralize the trained, conservative, or (morally) corrupt instincts of composers. The younger generation of avant-garde composers were born in the 1920s and were reared and educated during the Nazi era, when racial exclusion, nineteenth-century aesthetics and tonality, and electronic music instruments were packaged together into a grotesque mandate. In Germany, those in the older generation had to suppress their new music interests (as Eimert did), win the favor of the Nazi Party (as Trautwein did), or leave the country (as Schoenberg did). This bind was recast in the cultural Cold War, as the Soviet Socialist Realist doctrine again mandated conservative artistic positions and avant-garde art symbolized democratic freedom.[12] As Richard Taruskin summarizes, in the 1950s avant-gardism "seemed to embody a perfect artistic 'autonomy.' That autonomy easily translated into personal and political autonomy—that is, individual integrity—in the minds of many who were emerging from decades of oppression, an oppression that was still going on in the East."[13] Cage and Boulez began as kindred spirits, who in the early cultural Cold War mentality, used rigid systems to unlock and perpetuate their liberty—a paradox that reveals its own historically contingent logic.

The fellow travelers did not remain so for long. The first cracks appeared in December 1951, when Boulez wrote to Cage, "The only thing, forgive me, which I am not happy with, is the method of absolute chance (by tossing the coins). { . . . } I am a little afraid of what is called 'automatic writing' for most of the time it is chiefly a lack of control."[14] Boulez further registered his discontent along similar lines in 1954.[15] With the publication of "Alea" in 1957 Boulez publicly amplified his complaints and set the stage for the Darmstadt debacle.[16] However, to focus only on the progression of the aleatory debates, extending outward from the personal relationship between Cage and Boulez, obscures the degree to which Cage was a key figure to many of the European composers between 1949 and 1954. In this era, aided by Boulez's introductions, Cage and Tudor gained significant traction with Eimert, Stockhausen, and many other powerful impresarios and composers in the West German scene.

Widening Circles

Figure 2.1 shows a timeline of Cage's exposure by means of West German new music institutions between 1952 and 1954. Cage and Tudor garnered cachet in West Germany through Eimert's WDR *Musikalisches Nachtprogramm* and subsequently through other radio broadcasts (Otto Zoff on the SWF [*Südwestfunk*, or Southwest German Radio]) and lectures (Wolfgang Rebner at Darmstadt).[17] Radio was an extraordinarily important medium at that time,

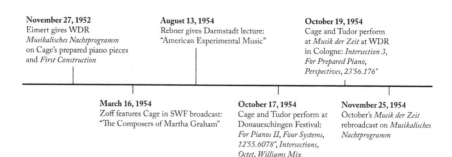

November 27, 1952	August 13, 1954	October 19, 1954
Eimert gives WDR *Musikalisches Nachtprogramm* on Cage's prepared piano pieces and *First Construction*	Rebner gives Darmstadt lecture: "American Experimental Music"	Cage and Tudor perform at *Musik der Zeit* at WDR in Cologne: *Intersection 3, For Prepared Piano, Perspectives, 23'56.176"*

March 16, 1954	October 17, 1954	November 25, 1954
Zoff features Cage in SWF broadcast: "The Composers of Martha Graham"	Cage and Tudor perform at Donaueschingen Festival: *For Pianos II, Four Systems, 12'55.6078", Intersections, Octet, Williams Mix*	October's *Musik der Zeit* rebroadcast on *Musikalisches Nachtprogramm*

FIGURE 2.1. Timeline of Cage and Tudor's West German exposure, 1952–1954.

and it would be difficult to overstate the impact of Eimert's particular endorsement of Cage on his *Nachtprogramm* in November 1952. Eimert's twice-monthly broadcasts, which aired from 11:15 p.m. to midnight and attracted a wide range of listeners, were critical in disseminating new music that had been forbidden or forgotten, as well as analysis of it. The show was something like a correspondence course for keeping current with new music; as Martin Iddon says, "In short, anyone who was anyone was listening."[18] Consequently, using the *Nachtprogramm* as something of a bully pulpit, Eimert had substantial power to shape the narrative and direction of the postwar musical avant-garde. This West German interest in Cage culminated in a pair of concerts in fall 1954 at Donaueschingen's *Musiktage* and Cologne's *Musik der Zeit*, where (at the latter) Cage and Tudor's stunning prepared-piano pieces were heard opposite the newest electronic music from the WDR studio.

In his 1952 broadcast, Eimert set the stage by introducing Cage to West Germany with a reasonably clear (though somewhat stereotypical) understanding of his aesthetic and philosophical premises, including mentions of gamelan, Meister Eckhardt, Buddhism, and silence.[19] Eimert portrayed Cage as a descendant of jazz music, Buddhism, and a lineage of American experimentalists such as Edgard Varèse, Henry Cowell, George Antheil, and Arnold Schoenberg.[20] Although Schoenberg was an Austrian who emigrated to the United States and gained citizenship in 1941, and although Antheil was immersed in the Parisian avant-garde in the 1920s, both played into Eimert's narrative of American rugged individualism and aesthetic freedom. As he wrote to Stockhausen contemporaneously, "Cage's works are interesting and completely unencumbered by conventional concepts."[21] According to the Europeans, Cage admirably stood outside of the musical tradition that they were all trying desperately to navigate and sidestep.

As Table 2.1 shows, most of the musical examples broadcast on Eimert's program were piano works—especially two-piano and prepared-piano works. Eimert contextualized these as examples of an "American experimental

TABLE 2.1. Repertoire played during Eimert's November 27, 1952 *Musikalisches Nachtprogramm* broadcast.

Musical Example and Composer	Piece as Named in Broadcast Transcript	Corresponding Work
1: Cage	"kleines Beispiel aus Cages Stücken für präpariertes Klavier"	*Three Dances* (for two amplified prepared pianos) (1944–1945)? *A Book of Music* (for two prepared pianos) (1944)? *Sonatas and Interludes* (1946–1948)?
2: Cage	"Festmusik für prepared Piano"	*Bacchanale* (1938–1940)
3: Varèse	*Ionisation*	*Ionisation* (1929–1931)
4: Cage	Konstruktion in Metall	*First Construction (in Metal)* (1939)
5: Cage	Konstruktion in Metall, 2nd example	*First Construction (in Metal)* (1939)
6: Cage [Ives]	"kleine Vierteltonpassage"	Ives, *Three Quarter-Tone Pieces for Two Pianos* (1923–1924)
7: Cage [Ives]	"ein Beispiel aus John Cages Vierteltonmusik für zwei Klaviere"	Ives, *Three Quarter-Tone Pieces for Two Pianos* (1923–1924)
8: Maderna	Konzert für zwei Klaviere und Instrumente	Concerto (for two pianos and instruments) (1948)

noise" heritage that extended from Varèse through to its fullest elaboration in Cage's *First Construction*; he concluded the broadcast with an excerpt from Bruno Maderna's two-piano concerto. Eimert probably focused on two-piano works because Boulez gave him a record in 1952 that must have contained Cage's *Three Dances, A Book of Music*, or both—a record of prepared-piano works for two pianos.[22] Boulez had already spoken about these pieces, as well as Cage's *Sonatas and Interludes*, in his introduction to Cage's 1949 performance at Tézenas's salon, so it stands to reason that Boulez had recordings of them in his possession.[23] Eimert also played from what he claimed to be a Cage work for two pianos tuned a quarter-tone apart. No such piece by Cage is known, and it seems likely that what Eimert mistakenly attributed to Cage—a work that perhaps also appeared on Boulez's record—was actually Charles Ives's *Three Quarter-Tone Pieces for Two Pianos*.[24]

Eimert characterized the prepared piano as the most recent stage in a long evolution of keyboard instruments, using the same type of historicizing narrative meant to justify electronic music and other new sounds to the "stubbornly conditioned ears of the public," in Varèse's famous phrase.[25] Eimert viewed Cage as a brother in arms in the quest to transcend the limitations of acoustic instruments, and yet, he did not hold Cage's electronic work in high esteem. As Eimert wrote rather pejoratively to Stockhausen, "His [Cage's] electronic tapes [*Imaginary Landscape No. 5* (1952) or *Williams Mix* (1952–53)?] are by contrast quite primitive and contain nothing more than a few feedback tones."[26] Nevertheless, Eimert found a conceptual and even spiritual kinship between Cage and European composers such as Boulez and Messiaen: all were searching for an "Authentic Music,"[27] a "music structured according to a crystalline logic without psychology, without memory."[28] In Eimert's reading, Boulez and the European avant-gardists sought this aim by magnifying Webern's pointillist aesthetics with integral serialism, whereas Cage and the American experimentalists pursued it by allowing the structure of the piece to spring from the interplay between new sonic materials, like the prepared piano and silence.

Preparing Electronic Music

At the time of Eimert's Cage broadcast, the WDR electronic studio space was anxiously anticipated. "What a shame that the construction of the WDR electronic studio is proceeding with such bureaucratic slowness," Eimert complained to Stockhausen in March 1952, "it is still months to completion."[29] Although the studio had been in the planning and construction phases since 1951, the first pieces would not premiere there until May 1953. While Eimert waited for the studio to become a fully functional space, he and Beyer were busy exploring the new timbres of the Melochord and montaging the sound catalogues of Meyer-Eppler and Schütz into their first pieces.

Meanwhile, Eimert wrote frequently to his protégé Stockhausen, who was, at the time, working as Pierre Schaeffer's intern at *Radiodiffusion Française* in Paris. Stockhausen was Eimert's main informant for contemporary French studio developments—an important role because Eimert was continually evaluating how much ground he was losing to the French, who had been making electronic music since the late 1940s. Stockhausen fielded anxious questions such as, "What is Schaeffer up to now? What about Messiaen?"[30] "It is important to me to learn about Boulez's electronic experiments,"[31] and "Write to me more about Boulez, please."[32] The West Germans anticipated their own electronic studio at the WDR with ebullient excitement but also plenty of competitive hand-wringing, primarily over their self-perceived lateness. It was in this environment that Cage's prepared-piano works were important models for the *terra incognita* that was early electronic music.

Eimert's combination of anticipation and anxiety was shared by many of those active in electronic music circles, whether in West Germany, France, or the States. In this era, composers and technicians confronted unfamiliar and unwieldy machines holding fast, on the one hand, to the expansive promises of new sounds while struggling, on the other hand, to find palatable ways to produce electronic music. In his own early experiments, Pierre Schaeffer searched for appropriate sound sources and sonic models for *musique concrète*. As Schaeffer wrote in his journal in June 1948,

> There is no instrument on which to play concrete music. That is the main difficulty. Or else we have to imagine a huge cybernetic-like machine that can achieve millions of combinations, and we're not there yet. As long as I have no more than two or four turntables that make only approximate transitions, I shall remain horribly imprisoned in a discontinuous style where everything seems to have been hacked out with a billhook. Is there a compromise? I instinctively turn to the piano. The preceding manipulations have in fact taught me that a piano could well replace all sound effects equipment. You can strike the strings directly, or scratch or lightly stroke them but you can also use the keyboard, not as a musical instrument, but as a convenient way of attacking the strings, which will have undergone some "preparation." [Schaeffer's footnote: the term "prepared piano" was used systematically by the American John Cage, whose works I was unaware of at this time. The use of the piano is similar in both cases, but with John Cage it leads to a music that still remains fairly abstract in its conception and performance].[33]

Dissatisfied with the denaturing effects that could be induced with the studio's turntables, Schaeffer imagined the prepared piano as an already complex, already noisy instrument that would serve as a super-percussion section and a sophisticated sound source for his *musique concrète* works. The footnote, apparently inserted retrospectively when Schaeffer prepared his journals for publication in 1952, suggests that he hadn't yet encountered either the concept or the terminology of Cage's prepared piano when he wrote this journal entry in 1948. We can surmise, however, that Schaeffer did hear Cage's prepared piano in one of the four Paris concerts in June 1949, where attending avant-garde composers called the sounds "profound." As Karel Goeyvaerts remembered, "The crisp sounds of his gamelan piano and the precise rhythm of the sonatas kept us spellbound. Messiaen claimed that this was his most riveting musical experience since he first discovered Çarngadeva's *Deçitâla*."[34]

Stockhausen, who must have encountered Cage's prepared piano on a recording in Schaeffer's studio in 1952, began composing his own preliminary *musique concrète* experiment in close quarters with Goeyvaerts and using the prepared piano as his sound source.[35] The experimental piece may have "ended in catastrophe,"[36] but the point is that Stockhausen, like Schaeffer, considered the prepared piano a promising sound source for electronic music. Boulez, too, seemed taken with the new sound world that Cage's prepared piano had opened up:

His use of the *prepared piano* is not merely an unusual area of percussive piano technique in which the sounding board is to be invaded by a strange, metallicizing vegetation. It has much more to do with calling into question acoustic ideas which have gradually become fixed in the course of Western musical evolution; for this prepared piano becomes, by way of a do-it-yourself tuning system, an instrument capable of producing frequency complexes.[37]

Boulez gets to the heart of the matter: the prepared piano was beguiling because its sounds unsettled the assumptions and expectations of listeners. The prepared piano married familiar old gestures to intriguingly new sounds. It displaced the predictable timbres of the acoustic piano, while remaining in a dialectical relationship with the historical progression of instrument development. This, of course, was the same dream that composers held for electronic music. In Boulez's formulation and in Schaeffer's (previously quoted), the prepared piano can almost substitute for the studio; both scenarios were capable of producing "frequency complexes." As the repertoire on the *Musik der Zeit* concert of 1954 suggests, it was only one small step from the new timbres of Cage's prepared piano to electronic music (see Figure 2.2).

The aural similarity between early WDR electronic music and Cage's prepared-piano music of the same era is compelling. Consider Eimert's *Glockenspiel* (1953), the eighth piece to be produced in the WDR studio, and the first piece for which Eimert is credited as the sole composer, without Robert Beyer. *Glockenspiel* shares a number of conspicuous sonorities with Cage's prepared-piano timbres, which is perhaps not surprising, as it was likely composed only a few short months after Eimert's *Nachtprogramm* broadcast. We might use Cage's *Bacchanale* (1938–1940) for comparison, because Eimert played it during the broadcast and could have had the piece in mind (and on record) as he composed *Glockenspiel*.

There are at least three sound-colors that are strongly shared between *Glockenspiel* (German for bells, chimes, or carillon) and *Bacchanale*: muted sounds, bell sounds, and metallic sounds. The muted sounds, produced when fibrous weather stripping is placed between the strings to dampen the vibrations, is particularly pervasive in *Bacchanale*, used in ten out of twelve preparations.[38] In *Glockenspiel*, the muted timbre is also pervasive, characterizing many of the low-frequency, gong-like strokes that begin the piece and are interspersed throughout. The many bell-like and metallic sounds shared between the pieces are produced on the prepared piano by inserting screws or bolts in the middle to low register, such as the third octave; one preparation (on D4) involves a "small bolt" whereas another (on B♭3) involves a screw with nuts plus weather stripping.[39] In the electronic studio, on the other hand, the bell-like and metallic timbres are almost surely a result of ring modulation, in which two frequencies are added together.

musik der zeit

I

DIENSTAG, den 19. Oktober 1954, 19.30 Uhr
im Kleinen Sendesaal

NEUE KLAVIERMUSIK AUS AMERIKA
gespielt von David Tudor und John Cage

MORTON FELDMAN   INTERSECTION 3

CHRISTIAN WOLFF   FOR PREPARED PIANO
Vier kleine Stücke

EARLE BROWN   PERSPECTIVES

JOHN CAGE   23' 56. 176" FÜR ZWEI PIANISTEN
(präparierte Klaviere)

Europäische Erstaufführungen

PAUSE

ELEKTRONISCHE MUSIK

KARLHEINZ STOCKHAUSEN   STUDIE II

HERBERT EIMERT   GLOCKENSPIEL

KAREL GOEYVAERTS   KOMPOSITION NR. 5

HENRI POUSSEUR   SEISMOGRAMME

PAUL GREDINGER   FORMANTEN I UND II

KARLHEINZ STOCKHAUSEN   STUDIE I

HERBERT EIMERT   ETÜDE ÜBER TONGEMISCHE

Erste Konzert-Vorführung der im Kölner Studio des NWDR
entstandenen Kompositionen

Die beiden Studien von Karlheinz Stockhausen sind Kompositions-
aufträge des NWDR Köln

Technik: Fritz Enkel, Heinz Schütz, Erhard Harfner

Ansage: Herbert Eimert

Zweiter Abend „Musik der Zeit" Freitag, 26. November 1954, 19.30 Uhr, Kleiner Sendesaal.
Werke von Sessions, Strawinsky, Gielen, Berio, Skalkottas.
Mitwirkende: Nancy Evans (Mezzosopran), Parrenin-Quartett, Hans-Jürgen Möhring (Flöte), Paul Blöcher (Klarinette), Willy Schulz (Baßklarinette),
Helmut Zernick (Violine), Paul Schröer (Bratsche), Hans Adomeit (Violoncello), Dora Wegner (Harfe).

FIGURE 2.2. Program for *Musik der Zeit*, October 19, 1954. Public premiere of the second group of electronic pieces from the WDR studios. WDR Historisches Archiv.

The input frequencies remain unheard under ring modulation, and the heard output is the sum and difference of the input frequencies, which creates an inharmonic relationship and thus a bell-like timbre.[40]

It is unlikely that Eimert arrived at these inharmonic, bell-like sounds through additive synthesis.[41] As Chapter 3 will show, it was not until the end of 1953 and early 1954 that the younger WDR composers, such as Stockhausen, Pousseur, Gredinger, and Goeyvaerts, collaboratively stumbled toward a workable solution for synthesizing inharmonic mixtures. We can speculate, based on the resources of the WDR studio and our knowledge of Eimert's compositional comfort zone, that the sounds for *Glockenspiel* were produced on the Melochord, which contained a number of generators and filters activated through knobs and a two-manual keyboard (refer back to Figure 1.1). The Melochord's bottom manual produced tones from a tone generator, whereas the top manual modified the sound. These modifications could include filtering (such as high-pass, low-pass, and bandpass); ring modulation; certain sound envelope characteristics such as plucked or blown attacks; and vibrato, noise, and reverberation. The various dynamic filters of the Melochord could certainly account for the muffled, muted timbres in *Glockenspiel*, and the instrument's ring modulator could have been used to produce metallic and bell-like tones. In summary, the timbral vocabulary of Cage's *Bacchanale*, Schaeffer's early *musique concrète*, and Eimert's *Glockenspiel* are remarkably similar. All of this gives aural evidence that Cage's idiosyncratic prepared-piano sounds provided an aesthetic model for Eimert—as well as for Schaeffer, Boulez, and Stockhausen—in their earliest attempts to create a new, electronic timbral world.

Cage as Celebrity

The initial exposures that Cage garnered in Europe in the late 1940s and early 1950s—in France by means of Boulez and Schaeffer on the one hand and in West Germany by means of Eimert and radio broadcasts on the other—seem to have accrued to substantial prestige by October 1954. Cage and Tudor were invited to play their prepared-piano works at Donaueschingen by Heinrich Strobel, "arguably the most powerful administrator in West Germany's new music community at the time."[42] Strobel was appointed music director of the SWF Baden-Baden in 1945, served as editor for the popular new music journal *Melos*, and organized the aforementioned long-standing prewar and postwar new music festival at Donaueschingen.[43] After receiving Strobel's invitation, Cage and Tudor, wanting to "stir up as much activity as possible" while in Germany, reached out to Eimert, expressing interest in also visiting the electronic music studio and arranging a "radio engagement" at the WDR.[44]

Cage ventured into rather fraught waters in trying to arrange events in both Donaueschingen and Cologne. Strobel had initially offered Cage a forty-five-minute concert, and Cage, rather presumptuously, countered with a proposal for *three* programs, one for piano, one for orchestra, and one for tape. Strobel stuck to his initial offer for one program. The orchestral aspect of Cage's proposal was abandoned entirely, and works for prepared pianos and magnetic tape by Cage, Morton Feldman, Earle Brown, and Christian Wolff were programmed together on a matinee concert (see Table 2.2).[45] In Cologne, Eimert's assistant Eigel Kruttge initially offered to include Cage and Tudor in an October 8 chamber concert, but Cage could not accept because he had promised Strobel that he would play nowhere in Germany before the Donaueschingen engagement on October 17. As Strobel explained,

> The attraction of your coming out in Germany, in presence of our large international auditorium would be lost, if you play anywhere in Germany before. I hope you understand that your Donaueschingen performance only can be realized if you give no performance before our concert, neither over another radio station {n}or anywhere else in Germany.[46]

These terms make clear what was at stake: Cage had considerable celebrity cachet, which Strobel was determined to draw to Donaueschingen (and away from Paris and Cologne). In courting Cage to appear at *Musik der Zeit*, Eimert (through Kruttge) tried to draw that prestige toward Cologne in an attempt to validate the WDR as the most important German (and international) new music center.

Although October 8 was out for an engagement in Cologne, Cage wrote again to Kruttge at the WDR, requesting a change of date or a change of planned program:

> Since I have not had a reply from you to my last letter, I am writing to say that I hope matters may be arranged in such a way that the concert plans you outlined may be realized. For that reason, please consider our needs as stated in my response to you flexible. I have asked Dr. Strobel whether he would be willing for us to appear in Köln [Cologne] before the 17th of October providing the performance does not include a work for prepared piano. If he agrees to this, you might be interested in a performance by David Tudor of my *Music of Changes* (about 42 minutes). [. . .] And, finally, if the honorarium I requested was too high, please let me know what you will offer. In any event, be assured that I am sincerely interested in cooperation with you.[47]

Having still no reply a month later, Cage wrote a third time. His anxiety at having overreached in these negotiations was palpable:

Although I have not heard from you in reply to my last two letters, I still hope that a concert such as you outlined may take place in Köln with our cooperation. Dr. Strobel is now interested in presenting my work for magnetic tape on the Donaueschingen program. But I would prefer to have it performed at Köln and will delay answering him, hoping for an early reply from you. My present situation is that described in my second letter to you: that is: that I would like to know from you what you will offer in the way of facilities and fee, rather than that the requests of my first letter be considered inflexible (with the exception of date [. . .]).[48]

Although Cage worried that he misjudged his requests for scheduling accommodations and a large honorarium, he also seemed to recognize his work was a valuable commodity. Cage clearly did not wish to appear as the *enfant terrible*, though his cooperative spirit was undermined as he tried to play the SWF off the WDR.

In the end, in a letter dated June 1, Kruttge acquiesced to Cage's requests for a change of date, and the Cologne evening concert took place on October 19, two days after the Donaueschingen matinee.[49] As Tables 2.2 and 2.3 show, the programs given at Donaueschingen and Cologne were remarkably similar. Cage and Tudor played the piano works of Cage (probably shortened versions of $34'46.776''$ and $31'57.9864''$) and several American collaborators in the first half, counterpointed by electronic music—by Feldman, Brown, and Cage in Donaueschingen and by the WDR studio composers in Cologne—in the second half.[50] Despite the similarity of repertoire, both festivals claimed they were offering premieres, with all the preeminence and symbolic capital contained therein.

Cage and Tudor's Donaueschingen concert was controversial, to say the least. As Joan Peyser writes, "Everywhere Cage and Tudor went, they were treated like a couple of clowns. At Donaueschingen the audience was angry and the press outraged. Complaints focused on the 'noise.'"[51] In another

TABLE 2.2. Program for Donaueschingen *Musiktage* matinee performance, October 17, 1954. Asterisked pieces were billed as premieres.

Composer	Title	Performer(s)
Christian Wolff	*For Pianos II*	David Tudor
Earle Brown	*Four Systems*	David Tudor
John Cage	*12'55.6078''* for two prepared pianos	David Tudor and John Cage
Morton Feldman	*Intersection*	Tape
Earle Brown	*Octet*	Tape
John Cage	*Williams Mix*	Tape

TABLE 2.3. Program for Cologne *Musik der Zeit* performance, October 19, 1954. Asterisked piece is billed as European first performance.

Composer	Title	Performer
Morton Feldman	*Intersection 3*	David Tudor
Christian Wolff	*For Prepared Piano: vier kleine Stücke*	David Tudor
Earle Brown	*Perspectives*	David Tudor
John Cage	**23'56.176" for two prepared pianos*	David Tudor and John Cage
Karlheinz Stockhausen	*Studie II*	Tape
Herbert Eimert	*Glockenspiel*	Tape
Karel Goeyvaerts	*Komposition Nr. 5*	Tape
Henri Pousseur	*Seismogrammes I*	Tape
Paul Gredinger	*Formanten I und II*	Tape
Karlheinz Stockhausen	*Studie I*	Tape
Herbert Eimert	*Etüde über Tongemische*	Tape

account, the Donaueschingen audience apparently responded to Cage and Tudor's performance "with a mixture of spontaneous pleasure and simultaneous outrage, shouting, laughter, and confusion."[52]

Cage and Tudor seem to have enjoyed a somewhat smoother reception at the *Musik der Zeit* concert in Cologne a few days later, not least because of the active rivalry between the two West German new music scenes.[53] For example, one reviewer rhetorically raised his eyebrows at a "piano with paper strips and paper clips," but focused his blurb on the importance of Cologne being first to host premieres, and ultimately first in the longer musical–historical purview.[54] In the logic of the cultural Cold War, the West German impresarios in charge of the Donaueschingen and Cologne concert series competed to be on the right side of history.

The honoraria that Cage and Tudor received for the concerts at Donaueschingen and Cologne can further clarify the esteem with which new music impresarios regarded Cage. Strobel and the SWF paid Cage and Tudor 2,000 Deutsche Marks (DM)—$4,330 in 2017 dollars—a lump sum that Cage and Tudor received in advance and used for their travel expenses.[55] From the WDR, Cage initially requested an honorarium of 3,000 DM—the equivalent of about $6,370 in 2017 dollars. Eventually, as Figure 2.3 shows, the WDR paid Cage and Tudor 2,000 DM, the same as the SWF. Beyond honoraria, both festivals also undertook considerable costs to rent and transport large Steinway grand pianos for the concerts.[56]

Cage and Tudor's substantial honoraria are wildly out of proportion to the stipends that anyone else drew. Goeyvaerts and Pousseur, who each had

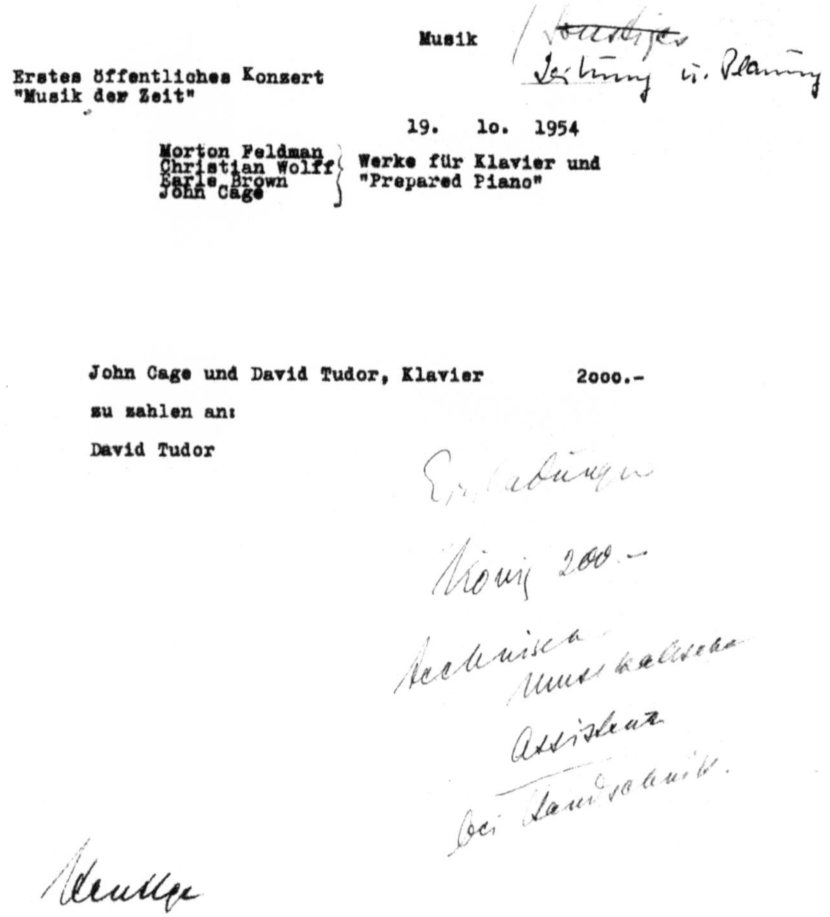
Musik

Erstes öffentliches Konzert
"Musik der Zeit"

19. 10. 1954

Morton Feldman
Christian Wolff
Earle Brown
John Cage
Werke für Klavier und "Prepared Piano"

John Cage und David Tudor, Klavier 2000.-

zu zahlen an:

David Tudor

FIGURE 2.3. Receipt for Cage and Tudor's 1954 *Musik der Zeit* honorarium. WDR Historisches Archiv.

their electronic pieces premiered in the second half of the WDR program, were paid 50 DM each, enough to cover their second-class train travel to and from Cologne. The sound engineer made 10 DM per hour; Gottfried Michael Koenig was paid 200 DM for "technical and musical" assistance. Although Cage and Tudor still had to defray international travel costs, they failed to draw such substantial honoraria again at subsequent concerts in West Germany. When they returned to the WDR and *Musik der Zeit* in October 1958 for a performance of the *Concert for Piano and Orchestra* after their visit to Darmstadt, they agreed to an honorarium of 750 DM, at least two and a half times less than what they were paid in 1954.

How might we reconcile the critics' and public's apparent disdain for Cage and Tudor's experimental buffoonery with the outsized honoraria West German administrators paid for their concert appearances? It would seem that in 1954, Cage and Tudor were underground European celebrities. In the new music scene, a number of institutions were competing for funds, notoriety, and international prestige.[57] Cage and Tudor's *succès de scandale* appearances in Donaueschingen and Cologne fueled the fire; they gained much more from being talked about—even if in the negative—than they did from being passively accepted, or worse, ignored. As the saying goes, there's no such thing as bad press. Strobel and the SWF embraced Cage's notoriety, leveraging his *provocateur* reputation toward the visibility his concert series stood to gain; the same could be said for Eimert and the WDR.

Cage and Tudor were reliable harbingers of the new, and they offered much by way of symbolic capital for image-conscious new music impresarios trying to mark their venue—Darmstadt, Cologne, Donaueschingen, Paris, etc.—as *the* place for European new music. Cage and Tudor made a lasting imprint on those powerful administrators, impresarios, and influential young composers who were largely controlling the new music scene. Those power brokers, in turn, promulgated Cage's ideas and works among the European avant-garde.[58] As the American experimental composer Earle Brown reflected, the most important introductions Boulez made for him in Europe were to Hans Rosbaud (a conductor of the SWF orchestra who was capable with new music scores), Otto Tomek (an editor at Universal Edition), and William Glock (a British critic, impresario, new music advocate, and controller at the BBC).[59] The institutional support for new music in West Germany turned on the judgments of a few powerful administrators who had the power to determine broadcast content, concert programs, funding streams, and guest appearances. Ultimately, Cage's embrace in institutional circles in West Germany in 1954 was far more consequential than a few negative reviews in the press.

The impact of Cage's music was further amplified at the WDR electronic studio, where his recordings were archived in the *Handapparat* library, an ad hoc collection of recordings deemed important by Eimert or other composers. The collection included electronic pieces produced in the studio as well as rare recordings of other recent music.[60] Koenig remembered first encountering Cage's prepared-piano music by means of WDR recordings, perhaps between the 1952 radio broadcast and Cage and Tudor's 1954 visit.[61] Visiting composers such as Mauricio Kagel, György Ligeti, Bengt Hambraeus, and Paul Gredinger commonly began at the WDR studio with a long listening session in the *Handapparat* recordings—Ligeti called this the "best shock of his life."[62] Through one or another of these avenues—live concerts, radio broadcasts, or recorded archives—the WDR-affiliated composers stoked their genuine interest in Cage's early music.

Widening Squares

We have already seen how the sound of Cage's prepared piano provided a timbral model for Eimert's, Schaeffer's, and Stockhausen's early electronic music. As it happens, Cage's early works may have also offered a crucial inspiration when it came to duration. In the electronic studio, composers confronted the new challenge of determining durations and temporal pacing of their music without the conventional rhythmic and metric structure of notation. Instead of quarter-notes, dotted-sixteenth-rests and so on, composers planned durations in clock time, often calculating seconds into corresponding centimeters of tape and vice versa—this is the "rhythmicizing" that Eimert spoke about in Chapter 1. This durational thinking was aided by the materiality of tape: a length of tape corresponded in a consistent and transparent way to the duration of a sound or silence.[63] On the one hand, this simple correspondence could be seen as more intuitive than the abstract, symbolic language of rhythmic notation; on the other hand, tape lengths are clumsy. At the standard tape speed of 76.2 cm/s, one can imagine that splicing and montaging durations longer than a second or two could very quickly become unwieldy.

One direct correspondence between Cage's early prepared-piano works and the WDR tape works is the use of durational notation, which Cage used in his "time-length" works (such as 31′57.9864″ and 34′46.776″). In these pieces, Cage forgoes the usual system of rhythmic notation, preferring instead an analog that is more like a written-out version of tape music, wherein visual distance corresponds to duration. As Figure 2.4 illustrates, the pitches that the pianist is to play are given on a traditional grand staff, but above, the pianist reads a graphic notation to determine articulation, dynamics, and temporal placement of attacks.

Scholars have advanced a number of possible explanations for Cage's evolving durational thought, from his extensive experience playing for dancers, to his increasing immersion in the paradoxes of Zen Buddhist teachings, to observing the way David Tudor used a stopwatch to accurately perform the durations in *Music of Changes*.[64] These explanations, while plausible, overlook the fact that Cage had been composing *Imaginary Landscape No. 5* and *Williams Mix* in the privately owned studio of Louis and Bebe Barron since early 1952.[65] It is probable that Cage's durational notation evolved out of his own experiences with composing tape music.

As a point of comparison, consider Stockhausen's *Studie II*, one of the only WDR pieces to include a score that is both a visual rendering and production directions. As Figure 2.5 shows, frequency blocks—additive synthesis mixtures—are shown on the top stave of *Studie II*'s score, tape lengths (in centimeters) on the middle, and decibel curves for dynamic changes on the bottom. Both Cage's time-length works and Stockhausen's electronic tape

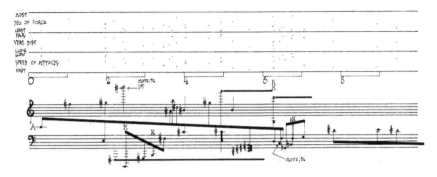

FIGURE 2.4. Cage, *31'57.9864" for a Pianist*, score excerpt from p. 1, showing durational notation. ©1960 by Henmar Press, Inc. Used by permission of C.F. Peters Corporation. All Rights Reserved.

music use a direct-duration system, whereby the length of tape or visual distance between events on the score correlates directly to the temporal unfolding of the music.

The similarities between Cage's and Stockhausen's handling of durations are deeper than the visual correspondences in their scores. In fact, it was duration—not aleatory pitch techniques—that most interested the young European composers, for instance in "Alea," where Boulez praised Cage's durations for inducing a rather undirected, improvisatory (read: Eastern) musical unfolding that is more like an open circle than a (Western) "closed circle of possibilities."[66] Boulez's momentary concession, a respite in his otherwise scathing critique, continued his long-standing endorsement of Cage's handling of duration. Already in his 1949 introduction at Tèzenas's salon, Boulez had praised Cage's innovative rhythmic structures, which "take into account [. . .] the passing of real time," and result in musical–temporal structures that are either "prismatic" or "crystallized."[67] Boulez seemingly had some understanding of square-root form even then, as he explained that Cage used both whole-number and fractional proportions in creating the temporal structure of his works.[68] Cage further clarified square-root form to Boulez in a letter in 1950, wherein he analyzed *First Construction (in Metal)*, one of the pieces well known to Boulez, Eimert, Stockhausen, and many others in the European avant-garde.[69] It is on these grounds that Boulez proposed that he and Cage were linked in "researching a work's structure by means of rhythmic structures."[70]

Cage used the proportional technique of square-root form between 1939 and 1956, and *First Construction* is a classic example.[71] The basic premise is this: the proportional scheme 4:3:2:3:4 governs the relationship between elements at all formal levels of the composition, including sections, phrases, and rhythmic motivic cells. These nested proportional relationships are

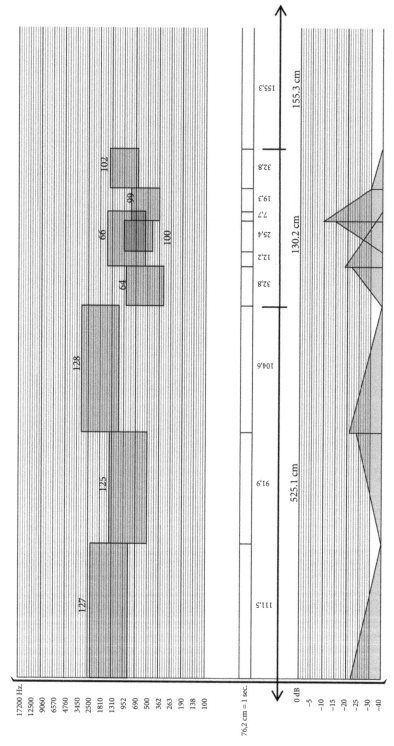

FIGURE 2.5. Stockhausen, *Studie II*, score excerpt, p. 4. Annotations label mixtures according to the precompositional chart and tape lengths in centimeters; cf. Tables 2.4 and 2.5. Stockhausen Foundation.

schematic, but also aurally salient. In *First Construction*, various percussion instruments alternate phrase by phrase, such that different instrumental timbres articulate the changes between phrases of 4-, 3-, and 2-bar lengths. Square-root form structures the piece's sounds within a tight, iterative, proportional hierarchy.

It appears that Stockhausen strove to replicate the microproportional–macroproportional relationships so familiar from Cage's square-root form in his first, discarded *musique concrète* piece. As he explained to Goeyvaerts, "I now wanted a structure, to be realized in an *Étude*, which was already worked into the micro-dimension of a single sound, so that in every moment, however small, the overall principle of my idea would be present."[72] Cage's early works were a model because, to paraphrase Stockhausen, Cage's musical structure was finally based on sounds themselves; the alternation between sounds and silences played a crucial role in the form of the composition.[73] According to Stockhausen, Cage's timbrally and durationally innovative work "heralds the multiplicity of relationships and changing states between material and material forms, whereby the smallest and the largest and the detail within the whole can be deeply bound together."[74]

As we will see in Chapters 3 and 4, proportions were of the utmost importance for the serial composers, who by 1953 began to focus on proportional relationships between terms in the series rather than using the series simply to order musical events. We will see in Chapter 4 that the kaleidoscopic durational structure of Koenig's electronic composition *Essay* could easily be related to the microdurational–macrodurational hierarchy on display in Cage's square-root pieces. Likewise, it should come as no surprise that Stockhausen worked extensively with both frequency and durational proportions in his early electronic music. In Stockhausen's first WDR piece, *Studie I* (1953), his frequencies were based on a proportional series involving the whole-number integers 4, 5, 8, and 12 (see Figure 3.3 in Chapter 3). Stockhausen continued his work with proportions in *Studie II* (1954). To generate the pitch (frequency) material for the piece, he used an irrational number, the twenty-fifth root of 5—that is, $\sqrt[25]{5}$, or 1.066495—to build a scale with a constant interval.[75] He then created five-frequency mixtures beginning at 100 Hz, using every scale step (1:1), every other scale step (1:2), and so on to 1:5. This created a proportional relationship whereby subsequent mixture groups were related to the basic unit by the proportions 1:2, 1:3, 1:4, and 1:5.

Stockhausen's durational structure in *Studie II* was likewise attentive to proportions, as can be seen in an excerpt between 0:27 and 0:34. Table 2.4 shows Stockhausen's frequency mixtures, their tape lengths in centimeters, their correlated durations in seconds, and their approximate temporal proportions. The end of this passage is shown, with score annotations, in Figure 2.5. Although we do not see the first two mixtures under discussion in Figure 2.5, Table 2.4 clarifies that the five mixtures at the beginning of the

TABLE 2.4. Mixtures, tape lengths, durations, and proportions in Stockhausen's *Studie II*, 0:27–0:34. For a visual representation of mixtures 127, 125, and 128, refer back to the score excerpt in Figure 2.5.

Mixture	Tape Length (cm)	Duration as Heard (s)	Approx. Proportion
129	98.1	1.287	1
126	119.0	1.561	1
127	111.5	1.463	1
125	91.9	1.206	1
128	104.6	1.372	1

TABLE 2.5. Mixtures, tape lengths, durations, and proportions in Stockhausen's *Studie II*, 0:27–0:38. For a visual representation of duration lengths and mixture conglomerates, refer back to the score excerpt in Figure 2.5.

Mixture	Tape Length (cm)	Duration as Heard (s)	Approx. Proportion
Subtotal 125–129	525.1	6.891	4
Subtotal 64, 66, 100, 99, 102	130.2	1.709	1
Silence	155.3	2.038	~1

excerpt are quite similar. They are all drawn from the same segment of the precompositional chart (mixtures 125–129), where the mixture frequencies are spaced every four scale steps. Furthermore, their durations are approximately in the proportions 1:1—the tape lengths vary up to 20 cm, but this produces a difference of at most 0.3 s. To my ear, these durations are close enough to be in the same proportion.

Table 2.5 clarifies the relationship between these five long sounds (mixtures 125–129) and the music that follows. Durationally, the five long sounds together are four times as long as the second event, which is a conglomerate of fast sounds (mixtures 64, 66, 99, 100, and 102). This conglomerate is about 130 cm long (~1.7 s) and exists in approximately equal proportion to the silence of 155 cm (~2 s) that follows it. Figure 2.6 shows this in schematic form. On the foreground level at the beginning of our excerpt, the five similar mixtures effectively have 1:1 proportional duration relationships with each other. At the phrase level, these five long sounds together exist in a 4:1:1 proportion with the fast-sound conglomerate and with the silence that bookends these two gestures.

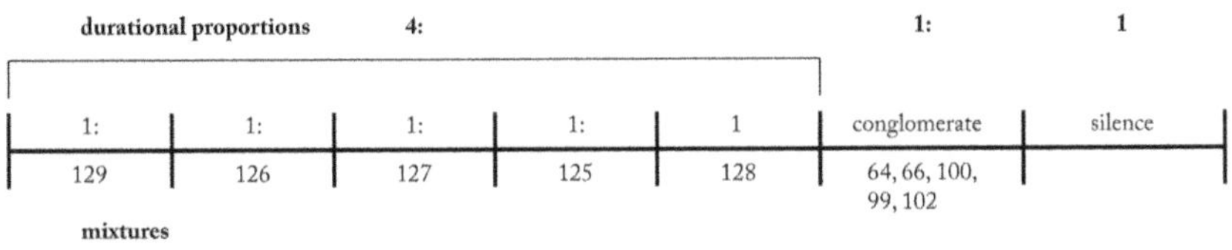

durational proportions   4:   1:   1

| 1: | 1: | 1: | 1: | 1 | conglomerate | silence |
| 129 | 126 | 127 | 125 | 128 | 64, 66, 100, 99, 102 | |

mixtures

FIGURE 2.6. Schematic representation of temporal proportions in Stockhausen's *Studie II*, 0:27–0:38.

This durational proportional structure is approximate, but perceptually functional. To add one further layer of complexity, recall that the five long sounds (mixtures 125–129) are all drawn from the frequency groups with the 1:4 ratios. Perhaps it is not coincidental that the frequency bands with the 1:4 ratio are deployed in a 4:1:1 durational relationship with the following gestures. It is here, in the proportional relationships between frequency and durations, that we can see Stockhausen manifesting his desire to bind together the smallest and largest detail within the whole work. The durational proportions of the *Studie II* excerpt, expressed as they are on both foreground (mixture) and middle-ground (phrase) levels, closely mirror the micro- and macro-orientations of Cage's square-root form in the *First Construction*. It was Cage's approach that provided Stockhausen with a feasible model for how to enjoin different compositional elements—particularly frequency and duration—into proportional relationships.

Studio Networks

As we have been analyzing the ways John Cage's works were sonic and structural inspirations for electronic music, it is worthwhile to remember that both the French and the West German electronic studios made such cross-pollinations and new relationships possible. Electronic studios—the WDR in particular—were steady anchors of the new music scene, fostering year-round dialogue on new music topics not least because of their continuous funding and guest-composer opportunities. Often, the interpersonal connections made in the studio—especially with collaborators who extended one's own toolkit—made significant and lasting impressions. This was certainly the case for Stockhausen, who, beginning with the 1954 Cologne visit, expressed more interest in David Tudor than in Cage himself.[76] As he reported to Pousseur,

> At the moment, David Tudor is here and is taking up the rest of "free" time. He is stimulating, and the cosmos of imagination of the Cage Group is a monster that is to be taken seriously. [. . .] This is the case

with Tudor (who is speaking for the "Cage Group" at the moment), Brown, Wolff, and Feldmann [*sic*].[77]

Cage's notoriety may have garnered the pair their first European concert tour, but by the time they arrived in Cologne in 1954, the younger composers were most interested in befriending Tudor, recognizing him to be a prodigious performer and invaluable resource. Stockhausen immediately cultivated an ongoing relationship beginning with a set of *Klavierstücke V–VIII*, which Tudor performed in New York on December 16, 1954.[78] After this, Tudor went on to perform Stockhausen's *Klavierstück XI* and Boulez's *Troisième Sonate*, as well as works by several other composers who were strongly associated with the WDR studio milieu.

To some degree, these connections were made at the Darmstadt *Ferienkurse*, where Tudor visited four times in quick succession (1956, 1958, 1959, and 1961).[79] Figure 2.7 shows the repertoire that Tudor played at Darmstadt in the years he visited, organized in a network graph by composer nationality.[80] The size of each node is proportional to the number of pieces, performances, or both, that Tudor played. Figure 2.7, however, shows only a limited picture of Tudor's international connectedness, as it collates only the repertoire that Tudor played at the Darmstadt *Ferienkurse*.

Figure 2.8 offers a more complete picture of European–American relationships as gleaned from Tudor's concert programs from 1954 through 1960, with node size again proportional to the number of times composition(s) were played.[81] Predictably, the largest nodes here are the American experimental composers in Tudor's inner circle, including Cage, Feldman, Brown, and Wolff. We also see that Tudor gave a fair amount of attention to Stefan Wolpe and Lou Harrison, as well as the music of Europeans such as Boulez, Bo Nilsson, Stockhausen, and Pousseur, whom Tudor encountered through WDR networks. Although these more famous composers formed the bulk of Tudor's repertoire, notice that Tudor played compositions by a huge range

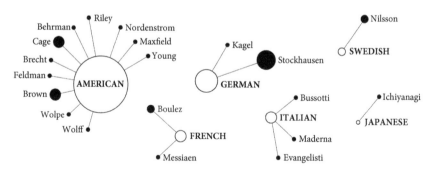

FIGURE 2.7. Composers whose works Tudor played in Darmstadt between 1956 and 1961, by nationality. Node size is proportional to the frequency with which Tudor played the composer's work.

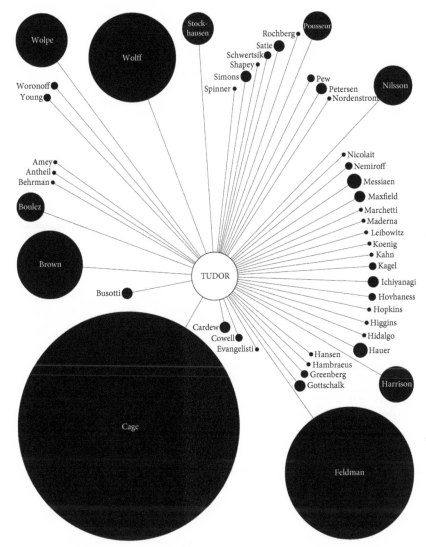

FIGURE 2.8. Tudor at the center of his international network, based on performances between 1954 and 1960. Node size is proportional to the frequency with which Tudor played the composer's work.

of Europeans, including lesser-known, WDR-affiliated composers such as Franco Evangelisti, Bengt Hambraeus, Mauricio Kagel, and Koenig.

Network graphs portray Tudor (and the others) as static figures, but in reality, Tudor moved between cities and scenes more than almost anyone else in the European or American avant-garde. From his 1954 Cologne visit on, Tudor was immediately understood as the sole pianist who could perform the technically and conceptually challenging repertoire of both the American and European avant-garde. This is precisely why Stockhausen, and many others, found that befriending Tudor was so satisfying and efficacious. Tudor's constant touring, along with his willingness to play new repertoire, afforded a huge range of composers many more good performances, and much more international exposure, than they ever would have gotten without him.[82]

Setting Tudor's prodigous talent aside for a moment, we should also remember the institutional mechanisms that allowed such creative partnerships to blossom. The WDR studio offered a physical space for collaboration, where Tudor and the composers first met to study scores, discuss ideas, try out experiments, learn about technological innovations, troubleshoot, and discover solutions to problems. In subsequent years, as Tudor moved between European studios, new music festivals, and his home base of New York City, he functioned as a musical translator, bringing the insights of American and European scenes together in his conversations, programs, and performances. Although Tudor was literally visible on stage and in the studio, his extraordinary contributions remain invisible in a historiographical paradigm that focuses on the innovations of composers.[83] In short, Tudor was a central figure in cross-pollinating the international avant-garde.

Conclusions

This chapter has suggested that we nuance our narratives about Cage, Tudor, and the European avant-garde in multiple ways. In summary, Cage and Tudor were relevant—especially to those in electronic music circles—earlier, longer, and far more deeply than is commonly acknowledged. In the early 1950s, the powerful and connected impresarios and composers in the West German and French new music scenes, including Eimert, Strobel, Stockhausen, and Boulez, all embraced Cage. They admired the aesthetic premises of his early music, going so far as to interpret Cage and the American experimentalists as symbols of freedom, democracy, and artistic autonomy. In the cultural Cold War environment of West Germany, impresarios were eager to appropriate Cage's considerable symbolic capital in order to mark their new music scene (Darmstadt, Donaueschingen, or Cologne) as the most progressive.

Beyond the prestige that Cage drew, his music was a sonic and structural inspiration for early electronic music both in France and West Germany. Eimert, Schaeffer, and other early advocates of electronic music hailed the prepared piano as a timbral model for the kinds of intriguing new sound worlds they wanted to create. Stockhausen, Boulez, Koenig, and others deeply admired Cage's proportional thinking, particularly with regard to duration. Cage's square-root forms provided a new inspiration for relating duration and pitch proportionally in the studio and for creating multifaceted, nested forms. For nearly a decade before the Darmstadt kerfuffle in 1958, Cage had been a kindred spirit for the WDR group. In his work with both timbre and proportional durational structure, Cage helped lay the groundwork for electronic music.

Perhaps more lastingly, Tudor was a key figure whose importance to both the European and American avant-garde cannot be overstated. He sustained a robust network that promoted new music compositions and performances, knitting together the new music scenes in locales such as New York City, Paris, Cologne, and Darmstadt. Although Cage continued to be important—if infuriating—to the Europeans in the late 1950s and 1960s (as discussed in Chapter 5), the composers' connection to Tudor remained unsullied. They—Tudor and a large, varied group of avant-garde composers—relied upon each other for creative validation and career advancement.

Multifaceted networks, which include performers, administrators, promoters, impresarios, critics, and composers, can reshape our under-standing of the intellectual dimensions, aesthetic concerns, and power dynamics of the Cold War new music scene. With these more expansive networks in mind, controversies such as Darmstadt 1958 become moments in which certain figures become visible as agents, in Latourian terms: they consolidate their power, accrue or spend their symbolic capital, sideline dissidents, recruit collaborators, and so on.[84] The WDR studio provided one of the most steady, institutional spaces in which such networks could constantly be formed, re-formed, and extended, as new collaborators joined and new issues emerged. In the next chapter, we will see that the WDR studio forged its key identity by perpetuating such a laboratory-like interdisciplinary working method, in which the younger generation of composers formed connections with scientific collaborators in order to advance their aesthetic work.

3 | Collaboration

The Science and Culture of Additive Synthesis

As is well known, composers in the early 1950s obsessively developed serialism, a compositional paradigm that sought to unify all aspects of the composition in a coherent, objective structure.[1] This pervasive interest was articulated collaboratively, such that the primary sources reflect each other like a hall of mirrors: the composers' shared interest in analyzing Webern for the seeds of integral serialism; their shared interest in unpacking and developing Messiaen's tentative experiments to organize pitch and duration in *Mode de valeurs et d'intensities*; their many conversations about how to unify the content and the structure of the composition into one rational form.[2]

The Darmstadt Summer Courses are the time and place where we usually imagine these conversations about serial technique convening.[3] As the Belgian composer Karel Goeyvaerts reminisced,

> The meadows of Marienhöhe were the scene of many long conversations. We all felt a great need for interpersonal contact, for in those post-war years, we all worked more or less in isolation. We were all very interested in what others were up to.[4]

The so-called Darmstadt composers did not merely exchange ideas for two weeks every August but corresponded with each other ardently throughout the year. In numerous letters, the friends discussed and debated several topics relevant to new music: who could capably perform and conduct their music, how to get their pieces programmed on festivals and concert series, how best to integrate the aleatory techniques of Cage, how to experience and incorporate the new insights of electronic music. Their correspondence was augmented by sometimes months-long stays at the WDR studio, where many of them composed their first electronic works.

In fact, the WDR studio was the most important physical and conceptual locus where integral serialism was theorized, debated, and practiced. The Cold War electronic music studios generally—in Germany, France, Italy, or the United States—were curious and compelling physical spaces full of new technologies, which held open the promise that composers could finally take full compositional control over timbre, as well as other compositional elements such as pitch, duration, and dynamics. At the WDR studio in particular, a laboratory ethos encouraged discussion, debate, and collective problem solving. These paradigms were essential for developing the studio's main aesthetic and technological signatures.

When the younger composers began to work at the WDR studio in 1953, they worked collaboratively to refine the techniques of additive synthesis, drawing on scientific discourses to inform their use of the studio's technologies.[5] The WDR offered an institutionally funded space much like a scientific laboratory, where the young composers worked experimentally to address hypotheses.[6] Even more important, these composers engaged a heterogeneous group of collaborators, leaning heavily on technicians and scientists as they learned to use the studio's machines.[7] The fruits of this labor—a group of closely related works—were premiered at the October 1954 *Musik der Zeit* concert (refer back to Figure 2.2). Finally, the failures and frustrations in the studio also led in new directions, as composers like György Ligeti took up unrealizable ideas in acoustic music, instead of in the studio.[8] In this way, the WDR studio was a locus where the main tenets of serial thought crystallized and where failures and breakdowns inspired new ideas for both electronic and acoustic music.

Acoustics and the Serial Paradigm

The younger generation of composers, including Stockhausen, Goeyvaerts, Pousseur, Gredinger, Koenig, Ligeti, Kagel, and others, enthusiastically embraced the sonic fantasies of the WDR studio's founders. They immediately began focusing their compositional attention on timbre, which describes a sound's quality or color. For example, timbre is the difference between an oboe and a clarinet when the two are playing the same pitch. Timbre is a complex phenomenon; it is less discrete than musical parameters like melody, duration, and register. Midcentury composers found timbre compelling, yet elusive and enigmatic. They wanted better tools than traditional notation and instruments, so they could better manipulate and integrate timbre into their music. The studio promised a direct engagement—sound *qua* sound— in which composers could create and control every aspect themselves.[9]

As the composers began with this sound synthesis project, they found themselves working at the intersection of aesthetic and scientific spheres.[10] Using a new studio technique called "additive synthesis," composers built timbres one partial at a time with a sine tone generator and reel-to-reel magnetic tape. Sine tone partials were recorded, mixed with more partials, and re-recorded. This layering process had to be repeated several times because, in 1953, the studio had only one sine wave generator and a four-channel tape recorder.[11] Additive synthesis applied the acoustical knowledge, following from Helmholtz's mid-nineteenth-century experiments, that a musical "tone" comprised a fundamental frequency plus a number of overtones, or partials, which had a decisive influence in shaping timbre.[12] In mobilizing acoustics to inform their use of the studio's electronic technologies, the composers participated in the rapid growth of electroacoustics, an evolution simultaneously underway in spheres such as telephony, radio broadcasting, and military engineering.[13] The studio's composers found themselves at an interdisciplinary intersection in which questions of science and engineering impinged on their aesthetic work. Although they claimed to care mainly about the music, as we will see, their musical progress in the studio depended on expanding their scientific and technical understanding. The composers began additive synthesis with a transparent idea, but they found that the sounds they produced and the techniques they used to produce them both needed considerable refinement.

Initially, the young composers were completely committed to additive synthesis for the integrated control it promised. As Stockhausen wrote,

> We return to *the element*, on which all sonic variation is based: the pure wave, which one can electronically generate, and which one calls the *sine-tone*. Every existing sound, every noise, is a mixture of such sine-tones—we call it a spectrum. Number-, interval-, and volume-relationships between such sine-tones account for the individual character of each spectrum. They determine timbre. And so for the first time, it was possible to *compose the timbre* of a music in the true sense of the word, that is to say from combining together elements, and so that the universal structural principle of the music will come into operation in the sonic proportions.[14]

In the early 1950s, Stockhausen and his colleagues fawned over the idea that the smallest and largest levels of the composition would be structurally united, that the musical form would be transparent, nested, and iterative. Stockhausen continued a fundamentally organicist dream, also operative in Cage's square-root pieces, that the proportional logic of the smallest details could be projected onto the entirety of the musical form. The question in the early days was how to determine the proportional logic. By using a "harmonic" scheme for additive synthesis—that is, by using evenly spaced partials—composers knew from Helmholtz that they could mimic the timbres of acoustic, or "natural" sounds like the violin, voice, or trumpet. By and large, they avoided this, as they opposed the idea that electronic music should re-create acoustic timbres. They wanted to jettison the historically conditioned assumption that only harmonic sounds are "musical."[15] Instead, the composers focused their energy on creating unusual, new timbres from "inharmonic" mixtures, in which sine tone partials are *unevenly* spaced. Such was the path toward sonic innovation, they believed.

The inharmonic mixtures favored by the composers posed no problem for the studio's generators, which could be tuned to any whole-number frequency. Using the hertz scale, composers worked with purely numerical proportions based on a serial scheme, leaving behind the built-in limitations of the equal-tempered scale, orchestral instruments, and conventional notation. In the studio, the affordances and limitations of the machines shaped the composers' musical choices and practices.[16]

While the composers sketched their proportional frequency mixtures, the technicians set up the recorders, created efficient tape loops, tuned the generators to specified frequencies, and even carried out the recording and re-recording process. The composer and technician often worked simultaneously, as Gottfried Michael Koenig explained: "The one is busy with the score, writing down frequencies, composing actually. And the other one could already make the preparations for the technical realization. Instead of doing it one after the other, one could do it in parallel. That helps of course, with time."[17] In the studio, serial composers applied proportions and the concept of "intervals" to frequency mixtures defined in hertz and durations measured in tape lengths. It was here in the studio that continuums, proportions, and intervals crystallized as the defining features of serial thought.[18]

Despite the linearity with which I am telling the tale, the early years of sound synthesis at the WDR were characterized by frustration, disagreement, and readjustment. For starters, the studio technology required some navigating, at least in the beginning. Stockhausen, as the studio's first technician, encountered a steep learning curve: "You know the whistling sounds you get on the radio when someone pushes the wrong switch—those are the sounds I was talking about, from the generators I mentioned. You can't mean this by 'pure tones' (sine wave)?"[19] Even when Stockhausen had gotten a handle on the sine tone generators, the manual layering of additive synthesis remained tedious. As Herbert Eimert reported to the young Italian composer Luigi Nono in September 1953, "Karlheinz [Stockhausen] works for 8–10 hours each day and has finished—in a quarter of a year!—something like three minutes of music. It is quite cumbersome and protracted work."[20]

These letters were written while Stockhausen was realizing his friend Goeyvaerts's first serial sine tone work from sketches.[21] Both of Goeyvaerts's early electronic works, *Composition No. 4*, "With Dead Tones" ("composed" in 1952, but not realized until much later) and *Composition No. 5*, "With Pure Tones" (1953), are strong expressions of the uncompromising integral serial attitude that held among the studio's composers. As Herman Sabbe describes, Goeyvaerts's entire compositional paradigm in the early 1950s was oriented toward projecting a "serial structure over the totality of the composition space so that the structure itself, as such, *is* the composition."[22] Accordingly, Goeyvaerts strove to unify the dimensions of space (frequency) and time (duration), such that the sounds of the composition existed in proportional, arithmetic relationships with one another.

In *Compositions No. 4* and *No. 5*, Goeyvaerts focused on static sounds.[23] He embraced the invariable, immobile, or "dead" drones of the sine tone generators, which produced steady-state tones without attack and decay envelopes. (Tapes were spliced at an angle to avoid the noise-burst produced by a vertical splice, which introduced a minimal attack and decay—that is, fades—to a sound. But Goeyvaerts's compositional idea focused on the steady-state or sustain part of the sonic envelope.) He used the same proportional schemes to govern both the inner timbral structure of the "dead" or "pure" sine tone mixtures and the duration of sounds deployed in time.[24] By compositionally excluding any internal, dynamic evolution of the sounds, Goeyvaerts suspended the static sound objects like particles in a block of ice.[25] Projected onto a formal level, the composer's sculptural attitude toward space and time is reflected in the nonretrogradable, quasi-immobilized compositional designs of *No. 4* and *No. 5*, in which the second half of the piece reverses the processes and proportions that were unfolded in the first half of the piece (see Figure 3.1).

Goeyvaerts realized the micro–macro proportional unity that Stockhausen had so fetishized, projecting the structure of single sounds onto the form of the entire composition. Indeed, Stockhausen admired Goeyvaerts's work immensely in this era.[26] As Stockhausen told Eimert, he was "able to see [in Goeyvaerts's work], for the first time, a foundation that is humanly comprehensible, the pure distillation of a musical idea."[27] Meanwhile, Stockhausen was thinking deeply himself about how to use proportions to structure his

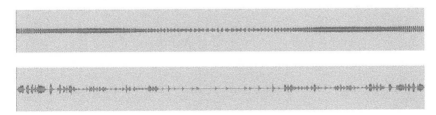

FIGURE 3.1. Goeyvaerts's *Composition No. 4*, "With Dead Tones" (above) and *Composition No. 5*, "With Pure Tones" (below), showing static structure on the formal level.

first electronic work, *Studie I* (1953).[28] Figure 3.2 shows a discarded sketch, in which Stockhausen intended to begin with a harmonic sound of evenly spaced partials (e.g., 200, 400, 600, 800, 1000, 1200 Hz . . .), and create a mixture by selecting every other partial (e.g., 200, 600, 1000 Hz . . .). He then intended to create different permutations of the mixture in which the partials were of variable loudness. In the mixture SV_{1a} the loudest partial (at 0 dB) is 2200 Hz, the next loudest is the 1400Hz partial (at −5 dB), and so on.

Perhaps not wanting to imitate acoustic timbres, Stockhausen became dissatisfied with these harmonic mixtures; the sketch excerpt transcribed in Figure 3.3 shows the inharmonic but proportional scheme that he actually used to determine the sound mixtures for *Studie I*. Here, Stockhausen used a series of five ratios involving the integers 4, 5, 8, and 12 to govern a six-frequency mixture. (The proportion 5:8 is included for logical consistency in the derivation but is set aside because Stockhausen uses a serial scheme that permutes a six-frequency mixture.[29]) Like Goeyvaerts, Stockhausen's compositional scheme focused on deploying logically derived proportions, rather than on controlling how the partials blended together as overtones in an acoustical sense.

Stockhausen and Goeyvaerts were certainly realizing their integrated, proportional compositional plans, but when they listened back to the results, they were disappointed. In correspondence with his best friend Pousseur, Stockhausen complained that Goeyvaerts's ideas were "exceedingly simple" and did not take enough account of the senses.[30] Goeyvaerts was likewise disappointed with the tape noise and failed fusion in his *Composition No. 5*: He could hear too many of the "component tones."[31] The same problem plagued

SV Klänge [Synthetic-Varied Sounds; S = synthesized from combined sine tones,
    V = varied amplitude between the sine tones]

SV₁   2200 Hz
       1800
       1400   **gleiche Lautstärke (siehe SH₁ homogen)** [same loudness (see Synthetic-Homogenous Sound₁)]
       1000
       600   **Harmonische 1 3 5 7 9 11** [odd numbered harmonic partials]
       200

SV₁ₐ		SV₁ᵦ		SV₁ᵨ	
2200 Hz	0 dB	1400 Hz	0 dB	200 Hz	0 dB
1400	-5	600	-5	1800	-5
200	-10	1800	-10	600	-10
1000	-15	200	-15	1400	-15
600	-20	2200	-20	1000	-20
1800	-25	1000	-25	2200	-25

FIGURE 3.2. Stockhausen, partial transcription of early (discarded) sketch for *Studie I*. Sketchbook, 3. Translations in square brackets are added by the author. Stockhausen Foundation.

I

1920 *12:*	800	1000	625	1500	1200
4: 800 *5*	333	417	260	625	500
5 1000 *8:*	417	521	325	781	625
625 *5:*	260	325	203	488	390
5: 1500 *12*	625	781	488	1170	937
4 1200	500	625	390	937	750

[...]

$$\frac{12}{5} \quad \frac{4}{5} \quad \frac{8}{5} \quad \frac{5}{12} \quad \frac{5}{4} \Big/ \frac{5}{8} \Big/\Big/$$

FIGURE 3.3. Stockhausen, partial transcription of sketch for *Studie I*. Sketchbook, 10. Proportions annotating first column are added by the author. Stockhausen Foundation.

Stockhausen's *Studie I*, wherein he and Pousseur agreed that the mixtures tended to sound more like chords than timbres.[32]

Composers discovered, after making these first experiments, that there was a problematic disconnect between the calculated, proportional deployment of partials and the rather uneven resulting timbres. It was much more difficult than expected to produce a convincing timbral fusion from an inharmonic mixture of sine tones.[33] As Eimert contemporaneously hypothesized, this was because our perceptual system deals poorly with sine tones, being used to the complexity of "natural" sounds, which include the fundamental plus partials, usually in harmonic spacing. Eimert suggested that the simple sine tones confuse the brain, causing it to imply corrective overtones where none exist or to rationalize the sine tones separately as combination tones stemming from different fundamentals.[34]

The studio composers' experimental foray into timbre perception would have been greatly clarified if they had returned to mid-nineteenth-century acoustics and grappled with the evolution of thought regarding complex tones.[35] In the 1840s, Georg Simon Ohm and August Seebeck debated about how the ear and the brain balanced fundamentals and partials during the perception of pitch and timbre.[36] Ohm, following Joseph Fourier, believed that the ear/brain analyzes and deconstructs complex waveforms into constituent partials. Seebeck, on the other hand, believed that the ear assembles pitch from discrete factors, following his observations that pitch can be perceived when upper partials are present but the fundamental is absent. Essentially, Ohm argued a deconstructivist position—ear/brain as spectral analyzer—whereas Seebeck argued a constructivist position—ear/brain as inferential hypothesizer. By 1863, Helmholtz had sided with Ohm, arguing that the ears perform real-time frequency analysis to understand the pitch of the fundamental, whereas the partials contribute to the timbre.[37] But Seebeck's alternative hypothesis was revived by J. A. Schouten in 1938, when scientists increasingly began to believe again in "pitch-residue theory"—namely that the ear will try to imply fundamentals and otherwise resolve contradictions between competing partial tones.[38] Eimert's discussion of combination tones recalls the pitch-residue theory, even as his understanding of timbre is indebted to a more traditional Helmholtzian perspective of fundamental plus overtones.

Part of Helmholtz's intervention in the Ohm–Seebeck debate in the mid-nineteenth century was to point out that the physical nature of a tone (acoustics) was not necessarily exactly coincidental with the ear's perception of a tone (psychoacoustics).[39] Scientific understanding of psychoacoustics was still developing in the mid-twentieth century, and although Eimert and others had basic acoustical knowledge, the WDR composers were seemingly not aware of all of the history or the latest thinking in psychoacoustics. As a result, in late 1953 and early 1954, composers continued to experimentally struggle through a months-long debate about proportions, partials, harmonicity, and fusion.

Paul Gredinger, a Swiss architect–composer produced only one piece at the WDR studio, *Formanten I and II* (1954), which used exclusively harmonic, evenly spaced partials. Although Gredinger subverted Stockhausen's preference for inharmonic partials, his harmonic partials made for much better fusion. The piece begins with a trombone-like tone, repeated three times with changing timbres, and exhibits many more such instances of shifting, morphing timbres over a series of repeated pitches.[40] Other sections of the piece vaguely mimic acoustic instruments such as the violin and clarinet. As *Formanten* shows, it was in fact easier to create perceptual fusion—composite timbres, rather than quasi-chords—with harmonic mixtures because the human brain is preprogrammed to synthesize timbres in various "natural" or "acoustic" scenarios.[41]

Gredinger's architectural training, as well as the collective studio preference for proportional logic, was evident when he invoked architect Le Corbusier's conception of the Modulor, a method "similar in purpose to our own," which attempted to discover a formal standard representing a "balanced and measured proportion of absolute beauty."[42] Gredinger had no resistance to harmonic partials, inasmuch as their use in the electronic *Formanten* married the proportional logic of Le Corbusier to the "absolute beauty" of "natural" acoustic sounds. It seems that Gredinger's success with timbral fusion—his attractive, continuously morphing timbres—went some distance toward fulfilling the sonic fantasies of the studio founders. Recall Meyer-Eppler's utopian dream, carried forward from Schoenberg's unrealized *Klangfarbenmelodie*, that electronic sounds would finally allow composers to create a continuous pathway between timbres like oboe and clarinet. Yet despite the aesthetic "success" of *Formanten*, neither Stockhausen nor Pousseur had much interest in Gredinger's synthesized "accordion tones," even if it was easier to create timbral fusion with harmonic mixtures.[43] Instead, they wanted to move further toward applying serial proportions throughout their compositions, to perfect their synthesis of inharmonic mixtures, to incorporate more noisy elements, and to create truly new timbres.

To move forward with these goals, Pousseur and Stockhausen needed to better understand what had gone wrong with perceptual fusion in *Studie I*. In a series of letters in December 1953, the two cast about for the source of the problem. (Despite his deep interest in electronic music, Pousseur was a secondary schoolteacher and couldn't come to Cologne for a long stay, so he communicated regularly with Stockhausen by letter.) Pousseur mistakenly believed that the partials in *Studie I* were sounding as "rungs on a ladder" because of their "relative rationality."[44] As he pointed out, the inharmonic mixtures of *Studie I* ironically had quite a few resonances with harmonic spectra. The ratios created the intervals of minor tenth (12:5 and 5:12), major third (4:5 and 5:4), and minor sixth (8:5 and 5:8).[45] Pousseur wrote that the six proportional overtones of a mixture, shown as the "real tones" on the top of the line in Figure 3.4 (384–160–200–125–300–240 Hz), produced a "common *audible* continued fundamental tone."[46]

Pousseur's first illustration from the letter (Figure 3.4) showed his logic. One can continue the process of relating frequencies by Stockhausen's ratios if one considers the proportional relationships between the lowest common factors in each ratio. The proportion between frequencies 384 and 160 is 12:5; the factor 32 unites these two integers. That is, 32(12) = 384 and 32(5) = 160, and likewise across the first row of frequencies. Then, having derived a second row of frequencies from the lowest common factors, Pousseur

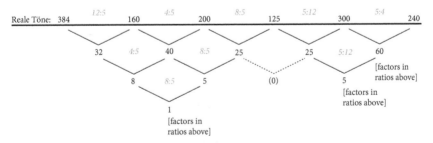

FIGURE 3.4. Pousseur, simplified illustration 1 from letter to Stockhausen regarding *Studie I*, December 17, 1953. Square brackets and proportions between factors (shaded) are added by the author. Stockhausen Foundation.

pointed out that the middle proportions in the series—4:5, 8:5, and 5:12—were preserved. Continuing his derivation of factors and proportions into a third and fourth line, Pousseur showed how a stratified proportional scheme lays out under the six-overtone mixture. It is true that the frequencies below the line in Figure 3.4 are imaginary (and, as it happens, those below about 20 Hz would be inaudible to humans). Pousseur nevertheless derived them by logically continuing the proportional scheme among factors. Perhaps following Eimert's pitch-residue logic, Pousseur argued to Stockhausen that they would be heard in the resulting music as "combination tones." Here, Pousseur made a vague reference to a psychoacoustic explanation: When two frequencies sound together, the listener can sometimes hear a third frequency that is the difference between the two original tones.[47]

In a second illustration (Figure 3.5), Pousseur tried to show why Stockhausen's mixtures might be producing additional combination tones. He arranged all of the frequencies—both the actual mixture frequencies and the possible combination tones—vertically, to show Stockhausen all of the harmonic relationships that inhere between the frequencies. The combination tones must be audible, he argued, because they are reinforced with octave and fifth relationships.[48] In these illustrations, Pousseur was stumbling toward an understanding of timbral fusion that was based on a combination of acoustic and psychoacoustic factors, as Meyer-Eppler contemporaneously explained in the 1954 WDR technical journal.[49] In this case, though, Pousseur was mistaken in his hypothesis that Stockhausen's problem was due to a muddied relationship between harmonicity and inharmonicity or between sounding mixtures and additional combination tones. But how did the acoustical proportions relate to timbral fusion? Why weren't they perceiving Stockhausen's mixtures as timbres?

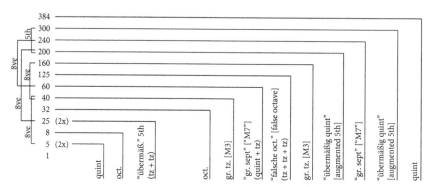

FIGURE 3.5. Pousseur, illustration 3 from letter to Stockhausen regarding *Studie I*, December 17, 1953. Translations in square brackets are added by the author. Stockhausen Foundation.

Synthesizing Meyer-Eppler's Psychoacoustics

At an impasse with timbral fusion, it was the tutoring and research of Werner Meyer-Eppler that allowed Stockhausen and Pousseur to finally break through. In late February 1954, Stockhausen mentioned to Pousseur, "For some time, I have been studying acoustics at length with M. Eppler, experimenting much and learning."[50] Stockhausen had known of Meyer-Eppler's work since at least 1952[51] and was probably already reading and digesting his important 1949 book *Elektrische Klangerzeugung* [*Electric Sound Production*] before attending his seminars starting in late 1953 or early 1954.[52] In *Elektrische Klangerzeugung*, Meyer-Eppler explained acoustical foundations that would have been essential to Stockhausen, including the spectral continuum among harmonic, inharmonic, and noisy sounds, and the ways in which timbre depends on relationships among loudness, partials, and attack and decay envelopes.[53]

Meyer-Eppler's specialty in phonetics added a particularly useful dimension, because it took perception and psychoacoustics into account.[54] From Meyer-Eppler, Stockhausen learned that perceptual fusion of mixtures is extraordinarily complex.[55] Following on Helmholtz's and Stumpf's late nineteenth- and early twentieth-century research into the perception of sound—research that had long compared musical timbres to vowels and consonants—Meyer-Eppler showed that vowels and consonants exist on a continuum from pitched tone to colored noise (see Figures 3.6a and 3.6b).[56] As Meyer-Eppler explained, musical sound exists within a similar continuum, and of course this knowledge can be used to manipulate overtone spectra in electronic sounds.[57]

Stockhausen's nascent alignment with such a phonetics perspective is reflected in a sketch for the sonic materials of *Studie I* (Figure 3.7). Stockhausen sorted the different types of linguistic phonemes into groups based on their timbral characteristics—voiced vowels (sine tones), voiceless consonants (impulses), and consonants (filtered noise). As Chapter 6 makes clear, Stockhausen and others deeply integrated experimental phonetics insights in a series of linguistic pieces beginning with *Gesang der Jünglinge* in 1955. In late 1953, however, it seems that Stockhausen used phonetics indirectly and experimentally as a way of studying timbral complexity. As Stockhausen wrote to Pousseur, he was learning how "spectra change at every moment: [partial] tones arise, abate, and change in volume."[58] Stockhausen was beginning to believe, as Meyer-Eppler advocated, that better compositional results could be obtained from subtractive synthesis—that is, from filtering complex colored- and white-noise spectra—than from adding complexity to mixtures produced through sine tone additive synthesis.[59] As Stockhausen wrote to Pousseur,

> The ideal "tone form" about which you speak is white or colored noise, a spectral band (think of the consonants t s f p etc. in our language,

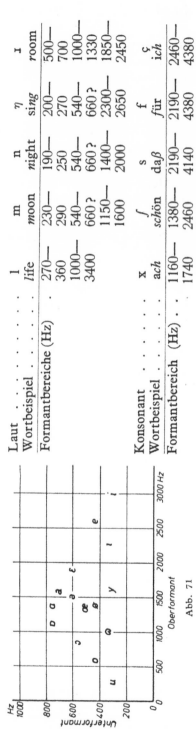

Laut	l	m	n	η	ı
Wortbeispiel	life	moon	night	sing	room
Formantbereiche (Hz)	270—	230—	190—	200—	500—
	360	290	250	270	700
	1000—	540—	540—	540—	1000—
	3400	660 ?	660 ?	660 ?	1330
		1150—	1400—	2300—	1850—
		1600	2000	2650	2450

Konsonant	x	ʃ	s	f	ç
Wortbeispiel	ach	schön	daß	für	ich
Formantbereich (Hz)	1160—	1380—	2190—	2190—	2460—
	1740	2460	4140	4380	4380

Abb. 71

FIGURES 3.6A AND 3.6B Vowel sounds and their characteristic formants (left); band-spectra frequency ranges of consonants (plosives and mostly nasals; right). From Meyer-Eppler, *Elektrische Klangerzeugung*, 81–83.

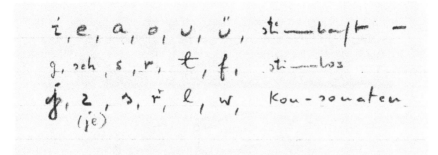

FIGURE 3.7. Stockhausen, sketch for *Studie I* (1953), showing vowels, voiceless consonants, and noisy consonants. Stockhausen Foundation.

bells, metal, etc., water). The combination tones do not help you: you continue to expect separate, different frequencies, but still single ones (even if there are more).[60]

Stockhausen's evolving perspective on timbre, which privileged the complexity of noisy sounds, was directly related to gaining much more information about phonetics and psychoacoustics.

Stockhausen further alluded to the work of Meyer-Eppler when he wondered whether spectral analysis could inform his compositions: "If one reverses the analytical process temporally, can wave-forms be synthetically produced from the analytical data?"[61] The WDR composers generally did not use spectral analysis in their work (such a process would come much later in the computer music era), but Meyer-Eppler's phonetics research did showcase a few examples of visible speech (see Figures 3.8a and 3.8b). These examples, drawn straight from the phonetics research underway at Bell Labs, gave Stockhausen a much more concrete idea of the complexity of sounds over time.

Although the limited machinery of the WDR studio precluded such reverse engineering of complex sounds, Meyer-Eppler's teachings did help Stockhausen understand why the steady-state sounds of Goeyvaerts and the harmonic sounds of Gredinger produced limited timbres and why his inharmonic mixtures resisted fusion. In short, additive synthesis oversimplified a complex phenomenon. When it came to timbres, the question was not just harmonic or inharmonic (i.e., natural vs. artificial) partials, but also this: How does any given sound subtly change over time? Stockhausen used the phonetics perspective to return to the question of the listener and human perception. How could he add complexity so that his new timbres could be easily processed by the brain, which was used to dealing with acoustically intricate linguistic phonemes?

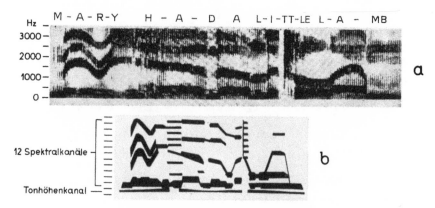

FIGURES 3.8A AND 3.8B Spectral representation of a spoken sentence (above) and simplified black-and-white sample with divisions into thirteen spectral channels (below). From Meyer-Eppler, *Elektrische Klangerzeugung*, Appendix XV.

Stockhausen took up with these questions in the compositional plans for *Studie II*. He used inharmonic mixtures of five tones each, derived from variously spaced frequency combinations of the irrational number $^{25}\sqrt{5}$. Decibel levels for each partial tone were given by way of a serial scheme.[62] Accounting for the complexity of perceptual fusion, Stockhausen also incorporated ad hoc techniques to manipulate attack and decay envelopes, dynamics, and reverberation. He and his technicians improvised envelope curves by using the volume knobs after each mixture was synthesized—these are shown on the bottom stave of the score (see Figure 3.9).[63] As a last step, the looped mixtures were played in a room and re-recorded to create ambient reverberation [*Hallraumeffekte*], which created an overlap in onset of the mixture envelopes that was particularly helpful for approximating the complex spectral evolution of sounds.[64]

The compositional logic of *Studie II* thus displays an awkward integration of proportional serial schemes (for pitch, duration, and mixtures) and experimental ad hoc techniques (for volume envelopes and reverberation). Despite Stockhausen's desire to create complex timbres, the serial (rather than acoustical) proportions he used to determine the frequencies and the initial dynamic levels of each partial probably inhibited rather than promoted fusion. During the latter stages of composing *Studie II*, Stockhausen attempted to "correct" for these limitations with ad hoc and approximate solutions—like turning volume knobs and reverberating looped mixtures—to add sonic complexity to his serial mixtures and make them more palatable as timbres.

This is the nascent beginning of what Stockhausen later called "statistical form," a technique based on approximations and gestural shapes instead of the explicit serial management of every single factor in the mixture (and the subject of Chapter 4).[65] While Koenig and Stockhausen developed

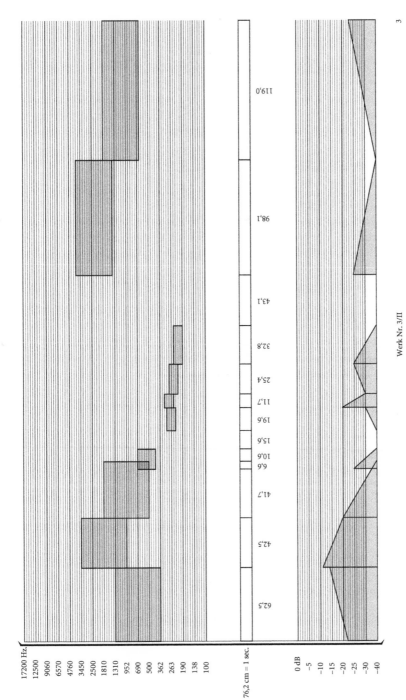

FIGURE 3.9. Stockhausen, *Studie II* (1954), score excerpt, p. 3. Frequency mixtures in hertz on top stave, tape lengths in centimeters on middle stave, and volume curves in decibels on bottom stave. Stockhausen Foundation.

Werk Nr. 3/II

3

many pragmatic new "statistical" techniques during the realization of *Gesang der Jünglinge* (1955–1956) and other works, in 1954 the idea of making approximations and technical compromises, especially to satisfy human perceptual schemes, was in its infancy.[66] As Stockhausen counseled Pousseur about *Seismogrammes*, "You must specify the 'blurring' at the beginning of the sounds more exactly, as there are thousands of possibilities for spectral evolution (transient effects) depending upon time quanta."[67] Stockhausen felt, however, that the additional dynamic, envelope, and reverberation techniques piloted in *Studie II* had resulted in much more sophisticated timbres than in *Studie I*. As he said to Pousseur, "For the first time, I freely feel that the whole complex can be tried out and composed (*practically*)."[68]

Stockhausen had ample opportunity to extend his knowledge, particularly as he realized Pousseur's *Seismogrammes I* (1954). The harmonic design of Pousseur's piece implicitly acknowledged the debate about harmonicity versus inharmonicity that was underway in 1953–1954, as well as the ongoing discussion about unresolved partial tones, absent fundamentals, and pitch-residue theory. In the first movement of the piece, Pousseur's sine tones correspond to partials above the seventh overtone that lie in the proportional relationship 7:13:19.[69] With this compositional scheme, Pousseur acknowledged the natural overtone series, but he used its upper reaches to create sounds that existed in complex intervallic proportions to one another.

By letter, Stockhausen gave Pousseur much practical advice based on his own experience and his increasing technical expertise with the studio's equipment. When Stockhausen offered some substantial criticisms, Pousseur responded with grace and resilience in the face of their collective uncertainty:

> If I can assure you of something, then it is that there was nothing in your pre-previous letter that was "not to my liking." If it appeared to be so, I would like to apologize. My not-so-perfect mastery of the German language is at fault, and I probably used one expression for another, so that perhaps it seemed like I was holding something back, which I could say only in a roundabout way "through the flowers," where in reality there is nothing. On my honor. Regarding my electronic work, I am quite impatient to hear, precisely because I am insecure about the result.[70]

In response, Stockhausen proposed changes that showed his growing investment in statistical form. As Stockhausen wrote, "In the future we should consider the envelope curves more as statistical phenomena—as a higher order group of microscopic changes in volume in dependence upon the smallest unit of time, in which there can appear just a few continuous evolutionary movements as patterns, as it is with pitch and duration, where it is clear that one would never permit chromatic scales."[71]

Later, after Stockhausen realized Pousseur's first movement, Stockhausen had a bit of time for experimenting himself, reporting that he had success- fully layered tiny individual tones in thick and fast sequences to make a "confetti cloud" [*Konfettiwolke*], which he then finished with an overarching dynamic curve.[72] This confetti cloud seems much closer to the effervescent sine tone glissandi of *Gesang der Jünglinge* than the more staid, academic mixtures that characterize *Studie II*. In working with Pousseur to realize *Seismogrammes*, Stockhausen developed and extended many nascent ideas, es- pecially relating to how statistical approximations might be usefully incor- porated into a piece.

A careful study of the group of "additive synthesis" compositions to come out of the WDR studio makes clear that the composers were engaged in a good deal of open experimentation and debate around questions of sine tone synthesis.[73] Different composers had different ideas about how to syn- thesize mixtures, especially whether one should use harmonic or inhar- monic schemes for the timbres. As Figure 3.10 shows, composers moved on a continuum between harmonic and inharmonic approaches, collectively negotiating their serial designs against the problems that inevitably arose in perceiving timbres from additive synthesis mixtures. Composers listened to each other's experiments, learned from each other's dissatisfactions, and made adjustments based on this information. Eventually inharmonic partials be- came *de rigueur* at the WDR studio, but this perspective evolved slowly and painfully over months.

Composers found that they needed to know much more about acoustics and perception in order to be more successful with additive synthesis of in- harmonic mixtures. Here the teachings and writings of Meyer-Eppler were crucial. Stockhausen and Pousseur in particular found that their dissatisfac- tion was not only a matter of technical inadequacy—such as mixtures limited to six or so partials because of tape noise—but also a matter of their incom- plete understanding of psychoacoustics. They paid much attention to the sonic results of their hypothesis, which informed their further experimenta- tion. Stockhausen's formidable technical knowledge—gained from a com- bination of his own experimentation, Meyer-Eppler's tutoring, and a deep knowledge of his colleagues' work—helped him become a well-informed and powerful leader in the studio.

Gredinger	Goeyvaerts		Stockhausen	Pousseur		Eimert		Stockhausen
Formanten (1954)	Composition No. 5 (1953)		*Studie I* (1953)	*Seismogrammes* (1954)		*Etüde über Tongemische* (1953–54)		*Studie II* (1954)

harmonic (evenly spaced) **partials** ◄ – – – ► **inharmonic** (unevenly spaced) **partials** ◄ – – – – – – – ► **noise elements**

FIGURE 3.10. Continuum of harmonicity to inharmonicity in the first group of additive synthesis compositions from the WDR studio.

Cultivating Shared Culture

There was a common aesthetic project underway at the WDR studio in the early-to-mid-1950s, illustrated by the consistency of the *Musik der Zeit* concerts in October 1954 ("additive synthesis" compositions, Figure 2.2) and May 1956 ("statistical form" compositions, Figure 3.11). Such aesthetic consistency was a result of the shared technologies, techniques, and technicians working together within a collaborative laboratory-like studio. In fact, this laboratory structure was part and parcel of the studio's design. As Nono said to his colleague Bruno Maderna in late 1953, Eimert intended to preside over a stable of composers, which he would unite and guide.[74] This was certainly accurate to a degree. Hatched in contrast to Schaeffer's rather authoritative, top-down studio leadership style, Eimert's favored studio structure was analogous to a university research laboratory, staffed as it was by a rotating cast of visiting young composers.[75] Eimert seemingly fancied himself a professor who loosely supervised his graduate students, providing them with space, technical resources, institutional funding, public exposure, and connections within the field.

Despite Eimert's supervision, however, his leadership had little to do with dictating the terms of the composers' engagement; he left the young composers rather free to try out their own ideas. Importantly, Eimert understood the serialist terms and endorsed the young composers' experiments, even though he himself tended to work more with the montaging of sound effects. Eimert's endorsement was incredibly important to the younger generation, but not because it insisted on a prescriptive, *a priori* dogma. The composers' ideas evolved in a continuous dialogue among scientists, composers, and technicians, rather than as a working-out of Eimert's preestablished prescriptions. Instead, Eimert's most important contribution was to create multifaceted opportunities for the younger composers to meet, discuss, and experiment collaboratively.

Eimert also found other ways to support the composers' creative work. He invited them to write broadcasts for his bimonthly nighttime music analysis broadcast, the *Musikalisches Nachtprogramm*, a widely heard program among the pan-European avant-garde and interested public alike. This gave composers a small stipend—perhaps the most important thing—but it also gave them exposure to their peers and the public and the time, space, and credibility for a continuing dialogue around their new ideas. The *Musik der Zeit* concerts, too, were explicitly designed to create engagement with the public, though finding support for electronic music—presumably among even an interested public—was an uphill battle.[76] Goeyvaerts said that electronic music was "at best tolerated" both by audiences and by administrators and staff not affiliated with the studio at the WDR. As Koenig remembered:

WESTDEUTSCHER RUNDFUNK KÖLN

musik der zeit

6. KONZERT

MITTWOCH, den 30. Mai 1956, 17.30 Uhr
im großen Sendesaal

ELEKTRONISCHE MUSIK

Im Studio des Westdeutschen Rundfunks entstandene Werke
Uraufführungen

BENGT HAMBRAEUS	DOPPELROHR 2
GOTTFRIED MICHAEL KÖNIG	KLANGFIGUREN II
HERMANN HEISS	ELEKTRONISCHE KOMPOSITION I
GISELHER KLEBE	INTERFERENZEN
KARLHEINZ STOCKHAUSEN	GESANG DER JÜNGLINGE (erster Teil)
HERBERT EIMERT	FÜNF STÜCKE
ERNST KRENEK	„SPIRITUS INTELLIGENTIAE, SANCTUS" Pfingstoratorium für Singstimmen und elektronische Klänge (erste Abteilung) Kompositionsauftrag des Westdeutschen Rundfunks Käthe Möller-Siepermann, Sopran; Martin Häusler, Tenor Sprecher: der Komponist

Ansage: **Herbert Eimert**

Klangliche Realisation: **Heinz Schütz, G. M. König, K. Stockhausen**

8. Veranstaltung **„Umstrittene Sachen"**: Mittwoch, 30. Mai 1956,
20 Uhr, kleiner Sendesaal
DIE UNERHÖRTE MUSIK
Komponisten ohne Publikum?
Referenten: Prof. Hans Heinz Stuckenschmidt und Prof. Wilhelm Maler
Leitung der Diskussion: Dr. Edmund Nick

FIGURE 3.11. Program for *Musik der Zeit*, May 30, 1956. Public premiere of "statistical form" electronic pieces from the WDR studio. WDR Historisches Archiv.

In the first years in Cologne, nobody knew electronic music; nobody liked electronic music. If electronic music was played in a radio broadcast [like the *Musikalisches Nachtprogramm*], mostly just before midnight, or in a concert hall [*Musik der Zeit*], people didn't like it, didn't know what do with it, hated it even. Musicologists were at that time only historically interested. Critics writing for the newspaper were many times musicologists, not always of course. Actually, some were willing to find out about the actual musical situation, especially after the Nazi time and the war and so on; but as Stockhausen said, "Nobody has anything to say, or knows anything about what we have done. We have to do it ourselves." [. . .] We felt we had to defend what we did, but also to explain it. That was the reason for making public statements about music in radio talks, lectures at schools, and so on. I thought it was the right approach, and I have always been interested in theories and philosophy.[77]

Despite the avant-garde composers' unbridled hunger for the new, critics and audiences were often hostile. As Stockhausen complained to Pousseur in late 1954, there was no possibility of playing their electronic music without lengthy spoken introductions. Even when prefaced with Eimert's explanations about the acoustical and musical foundations—owing to the *Nachtprogramm*, Eimert presumably spoke easily and willingly to the lay audience—the listeners were disruptive after only ten minutes of music.[78]

Stockhausen, in response to this situation, which he characterized as "depressing," teamed up with Eimert to found a journal. *Die Reihe* was pitched in tone toward a specialist audience of composer-peers rather than the quasi-interested public of the *Nachtprogramm* and *Musik der Zeit*. It would foster a print discourse about all of the new compositional developments in electronic and acoustic music. As Stockhausen wrote to Pousseur in December 1954,

A second bit of news: Schlee of Universal Edition will finance my journal. I will make this journal nominally together with Eimert, though I will effectively be doing all the work. I have suggested this: editorial department: Eimert, management and direction: Stockhausen. The title is not yet determined. For the first issue can you write an article (about 8 pages, preferably not more) on the subject of electronic music? The first issue is dedicated to the subject of electronic music. I would really like it if you took the position of "seen from the outside": what was effective and what is seen as new, what is clichéd and what is an active extension of the composition situation, what is a dumb task to do and what is an effective, principled new foundation, which things were spoken critically about, in short: what you see as the actual consequences of the first 1½ years of electronic composition.[79]

Die Reihe, though it was published in only eight volumes between the years of 1955 and 1962, was the most visible and authoritative collection of the midcentury composers' ideas, perhaps because it was also translated into English.[80] In the end, both Stockhausen and Eimert were listed as editors: Both spent considerable time corralling their friends and fellow composers—whomever they liked and endorsed—to write articles for small stipends on the themes Stockhausen and Eimert chose.[81]

Die Reihe and the *Musik der Zeit* concert series in Cologne were certainly important to the WDR-affiliated composers, but so too were similar ventures that sprang up across Western Europe. In Italy, Berio, Nono, and Maderna developed *Incontri Musicali*, a concert series based in Milan (with additional performances in Venice, Rome, and Naples), out of which later sprang a journal similar in tone and content to *Die Reihe*.[82] Berio and his colleagues spent considerable time commissioning their friends to write pieces for concert premieres, inviting them to contribute articles to the journal, and finding translators to render those contributions into Italian.[83] In France, Boulez nurtured his *Domaine musical* concert series, where all the most recent chamber music (composed by him and his friends) could be expertly performed for the Parisian intelligentsia.[84] In the pages of the *Gravesaner Blätter*, Hermann Scherchen chronicled the interdisciplinary conferences that took place in his private, self-funded electronic music studio and research center in Switzerland. Back in West Germany, festivals and concert series dedicated to new music proliferated, including Karl Hartmann's *Musica Viva* in Munich, Heinrich Strobel's *Donaueschinger Musiktage* in Donaueschingen, and similar series in Hamburg (*Das Neue Werk*) and Stuttgart (*Musik unserer Zeit*).[85] Most famously, of course, Wolfgang Steinecke grew the *Internationalen Ferienkurse für Neue Musik* in Darmstadt along with its associated journal, the *Darmstädter Beiträge*.[86]

In short, the exploits of the midcentury avant-garde composers were widely disseminated within a robust network of concert series and journals, which, by the mid-1950s, were increasingly addressed to each other (instead of to an interested public). A multifaceted web of institutional supports, increasingly available throughout Europe, facilitated their creative activity. Still, Cologne (and the WDR studio in particular) remained a crucial place wherein newer composers could have their work recognized, supported, and disseminated by increasingly powerful figures like Stockhausen and Eimert.

It was this milieu that the Hungarian composer György Ligeti hoped to enter when he began to contemplate leaving Stalinist Budapest. After a dangerous emigration in December 1956, Ligeti and his wife Vera remained in Vienna for a few weeks. He then secured a small stipend through Eimert and, in February 1957, began an internship at the studio.[87] He had apparently applied for numerous visiting professor posts, grants, and scholarships after the emigration, and Eimert's was the only affirmative response he received. Ligeti was extremely grateful for the opportunity.[88]

Considering the situation in retrospect, it is perhaps not surprising that Ligeti found a spot in Cologne. In Hungary, Ligeti had already heard Eimert's *Nachtprogramm* thanks to shortwave radio transmission—there is a vivid (if apocryphal) tale of Ligeti staying aboveground to listen during a bombing raid.[89] He had also begun to publish on new music topics in *Melos*, among other journals.[90] Eimert had explicitly committed to using the WDR studio's resources to host visiting composers; we have already seen that he had made it possible for visiting composers to accept a meager stipend, as those composers could supplement their income by producing additional content for the radio and for *Die Reihe*. As such, Ligeti wrote regularly for the *Nachtprogramm* as well as for broadcasts on the neighboring stations— the *Südwestfunk* (SWF) in Baden-Baden, the *Süddeutscher Rundfunk* (SDR) in Stuttgart, the *Bayerischer Rundfunk* (BR) in Munich, and the *Norddeutscher Rundfunk* (NDR) in Hamburg. Almost all of Ligeti's voluminous analyses of Webern were developed for this purpose, as were some of his discussions of Bartók, new music trends, and traditional, tonal music.[91] Ligeti also wrote three articles for *Die Reihe* and lectured extensively at Darmstadt in the late 1950s and the 1960s.[92]

Although Ligeti quickly gained his footing and established remarkable credibility as both a scholar and a composer, he had entered the world of electronic music in 1957 without much direct preparation.[93] A six-week stay at Stockhausen's apartment eased Ligeti's immediate transition to Cologne.[94] Once in the studio, he became fast friends with Koenig, who tutored him in the workings of the new machinery, allowed him to assist in the realization of *Essay* (1957), and helped him realize his own electronic compositional ideas. As Ligeti later recalled, "Koenig was the best and most helpful person that one can imagine."[95]

While at the studio, Ligeti composed three electronic works. Two of these, *Glissandi* (1957) and *Artikulation* (1958), are fairly well known,[96] whereas a third, *Pièce électronique No. 3* (1957), remained unfinished and is therefore relatively obscure.[97] Although he valued the experience, Ligeti never returned to electronic composition after leaving the studio in 1958. He explained,

> I find myself over the past years in a state in which I am a little bit dissatisfied with the acoustic results that one can make in the electronic studio; independent of which studio equipment is available, the perfection of studio equipment is beside the point.[98]

Although Ligeti did not find the electronic studio to be the right forum for his ideas, his experience at the WDR was crucial for his compositional and stylistic development. In fact, Ligeti's exposure to additive synthesis at the studio spurred his "sound-mass" style, which was introduced most famously in *Atmosphères* (1961). As I show in the next section, Ligeti transferred additive synthesis compositional techniques directly into the orchestral realm in *Atmosphères*, and in so doing, he brought the issue of timbre to the forefront of acoustic composition, as it was in the electronic studio.[99]

Translating Additive Synthesis

As with all of the composers discussed herein, Ligeti seems to have been viscerally inspired by the WDR studio's dream: to control timbre through additive synthesis. By the time Ligeti arrived at the studio in 1957, however, the heady optimism of the early 1950s had diminished, if only because composers kept running afoul of technical limitations. Ligeti's unfinished *Pièce électronique No. 3* provides compelling evidence of the limits of additive synthesis in the electronic studio. In Figure 3.12, the hand-drawn score shows Ligeti's concept of layering forty-eight individual sine tone voices together. The frequencies of the tones are given on the y axis of the graph, whereas the x axis corresponds to the temporal dimension. Ligeti used the graph paper to correlate the imagined duration of the figure with the length of tape necessary to produce it; his scale at the top of the page shows that each tiny 1-mm square on the graph paper corresponds to 5 cm of magnetic tape. The numbers across the x axis—50, 100, 150, and so forth—mark off tape lengths in centimeters. At 1360 cm long—and at the WDR standard playback speed of 76.2 cm/s—this excerpt should last about 17.8 s.

Despite the intricate notation and detailed compositional design, *Pièce électronique No. 3* was not realized in the analog studio. The forty-eight individual sine tones overwhelmed the studio's four-track tape recorder—the layering and re-recording necessary to make the mixtures created massive problems with synchronization and tape noise. Scholars have often made reference to the fact that Ligeti's third, unfinished electronic work was originally titled *Atmosphères*, until his orchestral work assumed that title.[100] The shared title is more than coincidental. Tellingly, when Ligeti failed to realize his ideas for *Atmosphères* in the studio, he recomposed them acoustically. Consider the opening figure of *Atmosphères*, shown in a graphic reduction in Figure 3.13. Of course, the translation from orchestral to electronic work requires notational transposition from pitch to hertz (or vice versa) but nevertheless, the conceptual and technical foundation of the passage remains additive synthesis.[101] Figures 3.12 and 3.13 illustrate the compositional thinking that defines Ligeti's signature sound-mass style. Namely, Ligeti treats each orchestral player not as a "finished" sound that stands alone, but rather as one element in a cluster. Of course, the resultant sound in *Atmosphères* is much richer and more complex than so many sine tones, because the orchestral pitches are composite tones with a fundamental and numerous overtones of their own.

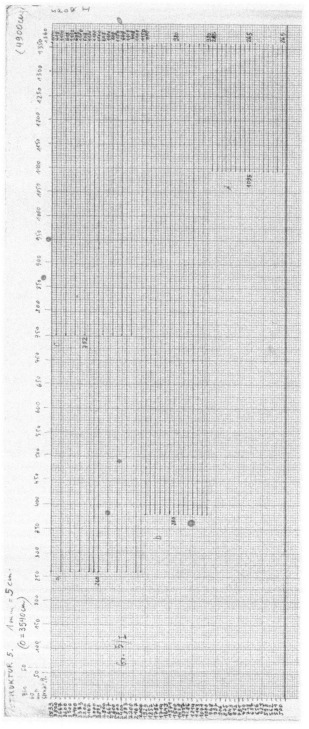

FIGURE 3.12. Opening figure from *Pièce électronique No. 3* (1957). György Ligeti Collection, Paul Sacher Foundation.

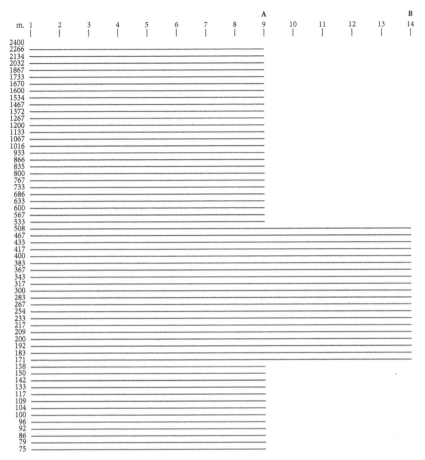

FIGURE 3.13. Graphic representation of *Atmosphères* (1961), mm. 1–14, pitches converted into hertz.

Beyond the static clusters, Ligeti also worked out an elaborate voice-leading technique to move sound masses fluidly in both pieces. As Figure 3.14 shows, in *Pièce électronique No. 3* Ligeti imagined individual voices leapfrogging over one another one at a time, to progressively higher or lower frequencies, causing the mass to migrate seamlessly in register. Figure 3.15 shows Ligeti's sketch for the upward spiral of the winds in *Atmosphères* beginning roughly at rehearsal letter F (mm 34–39). Ligeti uses the same voice leading in the acoustic micropolyphony, with the winds climbing over one another and the sound mass appearing to move itself almost magically.[102]

The leapfrog voice-leading technique results in a remarkable continuity of sound in both the electronic and the acoustic versions—the constant asynchrony between the individual voices' leaps means that it is nearly impossible to hear what voice is moving at what time. Although Ligeti transferred the

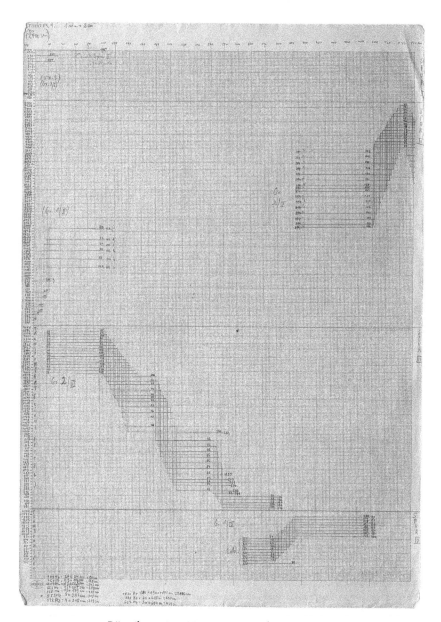

FIGURE 3.14. *Pièce électronique No. 3*, score, p. 4. György Ligeti Collection, Paul Sacher Foundation.

voice-leading technique from the electronic work to the acoustic work as literally as possible, he revised the temporal scope in *Atmosphères*. In contrast to the fleeting glissandos of *Pièce électronique No. 3*, the parallel passage from *Atmosphères* takes a surreal 50 seconds, a slow-motion drama that allows the listener to focus on the directional unfolding of the passage.

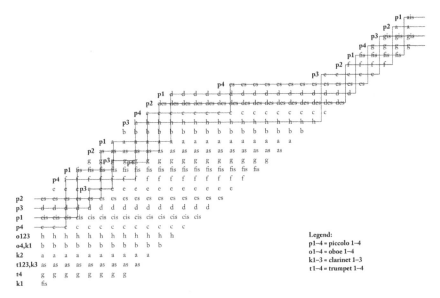

FIGURE 3.15. Transcription and adaptation of Ligeti's sketch for *Atmosphères*, mm. 34–39. Lines are author's annotations. György Ligeti Collection, Paul Sacher Foundation.

As a third demonstration of the kinship between *Atmosphères* and *Pièce électronique No. 3*, consider the penultimate section of *Atmosphères* (beginning at rehearsal letter T, mm 88–101). The strings play entirely in harmonics, creating a delicate, crystalline sound quality. Ligeti's sketches reveal that the entire passage is derived from the simultaneous combination of a number of different overtone series, in which the strings are assigned to play the "partials" above absent, but implied, "fundamentals." Figure 3.16a shows that Ligeti wrote out the overtone series in various octaves for pitch classes A, G, D, and C and assigned instrumentation to these series. Figure 3.16b, which appears later on the same manuscript page, sketches the implied fundamentals that would account for the partials in Figure 3.16a.

Ligeti chose harmonics that naturally occur on the instruments' open strings, ensuring that they would be playable at a fast tempo and that they would project as robustly as possible. These choices fed into Ligeti's compositional aim in the passage: to use the partials to produce the absent fundamentals as "difference tones" or "combination tones" or "residue pitches" in the listener's mind (or, possibly, by sympathetic resonance). As Ligeti explained, "My idea was that a sufficient number of overtones without the fundamental would, as a result of their combined acoustic effect, sound the fundamental."[103] Here we return to the Seebeck–Ohm–Helmholtz–Eimert

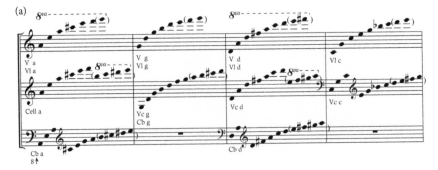

[Key: V=Violin; Vl=Viola; Cell and Vc=Cello; Cb=Contrabass]

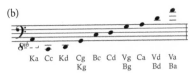

[Key: V=Violin; B=Bratsche/Viola; C=Cello; K=Kontrabass]

FIGURES 3.16A AND 3.16B Ligeti's sketch for overtone series used in *Atmosphères*, rehearsal letter T (above) and Ligeti's sketch for the implied fundamentals for overtone series (below). Author's commentary in square brackets. György Ligeti Collection, Paul Sacher Foundation.

debate about how the brain does or does not resolve conflicting partial tones, an idea that Ligeti first experimented with in the studio:

> I worked in this piece [*Pièce électronique No. 3*] with harmonic partial tones of imaginary fundamental tones, for example I selected one time a differential of 250 Hz, and another with 120 Hz, and so forth. If there is for example a tone of 4000 Hz, then the next partial is 4250, the following 4500, then 4750, and so on. There are different harmonic spectra in the piece, where the differentials of the partial tones are always constant. From that follows: through a difference of 250 Hz each, the partials produce an imaginary fundamental of 250 Hz.[104]

In his unfinished *Pièce électronique No. 3*, Ligeti imagined that, while the generators produced the upper partials, an ephemeral *Bassmelodie* of combination tones would emerge.[105] He translated this idea faithfully into the acoustic realm in *Atmosphères*, using ephemeral string harmonics for the upper partials.[106] Although I (and others) have never heard a *Bassmelodie* of absent fundamentals beneath the shimmering, gauzy, string harmonics, the concept reveals Ligeti's engagement with the imperfect psychoacoustical knowledge then in circulation at the WDR studio. The string harmonics of *Atmosphères* become significant on multiple levels—the partial tones (harmonic overtones) are themselves rendered in (string) harmonics. These ephemeral, gossamer sounds stand for the "impossible" sounds that could not be realized in the studio, despite the rhetoric of timbral utopia and dogged experimental research of the WDR studio composers. Ironically, these ideas had to be translated, renegotiated, and realized within the acoustic dimension.

Conclusions

This chapter has emphasized that the WDR studio of the early-to-mid-1950s was, above all, collaborative. Composers openly shared their ideas and their experiments and worked together to compose their pieces. Technicians created realization setups, suggested efficiencies, and transferred successful techniques between multiple composers. This cooperative, collaborative attitude toward composition stands in contrast to the "autonomous genius" model that composers propagated and that still often defines scholars' thinking and methodology.[107] Stockhausen, for example, was more than willing to claim credit as the intellectual force behind timbral synthesis.[108] His claim, although certainly not wholly true, is nevertheless somewhat tenable: since he was first hired as a technical assistant in the studio, Stockhausen learned how to operate the studio's machinery himself, which allowed him much more competence to troubleshoot, adjust, and realize his and others' ideas. Contrast this with a visiting composer who never became proficient at using the machinery of the studio and who had less time to musically integrate Meyer-Eppler's teachings on relevant topics such as phonetics and psychoacoustics. When we consider all the ways that "authority" accrues in a laboratory, it is clear that Stockhausen's authority stemmed in part from his technical ability, in part from his proximity to Meyer-Eppler and Eimert, in part from his assimilation of relevant scientific knowledge, and in part from his physical centrality in the studio space itself.[109] He was the center point connecting various collaborators.

That said, my analysis has also shown how Stockhausen benefited from fruitful collaborations with a number of other figures in his milieu—for example, Goeyvaerts, Gredinger, Pousseur, and Meyer-Eppler—though these important collaborators quickly became invisible. Goeyvaerts drifted out of Stockhausen's favor in the mid-1950s and left the field of music composition in 1957 after an emotional crisis. (He restarted his career as an "ordinary person" with a Belgian airline in 1958.[110]) Likewise, Pousseur remained distant physically, though not intellectually, as he also had a "day job." Gredinger never composed music again after *Formanten I and II* and instead became an important and influential advertising magnate.[111] Meyer-Eppler was primarily a scientist in Bonn—literally on the fringes of the Cologne composers' circle—but remained crucial in delivering information theory and phonetics insights, as we will see in Chapters 4 and 6. My excavations have aimed to make these figures visible again through careful analysis of correspondence, music, and writing.

Like many big-science laboratories, the WDR studio was greatly strengthened by heterogeneous collaborators who brought different expertise. Technicians were primarily oriented toward technical setup and practical translations, composers were oriented toward aesthetic debates, and scientists worked at the intersection of musical sound and scientific research. These different strands were drawn together in the WDR studio such that the music was informed by a synthesis of aesthetic paradigms, scientific knowledge, and technical constraints. In their early works, composers went through a trial-and-error process whereby they experimented with, and eventually discarded or revised, new ideas that were both aesthetic and scientific. A large part of this failure–revision cycle, demonstrating Andrew Pickering's "mangle of practice," had to do with negotiating the limits of the studio's technologies.[112] Composers strove for compelling new sounds, but were limited by tape noise, synchronization, and time. As Ligeti's failed *Pièce électronique No. 3* starkly demonstrates, the machinery imposed its own limits on the composer's designs.

In response to the mangle of practice, it may be easy to pessimistically conclude that the WDR studio never delivered on the timbral utopia it promised. The integral serial tenets turned out to be inadequate to fully address timbral synthesis on their own, as evidenced by perceptual failures of additive synthesis (e.g., *Studie I*). But as acoustical knowledge, techniques, and serial thought were further developed, composers found new ways to make progress with their ideas, often by translating them into acoustic music. Ligeti's *Atmosphères* stands as a prime example of this: a monumental intervention in avant-garde aesthetics, created by going to the bottom of the implications of the WDR studio discourses.

Ligeti was certainly not the only composer to translate his electronic inspirations and failures into acoustic music. Pousseur and Koenig simultaneously composed both acoustic and electronic music, using the same compositional paradigms and concepts.[113] Even for composers like Boulez and Nono, who did not visit for long stays in the 1950s, the studio remained critical as a nexus of ideas. The electronic music studio was compelling and frustrating in equal measure—it was both an ideal place to integrate timbre into composition, and a limiting scenario with several challenges. As composers and their collaborators mitigated these challenges, they often incorporated additional scientific information, making adjustments in their musical works accordingly. This process continues in earnest in the next chapter, when statistical form emerges as a substantial discourse out of the Cold War explosion of interest in information theory.

4 | Reclaiming Technology

From Information Theory to Statistical Form

In the mid-1950s, several composers in the European avant-garde began describing their music as "statistical," using new jargon with little overt definition. What did they mean? As this chapter will show, "statistical form" was the output of a series of studio-based translations, in which the composers learned the core concepts of information theory, revised them in the studio, and emerged with a "statistical" understanding of their electronic and acoustic music. Mediating this transfer was the scientist Werner Meyer-Eppler, the "primary German representative of information theory"[1] and a crucial link between military communication technologies and the aesthetic and technical concerns of the WDR composers. This chapter illuminates several inputs that flow into the concept of statistical form: Meyer-Eppler's teachings, critiques of integral serialism, and ad-hoc solutions to technical problems.

The uptake of information theory in the studio depended on a synthesis of scientific, aesthetic, and technical considerations. Yet, as we will see, studio composers often effaced their connections to information theory, preferring to speak about their music in abstract, aesthetic terms only. Scientist–musicians like Meyer-Eppler and his then-student Georg Heike wrote openly about the ways that information theory informed music, finding musical analogs with information-theoretic concepts like statistical prediction of language and the structure of communication systems.[2] By contrast, the WDR studio composers—especially Stockhausen—were secretive about their engagement with Meyer-Eppler and information theory and about their failures and inspirations in the studio. As Gottfried Michael Koenig cautioned, information theory could be a helpful interpretive lens, but it "never entered our discussions about composition theory and the production techniques of electronic music. [. . .] To say the Cologne composers had been inspired by it would be wrong."[3]

Indeed, when Stockhausen first introduced statistical form to the public in 1954, he spoke in purely aesthetic terms, tracing musical texture from Webern to Debussy—the studio discourses were completely cloaked.[4] The same was true in Stockhausen's 1957 article " . . . how time passes . . . ," which purported to think abstractly about musical time, pitch–duration relationships, proportions, and perception—ideas that were in fact conceived entirely in the studio. But as Koenig admitted, "the article in question contains hardly any references to composing; how it is done is not given away technologically."[5] Stockhausen and others kept the insights of the studio a carefully guarded secret, like a code that only a few insider collaborators could interpret.[6]

Despite the veiling of the studio's technologies, the composers' technoscientific bent was obvious to critics, who often disparaged the WDR composers as pseudo-scientists. In one scathing response to Stockhausen's " . . . how time passes . . . ," Dutch physicist Adriaan Fokker accused Stockhausen of mathematical errors, conceptual inaccuracies, and terminological obfuscation.[7] The American computer scientist John Backus, writing a "scientific evaluation" of several issues of *Die Reihe*, complained that it was rife with the composers' garbled mathematical formulas and "incomprehensible language."[8] This was not the fault of the translator, who had rendered "unintelligible German into unintelligible English."[9] According to Backus, the composers spewed "technical jargon without technical meaning," revealing their "inaccurate understanding of acoustics" and their meager understanding of other scientific domains.[10] Likewise, the American composer George Perle validated the "contemporary musical questions" explored in *Die Reihe*, but concluded, "In its content, Volume III of *Die Reihe* is worthless, and its manner, it is suspect. This is 'the simple truth.' "[11]

These insults are evidence of the boundary work that took place around the new electronic studio and the emerging interdisciplinary discourse of information theory.[12] Boundary work attempts to control or shape the dissemination of something (scholarship, research, creative practice, etc.) by policing the demarcations within and between fields. According to Thomas Gieryn, such boundary work can accomplish any number of aims, which include expanding authority, monopolizing resources, and protecting autonomy.[13] For instance, when scientists claim their own work is "science" while disparaging others' as "pseudo-science," they bolster their authority, as well as their access to resources like federal funding, peer review, and academic positions.[14]

In such debates, the WDR composers—who often spoke only in terms of purely musical logic, structure, and genesis—were policing an aesthetic boundary. In so doing, composers protected their claim to the lineage of the Western art music canon, building a sense of social identity that distinguished them—European avant-garde composers—as a group with similar concerns, goals, and methods, who were worthy of institutional support.[15] Simultaneously, scientists like Fokker and Backus policed the boundaries of technical and scientific domains, guarding against appropriation, misinterpretation, and distortion. They recognized the technoscientific jargon of the WDR circle, but, lacking access to the studio's machinery, discourses, and creative practices, they dismissed the composers' engagement as "pseudo."

Such boundary work was exceedingly common in the Cold War years, which saw explosive growth in the "new sciences" of information theory and related fields, including cybernetics, game theory, and, slightly later, systems theory.[16] Many of these theories evolved in the 1940s in dialogue with military communication systems and wartime technologies.[17] To take only one example, Norbert Wiener's cybernetics grew directly from his work at MIT to develop an antiaircraft missile defense system for the US military during World War II.[18]

As is well known, this intensive military engineering fueled an influx of new ideas and technologies into the academic and public spheres during the Cold War. At war's end, out of the public eye, military research groups were reconfigured to serve the dual goals of peacetime scientific advancement and Cold War superiority.[19] At the interdisciplinary Macy Conferences in the late 1940s and early 1950s, academics applied the insights of cybernetics to social sciences like psychology, anthropology, and psychiatry, and Wiener marketed his cybernetics ideas to the interested public in *The Human Use of Human Beings*.[20] Government funding was channeled toward projects like the University of Pennsylvania's ENIAC (the Electronic Numerical Integrator and Computer, the first American digital computer, 1945–1946) and Princeton's Institute for Advanced Studies (IAS) machine (an influential postwar computer, 1951–1952).[21]

In West Germany, the WDR electronic studio played an important role in such Cold War processes of reconfiguration and domestication. In the studio, the military engineering expertise of Meyer-Eppler was simultaneously veiled and put to scientific and aesthetic uses, as he translated information-theoretic insights into phonetics research and musical contexts. Furthermore, the studio's reclamations remasculinized West Germany in the eyes of the world. Like the pivot in cybernetics from missile defense to the Macy Conferences, the music of the WDR electronic studio became a beacon of cultural growth and advancement. It was on the grounds of electronic music that West Germany could stake its claims to cultural integrity and Cold War superiority. The visible boundary work around information theory and statistical form only testifies to the contentious nature of such a process of cultural reclamation.

In this chapter, I focus on the relationship between Claude Shannon's information theory and WDR electronic music because there are direct connections among Bell Labs, Meyer-Eppler, and the WDR studio. Although Wiener's cybernetics might work just as well to model electronic musical processes,[22] my interest here is in showing the direct lines of transmission that connect Shannon's information theory to midcentury music. I expose, in particular, the crucial roles of studio technologies. The uptake of information theory ideas was a result of the composers' perceptual dissatisfactions, as well as their practical successes and failures with the machinery in the studio (both already encountered in Chapter 3). In this way, the information theory discourses were not so much appropriated from the pop-cultural *Zeitgeist* as they were extracted from the technological constraints of the studio itself.

Stockhausen's *Jeux*

In Chapter 3, we uncovered the nascent beginnings of statistical form in the dialogue between Stockhausen and Pousseur in late 1953, in which they used volume curves and reverberation to add more complexity to their additive synthesis compositions. These technological foundations, however, were glossed over lightly in Stockhausen's public presentation of the ideas one year later in a broadcast titled "Von Webern zu Debussy: Formprobleme der elektronischen Musik" ["From Webern to Debussy: Formal Problems of Electronic Music"].[23] As Stockhausen wrote to Pousseur,

> Just a week ago I started work on the Debussy *Nachtprogramm*. (*Jeux* analyzed retrospectively, with respect to our new static problems of form). What do you think: a small piece by Debussy taken out of context, the word "statistical" mediating, to a small excerpt from [Eimert's] *Etüde über Tongemische*: voila—Debussy plus electronic music.[24]

The broadcast transcript does not survive, so it is hard to know how much Stockhausen discussed studio problems and electronic music on the radio. By the time the text was reprinted, however, the studio was rendered completely invisible—the title had been changed to "Von Webern zu Debussy: Bermerkungen zur statistischen Form" ["From Webern to Debussy: Remarks on Statistical Form"], and the text did not mention electronic music at all.

Instead, Stockhausen rehearsed the lineage of Webernian pointillism and integral serialism before pivoting into an analysis of the "statistical" fluctuations in Debussy's orchestral ballet score *Jeux* [*Games*]. Stockhausen identified and described rising–falling curves in pitch, loudness, and speed in Debussy's piece, suggesting that these gestures were more important than motives, harmonies, or traditional notions of form. Stockhausen was particularly concerned with textural continuums: "Between very large densities and pointillistic tone dispersions lie continually all variations of density. I am thinking of a *row of graded densities*[,] for vertical as well as for horizontal density."[25] These concepts are murky, not least because of Stockhausen's lack of transparency about the foundational context provided by the technologies and working procedures of the electronic studio.

When Stockhausen initially spoke to Boulez about the statistical form concept in November 1953, he likewise concentrated on a purely immanent serial logic:

> Dear Pierre,
>
> [. . .] I find myself more and more taken up with statistical composition: serial "improvisation" within limits of the serial spaces of time, of pitch, of intensity. [. . .] The serial groups of intervals (pitch—equally intensity and duration) divide the statistical spaces. We keep ourselves within limits [of these statistical spaces], while working in the directions of the intervals.[26]

Stockhausen was trying to describe musical approximations within limits, for instance, a glissando between fixed registral boundaries, trills within a serially determined duration, or a mass that gradually thickens. These were similar to the approximations and gestural shapes that he and Pousseur experimented with in their contemporaneous electronic music; recall the *Konfettiwolke* [confetti cloud] from Chapter 3. Instead of glossing the technical experiments he was undertaking in the studio, when speaking to Boulez, he implicitly drew upon the basic premises of descriptive statistics, which define data sets through distribution (range of values), central tendency (mean, median, and mode), and dispersion (standard deviation).[27]

Although Boulez was mathematically inclined, he struggled to grasp what Stockhausen could be proposing:

> Dear Karlheinz,
>
> Your last letter is really quite esoteric. I confess that in spite of all my application, and in spite of my habit to decipher the ellipses, I have been unable to unravel all of the enigmas that you put before me in your last letter. [. . .] What are you calling "statistical composition?" What do you mean exactly by "improvisation" within certain limits? What are you calling "statistical spaces?" What do you mean by "work in the directions of the intervals?"[28]

Stockhausen's terminology was esoteric, and his concepts were enigmatic to Boulez because they grew directly from the technical approximations that

Stockhausen, Koenig, and Pousseur used to produce electronic music at the WDR at the time. But absent Stockhausen's transparency, and without sharing the same experiences, Boulez found the ideas opaque.

Despite the initial confusion over the concept, many of the European avant-garde composers—especially those who had had some experience in an electronic studio—embraced statistical form. Pousseur, writing in 1955 about additive synthesis in electronic sound, suggested that inner partials are "statistic phenomena, a kind of source of probabilities," in contrast to the global and perceptible *Gestalt* of the composite sound or timbre.[29] Eimert suggested, in the same *Die Reihe* volume, that form in electronic music depends on "statistic structures" that organize sound according to densities.[30] Luciano Berio discussed *statistico* [statistical] and *probabilistico* [probabilistic] techniques in a 1956 *Incontri Musicali* article, suggesting that statistical conglomerations can lead composers to consider larger-scale proportions, which are more perceptually relevant, in their serial designs.[31]

Indeed, several composers found the musical approximations and large-scale shapes of statistical form quite useful for their acoustic compositions—so much so that statistical form supplanted pointillism and emerged as the second stage of serial technique.[32] In this case, the ambiguity of the new term was an advantage: it allowed several of the avant-garde composers to develop the concept according to their own interpretation, within their individual compositional poetics. Despite the richness of the composers' variegated applications, the concept of statistical form nevertheless had strong ties to Meyer-Eppler's information theory teachings.

Information Theory and Wartime Communications

Information theory—sometimes also called communication theory—developed primarily from the work of Claude Shannon in the late 1940s and early 1950s.[33] Shannon was an electrical engineer, PhD mathematician, and cryptographer working at Bell Laboratories, the research-and-development division of the AT&T telephone company.[34] Shannon's information theory, simply put, uses a mathematical equation to describe how much information is in a message. Although research into bandwidth and message size had been going on since the late 1920s,[35] Shannon's theory included the unpredictable elements of interference and noise as parts of the equation, where noise is anything that interrupts a signal. As such, Shannon's information theory equation described more accurately how information behaved in an imperfect or changeable communication channel. As Bell Labs engineer John Pierce summarized, information theory "tells us how many bits of information can be sent per second over perfect and imperfect communication channels in terms of rather abstract descriptions of the properties of these channels."[36]

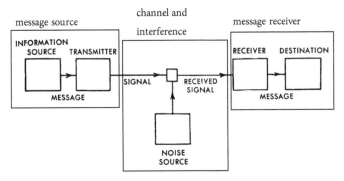

FIGURE 4.1. Shannon's schematic diagram for the communication system, with annotations.

Figure 4.1 shows Shannon's schematic drawing of the three-part communication system—the message source, the channel (with its potential interference), and the message receiver. In Shannon's telecommunication contexts, the message may originate with a human, and it is encoded using certain technology.[37] Landline telephones, for instance, reduce speech (the information source) to a few critical frequencies and change sound waves into electrical impulses (in the transmitter).[38] The message could become garbled already at this stage by a problem with the transmitter, such as poor control of amplitude and frequency modulation. But assuming that the transmitted message (signal) enters the channel, it might encounter still more limitations, such as interference (noise source) or inadequate bandwidth. Such distortions influence whether the message can be received and decoded on the other end. In the example of the telephone, the electrical signals are resynthesized into sound waves (in the receiver), and finally reach the human ear (the destination), which itself has limited capacities and capabilities.[39]

Shannon's information theory brought together considerations of message size, technological challenges (e.g., encoding, transmission, interference, and decoding), and human perceptual limits. It was a very synthetic discourse, simultaneously addressing technology, predictability, and perception. This synthesis was crucial, because it made the theory useful in a wide range of contexts.[40] One of those contexts was broadcasting, as shown in Figure 4.2—an illustration from Abraham André Moles's 1958 *Théorie de l'information et perception esthétique*.[41] A scientist and philosopher, Moles was the primary French proponent of information theory in the 1950s and 1960s and a crucial thinker about the relationships between information theory and music.[42] Although Meyer-Eppler was the chief figure to transmit information theory discourses in German circles, we will see that Iannis Xenakis and others in French circles benefited from Moles's knowledge. Moles's illustration in Figure 4.2 shows all the ways that broadcast sound has to be encoded,

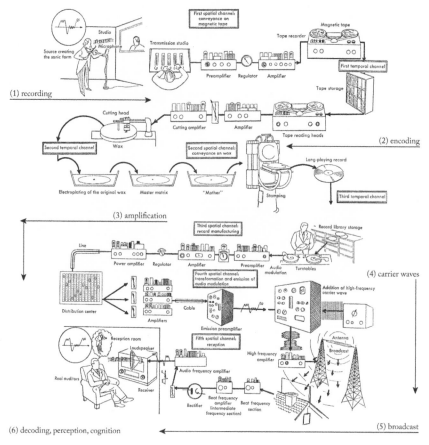

FIGURE 4.2. Moles's complex communication channel for recorded sound and broadcasting, with annotations.

transmitted, and decoded: it begins with acoustic sound waves recorded onto magnetic tape, vinyl records, or both; the sound is sent through amplifiers, cables, regulators, and distribution centers; it is broadcast, with the addition of carrier waves, in certain frequency ranges from antennas; it is received on a home "wireless" set (i.e., a radio); and finally, it is perceived and cognized in the listener's mind.

There are a lot of ways for the message to become noisy, garbled, unintelligible, or lost in the complex signal path. As Moles remarked, "Considering this dizzy chain of transformations, it seems remarkable that what remains at the end has some similarity to the original signal."[43] Domestically, in the Cold War era, information theory grew to address the challenges of telephony, broadcasting, and early computing; the roots of information theory concepts, however, were in military contexts of the 1940s and World War II.

Shannon worked for some time at Bell Labs on anti-aircraft and anti-missile teams, which used differential equations to predict the trajectories of V-1 rockets (also known as "doodlebugs" or "buzz bombs") aimed at London.[44] He then switched into military cryptography research, which he found quite similar. As he wrote, "There is an obvious analogy between the problem of data smoothing to eliminate or reduce the effect of tracking errors [in missile trajectories] and the problem of separating a signal from interfering noise in communication systems."[45] Shannon's wartime work moved in overlapping circles with Wiener (at MIT's Rad Lab) and Alan Turing (at Bletchley Park),[46] whose work used mathematical prediction and probability for Allied code-breaking efforts.[47]

This nexus suggests that military logistics of World War II regularly presented similar problems in slightly different contexts, such that the mathematical models used in Turing's code-breaking efforts had much in common with those that Shannon and Wiener developed to predict bomb-shell trajectories and handle domestic communication engineering problems. Furthermore, as the proliferation of information theory demonstrates, it was one small step from the various military uses, to the civilian and artistic reclamations of the postwar era. As Friedrich Kittler speculated, "the self-guided weaponry of the Second World War did away with the two fundamental concepts of modernity—causality and subjectivity—and inaugurated the present as the age of technological systems."[48] The consequence, according to Kittler, was that the electronic studio of the WDR and the music entertainment industry more broadly are, "in any conceivable sense of the word, an abuse of army equipment."[49] The WDR composers would not have agreed with Kittler that they were at the mercy of their technologies, without control, agency, or subjectivity; those composers likely remained ignorant about the wartime affiliations of their studio technologies, discourses, and collaborators. Yet they definitely did produce music that was thoroughly steeped in the sounds and the "technological systems" of World War II.

Meyer-Eppler's Reclamations

The WDR studio, informed by the teachings of Meyer-Eppler, was a primary site where information theory underwent an aesthetic reclamation. As we learned in Chapter 1, Meyer-Eppler was a Nazi Party member and physicist who, between 1943 and 1945, actively researched sonar, warning detection systems, circuits, radio transmissions, and encrypted speech for a U-boat military regiment.[50] Let us now focus on the Cold War translations that Meyer-Eppler performed as he domesticated this knowledge, by undertaking a second career in experimental phonetics, involving himself in electronic music circles, and transmitting information theory concepts to Stockhausen and friends.

After stumbling through a contentious British denazification process, by the mid-1950s, Meyer-Eppler had successfully pivoted into a second career and was lecturing on information theory topics in Gravesano, Switzerland (1955), in Munich and Darmstadt (1957), and in Brazil (1958).[51] This line of inquiry, which he had developed for nearly a decade, culminated in his second book, *Grundlagen und Anwendungen der Informationstheorie* [*Foundations and Applications of Information Theory*].[52] The book addressed a range of topics, from Shannon's equations to binary encoding to perceptual limits.

Meyer-Eppler and his French counterpart, Moles, encouraged the belief that Shannon's equations were an abstract model, a container into which situation-specific content (like music) could be poured. As Warren Weaver, one of the early proponents of information theory, wrote,

> This is a theory so general that one does not need to say what kinds of symbols are being considered—whether written letters or words, or musical notes, or spoken words, or symphonic music, or pictures. The theory is deep enough so that the relationships it reveals indiscriminately apply to all these and to other forms of communication.[53]

Information theory, as described in this highly general and schematic way, was especially useful to composers because it had so much to say about the receiving end of the communication channel—that is, the listener. Meyer-Eppler's teachings addressed not only the acoustical and technical problems of the electronic studio—for example, excessive noise from re-recording or amplification—but also music perception. In other words, information theory introduced tools to think about how audiences were hearing and receiving (electronic) music.

Like many of the Bell Labs scientists with whom Claude Shannon worked, Meyer-Eppler was well informed about psychoacoustic and perceptual issues.[54] Informed also by Stumpf's *Tonpsychologie*, Meyer-Eppler's writing makes clear a difference between perception [*Wahrnehmung*] (when information activates the sense organs), and cognition [*Empfindung*] (when the brain intervenes by comparing with previous experiences, creating patterns, and making predictions). According to Meyer-Eppler, the message first had to be perceptible in order for it to be cognizable. As such, he focused on describing the limits of sensory perception, writing, "The *boundary* of perceptual space can be investigated instead of *cognitively-produced structure*."[55]

Figure 4.3 illustrates Meyer-Eppler's thinking about perceptual boundaries. Human hearing occupies a band within a wider range of known frequencies—including the infrasonic and ultrasonic frequencies—that are imperceptible to humans. The same is true for the spectrum of visible light, which is contained within a larger range that includes infrared and ultraviolet spectra. To take this a step further, music has to fall within a certain range of values if the brain is to have any hope of making sense of it. If the frequencies

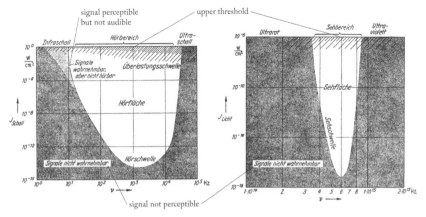

FIGURE 4.3. Meyer-Eppler's illustrations for the ranges of human hearing (left) and sight (right), both situated within infra- and ultra-dimensions of the spectra, with annotations. *Grundlagen und Anwendungen der Informationstheorie*, 198–99.

are too high or too low, or the durations too long or too short, etc., the listener is unable to "understand" the message. An electronic machine may be able to sense and record such ultra- and infra-dimensions of waves, but the human listener needs the signal to fall within the boundary of its own human receiving mechanism.

These may be simple insights, but they were nevertheless transformative. Meyer-Eppler drew attention to the fact that the sense organs have certain rather constant limits that cannot be willfully transcended. One could address the intelligibility of messages, Meyer-Eppler theorized, by addressing the perceptual limits of the human listener. Although the idea of perceptual boundaries is only one facet of information theory, such psychoacoustic insights spurred revolutionary new directions for the WDR composers.

Gestalten in Acoustic and Electronic Music

Stockhausen studied with Meyer-Eppler in Bonn at least weekly in 1955, taking eight seminars with him in total (see Table 4.1).[56] As the course titles suggest, Stockhausen was well exposed to Meyer-Eppler's teachings on psychoacoustics and perception, topics that seemed to speak directly to contemporary musical questions. Soon after landmark pointillist compositions such as *Structures* (Boulez, 1951), *Kreuzspiel* (Stockhausen, 1951), and *Kontra-Punkte* (Stockhausen, 1953), composers noted a problematic gap between their highly regulated, integral serial compositional designs and a rather disappointing aesthetic flatness. Moment to moment, pointillist music quickly started to sound the same. Ligeti expressed this elegantly: "The finer the

TABLE 4.1. Stockhausen's seminars with Meyer-Eppler at the University of Bonn.

Time Frame	Course Title	Course Title in English Translation
Winter 1954–1955	*Einführung in die Phonetik*	Introduction to Phonetics
	Kapitel psychologischer Akustik	Section on Psychoacoustics
Spring 1955	*Einführung in die Klangforschung*	Introduction to Sound Research
	Phonetische und akustische Probleme des Rundfunk	Phonetic and Acoustical Problems of Radio Broadcasting
	Praktische Phonetik	Practical Phonetics
Winter 1955–1956	*Phonetik und Phonologie des Deutschen*	Phonetics and Phonology of the German Language
	Informationstheorie	Information theory
Spring 1956	*Wahrnehmung und Empfindung sowie eine nicht näher bezeichnete Veranstaltung über Phänomenologie*	Perception and Cognition as well as a not-otherwise-specified presentation on phenomenology

network of operations with pre-ordered material, the higher the degree of levelling-out in the result. Total, consistent application of the serial principle negates, in the end, serialism itself."[57] Xenakis, Boulez, and Pousseur all made similar observations.[58]

These critiques often called attention to a related observation: if one used chance processes (instead of serial controls) to determine the musical events—as John Cage did in *Music of Changes* (1951)—the resulting music sounded just as flat and monotonous. As Ligeti continued,

> There is really no basic difference between the results of automatism and the products of chance; total determinacy comes to be identical with total indeterminacy. This is the place to seek the parallelism [. . .] between integral-serial music and music governed by chance (John Cage). The following is characteristic of both types: pause–event–pause–event–pause, etc.[59]

An information-theoretic perspective helped the composers further understand why music conceived in such different terms could sound so similar. Both serial and chance music are extremely information dense, each sound defined by its own pitch register, dynamics, articulation, and duration.[60] There is very little that is predictable about the pieces, because there are very few redundancies in the musical languages of either total serialism or chance composition.[61] Each bit of information is necessary to the integrity of the message.

The WDR composers, learning more about perception and psychoacoustics, began to understand that listeners cannot comprehend a message with so much information. As a result, many, if not most, of the midcentury avantgarde composers showed an interest in moving away from pointillist textures by the mid-1950s, regardless of the compositional technique (serialism or aleatory) that produced them.[62] Meyer-Eppler's teachings on the limits of perceptible sound functioned like an "involuntary benediction," in Robin Maconie's interpretation,[63] freeing Stockhausen and others from their excessive focus on the details—and pointing them toward larger shapes that would be perceptible as gestures and processes.

In this vein, we see Stockhausen working with textural density in *Gruppen* (1955–1957), for instance. Figure 4.4 reproduces the sketch for group 131, which matches up with rehearsal no. 156 in the score (as Stockhausen notes on the sketch) because of earlier interpolations of nonserial, freely composed material. This drawing represents the relationship of density, or orchestral thickness, on the vertical y axis and attack frequency, or acceleration, on the horizontal x axis—the same parameters that Stockhausen analyzed in Debussy's *Jeux*. The marimba and woodblocks—labeled as "Mar. + Holztrom"—are shown on the exponential curve. The attack frequency of these wooden percussion sounds increases to a peak and then quickly dies away, as illustrated by the circled articulations on the curve's trajectory. The sharp peaks above the curve map out density, or orchestral thickness. The densest vertical texture coincides with the most frequent percussion articulations. Perhaps counterintuitively, these high-density textures do not necessarily coincide with the loudest moments—the peaks simply represent the number of instruments playing at one time. Serial calculations are deeply

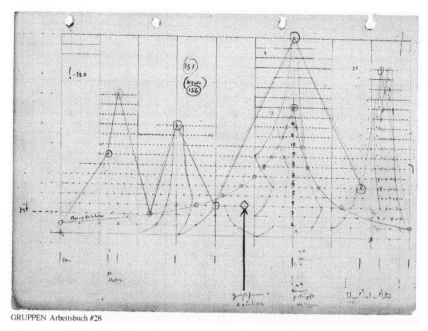

GRUPPEN Arbeitsbuch #28

FIGURE 4.4. Stockhausen, *Gruppen*, sketch for rehearsal no. 156. Stockhausen Foundation.

embedded in *Gruppen*,[64] but the sketches show also a gestural, conceptual approach to the material that is highly characteristic of the electronic studio.

Consider, for instance, a sketch from Ligeti's electronic *Artikulation*, which shows some of the general sound envelopes that he envisaged for the piece (see Figure 4.5). These generalized shapes may have been applied to

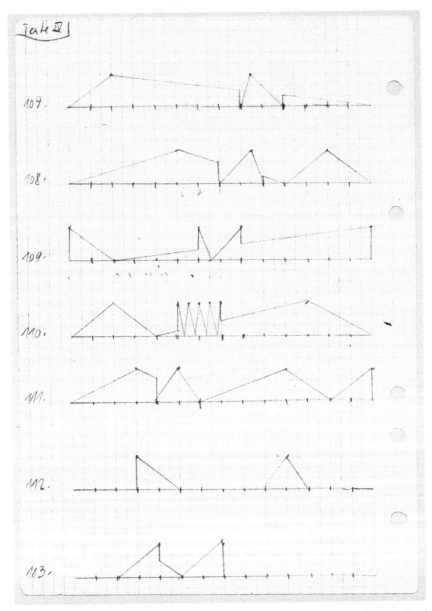

FIGURE 4.5. Ligeti, *Artikulation* (1957), sketch. György Ligeti Collection, Paul Sacher Foundation.

volume or density of sound, or they may have been mapped onto a frequency chart or sound mixture to give fluctuations in pitch or timbre. Because conventional music notation was, at best, of marginal use for electronic music, some composers—for example, Koenig—sketched in numbers that were essentially technical directions, or a realization score.[65] For others—like Ligeti—a gestural or conceptual sketch was quite useful for imagining the overall shape of a passage. Composers learned from Meyer-Eppler's perceptual teachings to take care that the major architecture of the piece would be audible. In these ways, the aesthetic shifts from pointillism to statistical form were reinforced by information theoretic ideas about message density, redundancy, and listener perception.

The Sampling Theorem and *Bewegungsfarbe*

The sampling theorem provides a second example of the way information theory was quite relevant and applicable to music. In Shannon's work with encrypted communications, it was practical to think of a written message in terms of "bits" (a contraction of "binary digits"), such as the dots and dashes of Morse code or the letters of the alphabet.[66] Encoding and decoding a message of discrete bits and predicting its size were—mathematically speaking, at least—straightforward maneuvers. Technologies like the telephone or the Vocoder, yoked to spoken language, introduced a difficulty: speech (or any sound) exists as a continuous wave, which introduces much more information and loads of mathematical complexity as compared with the discrete bits of written language.[67] As Shannon explained, "With a continuous source, the situation is considerably more involved. In the first place a continuously variable quantity can assume an infinite number of binary digits for exact specification."[68]

To solve the mathematical "problem" of the continuous wave, Shannon introduced the sampling theorem. Simply stated, the sampling theorem says that a continuous wave can be chopped up into discrete bits of information. The wave can then be accurately reassembled so long as it is sampled frequently and evenly enough, which, in most scenarios, is at the rate of "twice as many samples as the highest frequency present in the signal."[69] The mathematical, technological shortcut results in no noticeable information loss, even though sampling drastically reduces message size.

This is, of course, the premise of data compression by means of MP3.[70] The sampling theorem plays a perceptual trick, in a way. There *is* information loss when waves are sampled or compressed, but what are lost are frequencies that mostly lie on or outside of the boundaries of human perception. As such, the losses pass most humans' ears without notice. The sleight-of-hand accomplished by the sampling theorem recontextualizes the usefulness of

Meyer-Eppler's emphasis on perceptual limits of hearing. Sampling and compression technologies streamline and simplify data in a way that is mathematically useful; at the same time, the sonic changes are so miniscule as to be (nearly) imperceptible to humans.

In the studio, the midcentury composers likewise exploited the human perceptual mechanism—its (in)sensitivities, boundaries, and defaults—in similar ways. The human brain can hold a sequence of discrete samples apart only until they reach a certain speed; beyond this threshold, the brain creates the impression of continuity from a series of impulses. Film is one such situation that exploits the brain's inferential power, as Ligeti noted.[71] At sixteen or eighteen frames per second, the film flickers, but at a normal projection speed of twenty-four frames per second, it is impossible to perceive that the film is made of individual still frames even when we intellectually know that it is. The electronic studio was a prime location for composers to discover and rediscover this intriguing perceptual continuum.[72]

Stockhausen famously did so in " . . . how time passes . . . ," where he introduced a fairly major conceptual overhaul: pitch and rhythm are the same phenomenon, he argued. They are not just analogous parameters, relatable by the same proportions within in a serial scheme, but are of the same nature. Because both pitch and rhythm are periodic waves, rhythms can turn into pitches, and vice versa. As Stockhausen explained,

> This becomes clear if we steadily shorten the length of a phase (e.g., that duration between two impulses) from $1''$ to $1/2''$ to $1/4''$, $1/8''$, $1/16''$, $1/32''$, $1/64''$, etc. Until a phase-duration of approx. $1/16''$ [63 ms], we can still just hear the impulses separately; until then, we speak of 'duration,' if of one that becomes extremely short. Shorten the phase-duration gradually to $1/32''$ [31 ms], and the impulses are no longer separately perceptible; [. . .] one perceives the phase-duration as the 'pitch' of the sound. $1/32''$ phase-duration makes us, say, 'a "low" note.'[73]

Such transitions between pitch and rhythm were easy to create in the electronic music studio, where an impulse generator could be gradually sped up or slowed down to create the effect of moving between discrete pulses and pitch. Variable-speed tape recorders could likewise speed and slow sequences to induce the same effect.

In the studio, Stockhausen and others discovered that the boundary among rhythm, pitch, and timbre was arbitrary; or rather, that the boundary was perceptual—tied to the affordances and limitations of the human body. As Stockhausen reasoned,

Our sense-perception cannot react to a single phase quickly enough to perceive it as 'duration', so it summarizes several quanta to give the sensory quality 'pitch'. Steadily shorten the phase-duration still further, from 1/32″ to 1/64″, 1/128″, 1/256″, etc., and the note ascends as a glissando from 'low to high', and we can still speak clearly of recognizable pitches with phase-durations up to approx. 1/6000″. We can perceive still shorter phase-durations up to approx. 1/16000″, but exact pitch orientation gets lots in this time-sphere. Higher still, we do not 'hear' anymore.[74]

This discussion recalls Meyer-Eppler's hearing-limit graph in Figure 4.3. At some threshold, which Stockhausen believed to be about 60 ms, we stop perceiving a series of fast impulses as individual durations and start hearing them as a pitch. At that moment, we enter the low-frequency range, or the audible limit, the low point in the U-shaped lobe of Meyer-Eppler's hearing graph. As the impulses become shorter and shorter and the periodicity of the wave increases, the pitch rises, and we move into the middle of the lobe. At some point, the pitch becomes quite high, and we move into the liminal areas at the top of Meyer-Eppler's graph. Here Stockhausen replicated Meyer-Eppler's terminology almost exactly: these boundary-land sensations are perhaps perceptible (i.e., able to be sensed), but not hearable (i.e., not able to be fully cognized).

Koenig and Stockhausen cooperatively developed such insights about the pitch–rhythm continuum working side-by-side daily in the studio from mid-1954 through 1956. Koenig's *Essay* (1957) and Stockhausen's *Gesang der Jünglinge* (1956) are both deeply engaged with samples and continuities; both exploit the listener's perceptual boundaries, though with somewhat different techniques and results.

Essay is, in some sense, the epitome of serialism, as its pitches and durations are handled with a very specific serial plan.[75] Koenig began with a tape length of 76 cm as his basic unit—a sensible decision, as the tape speed at the WDR studio was 76.2 cm/s of sound. As Figure 4.6 shows, Koenig then used a "geometric series" to build seven further tape lengths. In a geometric series, terms are related by a constant ratio—here 3:2—to

1	2	3	4	5	6	7	8
76	114	171	256.5	384.7	577.1	865.7	1298.5

Tape lengths   *=3743.5 cm*

FIGURE 4.6. Koenig's *Essay* section durations, according to geometric series based on the ratio 3:2.

describe the relation between successive terms. As Figure 4.7 shows, Koenig then reordered these tape lengths according to a row that I have termed the *Grundreihe* [foundational row], as it appears to structure a number of parameters (though not all) in the composition.

Koenig then divided and subdivided each alphabetic section into quite small segments, also using geometric series. This process, as enacted for Section A, is shown in Figure 4.8. Koenig began with the tape length of Section A, which, after the serial reordering of Figure 4.7, was 384.7 cm. Enacting a geometric series again based on the ratio 3:2, Koenig created seven divisions within the length of Section A. These lengths (12, 17.9, 26.9, etc.) were then further subdivided with geometric series of new ratios: 12:11, 11:10, 10:9, 9:8, and so on. (Koenig would have continued to use the ratio 3:2 for all the subdivisions, but it resulted in too-small initial values in the series.[76]) Ultimately, the dividing and subdividing processes resulted in a panoply of small fragments ranging from 1.1 to 29.6 cm in length. (The

FIGURE 4.7. Koenig's *Essay* section durations, rearranged according to serial *Grundreihe* scheme.

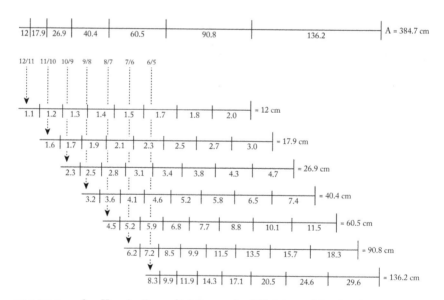

FIGURE 4.8. Koenig *Essay*, divisions and subdivisions of Section A.

divided and subdivided lengths were also reordered according to various serial rows, but that detail need not concern us here. A similar process was used to divide, subdivide, and order Sections B through H.)

The durations of *Essay*, based on the same geometric series at all levels of the hierarchy, create an exceptionally tight, proportional structure. The durational kaleidoscope, reminiscent of Cage's square-root form, is certainly fun to contemplate, but it is also important to ask how this prismatic structure interacts with the limits of perception. Koenig used his geometric series to subdivide down to a very small tape length—about 1 cm long. Table 4.2 shows a selection of some of these subdivided tape lengths (refer back to Figure 4.8), along with their durations. Recalling Meyer-Eppler's teachings from the 1950s, subsequent cognitive studies have shown that human perception has upper and lower limits. As Justin London explains, "We can entrain to a wide range of rhythms, but not all periodic stimuli afford entrainment; some are too fast, and others are too slow. Rapidly blinking lights can become a blur, and slowly (but regularly) dripping faucets will defeat

TABLE 4.2. Some subdivided lengths from Section A in *Essay*, with durations in milliseconds.

Tape (cm)	Duration (ms)
1.1	14.4
2.0	26.2
3.2	42.0
4.5	59.0
5.2	68.2
6.2	81.4
7.4	97.1
7.7	101.0
8.3	108.9
9.9	129.9
10.1	132.5
11.5	150.9
14.3	187.6
18.3	240.2
24.6	322.8
29.6	388.5

our attempts to predict when the next drip will fall."[77] Thus the question in *Essay* becomes this: How short is too short? To say it another way: How fast is too fast?

Given experimental research about perceptual limits, durations shorter than about 100 ms are probably too fast to be perceived as distinct objects, and instead create an impression of continuity in our mind; durations longer than 100 ms are probably long enough to be perceived as distinct entities, even when played in succession. This should be thought of not as a rigid boundary, but rather as a zone of transition. It is not as if we humans have a switch that flips when we reach the perceptual boundary, though numerous studies have suggested that 100 ms is a crucial duration for perceptual discernment.[78] Singers and drummers, when articulating at their fastest pulse, tend to perform sounds that are 100 to 120 ms apart. A host of studies points toward a similar conclusion: "the shortest interval that we can hear or perform as an element of rhythmic figure—is about 100 ms."[79] It seems that the 100-ms zone is constrained by the capabilities of the human body, whether it is perceiving or performing.

In this way, Koenig's *Essay* foregrounds the tension between humans and machines, a tension that had long colored the reception of electronic music. Studio techniques went beyond the physical limitations of human performers—whereas a human couldn't have played such fast successions, tape lengths of a centimeter could be montaged with minimal difficulty. Yet, such short fragments durations *do* run afoul of the listener's perceptual limits, because the brain cannot process them as individual moments. Instead, the successions that Koenig mapped out in *Essay*, as pictured in Figure 4.8, blend together into a strange, fluctuating sound somewhere between melody and timbre.[80] Koenig called this *Bewegungsfarbe*, or moving–sound–color. As he explained,

> What was interesting for me was the compression [*Stauchung*] and expansion [*Dehnung*] of the sound structure . . . . Through a process of shortening, the structure shrinks together into a so-called color-fleck, whereby the concept of *Bewegungsfarbe* originates (that is to say, coloration through a movement process). Ligeti, having assisted with my *Essay*, marked these effects also as "succession blurring," a term that describes the phenomena better than *Bewegungsfarbe*.[81]

Ligeti, as the technician for Koenig's *Essay*, learned this technique in the studio and subsequently applied it in his own acoustic works, presenting no small challenge to performers.[82] In pieces such as *Continuum* (for harpsichord, 1968) and *Coulée* (for organ, 1969) Ligeti wrote sequences calling for twenty articulations per second, or onsets that are only 50 ms apart, if performed accurately—a rate at which discrete notes blend together into a continuous, fluctuating timbre.[83] Realizing at least intuitively that the performer's physical boundary was similar to the listener's perceptual boundary, Ligeti knew that his performance directions and fast articulations brushed the limit of what most human performers can play. So Ligeti also used other tricks to approximate the *Bewegungsfarbe* effect, namely, increasing the number of performers, using a time delay, or both. In the "sound-mass" works like *Apparitions* (1957), *Atmosphères* (1961), and *Requiem* (1965), individual voices are layered and often staggered with short delays in micropolyphonic canons, which greatly increase the number of articulations heard within the same time frame and collectively produce a *Bewegungsfarbe* effect.[84] Whether in electronic music (Koenig) or acoustic music (Ligeti), composers in the WDR studio circle worked with the perceptual tricks induced by very short samples.

Returning to the comparison with Stockhausen's *Gesang der Jünglinge* (1955–1956), composed contemporaneously with *Essay*, we can first note that Stockhausen and Koenig (in the role of technician) began by montaging together small samples in the customary way. As Figure 4.9 shows, Stockhausen planned both the frequency and the duration of vocal samples—a biblical text sung by a boy soprano named Josef Protschka—according to a serial plan.[85] These montage techniques were commonplace at the WDR studio, and although they offered a lot of control over the sounding result, they were incredibly time consuming. Stockhausen and Koenig completed the first section of the piece with this precise montaging, but under pressure to finish in time for the May 1956 *Musik der Zeit* premiere, they needed a more

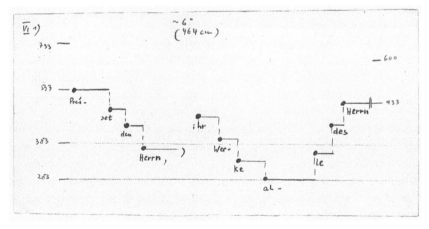

FIGURE 4.9. Stockhausen, *Gesang der Jünglinge*, sketch showing montage plan for vocal samples. Stockhausen Foundation.

efficient method to produce the remaining sections in the piece. Together they devised a new, improvisatory, gestural workaround that would produce very similar results with much more efficiency.

As composer Konrad Boehmer explained, this new technique used tape loops to superimpose a number of sine tones:

> Koenig was convinced that it would not be at all sensible to record thousands of centimeter-long particles of sinus [sine] tones and to then measure, cut, and finally glue them together. For this reason, he proposed a quasi-aleatoric production process in which he began with tapes of short magnetic and white taped sections and then recorded a sinus-glissando that would be automatically divided into distinct, small particles. If several such tapes are synchronised (with different "rhythms" and glissandi), one hears a "cloud" of tiny sound-particles with an all-embracing global direction.[86]

The reconstructive work of Sean Williams, which involves extensive experimentation with analog filters, generators, and tape machines, further clarifies this gestural methodology.[87] Stockhausen and Koenig improvised curves in real time by turning knobs on generators and filters to fill certain durational and frequency boundaries established in advance. These improvised gestures created effects like rising pitch or gradually slowing impulses. As Stockhausen explained, "[T]his resulted in an aleatoric layer of individual pulses which, in general, speeded up statistically. But you could never at a certain moment say, 'This pulse will now come with that pitch.' This was impossible to predetermine."[88] The sketch shown in Figure 4.10 shows the curves that guided these improvisations. When Stockhausen and Koenig recorded several such improvised curves on an efficient tape loop devised by Heinz Schütz, the team could create the piece's characteristic effervescent, free-floating glissandi quite effectively.

These gestural techniques, achieved with the affordances of the analog studio knobs, are the essence of Stockhausen's statistical form: approximations in which the general direction of the gesture is specified but its internal elements are freely distributed within limits. As this analysis shows, the studio machines themselves were extremely important in the evolution of the statistical form concept.[89] Equally important were the collaborative solutions that composers and technicians developed together to solve technical and musical problems. Studio composers had to work with the machinery in practical ways, and technicians were usually the ones who helped composers learn to do that. As Koenig wrote in *Die Reihe*, "Music and technique are so inter-related that only by a united effort can the artistic idea transcend the technical restrictions."[90]

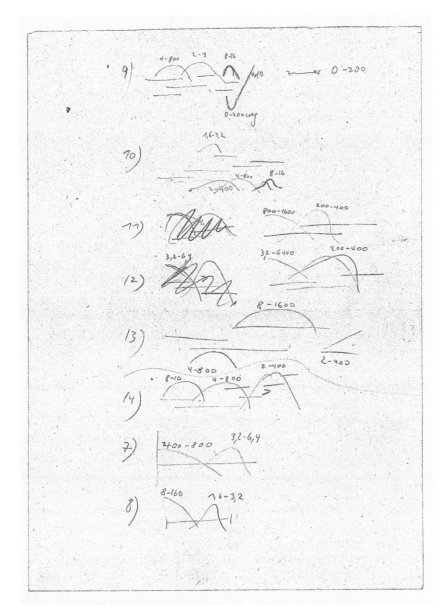

FIGURE 4.10. Stockhausen, *Gesang der Jünglinge*, sketch showing gestural curves for making statistical approximations. Stockhausen Foundation.

Cryptographic Probabilities

As we have seen so far, the WDR composers arrived at statistical form in their acoustic and electronic work through several related avenues, including both an aesthetic critique of pointillism and technical, gestural negotiations with technologies in the studio. These new perspectives were underwritten by way of Meyer-Eppler's teachings about information theory, sampling, and human perception. In sum, WDR studio composers used information-theoretic ideas to create a more efficient encoding of the message (i.e., a more efficient compositional technique) and a more reliably perceptible message (i.e., a more intelligible musical product).

One important aspect of information theory that we have not yet discussed concerns prediction and probability. As we have already noted, messages survive noisy interferences and are easier for listeners to comprehend when they include redundancies or repetitions. In Shannon's equations, the predictability and size of a message are directly related to its redundancies. One could reduce the size of a message by trimming redundancies or, in another approach, one could mitigate potential interference by adding redundancies or "expanding the verbosity of [the] discourse."[91] Smaller and more repetitive messages are more predictable, while larger, denser messages are less so. This correlation between message size and predictability builds upon the understanding that language, grammar, and syntax are themselves predictable, redundant structures. Shannon drew this insight directly from his work as a cryptographer.

During the war, the Allied forces spent considerable effort decoding German communications sent either through Morse code or by radio broadcast. This code-breaking work was famously done at Bell Labs (where Shannon led a team) and at Bletchley Park (where Turing and 9,000 other employees—most of them women—worked).[92] The Polish made important contributions in the late 1930s by linking six of the German Enigma enciphering machines together into a contraption called a *Bombes*, which Turing's machine extended. The Swedish cryptography program cracked the code for the German radio broadcasts encoded by Siemen's *Geheimschreiber* [secret writer], or "G-Schreiber," in the early 1940s.[93]

In these code-breaking scenarios, the very large number of possible solutions to the Enigma, Tunny, and G-Schreiber machines precluded the possibility of brute-force approaches, even with a "domestic army" assembled at Bletchley Park to crack them. Allied mechanical efforts—like the *Bombes* and Turing's machines—were essential, but the biggest breakthroughs exploited weaknesses in the Nazi's protocols and in the messages themselves. Believing their codes to be unbreakable, the Nazis occasionally reused code keys or sent similar messages, and often began messages with "testing" phrases such as "*Alles Klar?*" ["All clear?"][94] This introduced repetition or redundancy into the coded messages, and it was a key mistake, as this is where code-breakers began narrowing down and predicting possible solutions each day.

In addition Nazi errors, the codes were decipherable in part because language itself, as we have said, is predictable. To begin to decode the intercepted transmissions, the cryptographers exploited the fact that not all letters in the alphabet occur with the same frequency.[95] For example, the most frequently occurring letter in a code created from English is likely to stand for *e*.[96] This might be termed an intrinsic, or "first-order" probability of an event. Letters are also delimited by events occurring around them, or contextual, "second-order" probabilities—for instance, when the letter *q* occurs in English, it is very likely to be followed by a *u*. Words and sentences are further constrained by grammatical structures.[97] The fact that redundancies are built into languages means that messages are statistically predictable at different levels of the linguistic hierarchy.

This situation also holds true, to some degree, in music. Although music is not semantic in the same sense as language, there is a concern for syntax, redundancy, and predictability within musical structure.[98] For instance, we might hypothesize that the tonic chord in tonal music has an intrinsic, first-order probability of occurring most frequently. Music also has many contextual, or second-order, probabilities that can be extended into even higher levels of contextual probability through Markov chains (mathematical equations that model the probability for various scenarios). For instance, in tonal music, when a dominant-seventh chord appears, it is very likely to be followed by a tonic chord. In dodecaphonic and serial music, we can consider the predictability of an ordered series: as the row proceeds, there are gradually fewer and fewer choices.[99] The series is constrained by the progression through the twelve tones and thus becomes more predictable as the number of available pitches is reduced. Whether the next event is very predictable, somewhat predictable, or totally unpredictable depends on both the intrinsic and contextual probabilities of that event occurring.

By way of information theory, the contextual progression of music may thus be tied to the probability of certain events. The WDR composers, when they encountered information-theoretic ideas, began using them under a perceptual paradigm that emphasized gestures, contours, and *Gestalten* filled with efficient, nonserial approximations. But as this discussion of cryptography suggests, one could also get to a similar-sounding result by using probabilities, rather than approximations, to determine the progression of content. Information theory has much to say about probabilities, which can be usefully leveraged for music composition. In fact, Iannis Xenakis worked in exactly this way.

Musical Probabilities of Xenakis and Koenig

As early as his *Metastasis* (1953–1954) and *Pithoprakta* (1955–1956), Xenakis was known for his stochastic music—that is, music that uses probability theory to determine the course of events. Xenakis formalized his ideas in a series of articles that were published in the Swiss journal *Gravesaner Blätter*, which was edited by German conductor and electronic music impresario Hermann Scherchen.[100] With contributions in French, German, and English, the *Gravesaner Blätter* fostered an ongoing, international dialogue, culminating in interdisciplinary summits at Scherchen's home studio that brought together leading mathematicians and scientists, technicians and instrument builders, new music conductors and impresarios, and composers.

Xenakis was well ingratiated into the *Gravesaner Blätter* circle but was almost completely disconnected from *Die Reihe* and the electronic music discourses of the WDR studio. That said, Xenakis was no stranger to electronic music, and he worked extensively with *musique concrète* in Paris in the late 1950s.[101] Xenakis likewise was well exposed to developments in information theory, especially as transmitted by Moles. In the mid-1950s, Moles concerned himself with establishing links among information theory, electronic music, and aesthetics, especially by considering the limits of human perception. In his 1956 articles on information theory and music, published in volume six of the *Gravesaner Blätter*, Moles reaffirmed, after Shannon and Wiener, that the predictability of a message directly correlates with its size and coherence.[102] Prediction plays an enormous role in listeners' ability to comprehend musical structure, not least because of the cognitive importance of developing expectations, evaluating whether they have been met, and experiencing pleasure when a predicted course comes to fruition.[103]

Although Xenakis did not speak in terms of expectations, pleasure, and reward, he definitely worked to extend Moles's information-theoretic emphasis on predictability and comprehensibility.[104] Appearing in the same volume of the *Blätter* as Moles, Xenakis's essay "Probability Theory and Music" aimed to free serial music from its exceedingly linear, geometrical conceptions by using mathematical probabilities, especially "Gaussian" or "normal" statistical distributions.[105] Xenakis's equations produced results such as the graph-paper sketch from *Pithoprakta* shown in Figure 4.11. In this passage, individual string instruments play glissandi at varying velocities in varying ranges. Thinking of probabilities and statistical distributions of data allowed Xenakis to use equations to handle the *relative* separation or overlap of articulations in time [*Zeitdauern*], the *relative* thickness or pointillist texture in the vertical dimension [*Frequenzen*], and the *relative* velocity of glissandi [*Schnelligkeiten*].[106]

Note the similarity with Stockhausen's continuum concepts from his *Jeux* analysis and his *Gruppen* sketch (see Figure 4.4). Stockhausen, Boulez, Pousseur, Ligeti, and others worked contemporaneously and in parallel with Xenakis in using statistical form to move beyond excessively pointillist, linear textures. Whereas Stockhausen and others in the Cologne-WDR circle incorporated nonserial, gestural approximations, Xenakis adapted equations from statistics and physics. The Maxwell–Boltzmann distribution, which

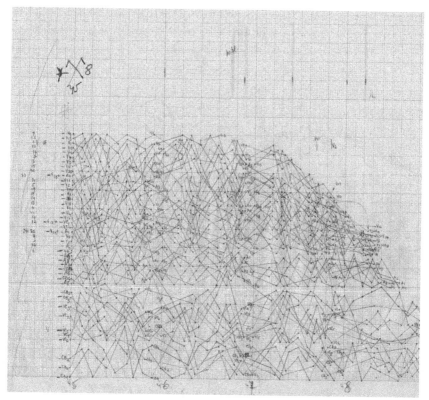

FIGURE 4.11. Xenakis, *Pithoprakta* (1955–1956), sketch. Collection Famille Xenakis.

describes the speed and movement of particles in a gas, allowed Xenakis to control the motion of the musical "molecules" (i.e., individual instruments) by programming them to change their velocity according to the "temperature" of the "sonic atmosphere" [*Klangatmosphäre*].

Although Xenakis's use of probability theory as a compositional device matured in the 1960s, the preceding example clarifies that he was already using probabilities and equations to govern the content and progression of his music by the mid-1950s. Xenakis's early training in mathematics and engineering, as well as his work in Le Corbusier's architectural studio from 1947 to 1959, were essential.[107] He was the primary architectural designer of the Philips Pavilion, a futuristic building constructed for the 1958 World's Fair in Brussels.[108] The Pavilion had white, curved walls and circus-tent-peak ceilings—much like the Denver Airport or the Sydney Opera House—which were designed according to parabolic equations. As Xenakis said,

> In the Philips Pavilion, I realized the basic ideas of *Metastasis*: as in the music, here too I was interested in the question of whether it was

possible to get from one point to another without breaking the continuity. In *Metastasis*, this problem led to glissandos, while in the pavilion it resulted in the hyperbolic parabola shapes.[109]

In other words, the architectural parabolic curves of the Pavilion are composed out musically in the glissandos of *Metastasis*. Underwritten by the Philips Electronics Company in the Netherlands, the Pavilion gave visitors a sensory glimpse of the future *inside* too, with a multimedia electronic sound-and-light spectacle. Edgard Varèse's eight-minute *Poème électronique* was the primary sonic event, set to an image track of Le Corbusier's design. A two-minute *musique concrète* interlude by Xenakis played as the tapes were rewound and visitors filed in and out of the building.[110]

We have established that Xenakis's early-to-mid-1950s sound-mass music and architecture stem from the same mathematical foundations, but where is there an overlap with information theory? For starters, the equations that Xenakis adapted—the Maxwell–Boltzmann and Gaussian distribution functions—are relatable to the paradigms of information theory. He may have known these equations from engineering and physics, but they connect mathematically to Shannon's information theory around concepts such as entropy, albeit from somewhat different angles.[111] In information theory, entropy is a measure of the amount of information in a message; as Shannon theorized, all possible information (the highest entropy value) is constrained by linguistic redundancies and statistical predictions. In physics, entropy is a measure of randomness within a system, such as the relative disorder of molecules within a gas. The concept of entropy is not used in exactly the same way in cryptography and thermodynamics, for example, but Xenakis's dual information-theoretic and physical-science experiences do intersect on certain shared or translatable concepts: randomness, statistical modeling, and predictability.

Furthermore, Xenakis's musical glissandi and architectural parabolas are in dialogue with the information-theoretic problem of continuity. As we have noted earlier, the sampling theorem is a mathematical shortcut that allows continuities to be reassembled from many discrete points. While Stockhausen and Koenig worked with such concepts to create the *impression* of continuity in pieces like *Essay* and *Gesang*, Xenakis seemingly came from another angle: rather than assembling an impression of continuity from impulses or spliced tape fragments in the studio, he used acoustic string instruments to produce glissandi, which were *actually* continuous sounds.

As Xenakis remarked, "serial music left out of account the problem of continuity–discontinuity."[112] This isn't strictly true beyond the pointillist music of the early 1950s, which many composers simultaneously self-critiqued—statistical form discourses addressed exactly this continuity problem. In any event, both Xenakis and the Cologne-WDR group were addressing the problem of continuities in the mid-1950s. It might be said that in *Pithoprakta*, Xenakis's glissandi addressed the pitch end of the continuum, whereas in *Gesang* and *Essay*, Stockhausen and Koenig's improvised impulse sequences focused more on the rhythmic end of the continuum. In reality, as Stockhausen argued in " . . . how time passes . . . ," pitch and rhythm are interrelated phenomena—speed (velocity, momentum) is a powerful variable that has a direct impact on both on the same continuum.

Xenakis went even deeper into information theory in the late 1950s by further integrating probability into his works. As he explained,

> If we link continuity with causality we again get at a basic problem of probability. [. . .] There is repetition, which plays such an important part in music. [. . .] The distance produced by more or less faithful repetition is once again an aspect of the question of continuity and discontinuity.[113]

Repetitions in coded messages were redundancies, which allowed for hypotheses of probable code keys. Repetition guided missile trajectory predictions, too: Is the shell likely to go where others have gone? How large is the range in which a shell could be expected to fall? In both scenarios, equations reduced extraneous "noise" and complexity, so that continuities and repetitions could generate predictions.

Xenakis used the same probability equations to describe musical information, especially in *Achorripsis* (1957), where they governed the distribution of timbres, durations, pitch trajectories, and glissando speeds.[114] He began with seven timbral groups, including flute, oboe, string glissando, percussion, pizzicato, brass, and string arco.[115] He then chose an arbitrary, mean density for events—0.6 events per time unit—and applied Poisson's formula, a differential equation like those that predicted missile trajectories, to handle the distributions. As a result, the Poisson distributions were applied successively to control pitch ranges, speeds of glissandi, and durations of sounds and silences.

This is all very similar to the experiments that Koenig undertook in the early 1960s, on the cusp of computer music and the digital revolution.[116] Information theory concepts like sampling and probability make visible a transition from analog to digital ways of thinking. Near the end of his life, Meyer-Eppler wrote about encoding music with binary digits (1's and 0's),[117] and both Koenig and Xenakis developed early prototypes of algorithmic composition. Koenig's early computer music research, such as *Project 1* and *Project 2*, worked with probabilities, limits, and distributions. Koenig's idea, which stemmed from his own critique of integral serialism, was to write a computer program in which the composer could create rules that would result in music.[118] He asked, "Would it be possible to make a piece completely according to the rules without being forced to make corrections after?"[119]

From a very early age, Koenig seemingly understood that music was quite rule-based. In his early training, in harmony and counterpoint classes, Koenig was stymied by a classmate who wrote a better orchestral *divertissement*. In analyzing the difference between his piece and his classmate's piece, Koenig remarked,

> At the same time [I was] angry at not being able to discover the program—I might almost say the algorithm—with which it was possible to compose music so easily and quickly. The "program" consisted simply of the instruction to change the harmonic function slowly (not more than one change in each bar), and only in simple harmonic progressions: tonic, dominant, mediant and so on. The melody had to keep within the respective function, which only made the whole affair still easier, and it was child's play to work out an accompaniment.[120]

Koenig noted that similar predictability conditions arose when, for a different assignment, he wrote an atonal chorale that used the parsimonious voice-leading rules of tonal chorales. As a result of the exercise, he understood the twelve-tone system and the tonal system to be similarly constrained. Koenig hypothesized that "well over the half of what is written in most scores consists of 'given' quantities[;] composers are much less original than they think."[121]

In the computer music programs of *Project 1* and *Project 2*, Koenig harnessed this predictability, while letting composers control parameters such as instruments, durations, attack styles, registers, and dynamic values. The composer's responsibility, then, was to constrain these parameters in such a way as to re-create a musical system; alternatively, the composer could create a system that aimed for the impression of (or the actual conditions of) complete randomness.[122]

This thinking relied on the same probability recognitions that Xenakis absorbed. Whereas Xenakis used probability equations to generate and deploy his musical materials, Koenig created algorithms that constrained and shaped musical forms, narrowing materials down into a probable system. In this way, Koenig was more attuned to the probabilities of a specifically formal logic, whereas Xenakis was attuned to expressing theoretical probabilities and distributions in (musical) sound. Nuanced differences aside, Koenig and Xenakis were working on two sides of the same probability coin.

Unfortunately, scholars tend to miss these connections, repeating a commonplace assumption that Xenakis, with his physics and engineering equations, was doing something fundamentally different from the devout serial obsessions of Stockhausen, Koenig, and the other Cologne–Darmstadt composers in the mid-1950s.[123] Perhaps this stems from an eagerness to understand Xenakis's creative thought—or the thought of Stockhausen, Koenig, or Ligeti, for that matter—on its own terms. After all, composers whom we might identify as members of a "school" still possess substantial agency to determine their individual poetics.

Our reigning assumption of great difference is misguided, however, inasmuch as it ignores the ways that Stockhausen (et al.) and Xenakis connected to information-theoretic discourses.[124] It is true that figures like Xenakis, Ligeti, Koenig, and Stockhausen came to "similar-sounding" music from different angles, but this is merely a testament to the breadth of information theory discourses, not a mark of fundamental difference. As I've demonstrated, Xenakis latched on to the probability aspect of information theory most strongly, whereas Stockhausen, Koenig, Ligeti, and others in the Cologne circle mined the musical implications of perceptual *Gestalten* and the sampling theorem. These are all legitimate components of information theory discourses. Beyond missing information theory as the common foundation, perhaps scholars tenaciously grasp onto the conclusion that Xenakis and the Cologne–Darmstadt composers are "quite different" because they seem to have repelled each other.

Although Xenakis appeared poised for entry into the WDR-Cologne scene at any moment, by all accounts, he remained an outsider.[125] His movement within the European avant-garde in the early 1950s certainly overlapped: he studied with Messiaen from 1951 to 1953, had his *Metastasis* premiered by Hans Rosbaud at Donaueschingen in 1955, and had his *Pithoprakta* premiered under Scherchen's baton at Musica Viva Munich in 1957 and again at Darmstadt in 1958.[126] Meanwhile, as we know, Xenakis attended the Gravesano summits and composed *musique concrète* in Paris extensively between 1955 and 1962.[127] Despite moving in intersecting artistic circles, Xenakis wavered between being *persona non grata* and a marginal figure in the WDR-Cologne group. For his part, Xenakis said that he was never welcomed:

> [VARGA:] Did it not occur to you that you might work in the electronic studio of the *Westdeutscher Rundfunk*?
>
> [XENAKIS:] No, because electronic music [as opposed to *musique concrète*] left me completely cold—and besides, Stockhausen was the absolute master. He had never invited me there. Pretending to ignore someone's work is a way of fighting it.[128]

When it came to the 1955 Donaueschingen festival where *Metastasis* was premiered, Xenakis's complained,

> Nobody invited me. The chairman of the conference was the convinced serialist Antoine Goléa, who didn't like *Metastasis*. [. . .] The French, the Germans and the Italians had formed an influential and exclusive club, that of serial music. Scherchen was then the only one who liked and supported what I was doing and who invited me to Gravesano to attend the meetings and give lectures.[129]

Later in life, Ligeti shed a bit more light on the situation, claiming that his own underexposure to Xenakis's very similar, contemporaneous sound-mass music in the late 1950s was due in part to "Stockhausen's endless self-centeredness [*unendliche Selbstbezogenheit*]. [. . .] He and Iannis Xenakis were the two composers who would absolutely not be known as colleagues. [. . .] For Stockhausen and Boulez, he [Xenakis] did not exist."[130]

Why might the more powerful Darmstadt composers have ostracized Xenakis in this way? Part of the answer may have to do with personality traits and old wounds that were never successfully resolved. But we can also infer from this collection of self-styled narratives that Stockhausen may have simply felt too threatened by Xenakis. Consider, for example, the way that Stockhausen claimed credit in a mid-1990s letter to a musicologist:

> I learned the term *aleatory* from him [Meyer-Eppler] and it was I who transferred it into music. A later use of this term (for example in an article "Alea" by the Frenchman Boulez), as well as in American music as "chance operations" or "indeterminacy" (Cage), has been *directly* mediated by me from information theory through personal interviews or indirectly through publications.[131]

Stockhausen's claim is astonishing in its breadth. Not only does Stockhausen collapse the distinctions among statistical form, indeterminacy, and information theory, he nearly ignores all collaborators—Meyer-Eppler and Cage are at least mentioned in passing, but the contributions of Koenig, Xenakis, Pousseur, and many others are completely veiled, lost in the darkness of Stockhausen's shadow.

It is true that Stockhausen took Meyer-Eppler's teachings on information theory and translated them into musical concepts; furthermore, Kagel, Berio, Ligeti, and others made much use of Meyer-Eppler's phonetics research—the subject of Chapter 6. It is simultaneously true that Koenig and Xenakis contemporaneously undertook similar projects, each from related spheres of experience and interest that were less directly mediated by Meyer-Eppler. In fact, many of the WDR-affiliated composers connected their techniques to information theory discourse in the mid-1950s, though their individual points of entry depended on their previous knowledge and expertise (e.g., architecture, studio machinery, human perception, and so on). Suffice it to say that although Stockhausen's compositions like *Gesang der Jünglinge* and writings like " . . . how time passes . . . " were no doubt influential, his claims in the preceding quotation are much too broad. Because Xenakis also expertly distilled and translated one of the central ideas of information theory, or perhaps because Xenakis would not play the role of a submissive, naïve visiting composer within the increasingly hierarchical WDR laboratory, he may have simply presented too much of a challenge to Stockhausen's self-proclaimed authority.

Conclusions

In the Cold War era, information theory was a highly adaptable, generalizable discourse with implications for numerous other scenarios, like genetics, linguistics, architecture, library science, sociology, computing, and electronic music.[132] As the analyses in this chapter have shown, WDR composers applied a number of crucial insights from information theory in both their acoustic and electronic music, centering around three topics: perceptible shapes or "statistical forms," sampling and continuity, and probability. We have said that composers critiqued their own early 1950s integral serial works, as well as Cage's total-aleatory works, with the insight that their "messages" were extremely information dense, comparable to random noise. From this realization, composers began explicitly planning to better accommodate human perception, especially by incorporating more large-scale shapes, gestures, repetition, and audible continuity into their music.

The electronic music studio was a critical site where such perceptual adjustments were negotiated and thought through, especially in dialogue with the technical affordances and limits of the machinery. As several of the pieces in this chapter demonstrate, studio composers launched their study of perception and continuity in cooperation with the studio's machines. They experimented with the gestural poetics of the analog dials, with the uncanny effect of montaging samples too short to hear separately at playback speed, and with approximations within the limits and boundaries (such as a filter's frequency ranges) imposed by the machines.

The studio's technologies formed a crucible of constraints and affordances, in which the central tenets of information theory were suddenly and transparently relevant. Composers and technicians, working in concert with the machines, synthesized much more than music in the studio. The resulting electronic and acoustic "statistical form" works are remarkable because they synthesize musical aesthetics, information theory, and the practical constraints of humans and technologies.

Information theory originated as a wartime discourse, its central ideas informed by military communication technologies, code-breaking patterns, and antiaircraft missile defense calculations. This context is rendered invisible in the abstract, mathematical equations of Shannon's theory itself and threatens to disappear completely from the expanding, contested, interdisciplinary discourse that information theory became in the 1950s. In the cultural sphere, information theory was subject to a process of domestication and neutralization, in which the "technologies" of war (defined broadly to include ideas) were repurposed to drive scientific, artistic, and cultural innovations in peacetime.

Recognizing that information theory, as transmitted by interlocutors like Meyer-Eppler and Moles, was a foundation of midcentury avant-garde music nevertheless helps us understand how the electronic studio reclaimed wartime technology. World War II—its traumas and technologies, its unresolvable conflicts and ambivalent choices—was not just a vague backstory for the midcentury avant-garde composers, though they were satisfied to let us assume as much. Avant-garde composers born in the 1920s and 1930s by and large talked about their musical innovations either in purely aesthetic terms or with technoscientific jargon; they rarely spoke directly about topics like the war or Meyer-Eppler's Nazi activities, if they even knew.

Despite these protective, enclosing, self-referential tendencies, the electronic music studio was a place where the material traces of war were managed, not least because military machines and ideas were put to use for art and cultural development. Composers did not profess that they were using information theory, nor would they agree that they were performing such domestications. Yet such reclamations happened on the cultural level anyway, more subtly, as information theory ideas were generalized and put into practice in various scenarios. It is this expanding interdisciplinarity that allows us to forget the original context, to reuse the ideas without attribution.

Such reclamations do not so much heal the wounds of war as accumulate new meanings and layers that distance us from the trauma. Like Benjamin's critique of Paul Klee's *Angelus Novus*, it is a horrible realization that we cannot "awaken the dead" or "make whole what has been smashed."[133] Electronic music hardly heals the gaping wounds left by the Holocaust. But in the studio, the European avant-garde composers nevertheless optimistically made do, allowing themselves like Benjamin's Angel to be swept into the future by the "irresistible storm of progress." Benjamin's Angel did not so much forget the wreckage of war—his face was turned toward it at all times—but he was compelled to watch it recede into the background.

There is a certain inevitability, a certain fatefulness, to Benjamin's Angel that resonates with the Cold War electronic studio. The composers and audiences who confronted wartime technologies and discourses in the studio did not, or could not, speak about them. Their offering, instead, was a pure, abstract, avant-garde music: sound itself, apropos of nothing, as they claimed. In the distanced and ambivalent reclamation of the midcentury electronic music studio, the destruction remains visible, for those who will look; but the soundtrack claims progress.

5 | Controversy

The Aleatory Debates Beyond Darmstadt

When we left Cage and Tudor in Chapter 2, in the wake of their 1954 European tour, we concluded that the pair had been enormously influential in the nascent studio milieu. Cage's prepared piano offered a new sonic template, and his square-root form provided an enviable model for how to use proportions to unify the composition. Tudor, moreover, functioned as the connective tissue between European and American scenes, his performances sounding out an international discourse of avant-garde musical experimentation. What should be made, then, of the visible rift at the Darmstadt Summer Courses in 1958, which grew between Cage and the Americans, on the one hand, and Boulez, Stockhausen, and the Europeans on the other hand?[1] Was this merely a tiff, a momentary spike in antagonism between increasingly well-established composerly egos? Was this feud more serious evidence of the parting of ways between the European and American groups?

It is valuable to return to these questions in the context of the electronic studio, because it is a way of asking how we can hold the European and American composers together—or apart, as the case may be—in thinking through the evolution of midcentury avant-garde music. What *was* the relationship between the European studio composers and the American circle, including Cage, Tudor, Feldman, Wolff, and Brown? How international was the musical avant-garde in the early Cold War era? And, perhaps most important for present purposes, what did the WDR and other electronic studios have to do with the circulation of these debates and discourses?

It is well known that the disagreement between the groups in the late 1950s centered around questions of aleatory, or how to incorporate chance elements into musical composition. It would be a mistake to think, however, that the debate reduced to a preference for serial control on the European side versus a preference for indeterminacy on the American side.[2] As Table 5.1 shows, multiple pieces were performed at Darmstadt in 1957–1959 that engage with some type of aleatory: chance, indeterminacy, statistical form, or

TABLE 5.1. Pieces played at Darmstadt in 1957–1959 that engaged with aleatory in some measure.

Composer	Piece	Primary Mode(s) of Aleatory (cf. Figure 5.1)	Year of Darmstadt Performance
Boulez	*Troisième Sonate*	mobile form, statistical controls	1959
Brown	Music for Cello and Piano	indeterminate time-space notation	1957
Brown	*Folio and Four Systems*	indeterminacy, mobile form	1958
Brown	*Pentathis*	statistical density	1958
Brown	*Hodograph I*	indeterminacy, graphic notation	1959
Brown	Music for Cello and Piano	indeterminate time–space notation	1957
Bussotti	*Pièces de chair II: Piano Pieces for David Tudor*	graphic score, indeterminacy	1959
Cage	*Music of Changes*	chance	1958
Cage	*Variations I* in various versions	indeterminacy, graphic score	1958
Cage	*Winter Music*	indeterminacy, chance	1958
Cage	Concert for Piano and Orchestra	indeterminacy, graphic score, chance	1959
Cage	*Aria* with *Fontana Mix* (RAI)	graphic score, indeterminacy, mobile form	1959
Cardew	Piano Piece 1959	indeterminacy	1959
Feldman	*Two Pianos*	indeterminate notation	1958
Haubenstock-Ramati	*Interpolations Mobile pour flute*	graphic scores	1959
Ligeti	*Artikulation* (WDR)	chance, statistical controls	1958
Pousseur	*Scambi I* and *II* (RAI)	mobile form, statistical controls	1957, 1958
Pousseur	*Mobile*	mobile form, indeterminacy	1958
Stockhausen	*Klavierstück XI* in various versions	mobile form	1957, 1958
Wolff	*Duo for Pianists I* and *II*	indeterminacy	1958

graphic notation, terms that we will define in more detail momentarily.[3] As this table broadly suggests, several European composers (including Boulez, Bussotti, Haubenstock-Ramati, Ligeti, Pousseur, and Stockhausen) had effectively moved past integral serialism and were now invested in chance techniques. It follows that Darmstadt was contentious in 1958 not only because of what Cage said about chance and control, or the *provocateur*-style insults he lobbed, but also because the European composers were more than offended bystanders; both groups were invested in the questions.[4]

This chapter presents several analyses of both electronic and acoustic works in which chance techniques play a role, so as to more fully elaborate the terms of the aleatory debates. Why were composers collectively so interested in how to use chance techniques for musical composition? What did composers mean to do when they incorporated chance into their works? What was at stake in opening up the musical form so as to let machines or performers take over the agency of the composer? As we will learn, the terms of the aleatory debates were wide ranging, as were the sources of inspiration. One immediate commonality between the European and American approaches to aleatory, however, is that both were heavily mediated through the new potentialities of the electronic studio. As was the case with serialism, electronic studios (both in West Germany and the United States) were important sites in which composers wrangled with the provocations of open forms, technological limitations, and machinic agency. These were at least some of the issues opened by questions of chance in music.

A Multiplicity of Terms

To begin to develop a nuanced understanding of the diverse landscape around aleatory, we first need to acknowledge that it, like statistical form, is a multifaceted and contested discourse.[5] Aleatory is a term that can refer to many different techniques, depending on the context, as Figure 5.1 shows. As such, the concept of aleatory invited many different points of engagement. Among the European avant-garde, aleatory was often a synonym for the information theory–derived, "statistical" approximations that Meyer-Eppler advocated, which, for example, Stockhausen used in *Gesang der Jünglinge*. In Cage's earlier music, aleatory often meant music composed through chance means, such as throwing dice or using the *I Ching* (the ancient Chinese *Book of Changes*). The Cage group did much to develop "indeterminacy," in which the composer left some part of the score—order of events, instrumentation, length of the piece, number of players, etc.—to the discretion of performers.[6] Graphic scores present a particular type of indeterminacy, wherein the performer has to decipher the often-artistic visual rendering in order to realize the piece in sound. Mobile form is likewise a type of indeterminacy, wherein the

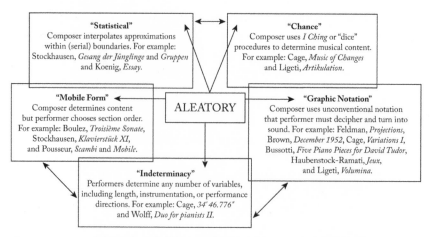

FIGURE 5.1. Multiple definitions and techniques associated with the term "aleatory."

performer creates a path through the piece (like a *Choose Your Own Adventure* book) by narrowing down choices from composer-determined segments and directions.

As the many facets of Figure 5.1 suggest, there are multiple stages at which chance or indeterminate elements can be introduced into a composition. Likewise, there are many different sources—literary, scientific, technological, philosophical—from which inspiration for aleatory processes can be drawn. Midcentury composers, including both the Cage group and the Europeans, actively worked with many of these options. Far from rejecting the aleatoric and indeterminate techniques in the wake of Darmstadt 1958, composers experimented with several different ways of incorporating aleatory in their own works of the late 1950s and early 1960s. The WDR studio was a prime locus for such experimentation.

Articulating Chance

Consider the case of Ligeti's second electronic piece, *Artikulation* (1958).[7] Ligeti produced the piece at the WDR in close proximity with Stockhausen, Koenig, and Kagel, who were simultaneously immersed in Meyer-Eppler's phonetics teachings (the subject of Chapter 6). Given the piece's title of "articulation," it is clear that Ligeti, like his colleagues, used a linguistic lens to focus his musical ideas. Yet the distance between the abstract electronic sounds of the studio on the one hand, and intelligible language on the other, raises the question: What did Ligeti mean when he claimed he was creating "pseudo-speech" and "imaginary dialogue without sense" in this electronic work?[8] Was the idea of "articulation" simply a fashionable metaphor in circulation among the WDR milieu? Or did Ligeti's electronic work correspond to language in deeper ways?

We can gain some perspective by retracing his compositional process.[9] Exploiting the different capabilities of the studio's oscillators, generators, and filters, Ligeti and his technical assistant Koenig first generated and recorded several different types of sound materials (see Table 5.2).[10] Second, they cut up those materials into precalculated tape lengths in an arithmetic sequence (in which terms of the series are related by a fixed constant).[11] So far, Ligeti's process fits well with the proportional durational plans that were standard compositional techniques of the WDR. Ligeti deployed his arithmetic durations in a balanced scheme, meaning that the shortest durations occurred the most frequently, providing a counterweight to the few segments of longer duration, which occurred infrequently. This scheme "corrected" the durational imbalance that Ligeti critiqued in the early integral serial works such as Boulez's *Structures Ia*, wherein short durations occurred only once and were thus inevitably overshadowed by longer durations, which demanded more of the listener's attention even when they too occurred only once.[12]

With the careful durational work accomplished, Ligeti and Koenig were ready to begin montage. Third—and surprisingly—they sorted the fragments

TABLE 5.2. Some of the sound materials for Ligeti's *Artikulation* (1958) in a mix of Hungarian and German, with translations and technologies added. György Ligeti Collection, Paul Sacher Foundation.

Anyaguk [substances]		
A. Magánhangzó—szerüek [vowel—like]	English Translation	Likely WDR Studio Machinery and Technique
1 Sinushang	sine tones	sine tone generator
2 Harm. spektrum	harmonic spectra	evenly spaced additive synthesis sine tone mixtures
3 Subharm. spektrum	inharmonic spectra	unevenly spaced additive synthesis sine tone mixtures; possibly ring modulation
4 Fehér Rauschen	white noise	white-noise generator
5 Oktavrauschen	octave-filtered noise	white noise fed through octave filter
6 Terzrauschen	third-filtered noise	white noise fed through third filter
7 20-Hz rauschen	20-Hz filtered noise	white noise fed through variable filter tuned to 20 Hz
8 Harm. spektrum hall-gliss	harmonic spectra with reverberated glissando	harmonic mixtures played back and re-recorded in reverberant room
9 Rauschhall	noise plus reverberation	generated noise played back and re-recorded in reverberant room

into boxes, drawing them out and pasting them together at random. They apparently performed this cutting, sorting, drawing, and pasting work in several iterations, imagining they were assembling "words" from fragmentary "phonemes," from which they built larger "sentences" and "texts."[13] (Refer back to Figure 4.5 to see a sketch of "texts.") Ligeti's aleatory montage process initially recalls Cage's procedure for composing *Music of Changes*, wherein he made his way through precompositional charts for tempo, pitch, duration, and dynamics by "tossing the coins" with the *I Ching*.[14]

Ligeti, however, subverted an all-encompassing aleatory. The crucial detail in this iterative process is that Ligeti sorted the fragments into boxes based on their sonic characteristics. For instance, at some stage, Ligeti seems to have grouped the fragments according to the criterion of pitch height, laying out four boxes for high, middle, low, and combination ranges.[15] At another stage, he seems to have grouped sounds by their material characters (sine tones, noise, etc.).[16] As Ben Levy has pointed out, the decision to sort fragments was quite consequential; the chance operations had less impact because the sorting criteria introduced statistical or probabilistic controls.[17] Essentially, Ligeti's sorting introduced boundaries (such as pitch height or sound type) within which the duration and order of events were freely permuted as fragments were drawn and pasted. This limited aleatory, or statistical aleatory, was much more in keeping with the statistical form experiments of the WDR composers—working within certain limits (frequency ranges, durational spans, etc.)—than it was akin to Cage's purist use of chance in *Music of Changes*.

To return to the linguistic questions, though, how did Ligeti's statistical aleatory process correspond with his metaphor of articulation? One resonance lies in the historical avant-gardes, especially in the nonsense texts produced in Dadaist circles in the late 1920s and early 1930s. In a piece such as Schwitters's *Ursonate* (1932), phonetic fragments were assembled into nonsense words, creating a sound poetry in which the sound of the phonemes replaced any coherent linguistic content. In *Artikulation*, by comparison, the sonic fragments (sine tones, impulses, noisy mixtures, etc.) were like Schwitters's phonemes, assembled into pseudo-speech texts to make the piece. The comparison depends on understanding the studio's electronic sounds as "consonants" (noisy sounds) and "vowels" (pure sine tones). If we buy this mapping, the assembly process then creates pseudo-speech combinations of phonemes (VC, CVC, etc.).

This sonic mapping—which is discussed at more length in Figure 6.8 of Chapter 6—recalls the exact terms in which Meyer-Eppler taught the composers about synthesized timbres. In Meyer-Eppler's seminars, phonemes were models for the complex electronic sounds the composers wanted to produce, meaning that phonetics and music informed each other. As the structural linguist Roman Jakobson contemporaneously argued, there is a strong relationship between a language's sound and its structure.[18] Jakobson and Halle devoted significant attention to sonic features such as the formant structure of vowels, degree and type of noise in consonantal sounds, compact versus diffuse noise bands, presence of low-frequency fundamentals, and the relative roughness or smoothness of timbre—in short, the same ways composers described sounds in the electronic studio. These sonic characteristics allowed a listener to distinguish among, say, French, Dutch, and Hungarian without understanding any of the semantic meaning. Language could be quasi-musical, and music could be quasi-linguistic.

The sonic comparison between phonemes and electronic sound momentarily suspended the question of content and meaning. And yet, Meyer-Eppler's phonetics teachings also branched outward to address questions of syntax and redundancy. Stockhausen remembered an in-class exercise in which "we would take a newspaper and cut the text up into smaller and smaller units—three syllables, two syllables, one syllable, sometimes right down to individual letters. Then we would shuffle the pieces like cards, arrange the new text and study the degree of redundancy that would decrease the more you cut up the original newspaper text."[19] Meyer-Eppler's exercise demonstrated that languages have characteristic structural and sonic features based on their redundancies—an essential information theory insight.

Ligeti's statistical sorting of the fragments by sound type in *Artikulation* capitalized on this idea, reintroducing the sonic redundancies that define the structure of languages. His limited aleatory produced surface variation but allowed him to retain control over the unfolding of the phrases through carefully managed similarity relations. It is in this way that Ligeti could claim that *Artikulation* created, both metaphorically and sonically, pseudo-speech. Like his colleagues, Ligeti worked in concert with the studio's technological possibilities, synthesizing not only sounds, but also rich intellectual discourses, including Cage's purist aleatory, Meyer-Eppler's phonetics, Koenig's and Stockhausen's statistical controls, information theory, and Jakobson's structural linguistics.

Open Structures, Fixed Media

Another contemporaneous electronic piece to produce a synthesis from these discourses is Henri Pousseur's *Scambi* (1957). Pousseur composed it at the Studio di Fonologia, housed at RAI in Milan after receiving an invitation from Luciano Berio. According to their correspondence, Pousseur visited Milan between March 1 and May 31, 1957, and was paid a stipend of 150,000 Lire ($2,078 in 2017 dollars), a sum that his host Berio described as generous.[20] The equipment of the Studio di Fonologia was, on its face, similar to that of the WDR, including oscillators, generators, filters, and tape machines. Beyond these surface similarities, however, the technical situation in Milan was considerably more individualistic.[21] The Italian radio was reluctant or unable to fund a dedicated electronic music studio in the immediate postwar era, but Alfredo Lietti, the studio's main engineer, was permitted to construct whatever instruments he could from spare communication technology parts in the warehouse.[22] A physicist who had worked as a military communication officer at the RAI during World War II, Lietti was very much an Italian analog to Meyer-Eppler. The RAI's unique equipment was a silver lining in the scarce postwar period; as we will see, Lietti's handbuilt machinery had an enormous impact on the studio's functionality and on the composers' musical thinking.

Because the machines at the Studio di Fonologia were mostly one-of-a-kind, Berio described some of the studio's quirks and capabilities in a letter to Pousseur before his visit.[23] He made particular reference to a machine that was novel for its decoupling of the usual lock-step correlation between tape speed and pitch. The *Tempophon*, made by the company Telefonbau und Normalzeit, could change the duration of a sound while preserving the pitch. The *Tempophon* achieved its effect by removing samples of recorded sound, thus changing the length while maintaining the pitch by means of the remaining "snapshot" samples.[24] Such a machine was useful in radio broadcasting and film dubbing scenarios, in which it might be necessary to stretch an advertisement to fill a few more seconds or to shorten a clip of dialogue to synchronize with the image track. The *Tempophon* could be reappropriated for musical time-stretching too, though Berio warned Pousseur that for long sounds, the *Tempophon* sometimes produced an unpalatable result: in removing samples of recorded sound, the machine mangled timbre in a way that the ear could detect all too easily.

Each of the nine oscillators of the Studio di Fonologia—all built by hand by Lietti—operated in slightly different frequency ranges (Figure 5.2). There were several variable-pass and bandpass filters as well, which could be used either to shape oscillator-generated sounds or, more commonly, to filter white noise. Lietti equipped the Studio di Fonologia with more and different filters than the WDR studio had at the time. As such, opposing the WDR studio's additive synthesis methods, the composers working in Milan turned toward "subtractive synthesis"—that is, producing musical sounds by filtering them out of a much larger band of noise.

Another of Lietti's original devices, which was crucial for Pousseur during the composition of *Scambi*, might be termed a "dynamic filter" or an "amplitude selector" [*selezionatore d'ampiezza*].[25] Amplitude is a measurement of the loudness of sound waves. As can be discerned from Berio's illustration in Figure 5.2, the amplitude selector culled certain frequencies—those above a certain loudness threshold—from a more complex sound or a band of noise.[26] In modern parlance, the amplitude selector is a noise gate. It was used to

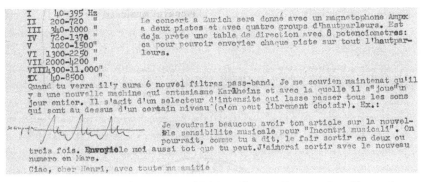

FIGURE 5.2. Berio's description of RAI oscillators, filters, and an illustration (in ink) of the effect of Lietti's amplitude selector. Henri Pousseur Collection, Paul Sacher Foundation.

eliminate excess noise in radio broadcasting scenarios, where it could extract the desired signal (music, speech, etc.) above a certain loudness threshold while suppressing low-volume unwanted noise (such as the hiss of tape noise). In his letter, Berio reported that Stockhausen was very excited about the filtering made possible by the amplitude selector; to judge from *Scambi*, Pousseur shared this enthusiasm.

Pousseur began *Scambi* with white noise and used the amplitude selector at nearly every stage of the compositional process. White noise can be defined as "all frequencies at random amplitudes over the full range of human audio perception."[27] The amplitude selector introduced a new way of filtering this noise. Instead of limiting the frequency range (as a high-pass, low-pass, or bandpass filter would have done), the amplitude selector culled only the loudest frequencies in the noise band. As Pousseur explained, he filtered eleven bands of white noise from across the frequency spectrum, changing the settings of the amplitude selector to "isolate from the same sound-reserves a more or less dense, short-lived 'foam.'"[28] The metaphor of skimming foam from the top of a liquid is apt. If the amplitude selector was set very high, the "foam" consisted of only the loudest frequencies, producing a texture of dry impulses separated by silences. If the amplitude selector was set lower, further into the noise band, more frequencies were allowed to pass, and the resulting sound was "a sort of 'bubbling' in which the elements fuse together."[29]

Pousseur's selective filtering, in harmony with the basic concept of statistical form, meant that only a general direction could be predicted in advance.[30] As he said, "it was impossible to determine the precise point at which the sound suddenly appeared, or disappeared: to a large extent this depended on more or less subtle dynamic differences which constantly occurred in structures which were in part aleatoric."[31] Pousseur's extensive filtering of white noise likewise recalled his and Stockhausen's shared interest in the "ideal tone form" of complex sounds, like the noisy consonants of *p, t, f,* and *s,* as discussed in Chapter 3.[32] Although I will develop the idea more in Chapter 6, we continue to glimpse the ways in which Meyer-Eppler's phonetics teachings had substantial and lasting impacts among the European avant-garde.

Returning to *Scambi*'s composition, the practical work of subtractive synthesis done, Pousseur then worked with the echo chamber (an idea he and Stockhausen developed during the *Studie II* and *Seismogrammes* experiments) to further modify the sounds with reverberation. As Pousseur explained, this systematic work resulted in "a new, close relationship, an organic link between the dimensions of time and space."[33] Having produced a range of sonic textures, it was nearly time to montage the sound samples together. Unfortunately, this created something of a compositional crisis. Having spent a long time communing with the amplitude selector to produce sound materials that he heard as "organically unfolding," Pousseur was unsure about how to proceed:

> I was reluctant to use scissors at this late stage; the finished material now had its own complex integrity, which would have been interrupted, physically injured as it were (at least that is how I felt about the organic cohesion of the material). From the point of view of form, the slightest cut would have had unforeseen consequences.[34]

Pousseur thus found himself at a compositional impasse, having worked so hard to develop his sounds along textural continuums (from dry to bubbling) that he could no longer imagine segmenting and montaging them. On the one hand, he was enthusiastic about what he had produced, having used subtractive synthesis and reverberation to efficiently produce sophisticated sounds. But on the other hand, he was running out of time and recognized that various tapes of filtered sounds do not make a piece.

For a solution, Pousseur turned once again to the amplitude selector. He passed his "finished" sounds through the machine another time, filtering them at various levels. This final filtering introduced silences and pauses into the "finished" sounds, which arbitrarily marked sections and phrases—places where, with the machine's help, Pousseur could again insert himself and make cuts without doing violence to the sounds. This was not so much a relinquishing of control as a further statistical manipulation of the material, achieved by continuing with the technological processes he had used throughout the composition of the piece. As he explained, "The production of 'general pauses' depended on the nature of the existing material: did not the quality of the material itself determine how it went through the selector!"[35] For the serial-minded composer, there was an elegance to his solution: the sounds of the piece and the sectional divisions of the piece were determined by the same machinery and the same statistical logic.

At the formal level, the order of *Scambi*'s thirty-two sections is not fixed in advance.[36] This means that anyone can realize a version of *Scambi* by assembling Pousseur's sound materials (which he regarded as "the work").[37] To help the would-be layperson composer, Pousseur described the start and end of each sound as exhibiting either an "on" or an "off" state in the parameters of pitch, speed, homogeneity, and continuity. Sounds began and ended with either a high pitch or a low pitch, a continuous texture (burbling) or a discontinuous texture (impulse), a slow or a fast speed of internal change, etc. These descriptors could then be used to inform sonic linkages in different versions of the piece—for example, a sound that ended with a high, fast, homogeneous texture could be joined with another beginning with the same sonic characteristics. Pousseur's two realized versions prioritized such continuities, whereas two additional versions produced by his RAI studio colleagues Berio and Marc Wilkinson emphasized textural discontinuity between sections.[38]

At first glance, it seems ironic that Pousseur pioneered an "open" or "mobile" form in fixed media. As we have said, Pousseur was running out of time, and it could be that leaving the form "open" was simply a pragmatic decision of last resort. Given that several versions were produced, however, it seems that Pousseur was genuinely interested in the possibilities of a mobile form. He wanted to involve a co-realizer, a collaborator on par with a performer like Tudor, who contributed innumerable insights in realizing an indeterminate score by Cage, Wolff, Feldman, or Brown. As Pousseur said, he was exceedingly happy with Wilkinson's and Berio's iterations even though they did not conform at all to his own idea of timbral continuity.[39] Yet *Scambi* doesn't really involve a performer in the same way that an indeterminate instrumental score does. In contrast to Earle Brown's dream of an "infinite number of realizations"[40] in his performer-indeterminate piano work *Folio and Four Systems* (1952–1954), for example, just how open can *Scambi*'s form be, when it has to be frozen on magnetic tape?

This conundrum between fixed media and indeterminate, improvisatory unfolding is softened in the digital age, when software and digital audio workstations make it easy to arrange and rearrange sound samples. Pousseur was almost prophetic in this sense, saying, "I can easily imagine a day when works such as these will be offered to the public itself. All that is needed is one or, if possible, two or three tape-recorders at home—this can always be done if several 'amateurs' get together—a little splicing-glue and leader tape."[41] Here we witness another Cageian affinity: all people are potential musicians. One need not be a composer with specific training; an amateur "realizer" can assemble these fragments into a performance, because art is life and life is art.[42]

Pousseur's *Scambi*, like Ligeti's *Artikulation*, bears marks of the struggle between serialist plans, Cageian deconstructions, and technological affordances and constraints. Both *Artikulation* and *Scambi* stand in a liminal space, where aleatory is held at arm's length—embraced in some ways, eschewed in others. *Artikulation* and *Scambi* both exhibit a technologically mediated brand of statistical aleatoricism. At the formal level, both pieces are marked by aleatory assemblage and openness in their form. At the same time, both pieces depended on careful precompositional planning and compositional controls, where boundaries were determined by the studio's machines and sonic possibilities.[43] Cage's ideology recedes further into the distance when we consider the iterative compositional processes and the frozen, fixed-media results.

In the final analysis, the European studio composers' fascination with aleatory tracks less toward a Cageian, performer-centered indeterminacy than it does toward the statistical constraints of the studio. It is by thinking with the studio's machines that Ligeti and Pousseur found the creative direction for *Artikulation* and *Scambi*.[44] As these hybrid works suggest, each European composer encountered the aleatory discourse at his own port of entry, experimenting with indeterminate, statistical, chance, and mobile techniques, depending on his own situation. The working-through of the plethora of aleatory concepts in fact continued in the acoustic works of the late 1950s and the 1960s.

Pianistic Precursors and Rejoinders

Beyond the studio, the question of open, mobile forms preoccupied the European composers in several of their contemporaneous piano works. Stockhausen's *Klavierstück XI* (1956), technically the "first-born" of the group of pieces discussed here, shows clear connections to Cage and Feldman, as well as to the WDR statistical form techniques of *Gesang der Jünglinge* and *Gruppen*. Pousseur's *Mobile* (1958) for two pianos addresses similar concerns as *Scambi* in an acoustic, performer-controlled environment. Boulez launched his own experiment with mobile form in the *Troisième Sonate* (1957–1958, rev. 1963), where he used statistical controls (like those Ligeti introduced in *Artikulation*) to place limits on the performer's choices.

Klavierstück XI is perhaps more famous for its large-format, quasi-graphic score than anything else.[45] Cage made fun of it at Darmstadt 1958, saying that *Klavierstück XI's* "single unconventional aspect" was its clumsily large score (measuring 54 × 94 cm), which required a cardboard tube for transport and clips to attach to the piano.[46] The single page contains nineteen musical fragments of varying lengths, such that the pianist can begin with any one and proceed to any other that catches her eye. The playing style for the next segment is provided by remarks at the end of the previous fragment; thus, the tempo, dynamics, and articulation of any segment will depend on where the segment is approached from. The piece ends when the pianist has repeated any segment for a third time.

Because it prescribes no grammar or hierarchy and few conditions for making connections, *Klavierstück XI* resonates with the free-assembly mobile form of *Scambi*. As an acoustic piano piece, however, it is somewhat more efficient—using a human performer to avoid the fixed-media versus open-work conundrum—though not totally. It would be unusual for a pianist to perform the work without sketching out or practicing a possible order ahead of time, despite Stockhausen's having expressly prohibited this in the score directions.[47] Typically the performer would, at the least, familiarize herself with the sounds and shapes of each fragment as well as the possible tempo and articulation variations; and these preparations would be hard to keep separate from the practicing of various transitions and paths. The human performer's desire for preparation is, paradoxically, bound to limit her true freedom to assemble the piece on the fly. Stockhausen's interest seemed to linger on the multiple, embodied possibilities anyway—his score directions suggest performing the piece multiple times on the same concert, presumably to give both the performer and audience multiple experiences for comparison.

Stockhausen's thinking about the performative dimension in *Klavierstück XI* can hardly be separated from the perspectives and preferences of David Tudor, for whom the piece was written. Stockhausen broached the compositional idea with Tudor during his 1956 visit to Europe, and Tudor replied that it was very close to a procedure that Morton Feldman was simultaneously undertaking in *Intersections*. As Tudor tells it,

> most of the series [Feldman's *Intersections*] had boxes which you read from right to left across the page, but there was one in which you could go from any box to any other, which was the furthest he ever went with the idea of freedom. I had already started work on a realization of this score, and had the parts with me in my bag, when I came to Europe and met Stockhausen, who said, "what if I wrote a piece where you could decide where you wanted to go on the page?" I said I knew someone who was already doing one, and he said, "In that case I shall not compose it." So I retracted and said it was just an idea my friend had been thinking about, and told him he mustn't consider any other composer but should go ahead and do it anyway.[48]

Stockhausen clearly did go ahead with it, but he also introduced a logic for the piece that was much more resonant with his own WDR studio experiences. He rationalized the potential iterations of *Klavierstück XI* by arguing that the fragments of the piece were drawn from an overarching unity, a statistical *Gestalt*, in which order was inconsequential:

Piano Piece XI is nothing but a sound in which certain partials, components, are behaving statistically. [. . .] If I make a whole piece similar to the ways in which (a complex noise) is organized, then naturally the individual components of this piece could also be exchanged, permutated, without changing its basic quality.[49]

Stockhausen's vocabulary—noise, partials, complexity, permutations—strongly relates to statistical form jargon.[50] In fact, as Stephen Truelove's reverse engineering of the sketches has shown, *Klavierstück XI* was informed by the pitch–duration continuum that preoccupied Stockhausen in *Gesang der Jünglinge* and *Gruppen*.[51]

Stockhausen began, as Truelove contends, by making rhythmic "scales" with increasingly smaller subdivided durations. He then reordered and consolidated these durational motives into a "Final Rhythm Matrix" using serial procedures. Nineteen of these durational motives produced the rhythmic content of the musical score. Finally, to map pitch material onto the rhythmic motives, Stockhausen translated durational proportions into intervals. The durational proportion 3:2 (which says to the performer, "three of this note value in the space of two") was translated into the pitch interval of a perfect fifth; the proportion 2:1 became an octave—or, more likely, it was adjusted into what WDR composers would have called a "Webern octave" of a major seventh or a minor ninth.[52] As such, the pitch relationships were (more or less) expressed from the same proportional logic as the durational relationships. Stockhausen's extensive work in the electronic music studio, which gave rise to the duration-into-pitch insight,[53] accounts for his conclusion that *Klavierstück XI* is a magnified "complex noise" of "statistically-behaving partials." Taking the bird's-eye view, he argued that the mobile form was, in the end, rather inconsequential.

It is here that we can begin to understand the gap between the Cage group's approach to indeterminacy and Stockhausen's approach to the same. Although he ostensibly experimented with mobile form in *Klavierstück XI*, the piece's indeterminacy failed to fully engage the creative possibilities of the human performers. It had the superficial trappings of the "self-renewing kind of mobile complexity" that Boulez and his European contemporaries courted,[54] but more accurately, the piano piece was a composing-out of Stockhausen's proportional preoccupations. Oriented toward the electronic studio and statistical form, Stockhausen did not quite intersect with performer-centered indeterminacy on Cage's terms.

Likewise for Pousseur, the studio experiences were the precipice of further experiments with indeterminacy, formal openness, and mobility. In his 1958 Darmstadt presentation "Theory and Practice in the Newest Music," Pousseur brought together issues of meter, notation, proportions, sonic periodicity, and indeterminacy.[55] Pousseur continued to explore performer-centered indeterminacy in his acoustic compositions of the late 1950s and early 1960s as well.[56] A brief analysis of *Mobile* (1957–1958) will show that Pousseur hardly rejected Cage's ideas and interventions, but instead continued to manipulate and plumb them in his acoustic works.

The score for *Mobile* includes ten sections that are, to varying degrees, through-composed, as well as three *cahiers mobile* [mobile notebooks], each of which contains three musical fragments. Figure 5.3 shows how the mobile sections (notated with arrows) are interleaved between the fixed sections (notated with roman numerals). The *cahiers* can be selected by the pianist in any order (i.e., *cahier* no. 1 does not have to be chosen first), but as the solid arches in Figure 5.3 show, once a *cahier* has been chosen, its three excerpts are generally played out before the pianist moves on to another.[57] The tenth and final section is *ab libitum* in durations, dynamics, use of pedal, and articulations.

As Pascal Decroupet has pointed out, the piece is based on a dialectical relationship between the mobile and fixed sections.[58] The fixed sections can be described according to their musical characteristics—register, dynamics, textural thickness (e.g., single tones vs. chords), gestural unfolding (e.g., one tone at a time vs. melismatic flourishes), and articulation (e.g., staccato, tenuto, legato). In making choices about how to interleave the mobile sections, which can also be described in these ways, performers can opt for consistency or contrast, very much like in *Scambi*. A good example of how this works is in section III, which is mainly characterized by wide-ranging registers, a texture of single, tenuto articulations, and free dynamics. Piano A could introduce maximal contrast in and after III with *cahier mobile* no. 1, which features mostly melismatic flourishes at dynamic extremes in the top half of the piano's register. Alternately, Piano A could aim for minimal contrast—maximal coherence—by interrupting III with *cahier mobile* no. 2, whose *structures de préparation* are two- or three-note chords in widely varying registers and tenuto articulations. Whether Piano A went for maximal contrast or maximal coherence might depend on Piano B, who has a similar set of considerations; or it might depend entirely on chance: Pousseur allows for the pianists to either plan the *cahiers mobile* in advance or select them on the fly.

It is intuitively true that the live-performed *Mobile* allows for more flexibility than the fixed-media electronics of *Scambi*—unless of course an improvised iteration of *Scambi* was performed with twenty-first-century live electronics. At the same time, however, the framework of *Mobile* introduces certain limitations, namely to do with performer coordination. The two pianists, who are both making interpolations and digressions from the notated score simultaneously, face a steep challenge in coordination. This is especially apparent in sections II and IV, in which both pianists play from one of their *cahier mobile*.[59] Each partner's materials, which could be chosen on

Piano A Form

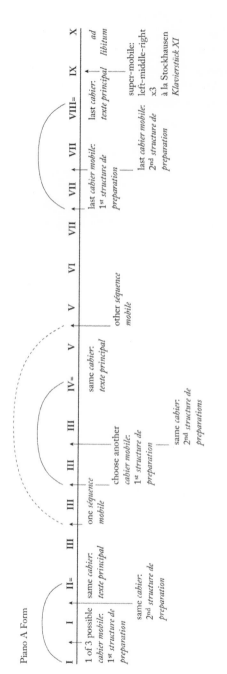

Piano B Form

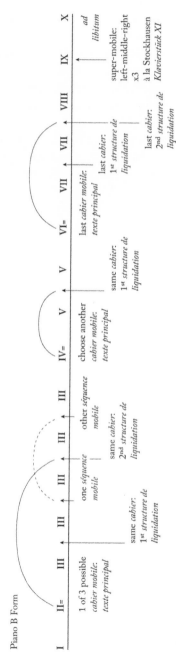

FIGURE 5·3. Form in Pousseur's *Mobile* (1958) for two pianos. Through-composed fixed sections (roman numerals) are interleaved with "mobile notebook" excerpts (at arrows). Arches show material drawn from the same *cabier mobile*; dotted arches show *sequence mobile* materials.

the fly, are not visible to the other. This introduces complexity, relativity, and uncertainty as to when the pianists might meet up and reground themselves as an ensemble. The uncertainty only compounds as they approach the final movements, which include both the "super-mobile" section IX, in which the performers wend through nine separate excerpts, and the *ad libitum* section X, which invites the performers to improvise with nearly all parameters (including pedal, articulation, dynamics, relative durations, pacing, and tempo).

In these ways, the true mobility of *Mobile* lies not in its variable form, but in the uncertainties introduced by the coordination required of its human performers. If Pousseur revived the continuity–contrast question he had been contemplating in *Scambi*, he did so in a way that remarkably reintegrated the performer's human capabilities. For instance, the tempos in *Mobile* were based on a proportional, pitch–duration scheme reminiscent of the studio, which could be precisely realized in measured tape lengths. Yet Pousseur embraced the inexactitude of human performers, writing, "This chronometric system does not represent inflexible proportions, strictly foreseen by the composer, but permits performers to realize (in a way natural to each) time structures independent of any direct reference to periodicity."[60] For Pousseur, the embodied—and thus surely inexact—performance of temporal proportions was a desirable escape from serial music's obsessive interest in periodicity. Likewise, the uncertainty of duet coordination between the improvising players reveals an embrace of Cageian ideals. Pousseur both established periodicity, through temporal proportions, and undermined it, through the indeterminacy of improvised performance and embodied mobility.

This analysis suggests that Pousseur took the indeterminacy of the Cage group seriously. Boulez, on the other hand, remained skeptical that performer-centered indeterminacy would make music more interesting. Suspicious of highly open graphic scores and performance-art scenarios, Boulez complained,

> The notation becomes—subtly—imprecise enough to allow the performer's instantaneous, shifting, iridescent choice to slip through the hypothetical grid. [. . .] You see what it comes back to? Always a refusal to choose. [. . .] [The composer] escapes choice, not by numbers, but through the performer. One transfers one's choice to him.[61]

Boulez insisted that any chance-based innovations must be "guided" by the composer into an "effective collaboration."[62] The composer is figured here as the creative genius structuring the scene—the man behind the curtain, as it were. For Boulez, performers mustn't have too much freedom, because their " 'instant' imagination misfires more often than it fires."[63]

It is from this position of controlling the variables that Boulez experimented with mobile form in his *Troisième Sonate*. In sum, the five-movement piece pivots around a central, unchanging movement III, as is shown in Figure 5.4.[64]

mobile	fixe	mobile		mobile	fixe	mobile
I II		IV V		I IV		II V
II I	III	V IV		II V	III	I IV
IV V		I II		IV I		V II
V IV		II I		V II		IV I

FIGURE 5.4. Mobile form possibilities in Boulez's *Troisième Sonate* (1957–1958).

The permutational form is further constrained as movements II and IV will remain always equidistant from it, as will movements I and V. The concept of the whole piece remains unrealized, though, as movements I (*Antiphonie*), IV (*Strophe*), and V (*Séquence*) were never published, existing only in various stages of sketch drafts and manuscript copies since their tentative premiere at Darmstadt 1959.[65] This leaves movements II (*Trope*) and III (*Constellation-Miroir*) as the piece's published representatives, both of which include embedded levels of formal mobility in and of themselves.

Boulez offered the performer a few choices on the foreground level (*à la* Pousseur) in movement II (*Trope*), wherein "optional structures," enclosed within parentheses in the score, may be either played or omitted.[66] Further, the performer can begin with any of movement II's four sections—"Parenthèse," "Glose," "Commentaire," or "Texte"—continuing to the next sections in the circular order that Boulez specifies in the score. "Commentaire" can possibly be heard in two different places, but the performer must choose one or the other; as such, the path is mostly determined once the performer chooses her point of entry.

These score options seem to take the questions of open and mobile forms seriously, but do they affect the music? As William Harbinson has argued about movement II, there is little difference in sound among the various permutations: "The movements contain graduated degrees of register, density, and predominant dynamic level; thus, a 'gentle curve' [Boulez's term] of varied arc results from any of the eight possible orderings."[67] Anne Trenkamp has argued something similar about movement III.[68] Boulez's extravagant red and green notation, replete with signposted shapes at the beginning and end of each stave, ostensibly offered the performer a number of paths through the piece. But as Trenkamp suggests, "the multiplicity of signs gives the illusion that the pianist has more choices than are really important or available."[69] The order of segments (phrases) is permutable, but not entirely free; Boulez further limited performer choice by grouping segments into units (sections). The performer's chosen foreground permutations at the phrase level are then neutralized at the section level, where the composer has already mandated controls based on texture, register, and pitch similarity. These middle-ground controls, which recall the constraints that Ligeti introduced by sorting his electronic sound materials, limit the impact of random selection. As Trenkamp concludes, "While there is choice among individual segments, the organization of these segments into units prevents random chance and provides a sub-formal structure. [. . .] Boulez has loaded the dice."[70]

Like *Klavierstück XI* and *Mobile*, the form of *Constellation-Miroir* is even less mobile when the performer is involved. For practical reasons, performers generally decipher the red and green symbology, determine the possible paths, and rehearse them in advance. As the pianist Claude Helffer reported, "After three or four attempts I was satisfied with the routes I had chosen and no longer had any desire to search for different ones. Before starting to play *Constellation-Miroir* I now have three possibilities in mind—routes for which I have already provided."[71] It is worth mentioning that in all likelihood this limited mobility didn't bother Boulez at all: as his comments in "Alea" suggest, a structure that permitted more performer freedom was not palatable. Different versions of the piece sound oddly similar, and pianists practiced and performed well-worn paths, but so what? The composer's "voice" cuts through, preserving musical integrity instead of leaving it entirely to the whims of the performer. These are exactly the conditions that Boulez courted in "Alea."

Like the work of his contemporaries, Boulez's *Troisième Sonate* reacts to and synthesizes numerous threads. These include literary open forms (Stéphane Mallarmé and James Joyce in particular),[72] Cage's varied chance and indeterminacy practices (as critiqued in "Alea"), and the particular constraints and attitudes of the midcentury electronic studio (the movements as "formants").[73] This multiplicity of inspiration broadens our understanding of the aleatory debates and recasts our tendency to overemphasize the Cage–Boulez disagreements. Yes, Cage was an important interlocutor, whom Boulez explicitly addressed in "Alea" and implicitly addressed in the *Troisième Sonate*. But it is also true that the aleatory discourse is rich and multifaceted, and so too are composers' artistic engagements with it.

Brownian Motions

Although we have been focusing on the ways that several European composers incorporated aleatory inspirations (from Cage, to literature, to linguistics, to the studio machines), it is also worthwhile to ask whether the Cage group was similarly omnivorous in their creative consumption. To put it even more succinctly: Were the American experimentalists watching how the Europeans incorporated chance into their works too? In fact, we can see such a dialectical, trans-Atlantic, studio-fueled conversation unfolding in the work and activities of Earle Brown, one of the American experimental composers in the New York–based Cage group.[74]

Brown first met Boulez in New York in 1952, later spent several months in Paris, Milan, Cologne, and elsewhere in Western Europe in late 1956 and early 1957, and twice lectured on notation and form in new music at Darmstadt (1964, 1965).[75] In Cologne in 1957, Brown fell in with Heinz-Klaus Metzger, Sylvano Bussotti, and especially the musicologist Hans G. Helms, who embraced and promoted his "anti-authoritarian, liberated" concepts and scores.[76] Brown's works were commissioned by Boulez, Steinecke, and others, and were performed several times in Europe, including by Tudor at Donaueschingen and Cologne in 1954 (see Tables 2.2 and 2.3), and played by Tudor, Maderna, and others at Darmstadt (see Figure 2.7 and Table 5.1). Because of such experiences—and especially because of his close association with the cross-pollinator Tudor—Brown's graphic scores and improvisatory, indeterminate musical ideas were well known among the European avant-garde.

During his visit to Paris in 1956, Brown said that he and Boulez argued at length over open form ideas: "I think he [Boulez] learned a lot from it because his music sort of opened up and softened up a bit after those conversations, and that's when, after I was there in Paris, and we had all those talks, he did 'Alea,' the article."[77] Likewise, Brown was quite sure that Tudor's performances of his early piano works had an impact on both Boulez's *Troisième Sonate* (1957–58) and Stockhausen's *Klavierstück XI* (1956). As he said, "both [were] influenced—I'm quite positive—by a piece called *Twentyfive Pages* which I wrote in 1953, which was about seven [*sic:* three to four] years before they did their stuff."[78] Fascinating as these narratives are, it is not useful to use Brown's memories to definitively establish (or deny) "firstness," and I am not very interested in arbitrating the debate over who influenced whom. Instead, I would like to focus on the ways that Brown's claims reveal that the aleatory debates were an elaborate, ongoing conversation that stretched across several local and regional new music scenes in the mid-to-late 1950s.

The graphic scores and mobile forms that Brown produced in the early-to-mid-1950s were, in fact, strongly resonant with the statistical and indeterminate questions the European composers were contemporaneously exploring in the WDR and RAI studios. Consider Brown's score directions for *Folio and Four Systems* (1952–1954): "*Time* is the actual dimension in which music exists when performed and is by nature an infinitely divisible continuum. [. . .] Similarly, all of the other characteristics of a sound—frequency, intensity, timbre, modes of attack-continuation-decay—are infinitely divisible continua and unmeasurable."[79] This jargon-heavy note, with its emphasis on continuums and the acoustic features of sound, could just as easily be a program note for one of the WDR electronic works. Likewise, Brown's *Pentathis* (1958)—though it is a conventionally notated, purely acoustic work for chamber orchestra—exploits the continuum between "pure tone" and "noise" familiar from the electronic studio and constructs "accumulated densities and configurations."[80] These phrases betray Brown's familiarity with the temporal continuum and statistical form discourses popularized in and around the WDR studio, and moreover, his familiarity with analog studio technologies themselves.

Brown's first exposure to electronic music came early—between 1951 and 1953—when he worked with Cage and Tudor in the New York studio of Louis and Bebe Barron.[81] He subsequently worked as a recording engineer for Capitol Records (1955–1960) and as a producer for the Contemporary Sound Series at Mainstream Records (1961–1973).[82] When it came to the Cage group's early 1950s "Project of Music for Magnetic Tape," the Barrons recorded six different types of mostly *musique concrète* sounds (city, country, electronic, manually produced, wind produced, and small), collecting an enormous stock of raw material. Then Brown joined Cage and Tudor for the almost interminable work of splicing together Cage's *Williams Mix*, Feldman's *Intersection*, and Brown's *Octet I*. As Brown remembered,

John, David and I were each paid forty dollars a week! David seldom showed up to cut and splice. Number one, it bored him. And two, he was practicing our piano music—John was setting up concerts, and David had to practice all the time. [. . .] We had splice bars, razor blades and a degausser. We were recording at 15 inches per second and had the scores on quarter-inch graph paper, the same size as the tape. With splicing tape and talcum powder, we just followed the score. John always compared it to following a dressmaker's pattern: cut it out and stick the pieces together. That went on for about four years.[83]

Brown's comments suggest, rightly, that the manual studio work of tape splicing was boring and repetitive. At the same time, however, the studio was a crucible for Brown's nascent thinking about the dimensions of musical sound, duration, and notation.

As is evident in the *Folio* series, which is made up of several single-sheet graphic scores titled by month and year, magnetic tape actually revolutionized Brown's thinking. In *October 1952*, for example, conventionally notated rests disappear, leaving the performer to interpret the spacing of the score as a literal representation of sound and silence (Figure 5.5). This recalls the direct durational paradigm of magnetic tape; bypassing metric notation, physical proportions describe the relationship between sound and silence.

December 1952 goes even further in this direction, with an entirely graphic, spatial map of boxes and lines slightly reminiscent of a deconstructed Mondrian canvas (Figure 5.6).[84] Sonic events scattered about the page in *December 1952* are analogous to tape fragments, which can be spliced together

FIGURE 5.5. Earle Brown, direct durational spacing in *October 1952* from *Folio and Four Systems*. © 1961 (renewed) by Associated Music Publishers, Inc. (BMI) International Copyright Secured. All Rights Reserved. Reprinted by Permission.

with any others. It is up to the performer to sonify the fragments, using loudness, density, register, and duration in accord with her interpretive reading of the graphic blocks; and likewise the performer chooses how to montage these sound fragments together.

It is no coincidence that Brown's indeterminate notation and mobile form work gelled, by his own account, in the very next work *Twentyfive Pages* (1953), composed at the end of his tenure in the Barron studio. Here, Brown extended his graphic scoring techniques to produce a three-dimensional representation of sound—insofar as is possible in a score—by allowing the performer to use score sheets in any orientation and any order. This placed the

FIGURE 5.6. Earle Brown, *December 1952* from *Folio and Four Systems*.
© 1961 (renewed) by Associated Music Publishers, Inc. (BMI) International
Copyright Secured. All Rights Reserved. Reprinted by Permission.

performer inside a spatialized, nonlinear musical scene. As Brown said, "My
music is definitely *mosaic* not narrative."[85]

Brown's graphic scores ask the performer to enter a "relational space"
where they must create and react to the sound itself, recalling the direct
engagement with sound that was possible for the first time in the analog
studio.[86] The connection is even more transparent in the score of *Four Systems*
(Figure 5.7), which Brown hastily composed for Tudor's birthday in 1954.[87]
More than musical staves, the "systems" here might just as well be understood as graphic representations of magnetic tape, in which the inscribed
sounds are made visible so that the performer can again make them audible.[88] If the graphic score stands in for magnetic tape and the piano for the
oscillators and filters, then the performer is the playback and speaker dif-
fusion system. As the score note suggests, Brown's musical thinking was
attuned to the constraints of both the human and electronic systems—the
physical boundaries of the tape, keyboard, or hand, and the sonic boundaries
of the oscillator's frequency ranges and human ears.

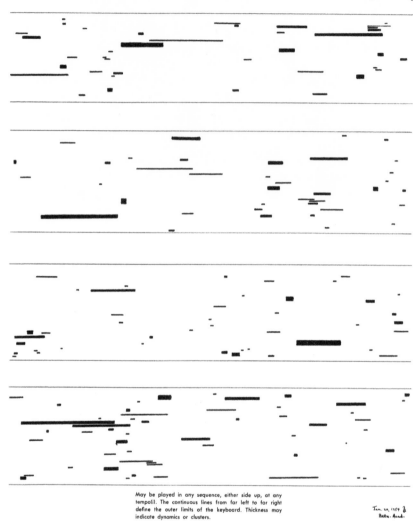

4 SYSTEMS

for David Tudor on a birthday
Jan. 20, 1954

May be played in any sequence, either side up, at any tempo(i). The continuous lines from far left to far right define the outer limits of the keyboard. Thickness may indicate dynamics or clusters.

FIGURE 5.7. Earle Brown, *Four Systems* (1954). © 1961 (renewed) by Associated Music Publishers, Inc. (BMI) International Copyright Secured. All Rights Reserved. Reprinted by Permission.

Brown's development of graphic indeterminacy and open forms owes much to the new logic of the analog studio, where sounds could be fragmented and detached, recombined, and diffused in speakers that were spatially spread about. At the same time, Brown's works push back against the constraints of fixed media. He was infatuated with the idea that graphic notation invited infinite subtle, interpretative variations. Regarding *October 1952*, he said, "If fifteen different pianists played that, you'd recognize the piece, but it would never be the same twice. That just intrigued me, just knocked me out: *never the same twice, but always the same thing.*"[89] Likewise, Brown embraced the human improvisatory possibilities of mobile forms. As he explained,

> But once you get into abstraction, where multiple interpretations are possible, that's where *open form* occurred to me [. . .] With Joyce it's the same. It's impossible for two people to agree on what *Finnegans Wake* means. [. . .] The thing to do is create a world in which each person interprets it differently. Because that's what they're going to do anyway.[90]

These comments and attitudes subvert and problematize the frozenness of fixed media.[91] Brown embraces the genuinely human skills of flexibility, improvisation, and interpretation. Contrary to Boulez, he trusts the performer to play with sounds—in much the same way that a composer does in the studio—but absent the goal of discovering the definitive interpretation that can be fixed on tape or repeated in live performance. For Brown, the beauty of the open form lies in the work's always being made anew.

Conclusions

In this chapter, we have considered a range of electronic and acoustic pieces that take the question of aleatory in its variations—mobile form, statistical form, indeterminacy, and graphic scores—very seriously. Electronic studios were important sites where these questions were raised, discussed, and investigated, not least because the studio technology itself invited or necessitated aleatoric perspectives. Although we have considered a range of sources for the aleatory debates, including linguistics, phonetics, studio technologies, and performer limits, there are a number of additional facets that we could add to the analysis. The Cage group's work, in particular, is indebted to parallel questions circulating in visual and performance art among the New York school of artists, with whom they regularly socialized and collaborated.[92] The European group, likewise, was heavily influenced by experimental literature, especially that of James Joyce (more on that in Chapter 6). More must be said about improvisation and jazz as essential discourses with which the midcentury composers engaged, on both sides of the Atlantic.[93] Future work should by all means continue to expose and elaborate these important facets of the network.

My intention here has been to take a first step to expand and nuance the terms of the aleatory debates beyond the well-worn American–European polemic, as crystallized in Boulez's and Cage's mutual critiques. It's time we reconsider the *who*, the *where*, and the *how* of various types of aleatory interventions. As the network of chance technique expands, we see that electronic studios were the literal meeting points that nurtured experimentation and extended dialogue.

Furthermore, it's time we understood debate and disagreement as a sign of shared investment.[94] Instead of viewing controversy as evidence of fundamental difference, it's helpful to consider the way debate makes the stakes visible, helping actors on both sides to clarify their own positions, investments, and next moves. In the case of the midcentury composers, their momentary squabbles and polemical insults paled in comparison to the enrichment they received from sharing in an ongoing, contested discourse. A brief example: after Darmstadt in 1958, Cage traveled to Milan for several months, where he worked at the RAI electronic studio. Berio wrote to Pousseur, "Everything is wonderful" as friends arrived.[95] As Berio's "Palace of United Nations of Music" illustration in Figure 5.8 suggests, he was still very much invested in the creative, intellectual energy of this international avant-garde network, which absolutely included Americans like Cage and Tudor.[96] Likewise, as Brown said,

> In Darmstadt [1958] we were working together: there was no aesthetic split; well, there was an aesthetic split, but there was no personal split. We were very good friends with each other. I was good friends with Karlheinz, Pierre, Luciano, and Maderna—they were the key people—Ligeti, etc., and we had no animosity whatsoever.[97]

Although interpersonal grudges hold in a few specific cases, it is time to reevaluate the significance we attach to the story of the American–European split on the whole. The aleatory debates reveal a network that is international, professionally heterogeneous, and indebted to the technologies available in the laboratory environments of the Barron, WDR, and RAI studios.

The aleatory debates, as analyzed here, also expose an intense dialogue between the agency of human performers and studio machines, which is played out in the paradox of open forms and fixed media.[98] The apparent contradiction in terms was obvious to every composer who worked on both acoustic and electronic sides—which is to say, everyone. As Cage remarked, "Everyone now knows that there's a contradiction between the use of chance operations and the making of a record. [. . .] [I]f you want music to come alive [. . .] you must not *can* it."[99]

In light of this paradox, it is initially ironic that composers like Ligeti and Pousseur explored open forms in fixed media; yet hearing such fixed-media experiments in dialogue with acoustic works reveals important facets

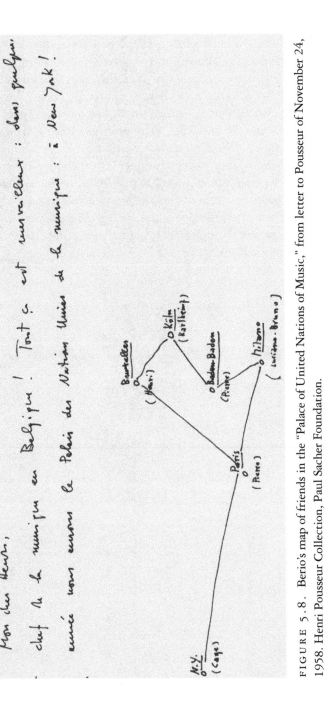

FIGURE 5.8. Berio's map of friends in the "Palace of United Nations of Music," from letter to Pousseur of November 24, 1958. Henri Pousseur Collection, Paul Sacher Foundation.

of the aleatory questions: statistical sorting, which limited sonic possibility (Ligeti, Boulez); performers' or realizers' constrained choices, which grew from practical considerations (Pousseur, Stockhausen, Boulez, Brown); and technological interventions, which pushed humans further into the background (Pousseur, Ligeti, Brown).

The aleatory debates expose the distributed agency of studio environments. In exploring how to incorporate chance, composers grappled with how to navigate their own agency in dialogue with that of technicians, machines, and performers. On the one hand, composers exhibited a strong desire to work through the studio's affordances, even in some cases turning over their own compositional agency to the machines. On the other hand, composers also continued to exploit prodigious live performers to escape the constraints of fixed media, and to circumvent the analog studio's limits. As we will see in Chapter 6, the further exploration of the distributed agency between humans and technologies reveals important insights that could hardly have come from acoustic music alone.

6 | Technosynthesis

From Vocoder Speech to Electronic Music

Stockhausen's *Gesang der Jünglinge* (1955–1956) is considered a master-work that compellingly demonstrates the artistic potential of midcentury electronic music. The pure, youthful, boy-soprano voice of Josef Protschka brushes against abrasive metallic smears, shadowy low-frequency rumbles, dry and brittle shaker noises, and spongy sine tone mixtures, all coaxed from the WDR studio's generators. At some moments, the listener is funneled into the boy's ethereal hum—unmanipulated and close-miked—and the piece seems to reveal its true center. At other moments, the listener is spun outward in a joyfully untethered chorus of swirling, layered voices and spatially diffused, impulsive sine tone flourishes. *Gesang*'s biblical text fragments coalesce into an *Ur*-language before dissipating into the synthesized ether again. As if sonifying cultural anxieties, the voice negotiates the commentary of the machine. *Gesang*'s sonic counterpoint exposes the central, nagging problematic of midcentury electronic music: What is the place of the human in an increasingly technologically mediated world?

Stockhausen's exposure to experimental phonetics and speech synthesis experiments by means of his mentor Werner Meyer-Eppler underwrote his exploration of the relationships between the human voice and synthesized sound in *Gesang*.[1] The piece is perhaps the most famous to showcase such issues, but it is far from the only one; *Gesang* belongs to a network of faux-language works that use experimental phonetics and speech synthesis research as a technical and aesthetic point of departure.[2] Some of these pieces—such as Mauricio Kagel's *Anagrama*, György Ligeti's *Aventures* and *Nouvelles Aventures*, John Cage's *Aria*, and Dieter Schnebel's *für Stimmen*—are purely acoustic works, which use phonetic symbols and the voice to explore deconstructed, sonic linguistic seeds. Others—such as Luciano Berio's *Thema (Omaggio a Joyce)*, Bruno Maderna's *Dimensioni II*, Kagel's *Transición I*, Ligeti's *Artikulation*, and Cage's *Fontana Mix*—use electronic studio technology to deconstruct sampled vocal sounds into elemental fragments that are then isolated, manipulated, and recombined.[3]

This network of similar pieces responded to common sources of inspiration—namely, speech synthesis discourses, phonetic linguistics, James Joyce's experimental literature, and studio technologies, all of which enabled the deconstruction and reconstruction of sounds. This chapter shows how the technoscientific research on speech synthesis—begun for both domestic and military purposes in the 1930s—was parlayed into a wide-ranging aesthetic experiment among the European avant-garde in the 1950s and 1960s. The WDR-affiliated composers incorporated knowledge of research from Meyer-Eppler at the University of Bonn, from Bell Labs in the United States, and from the Harvard-based linguist Roman Jakobson; the RAI studio composers in Milan came to similar artistic positions from related intellectual and technological inspirations.

As this chapter also shows, the composers in both Cologne and Milan were actively reading Joyce as well as structural linguistic texts together and discussing their implications. In these ways, the studio environments reveal a highly interdisciplinary nexus, in which scientific, technological, and pragmatic developments intersected with literary and musical experiments.[4] Not only did the WDR and RAI composers appropriate experimental phonetics research, but their aesthetic work fed back into the cultural sphere. Midcentury electronic works sound out a heterogeneous network, whose cumulative effect was to repurpose technologies for the common good.

Meyer-Eppler's Phonetics

As we know from Chapters 1 and 4, Meyer-Eppler's research turned from military engineering, physics, and acoustics toward experimental phonetics and information theory in the postwar era.[5] After denazification, he began working (with his colleague Paul Menzerath) to rebuild the Phonetics Institute at the University of Bonn, qualifying for a faculty position with a second *Habilitation* in phonetics in 1952. Meyer-Eppler's turn toward experimental phonetics was less a total professional overhaul than a rebalancing and reorientation within his existing research areas. Already in *Elektrische Klangerzeugung* (*[Electric Sound Production]*, 1949), Meyer-Eppler joined phonetics researchers who included Hermann von Helmholtz, who imitated vowel sounds with tuning forks (1867); Dayton Miller, who did the same with organ pipes (1922); and Carl Stumpf, whose *Die Sprachlaute* (*[Speech Sounds]*, 1926) was informed by extensive ethnographic research of many Western and non-Western languages and musical practices, as recorded on wax cylinders by Stumpf, Erich Moritz von Hornbostel, and their colleagues in German prisoner-of-war camps during World War I.[6]

Meyer-Eppler placed himself within an experimental phonetics lineage, which saw scientists trying to better understand the operation of the human larynx by constructing artificial larynges that could produce vowel sounds.[7] Comparable to the turn from acoustics to electroacoustics,[8] phonetics research took on a particularly technological bent at Bell Labs in the United States in the early 1920s, where researchers like John Stewart and Harvey Fletcher produced vowel and consonant sounds using an electrical buzzer, as part of a multifaceted speech and hearing research project that aimed to improve telephony.[9] Communications research at Bell Labs and elsewhere depended, on the one hand, on technological innovation in electronic circuits and machines, and, on the other hand, on a growing understanding of human perceptual mechanisms, which included research performed on Deaf and hard-of-hearing populations.[10] In this way, experimental phonetics was very much an interdisciplinary intersection, where speech synthesis drew directly from perceptual research and communications engineering.

As glimpsed in Chapter 3, research in psychoacoustics and experimental phonetics had long run in overlapping circles with musical discourses, and authors such as Helmholtz, Miller, and Stumpf overtly addressed the musical implications of their scientific work.[11] Furthermore, electronic instrument builders such as Trautwein, Bode, and Theremin knowingly used electronic circuitry akin to that found in communication technologies to produce and filter their electronic sounds.[12] For example, the electronic circuits of the Trautonium filtered an overtone-rich sound—essentially the same process used to produce vowels and consonants in the human vocal tract and to synthesize speech in the Vocoder.[13] Later, twentieth-century theorizing—as well as related computer music work at Bell Labs and elsewhere—continued the trend of using phonemes to model music timbre.[14]

Meyer-Eppler's early 1950s phonetics and electronic music work, with its marriage of technical, perceptual, and aesthetic concerns, makes visible the intertwined development of communication technologies and electronic music. He was intimately familiar with the Vocoder, having met in 1948 with Homer Dudley, the Bell Labs engineer who headed up the Vocoder research team.[15] Meyer-Eppler's sonic archive contains numerous tracks of Vocoder-produced synthetic speech and sound effects.[16] These were evidently the demonstration tracks that Dudley played on tour, as the sounds were discussed in a number of articles and press reports.[17] As Dudley described:

Keeping careful time with the puffs of a locomotive, the demonstrator can make the locomotive puff intelligibly "We're – start – ing – slow – ly – faster, faster, faster" as the puffs come closer together. Or

a church bell may say "Stop – stop – stop – don't – do – that." [. . .]
These tricks and others have suggested uses for the Vocoder in radio
and sound pictures.[18]

As the preceding example suggests, public demonstrations often showcased
the Vocoder imitating the sounds of speech, trains, airplanes, organs, and
string quartets. The Vocoder's sounds blur the lines between "speech" and
"music," inviting the audience into the imaginary world of filmic and radio
sound effects.

Meyer-Eppler seized on these implications, employing the Vocoder for
sound effects in *Der alte Roboter* [*The Old Robot*], a radio drama that was
broadcast from the NWDR-Cologne in 1951.[19] Vocoder sound samples also
appeared in the earliest WDR electronic music, such as Eimert and Beyer's
Spiel für Melochord (1952), which, as we saw in Chapter 1, was collaged from
a sound catalogue prepared by Meyer-Eppler. As Elena Ungeheuer put it, "in
Meyer-Eppler's hands, speech synthesis via the Vocoder [. . .] became the
starting point for the fabrication of electronic music."[20] This kind of science-
to-music transfer was possible because the communication technology developed at Bell Labs was similar to the aesthetic technology developed in early
electronic music instruments and in the Cold War studio. Both depended on
the same circuitry, the same sound-production mechanisms, and the same
perceptual and technical research.

As we noted in Chapter 4, Stockhausen took eight seminars with Meyer-
Eppler between 1954 and 1956, the same time that he was composing
Gesang der Jünglinge (see Table 4.1).[21] Phonetics, because it was so deeply attentive to the timbre of linguistic sounds, gave Stockhausen many ideas for
constructing his electronic sounds. As Stockhausen wrote, in *Gesang,*

> the extremes of the targeted scale are thus: sound/vowel—consonant/
> noise; in the sonic area between *u* and *i* [we find] the darkest and
> lightest colors; in the sound-noise opposition between pure harmonic
> spectra and aleatoric noise bands, as well as in the noise area between
> *ch* and *s* (voiceless), [lie] the darkest and lightest colors.[22]

In other words, the phonetic continuum between vowels and consonants
was a perfect analog for the musical continuum from pitched tone to
noise in the electronic studio. This sonic continuum was one of the major
insights Stockhausen and other composers took from Meyer-Eppler's phonetics teachings. Stockhausen went even further with phonetic explorations
in several acoustic works from the late 1950s and 1960s, including *Carré*
(1959) for spatially deployed orchestras and choirs, and *Stimmung* (1968),
which composed out timbral morphing by way of changing vowels (see
Figure 6.1). The singers use different vowel shapes to emphasize certain
partials in the sound, such that the human vocalists become simulacra

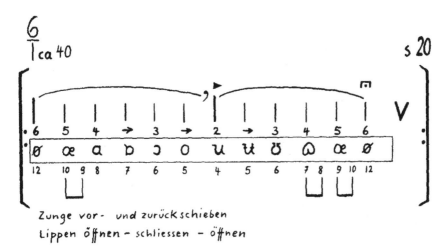

FIGURE 6.1. Stockhausen's *Stimmung* (1968), vowel–timbre morphing from a male voice part. Stockhausen Foundation.

of studio equipment, "tuning in" partials as if they were themselves oscillators.[23]

In exploiting and disseminating Meyer-Eppler's teachings, Stockhausen had crucial help from Mauricio Kagel, a young studio apprentice who began at the WDR in late 1957. A Jewish-Argentinian émigré in Cologne on a DAAD (*Deutscher Akademischer Austauschdienst*, or German Academic Exchange Service) grant, Kagel had already composed a *musique concrète* work as part of an experimental artistic collective in cosmopolitan Buenos Aires.[24] Kagel was erudite (including study with Jorge Luis Borges and Witold Gombrowicz and two encounters with Pierre Boulez), but the WDR studio experience nonetheless must have presented a bit of a shock. Kagel's sketches and notebooks from the period are a mish-mash of Spanish, German, and occasionally English—like Ligeti, he was learning German at the same time he was learning the electronic studio equipment. The first volume of his *Arbeitstagebuch* [daily working journal] contains over seventy pages of single-spaced typed notes detailing his studio experiments in June and July 1958.[25] Kagel's notebooks give an excellent picture of how he came to terms with the machinery of the studio, moving from basic technical definitions and mechanical functions to hypotheses and musical propositions to experiments, ending with results and reflections. His experimental practice with the studio equipment very much mirrors scientific laboratory experiments.[26]

Kagel's scientific investigation was no doubt aided by taking a seminar in Bonn with Meyer-Eppler for twelve weeks between November 1958 and February 1959. Meyer-Eppler's course, taught from the foundational *Elektrische Klangerzeugung*, began with an in-depth technical and mathematical investigation of acoustical principles and electronic technologies. In the first several weeks, Kagel took notes (mostly in German) on topics such as wave types, periodicity and aperiodicity, sine and cosine functions as related to Fourier analysis, Gaussian functions and statistical dispersal, combination tones, ring modulation, filtering, and amplitude modulation.

In week nine, Meyer-Eppler's lecture delved into phonetics. Kagel seemingly took from this the insight that music and speech exist together on a continuum. As he wrote in his notes, "speech takes on the character of music and music the character of speech. Musical formants are modulated into speech formants."[27] This resonates with Stockhausen's and Ligeti's translations (in *Gesang* and *Artikulation*, respectively) of the vowel–consonant continuum of speech into the sine tone–noise continuum in the studio. Kagel's insight is directly connected in his notes to the Vocoder; it is likely that Meyer-Eppler played Homer Dudley's musical-synthesized-speech tracks to illustrate the music–speech continuum.[28] After encountering such a fascinating technology—or at least recordings of it—Kagel's notes further question how to bring the Vocoder's speech synthesis into music: Should he use additive mixtures (additive synthesis) or multiplicative mixtures (ring modulation)? Why do pure sounds (vowels) behave so differently than noisy sounds (consonants) under manipulations like ring modulation and reversed tape direction? These are the kinds of musical questions that Kagel, Stockhausen, Ligeti, and others extrapolated from Meyer-Eppler's phonetics teachings. We will soon see exactly how Kagel engaged these questions musically in *Transición I* and *Anagrama*, but first let us learn more about speech synthesis and the various uses for the Vocoder, its connections to structural linguistics, and, most important, the ways in which these interdisciplinary discourses had an impact on midcentury electronic music.

Speech Synthesis and the Vocoder

Dudley's Vocoder, short for "voice coder," was a machine that could both analyze human speech (substituting for the ear) and resynthesize it (substituting for the vocal system). As shown in Figure 6.2, the speaker's voice was turned into electrical signals in the microphone; a frequency analyzer then determined the fundamental frequency and sorted the remaining overtones into ten channels that covered different frequency ranges (in hertz).[29] The frequency analyzer gave information on how much power was contained in each spectral band, so that the synthesizer could balance the relative strength (amplitude) of the various partials. During resynthesis, a buzz sound from a relaxation oscillator and a hiss sound from a noise generator approximated the vowels and consonants of speech, respectively. The resynthesized speech

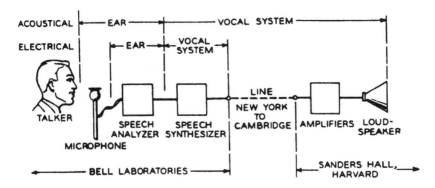

FIGURE 6.2. Dudley's schematic showing how an electrical circuit for speech analysis and synthesis corresponds to the aural and vocal functions of the human body.

could be then transmitted by phone lines or radio waves, or passed through amplifiers and loudspeakers, depending on the situation.

One considerable advantage of the Vocoder's analysis–resynthesis process was that it significantly reduced message size, a considerable concern in early telephony.[30] It did so by drastically simplifying speech from a complex range of frequencies—spanning thousands of hertz—down to only eleven frequencies that were most necessary for comprehension and resynthesis on the other end.[31] These are largely the domestic terms in which Vocoder technology was explained to the American and British publics in the late 1930s and 1940s: the simplification of speech would allow the expansion of the domestic and trans-Atlantic telephone networks. In postwar British news reports, likewise, Vocoder technology was valuable because it allowed "several messages to be transmitted over the same line"[32] and resynthesized at the other end, which "makes the system attractive for long submarine cables which are very expensive and have limited capacity."[33]

In the United States, the Vocoder's "robot voice" was also presented to the public in 1939 as a novelty, whose primary use was entertainment. Hollywood reporters imagined sci-fi sound effects, animal cartoon voices, character aging, choral effects, voice-overs for actors who couldn't sing, and the correction of speech defects like monotony and oversibilance.[34] At the 1939 World's Fair, Bell Labs deliberately emphasized an entertaining, domestic veneer. Young, effervescent "Voderettes" controlled the robotic voice of the "Pedro the Voder," an artificial talking machine (see Figures 6.3 and 6.4).[35] The Voderettes, operating finger keys and a foot pedal, demonstrated speech synthesis (but not analysis) by filtering the Voder's oscillator-generated hisses and buzzes into linguistic phonemes.[36] After six

FIGURE 6.3. Synthesizing speech with the Voder at the AT&T Exhibit, World's Fair 1939–1940. New York Public Library.

FIGURE 6.4. Women telephone operators staffing the AT&T Exhibit, World's Fair 1939–1940. New York Public Library.

to twelve months of daily training, the "girls" were proficiently synthesizing a vocabulary of about 2,500 words; the Voderettes made the machine speak. Their presence added an element of sex appeal to the Voder's robotic, artificial voice, as well as a veil of domesticity and safety to the project of artificial speech synthesis.[37]

The novelties of the World's Fair—the beautiful Voderettes, Pedro's uncanny robotic voice—served as convenient distractions from the violence growing in Hitler's Germany where, in the spring of 1939, the regime was exterminating the disabled, persecuting Jewish business owners, expanding the *Kriegsmarine* [naval fleet], and preparing to invade Poland. In fact, speech synthesis research was deeply intertwined with encryption and military communication, though this was largely kept secret from the public.[38] At sites like Bell Labs (in "Project X" and "SIGSALY") and Bletchley Park (in "Delilah") researchers pursued a technology that would securely encrypt speech in earnest.

Both the American and Nazi militaries had very good machines for encrypting written communications (the Tunny, the G-Schreiber, the Enigma, etc.), but the early systems for encrypting *spoken* communications (inverters and scramblers) were highly insecure and easy to crack.[39] The Vocoder promised a much more secure method: each channel of analyzed speech frequencies was transformed into random noise with a one-time-use record produced by the Muzak corporation. On the other end, a duplicate Vocoder played a duplicate noise record completely in sync, providing a decoding key. Noise was removed, the transposed frequencies were returned to original frequencies, and the simplified speech was reconstructed by the oscillators and filters.[40] The Vocoder's simplified speech was easy to encode and decode, so long as the receiver possessed the right key; without this, it was nearly impossible to filter the message from random noise.

Although the Vocoder promised an essential advance in military communications, these particular functions were only hinted at in public. At least one American reporter mentioned that the machine could be used for " 'scrambling' messages in wartime,"[41] but quickly skipped on to the more enticing dimensions of movie sound effects. Dudley mostly deferred the question in his publications, vaguely saying in 1939 that applications may include "new types of privacy systems," but that further "engineering possibilities [. . .] are hard to predict at the present time."[42] By and large, the military dimensions of Vocoder technology remained hidden behind the façade of entertainment and domestic progress.

The military uses of the Vocoder and similar speech synthesis technologies were well known to Meyer-Eppler, given his participation in Nazi military science and engineering. His research reports for the U-boat division in 1943–1945 concerned sonar, electrical circuits, and wave transmissions, though toward war's end, his growing knowledge of signal extraction and information theory pointed directly toward voice encryption. In late 1959 and early 1960, in fact, he authored two further reports titled *Zur informationstheoretischen Systematik der geheimen Übermittlung von gesprochener Sprache* [An Information-Theoretic Classification for the Secret Transmission of Spoken Messages] and *Verfahren zur Sprachverschlüsselung* [Techniques of Ciphering].[43]

Despite this, the Vocoder's military entanglements (and likely Meyer-Eppler's personal entanglements) remained latent in Cold War electronic music and unknown to composers like Stockhausen and Kagel. If the war years necessitated exploring the secretive, militaristic aspects of speech synthesis technologies at government-sponsored research sites, then the postwar years offered much more freedom of application. Working with the same technologies, mathematical problems, and perceptual research as the Bell Labs engineers, Meyer-Eppler and the WDR studio composers repurposed wartime machinery and ideas for use in Cold War electronic music. The military dimensions remained invisible so long as Meyer-Eppler et al. could reclaim the technologies, theories, and sounds for artistic use. By focusing his attention on the artistic uses of the Vocoder and on the scientific advancement of phonetics, Meyer-Eppler kept the militaristic dimensions of his past all but invisible.

From Jakobson to Joyce

Beyond, or at least adjacent to, military engineering circles, another context in which the Vocoder and Voder were broadly important was structural linguistics. There were several lines of transmission among scholars who worked and moved freely between Bell Labs, Harvard, MIT, and other East Coast laboratories.[44] This is especially visible in the work of the Harvard-based phonologist Roman Jakobson. He was among a group of expat intellectuals—which also included Adorno—whom the American Rockefeller Foundation funded to undertake social, humanistic, and scientific research, with an eye toward nurturing wartime and Cold War superiority. Morris Halle, Jakobson's coauthor for the first section of *Fundamentals of Language* (1956), was a Harvard-trained linguist and student of Jakobson who went on to an influential career in generative phonology at MIT.[45] These two traveled in overlapping circles with many of the primary figures in linguistics as well as in military and communication engineering—including Claude Lévi-Strauss, Warren Weaver, Claude Shannon, and Norbert Wiener—all powerful scholars associated with the fast-growing, interdisciplinary information theory and cybernetics discourses.[46]

Jakobson's research moved from early investigations of the Russian language toward increasingly influential Saussurian generalizations in the mid-1950s and 1960s. As phonologists, Jakobson and Halle argued that phonetic sounds played a structural role in creating linguistic characteristics. In their view, the core structural identity of a language was sonic:

> This so-to-speak inner, immanent approach, which locates the distinctive features and their bundles within the speech sounds, be it on their motor, acoustical or auditory level, is the most appropriate premise for phonemic operations, although it has been repeatedly contested by outer approaches which in different ways divorce phonemes from concrete sounds.[47]

For Jakobson and Halle, linguistic structure cannot be disentangled from sound. Linguistic structure must be analyzed all the way back to the acoustical structure of the phonemes.[48] As a result, Jakobson and Halle devoted significant attention to sonic features such as the formant structures, noise bands, and timbre of vowels and consonants.

Jakobson and Halle's deep connections to acoustics made their linguistic arguments particularly susceptible to analogy with music:

> And just as musical form cannot be abstracted from the sound matter it organizes, so form in phonemics is to be studied in relation to the sound matter which the linguistic code selects, readjusts, dissects and classifies along its own lines. Like musical scales, phonemic patterning is an intervention of culture in nature, an artifact imposing logical rules upon the sound continuum.[49]

For Jakobson and Halle, as was said in Chapter 5, musical structure was the best metaphor for linguistic structure: musical forms organized raw acoustical stimuli into legible music in the same way that phonemes organized raw acoustical stimuli into legible languages.

Concepts like acoustical change along a sonic continuum—especially as a structural linguistic or musical principle—were central in both Jakobson and Halle's phonetic theories and the midcentury electronic studios. Furthermore, Jakobson and Halle's *Fundamentals of Language* was littered with the vocabulary of information theory: linguistic messages were conceptualized in terms of codes, and listeners were analogous to cryptanalysts.[50] As such, Jakobson and Halle understood phonemes, à la Claude Shannon, as "bits" of information, which had to be accurately transmitted and decoded in the mind of the listener in order to be intelligible. Jakobson and Halle's position—an explicit embrace of Shannon's concerns of message size, redundancy, encoding, and decoding—resonated strongly with the information-theoretic perspectives of midcentury electronic music composers.

Indeed, the WDR-affiliated composers probably encountered Jakobson and Halle's ideas, at least secondhand, by means of both Meyer-Eppler and the scholar and experimental composer Hans G. Helms.[51] A journalist and poet, Helms had studied with Jakobson at Harvard in the early 1950s. Meyer-Eppler's immersion in American speech synthesis discourses is evident in his 1959 book *Grundlagen und Anwendungen der Informationstheorie,* where he cites Jakobson and Halle among Gordon Peterson and Harold Barney and several other Bell Labs–affiliated researchers.[52] Perhaps even more important for the young composers was an influential peer-led James Joyce reading group—something of a secret society—that Helms hosted in his Cologne apartment in 1957.[53] In the context of Helms's reading group, Jakobson's linguistic, acoustic, and musical ideas were placed into dialogue with the WDR composers' studio experiments and the playful, multilinguistic prose of *Finnegans Wake.* In this way, both Jakobson's phonology and Joyce's experimental, deconstructed prose provided important intellectual touchstones for the composers' musical work. In fact, groups in both Cologne and Milan were simultaneously reading Joyce, studying structural and phonetic linguistics, and experimenting with the studio technology.

At the RAI studio in Milan in 1957, a second James Joyce reading group brought the composer Luciano Berio and the soprano Cathy Berberian (Berio's then-wife) together with the emerging literary scholar Umberto Eco.[54] Reading Joyce's *Ulysses* alongside Ferdinand de Saussure's *Cours de linguistique général,*[55] the three developed both a radio documentary and a related electronic music piece by deconstructing Berberian's recorded reading of the "Sirens" episode.[56] In 1958, Berio corresponded with phonetics researchers at the University of Milan, receiving a copy of a lecture called "Electroacoustic Analysis of the Consonants," which was delivered at the Italian Society for Experimental Phonetics.[57]

There was certainly dialogue between the Milan- and Cologne-based groups as well. The Italian composers had long internalized the central insights of Meyer-Eppler's work, both through their own encounters with him and their conversations with their Cologne-based colleagues. Bruno Maderna, who lived between Milan and Darmstadt, West Germany, in the 1950s, was among the first to experiment with electronic music in 1952 at Meyer-Eppler's office at the Phonetics Institute in Bonn as discussed in Chapter 1.[58] Letters exchanged by composers such as Stockhausen, Berio, and Pousseur show the constant exchange of technical, scientific, and musical ideas in the mid-to-late 1950s. Another example of the dialogue between West Germany and Italy is a pair of quite similar concerts—given in Cologne in March and Milan in June of 1958, respectively—which included several of the same phonetics–music pieces.[59] This exchange continued in 1959, when Maderna produced an electronic piece based on a phonetic text supplied by Helms. The constant written correspondence among several of the composers, as well as their frequent travel around Europe, reinforced the transmission of ideas between the groups.

The phonetics–music dialogue between the Cologne-based and Milan-based composers was particularly extended and rich because both scenes drew from the same pool of ingredients. In both locales, composers used the studio technology to create artistic responses to phonetics discourses. Composers were informed by extensive collaborations with literary and scientific intellectuals, who contextualized, extended, and corroborated their musical experiments. The sources for the Cold War phonetics–music works are multifaceted, not least because of the substantial overlap among linguistic, technological, and musical approaches to speech. The works incorporate a range of inspirations, especially because composers' musical studio experiments fit hand-in-glove with their concomitant explorations of literature, linguistics, scientific psychoacoustics, and speech synthesis technologies.

The Phonetic Nexus

This burgeoning discourse brings us to a fuller elaboration of the interdisciplinary nexus that is speech synthesis.[60] Beginning in the "Research" zone of Figure 6.5, experimental phonetics takes human vocal production as a foundational disciplinary question. Likewise, psychoacoustic research empirically studies the limits of human perception. These scientific investigations give much more insight into the function of the human body on their own, but are also called on to inform work in related "applied" scenarios.[61] In scenes such as the Macy Conferences, the Ratio Club, Harvard University, and the MIT Artificial Intelligence lab, we see considerable interpenetration between empirical laboratory research on the one hand and applied humanities, technology, and social-sciences contexts on the other hand.[62] Jakobson, for example, took his Harvard students to visit Bell Labs, because he understood the Vocoder as the technological complement to his phonology.[63] In short, research agendas are shaped internally by disciplinary discourses, but are also shaped by a feedback loop with adjacent spheres: Experimental phonetics research informed the evolution of phonetic and structural linguistics, and the research of linguists informed the newest experimental designs of scientists and the speech synthesis prototypes of engineers.

Proceeding to the "Engineering" zone of the figure, considering sites like Bell Labs, the rather fluid exchange among abstract, experimental research and more practical concerns continues. On the one hand, Bell Labs researchers were free—both by funding and corporate mandate—to explore theoretical questions that did not have an immediately apparent practical implication.[64] On the other hand, Bell Labs teams were simultaneously oriented

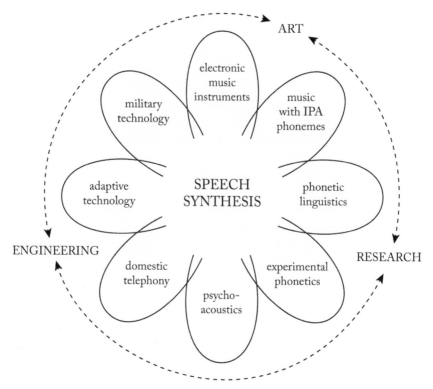

FIGURE 6.5. Speech synthesis at the intersection of a number of related constituencies.

toward solving AT&T's engineering and design problems. Domestically, engineers turned scientific research toward creating efficiencies in projects like the transcontinental and trans-Atlantic telephone network. Less visibly, research teams replicated the mechanisms of the human body with machines like the Vocoder, while simultaneously creating adaptive interventions like the "hearing glove" and "visible speech" spectrograms for Deaf and hard-of-hearing populations.[65] In secret but overlapping circles, engineers addressed the urgent problem of secure military communication.

In the "Art" zone of Figure 6.5, a similarly fluid exchange characterized the evolution of electronic music, which had long intermingled questions of perception, engineering design, and aesthetics. Early electronic music instruments materialized experimental scientific insights, often using similar electrical designs as contemporary communication technologies.[66] In some early recordings from the 1930s, the Trautonium—which operates by way of subtractive synthesis, or the filtering of complex sounds—was used to mimic vowel sounds, much like the Vocoder.[67] Likewise, the warbling vibrato of the Theremin, produced as the performer waves her hands in the magnetic field between two antennae, married human gesture with radio-broadcasting technology.[68]

In the Cold War era, the question was not whether electronic music instruments *could* make use of scientific discoveries and engineering advances—clearly instrument builders could and did do so; the question was whether it would be aesthetically interesting to do so. Many of the Weimar-era electronic instruments were used in musically retrogressive ways; the Theremin, Trautonium, and Ondes Martenot were used to play arrangements of old works (like those of Beethoven, Chopin, Schubert, Schumann, Strauss, etc.), or in some cases, new works that nevertheless mimicked nineteenth-century aesthetics and forms.

For the Cold War composers, then, the question was how phonetics and speech synthesis insights could lead to music that was *truly* new, genuinely avant-garde. The studio composers provoked audiences in their phonetics–music works, drawing listeners into a conceptually and philosophically rich sonic space that exposed several questions: How would the human interface with technologies in the electronic studio? What were the foundational seeds of linguistic meaning and structure? And even bigger, what did it mean to be a human being in such a technologically infused Cold War climate?

Abstraction and the Sonic Continuum

These questions arise and abate in several similar pieces, spread between electronic and acoustic formats and composed in both Cologne and Milan, to which we now turn our analytical attention. Let us begin in the WDR studio in 1958, where Mauricio Kagel directly adapted the scientific insights of Meyer-Eppler's phonetics in a pair of pieces apparently composed simultaneously: *Anagrama* (for vocal soloists, a speaking choir, and chamber ensemble) and *Transición I*.[69] Sketches suggest that the pieces are conceptually entangled.[70] On the one hand, sketches for the acoustic *Anagrama* include discussions of the noise generator, reverberation, filtering, and ring modulation; sketches for the electronic *Transición I*, on the other hand, include long digressions about phonetic sounds produced by a human voice—for example, the timbral and musical characteristics of vowels, voiced and unvoiced consonants, and International Phonetic Alphabet (IPA) charts.[71] This is evidence that Kagel was working with phonetics-to-music translations concomitantly in acoustic and electronic formats, exploring the same issues for both human vocalists and studio technology.

Kagel's interest in phonemes, in both electronic and acoustic contexts, relates heavily to timbral variation. As his illustration in Figure 6.6 shows, when one changes the vowel in the mouth, the timbre of the sound changes as well, even if the pitch does not. This allows for constantly morphing

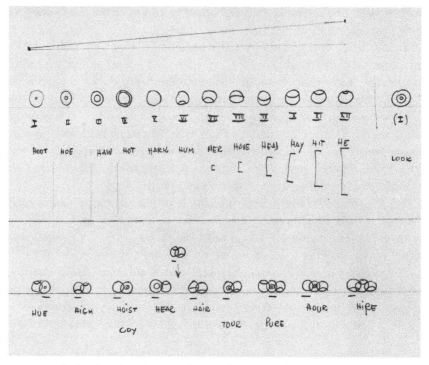

FIGURE 6.6. Kagel, *Anagrama*, sketch of vowel–timbre changes. Mauricio Kagel Collection, Paul Sacher Foundation.

timbral play with a wide range of possibilities; Figure 6.6 illustrates monothongs (single-sound vowels), diphthongs (two vowel sounds back to back) and trithongs (three vowel sounds back to back), graphing out the timbral changes induced by the mouth–filter.[72] This sketch strongly recalls the recorded vowel–timbre continuums (e.g., *u-ü-i-ü-u, o-ö-e-ö-o, u-o-a-o-u*) that Meyer-Eppler collected in his sonic archive and illustrated graphically in *Elektrische Klangerzeugung* (refer back to Figure 3.6), played at Darmstadt in 1950, and likely played in his subsequent seminars.[73] Kagel used these timbral vowel changes to create the music of both *Anagrama* and *Transición I*.

As Figure 6.7 shows, this morphing vowel-play appears near the end of the third movement of *Anagrama,* when we hear the singers performing timbral transformations on a single pitch by changing the sung vowel. As the written instructions indicate,

> Each vocal soloist sings on (and around) the same pitch until the end of the movement. He or she should perform continual transformations of vowels (with the exception of 'A') in different combinations and successions. The transformations between vowels are always formed differently: quickly, decelerating, slowly accelerating, and so on. Short

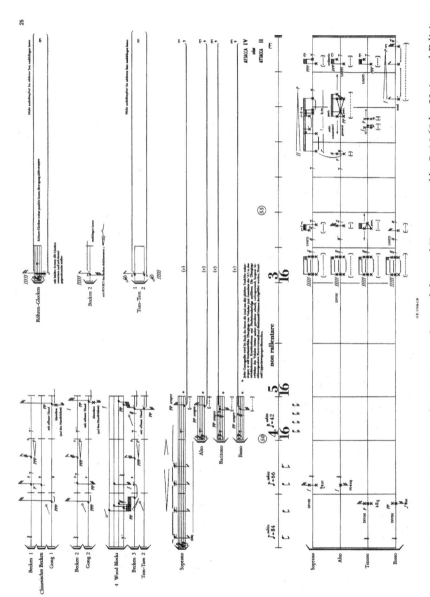

FIGURE 6.7. Kagel, *Anagrama für vier Gesangsoli, Sprechchor, und Kammerensemble.* © 1965 by Universal Edition (London) Ltd., London/UE 13106.

crescendos and diminuendos can be spread throughout; exaggerate mouth- and lip-movements.[74]

The electronic work *Transición I* opens with a similar effect, which, for about a minute, mixes "vowels" and "consonants" as listeners are led along the continuum between pitched tone and noise. Consider also the section of *Transición I* heard between 9:00 and 9:25, in which these morphing timbres are interrupted by pitched and percussive interjections. All this to say that Kagel extended the vowel–timbre insights of Meyer-Eppler through human singers and into the sonic space of the studio, in much the same way that Stockhausen described doing during the composition of *Gesang*. Linguistic phonemes—particularly timbrally rich vowel mixtures, but also noisy consonant interjections—became the raw sonic material for Kagel's electronic and acoustic music.

Berio and Berberian drew a similar sonic continuum out of their deconstruction of the "Sirens" episode of *Ulysses* while composing *Thema (Omaggio a Joyce)* at the RAI studio in 1958. Although *Thema* is a work for tape, it only manipulates Berberian's recorded voice and does not use any electronically produced sounds.[75] The prominent *s*-sound motive, however, obscures this fact, because it approximates the sounds of the noise generator. As Berio explained, "S—the basic colour of the whole piece, evidently very similar to a strip of white noise—could easily evolve into F, F into V, SZ into ZH, etc., using filters or adding a *fundamental* tone."[76] Figure 6.8, which relates vowels and consonants to different kinds of electronic sounds, fleshes out Berio's (and indeed Stockhausen's and Kagel's and Ligeti's) observations about the sonic analogies between electronic sounds and phonemes.[77] Noisy sounds (whether from an *s* sound or from noise generators) can be pushed toward more pitched sounds by narrowing the sound bands with filters or adding fundamentals, or pushed toward percussive interjections by means of layered impulses.

Notably, the noise-filtering process (subtractive synthesis) that Berio described to transform the *s* sound is exactly the process used by the Voder operator, who begins with a noise source from a generator and filters noise bands into the phonemes of speech. Whereas the Voder operator strove to

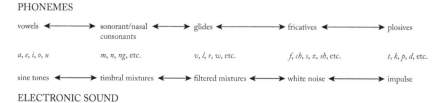

PHONEMES

vowels ⟷	sonorant/nasal ⟷ consonants	glides ⟷	fricatives ⟷	plosives
a, e, i, o, u	*m, n, ng*, etc.	*v, l, r, w*, etc.	*f, ch, s, z, sh*, etc.	*t, k, p, d*, etc.
sine tones ⟷	timbral mixtures ⟷	filtered mixtures ⟷	white noise ⟷	impulse

ELECTRONIC SOUND

FIGURE 6.8. Correspondences between types of phonemes (above) and sounds produced with common electronic studio equipment and techniques (below).

create intelligible phonemes and string them together into words, however, the composer often went in the opposite direction, abstracting and deconstructing speech. For the composer, the sonic continuum pictured in Figure 6.8 invited an artistic exploration of the space in between adjacent sounds. Artistically, it was interesting to play along this continuum, to explore the boundaries, and to thereby create a sonic dialogue between language and music.

As Berio, Berberian, and Eco believed, the electronic studio was—perhaps not surprisingly—the ideal place to explore these linguistic–musical deconstructions. "Through the means offered by electronic music," Berio later reflected, "we can push the integration and continuity between different acoustic structures to their extreme limit, and we can move from a *phenomenon* to a hypothesis and its demonstration—as well as the reverse."[78] The studio technology itself allowed the composer to get inside the acoustical features of the language in a crucial new way—to mine the language, extracting and isolating its raw materials. As Berberian further explained,

> The fact that with a tape-recorder you can record one or more sounds, isolate them from their context, listen to them as they are, a sound, modify and combine them with other acoustic elements from different contexts; all this has given the musician (and the singer) the possibility of a different listening of reality and of all those acoustic facts that normally would escape us."[79]

In the electronic studio, Berio and Berberian moved from a contextual phenomenon—phonemes in language—into a sensory–aesthetic hypothesis that was demonstrated with the help of technology. It was the studio's technology, and the tape recorder in particular, that allowed them to crack language open, to see what it really contained, and to imagine how it can be further deconstructed, synthesized, and remade as music.

Traces of the Human

For Berberian and Berio, as well as for Stockhausen and Kagel, electronic studio technologies like generators, filters, and tape recorders were agents of both deconstruction and reconstruction. On the one hand, *Anagrama* and *Thema* translate their inspirational nodes (phonetic linguistics, Meyer-Eppler's teachings, speech synthesis technologies) into pure, abstract sonic structure. On the other hand, the phonetics–music pieces sometimes play with signification. In *Thema*, for example, we also hear a range of Berberian's recognizably linguistic sounds, from intelligible phrases to deconstructed and isolated phonemes to linguistic onomatopoeias that mimic musical glissandi, appoggiaturas, and trills.[80] In using the recorded voice to develop the "latent polyphony" of Joyce's playful text, Berberian's sounds often remain obviously linguistic, gestural, and embodied.[81] Likewise, Kagel's *Anagrama* is full of the noisy by-products of speech, such as clicks, tongue fluttering, and lip smacks. In the opening two minutes of movement II, we hear hisses, buzzes, shouts, whoops, and isolated phonemes; in movement III, we hear laughing, tongue rolls, clicks, and warbles. These extra-linguistic sounds draw us in, pushing us to confront the odd sounds that can issue forth from human singers.

Kagel's compositional foundation in *Anagrama* is thoroughly wedded to that most human capacity: language. The piece is based on the palindromic Latin phrase *in girum imus nocte et consumimur igni* [we circle in the night and are consumed by fire].[82] Kagel used the palindrome's unique letters (*i, n, g, r, u, m, s, o, c, t,* and *e*) for an anagram, rearranging them to serially organize several of the musical parameters.[83] In the sketch page shown in Figure 6.9, Kagel used IPA and his knowledge of several languages to analyze timbral permutations of vowels *a, e, i, o, u*. (A similar chart exists for consonants in the anagram.) When it came to the composition, however, Kagel excluded the vowel sound *a* (as we saw in conjunction with the performance directions for Figure 6.7), concentrating exclusively on the phonetic sounds provided for by the anagram. As Kagel explained: "The phonemes make the anagram into a function of *evolution*. Phonetic structures develop and form the shape of the phonetic structures of Italian, French, etc."[84] Kagel viewed phonetic

FIGURE 6.9. Kagel, *Anagrama*, phonetics chart. Mauricio Kagel Collection, Paul Sacher Foundation.

sounds of the anagram as the *Ur*-seeds from which linguistic and quasi-linguistic utterances could be formed; in a process of recombination, the piece uses various nonsense utterances of consonants and vowels (CVC, VCV, etc.), alongside interjections in German, French, Spanish, and English.[85]

Another such example of semisensical linguistic play is Bruno Maderna's electronic piece *Dimensioni II*, later titled *Invenzione su una voce* [*Invention on a Voice*].[86] Maderna recorded Berberian performing an IPA text written by Helms, likely giving her free reign to vary pitch, inflection, and timbre.[87] He then further manipulated Berberian's voice with tape techniques, such as drastically speeding up and slowing down the tape. The piece begins with ambiguous squeaks, soon revealed to be Berberian's laughter played at high speed, and ends with Berberian's voice being played so slowly that she sounds like a man. In this way, the piece concatenates *musique concrète* moments, in which the sonic polyphony arises from Berberian's defamiliarized speech, with *elektronische Musik* interjections (including reverberant sine tone flourishes and mixtures reminiscent of Stockhausen's *Gesang der Jünglinge*).[88]

As expected, given Helms's phonetic text, we hear isolated phonemes or consonant strings (e.g., "*tkssss, hmmmm*," 2:33–2:36), but we also hear snippets that recall languages like French ("*me suis châle je que le*," 3:57–4:01) and English ("*good-good*," 12:13–12:27). The piece's faux-linguistic plurality resembles Helms's own contemporaneous *Fa:m' Ahniesgwow* (1959), a spoken-word piece produced at the WDR studio.[89] It also recalls the linguistic plurality so characteristic of Joyce's *Ulysses* and *Finnegans Wake*, the texts these collaborators were reading together.

Like many of the phonetics–music works, the emotional tenor of *Dimensioni II* varies wildly, from laughter and spurious cartoon-like quips, to an aggressive, angry climax (12:40–14:55) that places Berberian's voice at the center of an unrelenting, abusive, noisy melee. The provocative emotional landscape of this and related pieces—for example, Berberian and Berio's *Visage* (1961) and Ligeti's *Aventures* (1962–65)—can be traced to at least two causes.[90] One is that composers push the boundary between linguistic absurdity and signification. Traces of language anchor the pieces in the human dimension, where recombining phonemes remains a distinctly human form of play. Yet in eschewing syntax, most of these works overthrow the comfort that comes with intelligibility, leaving the listener instead with a sound poetry of strange, quasi-linguistic sounds combined in baffling and absurd ways. In many listeners, this provokes feelings of confusion, frustration, alienation, and even disgust. We feel destabilized when works retain several of the gestural, emotive, and phonetic traces of language, with little of the syntax: the human body remains, but it is emptied of a mind.

These works likewise provoke in a second way: by blurring the distinct separation between humans and their technologies. In pieces like *Thema, Dimensioni II*, and *Visage*, the human voice, and by extension Berberian's body, is at times overwhelmed by the noisy, violent, intrusive techno-logical sounds.[91] This recalls the critic of *Gesang der Jünglinge* (quoted in the Introduction), who was horrified by the way the "God-given voice of Man" was trampled, invaded, and debased by the "perverse manipulations" of the studio's technologies.[92] The electronic works bring the human voice into contact with technologies that threaten to damage or even obliterate it, activating Cold War technophobic anxieties. These pieces are not just about pure sonic continuums, but about the way in which the human voice—in this case, Berberian's voice—interacts with the technologies of the studio. The human body remains only as a shell, as a vessel within which the machinery can do its work.

This kind of substitution characterizes speech synthesis technologies like the Voder and Vocoder, where, behind the screen of the Voderettes' youthful bodies, generators speak in place of the larynx and filters replace the mouth. For electronic music composers, the filters of the studio could stand in for the human body, and the human body could replace the studio machinery. As Ligeti said about the quasi-linguistic utterances of *Artikulation*, "Do you see how similar it is to speech? [. . .] My mouth is a filter. There is not much difference between an electronic filter and a mouth filter."[93] This body–machine interchangeability is premised, as Jakobson argued, on the fact that the baseline acoustical features of a language—its phonetic structure—can be analyzed and replicated by electronic machinery.

The question is not whether the Vocoder can replace human speech, but what would be lost if we were to allow such a replacement. Technically, the Vocoder can and does speak for the human. But it is distressing to imagine that this means the Vocoder can replace the human: the machine is cold—it lacks inflection, it lacks gesture, it lacks body. Moreover, the Vocoder was encoded, if invisibly, with the ambivalent residues of its military entanglements. At the cultural moment of the Cold War, speech synthesis was intriguing, but also a bit dangerous. In using speech synthesis technologies, the implicit question is this: If we give our speech to a machine, do we give away our humanity?

The Woman in the Machine

It is with these anxieties in mind that we turn toward Cathy Berberian's role as the central collaborator for a whole subset of phonetics pieces produced in and around the RAI studio in the late 1950s and 1960s.[94] Berberian was no doubt an iconic voice, a muse, and a prodigious collaborator on par with David Tudor.[95] In the characterizations of studio technician Marino Zuccheri and musicologist David Osmond-Smith, she was in fact the RAI studio's most important technology, its "tenth oscillator."[96] Recall that Alfredo

Lietti, who reconstructed oscillators and filters by hand from discarded wartime broadcasting machinery, stocked the RAI studio with much unique equipment.[97] The fact that Berberian's voice appears in nearly every piece to emerge from the RAI studio is reason enough to think of her as the tenth oscillator, but in examining John Cage's *Fontana Mix* and *Aria* more carefully, we can see that Berberian actually functions as a human simulacrum of the studio equipment.

Cage composed both *Aria* and *Fontana Mix* at the RAI studio between November 1958 and March 1959, the same time during which Berio, Berberian, Eco, and the technician Zuccheri collaborated on *Thema*.[98] To create *Fontana Mix,* Cage and Zuccheri ambled about the city with a microphone and tape recorder, harvesting sound from the Duomo, the tram, the zoo, and so on.[99] Cage then catalogued and modified his *concrète* sound materials according to graphic transparencies that he produced (see Figure 6.10), which offered spatial, geometric coordinates for mapping onto variables such as frequency, amplitude, and duration.[100] As a final step, Cage and Zuccheri montaged *Fontana Mix* from the tiny fragments that Cage cut from the original tapes.[101] The result is noisy and chaotic, reflecting the extensive montage process that was familiar to Cage from his work in the Barron studio in the early 1950s, and which was also contemporaneously important to Berio and Maderna.[102]

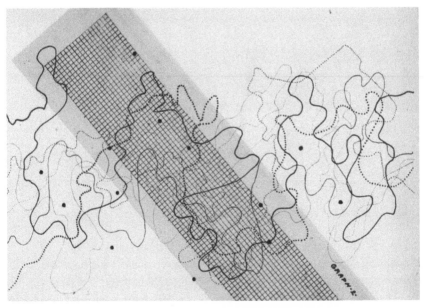

FIGURE 6.10. Cage, *Fontana Mix* (1959), showing superimposed line sketch, dot map, and graph for measuring. © 1960 by Henmar Press, Inc. Used by permission of C.F. Peters Corporation. All rights Reserved.

So far, Cage's compositional process had not used Berberian's voice or the nine oscillators and special filters that were uniquely available at the RAI. Cage incorporated more of these resources, however, by means of a strong connection with Berberian in *Aria*, an entirely acoustic piece composed—and often performed—simultaneously with *Fontana Mix*.[103] Both *Aria* and *Fontana Mix* feature montage as a central technique, yet scholars have generally paid less attention to *Aria* and Berberian's role in producing it than they have to the indeterminate, graphic superimpositions of *Fontana Mix*. James Pritchett and David Nicholls, for instance, are highly attentive to the ways that the graphic notation Cage pioneered in *Fontana Mix* is a "tool" for structuring sound (see Figure 6.10) but give no attention to the way that Berberian's voice is similarly exploited by Cage as a tool in *Aria*.[104] In reality *Aria* and *Fontana Mix* are acoustic and electronic sides of the same coin.

Aria rockets among linguistic excerpts in Armenian (Berberian's ethnic heritage), Russian, Italian, French, and English, along with occasional isolated phonemes.[105] The colors shown in the score excerpt of Figure 6.11 represent different singing styles—blue = jazz, red = contralto, orange = oriental, yellow = coloratura, purple = Marlene Dietrich, and so on—and the wavy lines represent approximate pitch and pacing for the phrases. Black squares

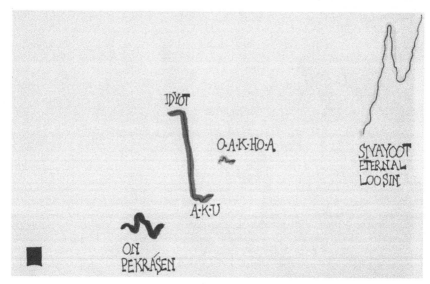

FIGURE 6.11. Cage, *Aria* (1958), score, p.5. Pitch and duration are indeterminate and relative, based on singer's interpretation of wavy lines. Black square represents extra-musical noise; ON PEKRASEN in the style of jazz, IDYOT to A.K.U in the style of contralto, O.A.K.HO.A in an "oriental" style, and STYAYOOT ETERNAL LOOSIN in the style of coloratura. © 1960 by Henmar Press, Inc. Used by permission of C.F. Peters Corporation. All rights Reserved.

indicate the nonlinguistic or extra-musical noises—including clicks, hoots, sighs, and exclamations ranging from sexual pleasure to disgust (for which Berberian would become famous by the time of her own *succès de scandale* composition, *Stripsody* [1966]).[106] Already in *Aria*, though, Berberian was performing "human tape-montage," spitting out fragments in various languages and styles.

In *Aria*, Berberian codified a technique that would become her artistic signature.[107] Berberian's "vocal mimesis" reembodied the otherwise cold, inhuman studio machinery.[108] She was perhaps a bit like a human Vocoder, but she was, of course, much more prodigious. If visitors to the 1939 World's Fair were surprised that Pedro the Voder could speak, Cold War composers were equally surprised at the fidelity with which Berberian could recreate tape montages. Her virtuosity, coupled with her voracious exploration of all the sounds a human voice can make, superseded the studio's idiosyncratic and unusual generators and filters to become its most important sonic resource.

That her voice was contained within a young woman's body was no doubt central to the fascination.[109] Berberian not only rehumanized the studio's technology, but, more broadly, she performed a gendered neutralization of speech synthesis technologies, a neutralization that the Voderettes also performed as they operated the robotic voice of the Voder. Composers and listeners were free to be curious about the Voder, or about the studio's machines, because they could so easily read the Voderettes and Berberian as safe, domestic substitutes for an otherwise unfamiliar and vaguely threatening technology. Performing her amazing mimesis, Berberian was like the machines, only better.

Conclusions

The composers' embrace of phonetics and linguistics discourses at the WDR and RAI studios further fueled their longtime preoccupations with acoustics and timbre. The studio technology, Meyer-Eppler's teachings, and James Joyce's literature combined to catalyze both linguistic deconstructions and reconstructions. Composers obsessively used the technologies at hand—including tape, generators and filters, and Berberian's voice—to "crack open" linguistic sounds and to "hear inside" them. In the experimental artistic space of the studio, composers used musical experiments to unmoor themselves from linguistic syntax and explore provocative recombinations, challenging human sounds, and nonsense sonic poetry.

In their investigations of phonetics and speech synthesis, the European avant-garde composers, though only in a glancing blow, encountered technologies and discourses that were central to the military. To take a Kittlerian line of questioning, does it matter in the Cold War era that both magnetic tape and the Vocoder had been military technologies?[110] Does it matter whether Stockhausen, Kagel, Ligeti, Berio, and others knew of Meyer-Eppler's military entanglements? Are residues of violence sedimented into speech synthesis discourses, even when those dimensions remained latent and veiled? And need the midcentury avant-garde composers grapple with such ambivalence?[111]

These are questions that are answerable only on a speculative level, if at all. I would not argue linearly that the Vocoder embodies military residues and that the avant-garde composers responded to this sedimentation. Instead it is more useful to pivot into a networked perspective that explores the consequences of the interdisciplinary speech synthesis nexus (see Figure 6.5). One observation that we definitely can make is that Dudley, Meyer-Eppler, and others who knew about the Vocoder's military dimensions repeatedly foregrounded its civilian and artistic uses. Over and over, those who knew about the secret projects of encryption deferred the question, perhaps because those projects were classified. Instead they discussed improvements to the domestic telephone network, imagined the Vocoder as an adaptive technology, used beautiful young women as an entertaining veneer, and pointed out its many connections to electronic music.

These kinds of deflections were easy, insofar as the phonetics nexus was always rife with overlapping interests. Technologies like the Vocoder, though they may have started as military engineering projects, were never simply performing one function. As a technology like the Vocoder moved to the center of an interdisciplinary nexus, its embeddedness in any one disciplinary corner was weakened. Although the Vocoder, like information theory, was connected simultaneously to the military, to domestic communication engineering, to avant-garde music, and to structural linguistics, the specifics of any one of these histories could be easily veiled and neutralized. Despite its many possible attachments, it was defined by none of them. The users of the Vocoder could claim or deny any of the attachments, re-creating the meaning of the machine with each new use. The technology became raw material available to anyone, fodder for reappropriation.

The electronic music discussed in this chapter played an important role in this Cold War cultural process of neutralizing technologies. When composers used speech synthesis technologies and phonetics discourses in their music, the civilian, military, and adaptive applications remained hidden behind the curtain, as it were. In aestheticizing speech synthesis, Cold War avant-garde music performed an effacement somewhat similar to the neutralization performed by the Voderettes. The works discussed here translated phonetic concepts into pure sonic structure, infused them with the aesthetic trappings of high-art music, and domesticated them with Berberian's body and voice.

Despite the success of these cultural pivots, screens, and neutralizations, the reclamations of Cold War electronic music are in no way airtight. The phonetics–music pieces under discussion here exhibit many moments of perilous slippage. Their absurdity, their nonsensical recombinations, and their anxiety-producing provocations all point toward the tenuousness of the project of domesticating artificial speech. Stockhausen's *Gesang der Jünglinge* sonically grapples with the relationships between the human and the machine, between the sacred and the profane. Kagel's *Anagrama* and Ligeti's *Aventures* goad the listener between the extremes of sonic abstraction and theatrical absurdity. Berio's, Maderna's, and Cage's works deconstruct and threaten to obliterate Berberian's voice on the one hand, and use her gendered prodigiousness to buttress their technological experimentation on the other. These pieces make Cold War anxieties audible, stoking the latent discomforts of a culture both technologically saturated and technologically phobic.

Like the interdisciplinary cross-currents of phonetics, it is impossible to wipe away such musical ambivalences. It is as if the composers are asking, "If we humans are going to have to live with/among/between such technological impositions in our lives, how can we regain control? How can we get the machines to work for *us*?" Listeners may wish for a sure, reassured response to these anxious questions, but the phonetics–music works fail to provide it. Instead, these works lay bare our fundamental humanness—which is to say we encounter our human failures to cope with the implications of the machines. When we listen to the phonetics–music works, we often cannot decode the tangle that has been put before us. We stumble over the nonsense, we are disgusted by hearing all that which is extra-musical, and we are provoked by sounds that threaten to obliterate and overwhelm.

These moments of imperfect reclamation—the partially failed attempts to aestheticize, domesticize, and neutralize speech synthesis—make these works provocative and essential. Language remains a fundamental human trait. When the Cold War composers situated us in the speech synthesis nexus, they provoked an ongoing investigation of the intersections of bodies and machines. They asked us to consider the cultural work that electronic music might do, as it sonified the feedback loop between artistic products and military empires. That the phonetics–music works only partially succeed as music, and only partially succeed as reclamations, is evidence of the fraught nature of such a complex process of neutralization and domestication. Attempted, incomplete, tenuous: these are the cultural reclamations of Cold War electronic music.

| Epilogue

This book has argued that electronic music studios performed essential cultural work in the Cold War era. The WDR and RAI studios embraced the progressive rhetoric of the cultural Cold War, reaping institutional funding and revivifying radio stations that had previously been Fascist propaganda centers. Composers, working together with their invisible collaborators, domesticated military technologies like the Vocoder, noise and sine tone generators, and magnetic tape, repurposing them for the dream of creating high-art music out of brand-new sounds. Most important, studios reclaimed the core tenets of wartime discourses—information theory, cybernetics, and experimental phonetics—as the conceptual foundation of their compositional projects. I would not say that the military–industrial–research complex drove innovation in electronic music; and yet, the midcentury studios' tools, technologies, and discourses were dialogically linked to innovations in science, communication technology, and military engineering.

The WDR and other electronic music studios were heterogeneous networks, which imbricated institutional priorities, technologies, scientific discourses, aesthetic paradigms, and different kinds of professionals. The studio's institutional culture—its greatest asset—replicated the collaborative structure familiar from wartime and Cold War laboratories. Fred Turner could have been speaking about the WDR studio when he wrote,

> In the research laboratories of World War II and later, in the massive military engineering projects of the Cold War, scientists, soldiers, technicians, and administrators broke down the walls of bureaucracy and collaborated as never before. As they did, they embraced both computers and a new cybernetic rhetoric of systems and information. They began to imagine institutions as living organisms, social

networks as webs of information, and the gathering and interpretation of information as keys to understanding not only the technical but also the natural and social worlds.[1]

In Turner's telling, scientific–military research labs such as MIT's Rad Lab, AT&T's Bell Labs, and Stanford's Artificial Intelligence Lab were sites of innovation precisely because they were "free-wheeling, interdisciplinary, and highly entrepreneurial."[2]

The same could be said of both institutional and private electronic music studios, which were loci of experimentation for intellectuals and artists, whether in Europe, Asia, South America, or the United States. At Bell Labs, for example, engineers John Pierce and Max Mathews engaged in a deep dialogue with composers such as Lejaren Hiller, James Tenney, Jean Claude Risset, and John Chowning, who together used early computers to synthesize timbres and compose music. These interactions informed the technoscientific research paradigms that were then pushed further at computer music centers such as IRCAM in Paris, CCRMA at Stanford, and the Experimental Music Studio at the University of Illinois, among others.[3]

Likewise, collaboration defined the San Francisco Bay area scene in the 1960s. The composers Pauline Oliveros, Morton Subotnik, and Ramon Sender developed their experimental aesthetics in dialogue with several countercultural interlocutors, as well as with instrument builder Don Buchla, whose penchant for physics and NASA engineering projects informed his modular electronic music system.[4] Robert Moog's synthesizers were informed by a similarly heterogeneous network, which included high-art composers, popular music performers, electrical engineers, and sales and marketing professionals.[5] Electronic music benefited from the funding, space, technology, and ideas culled from Cold War military and industrial interests, to be sure; but studios were sites of innovation when they synthesized the contributions of their various technologies and human actors.

Cold War electronic music certainly drew from related spheres such as phonetics, architecture, and communications engineering, but it also fed back into them. For instance, electronic music continued to inform experimental phonetics in the latter half of the twentieth century in Cologne and elsewhere. Georg Heike, one of Meyer-Eppler's students and successors at the Phonetics Institute in Bonn, continued a direct dialogue with the WDR studio composers after Meyer-Eppler's death in 1960, publishing articles that drew further connections between the principles of information theory and serial music.[6] Heike's mid-1970s and 1980s research on a digital speech synthesizer, undertaken while he was the director of the Cologne Phonetics Institute, plumbed the connections among speech, phonemes, and music.[7] The musical techniques and aesthetic commitments of the WDR studio and the European avant-garde informed Heike's scientific research agenda.

This rich cross-pollination continues in the "synthrumentation" of Clarence Barlow, an avant-garde composer associated for some time with a second-generation Cologne circle.[8] In synthrumentation (a portmanteau of synthesis and instrumentation), Barlow uses the acoustic instruments of the orchestra to imitate vowel and consonant sounds.[9] Likewise, the composer Peter Ablinger uses the piano to replicate speech, playing on the brain's willingness to infer linguistic continuities and *Gestalten* from suggestively incomplete frequency spectra.[10] On the one hand, in their music, composers such as Barlow and Ablinger create acoustic, instrumental Vocoders. Contemporary cognitive scientists, on the other hand, use musical knowledge, aesthetic norms, and computer music discourses to shape research agendas, experimental design, and software.[11]

Adjacent to these technoscientific exchanges, midcentury electronic music's effects likewise reverberated in artistic and cultural domains. A brief vignette, analyzing the architectural designs that Rainer Fleischhauer and Jörn Janssen published in the seventh volume of *Die Reihe*, can further illuminate the Cold War cultural stakes.[12] The two architects had spent several lunches in the WDR canteen, fruitfully exchanging ideas with Koenig and Stockhausen. In the resulting "Project for 200,000 Inhabitants" the architects imagined "a solution for the re-building of Karlsruhe after its destruction in 1944."[13] The eight-and-a-half-mile-long city—inspired by Stockhausen's melding of space and time—integrated music, literature, art, science, and technology with community-oriented living. Electronic music, with its integrated, serial logic, informed both the spatial proportions and the conceptual modeling of daily life in this hopeful, reconstructed city.

In the new Karlsruhe, a single, large, communal electronic music and art studio supplanted the theater, the opera house, and the concert hall— institutions that were obsolete in the technologically obsessed Cold War world. The studio, meant to be "used alike by the audiences and the performers and their instruments," was both a private research lab and public performance space, where amateurs and professionals could meet for technological experimentation, collaboration, and exchange.[14] One can imagine laypeople gathering here to "play composer," perhaps to montage a new version of *Scambi* from Pousseur's source materials; and then the amateur composers become the audience as their iteration is projected—with accompanying images, even—into the present space and time.

Fleischhauser and Janssen's rendering capitalized on electronic music's multiple functions: the WDR's basement-level "emergency studio" was a hedge against the nuclear reality of the Cold War, but in the meantime used for producing avant-garde music and spoken word; the RAI studio's machines were assembled from discarded wartime broadcasting equipment and used to produce radio dramas that were only lightly revised into electronic music compositions. The boundaries of electronic music were constantly blurred, as use value for both technologies and artistic products fluctuated in various spheres.

Far from resisting such cross-currents, the studio centralized and managed them. As Reinhold Martin argues, architectural spaces are a powerful conduit for manifesting such organizational patterns and social values: "The system's phantasmagorias [. . .] constitute an indelibly real system of images, with indelibly real consequences."[15] Fleischhauer and Janssen's utopian plans materialize the logic of the cultural Cold War. The studio is a place where technologically inflected art-making infuses daily life. In the Cold War imagination, the studio is the place to address and redress relationships among technology, art, culture, and society, thereby advancing the human condition.

Such quixotic visions gesture toward the emergence of an interdisciplinary, practice-based avant-garde in the 1960s.[16] Although the WDR studio—and other institutionally funded centers like the Darmstadt Summer Courses and the Donaueschingen festival—remained important as steady patrons of new music, experimental electronic music became increasingly possible in home-based, privately funded, and contingent spaces. With the rise of collectives such as MEV (*Musica Elettronica Viva*), AMM (a British free-improvisation group), the Scratch Orchestra, Fluxus, and the like, avant-garde innovations transitioned, at least in part, to (semi-)private sites. In Cologne and elsewhere, electronic music composers and artists began gathering in alternative spaces, such as Helms's reading circle in his home, Mary Bauermeister's *atelier*, or Galerie 22 in Düsseldorf.[17] Artistic interdisciplinarity has long defined avant-garde communities, but in the second half of the twentieth century, electronic music's new technological scenarios pushed the experimental, collaborative ethos even further.

Part and parcel of this evolution was the audible migration of sounds and techniques through an increasingly porous high-art–low-art divide.[18] It has by now become a matter of cultural lore that the Beatles drew on electronic music, including that by Stockhausen and Berio, on albums such as *Revolver* (1966) and *Sgt. Pepper's Lonely Hearts Club Band* (1967).[19] Avant-garde electronic music and experimentation with synthesizers had far-reaching effects on rock artists such as the Beach Boys, Frank Zappa, Jefferson Airplane, the Grateful Dead, Stevie Wonder, Emerson, Lake & Palmer, Can, Tangerine Dream, and Kraftwerk.[20] Electronic sound, enabled by synthesizers, likewise became increasingly ubiquitous in film scores and television advertisements.[21]

The timbral utopia dreamed up at the WDR studio became the driving force behind the evolution of much high-art music, too. Composers took electronic ideas into the acoustic realm as a way of mitigating breakdowns, frustrations, and failures, as well as capitalizing on studio epiphanies. Spectralism owes much to the timbral synthesis projects imagined and begun in the WDR studio and carried much further at Bell Labs and IRCAM in the 1970s and 1980s. New Complexity engages in a dialogue with the perceptual and performative limits first transcended thanks to studio technologies, whereas Minimalism makes extensive use of tape music's samples and loops. These are broad strokes, to be sure; we do not need to posit that the WDR studio is the fountainhead of every interesting development of the latter half of the twentieth century. It is clear, however, that the ideas, techniques, and sounds of Cold War electronic music proliferated outward in a series of ripples.

More speculatively, Cold War electronic music sonified the culture's psychological repressed, disclosing much more than deeply held aesthetic convictions.[22] The analog electronic studio brought wartime detritus out into the aesthetic sphere, exposing but also salving cultural wounds. Electronic music sonified the optimistic striving of the Cold War moment, attempting to quell anxious and fearful murmurs with its domesticizing, containing, and repurposing. Electronic studios soothed old wounds in a backward-looking catharsis and, at the same time, created forward-looking dreams of a new musical and social order. Such cultural work, as Tara Rodgers suggests, is at the core of the concept and metaphor of "synthesis."[23] The cultural work of electronic music stemmed from its unending dance with the affordances of technologies. The analog studio of the 1950s is one rich chapter that illuminates the dynamic impacts of electronic music, but it is not the end. The story of the profound consequences of electronic music will continue to be told.

Introduction

1. This anecdote relies on details supplied by Gottfried Michael Koenig in interview with the author in May 2015 and in private email communication on June 9, 2016. See Iverson, "From Analog to Digital," 43–55.

2. The WDR studio's equipment will be installed at the Haus Mödrath—Räume für Kunst beginning in early 2019. http://www.haus-moedrath.de/de/studio.html (accessed July 29, 2017).

3. Chadabe, *Electric Sound*; Holmes, *Electronic and Experimental Music*; Manning, *Electronic and Computer Music*.

4. Adorno, "The Curves of the Needle," 271–76; Benjamin, "The Work of Art in the Age of Mechanical Reproduction," 217–51; Rothenbuhler and Peters, "Defining Phonography: An Experiment in Theory," 242–64; Hayles, *How We Became Posthuman*; Katz, *Capturing Sound*; Sterne, *The Audible Past*; Sterne, *MP3*; Taylor, *Strange Sounds*; Taylor, Katz, and Grajeda, eds., *Music, Sound, and Technology in America*; Volmar, "Listening to the Cold War," 80–102.

5. Beal, *New Music, New Allies*; Shreffler, "Berlin Walls," 498–525; Shreffler, " 'Music Left and Right,' " 67–87; Shreffler, "Cold War Dissonance," 40–60; Taruskin, *The Oxford History of Western Music*, vol. 5, 1–54.

6. Birdsall, *Nazi Soundscapes*; Bohlman, *Jewish Music and Modernity*; Currid, *A National Acoustics*; Kater, *The Twisted Muse*; Lacey, *Feminine Frequencies*; Potter, *Most German of the Arts*; Rehding, "Magic Boxes and *Volksempfänger*," 255–71. Useful counterpoints from the French situation include Fulcher, *The Composer as Intellectual* and Fulcher, "French Identity in Flux," 261–95.

7. Baade, *Victory Through Harmony*; Fauser, *Sounds of War*; Sprout, *The Musical Legacy of Wartime France*.

8. Calico, " 'Für eine neue deutsche Nationaloper,' " 190–204; Fosler-Lussier, *Music Divided*; Kelly, *Composing the Canon in the German Democratic Republic*.

9. Carroll, *Music and Ideology in Cold War Europe*; Fosler-Lussier, *Music in America's Cold War Diplomacy*; Fulcher, *Renegotiating French Identity*; Mesch, *Art and Politics*; Rosen, "Music and the Cold War"; Ross, *The Rest Is Noise*, 373–446; Rubin, *Archives of Authority*; Saunders, *The Cultural Cold War*; Schlosser, *Cold War on the Airwaves*; Taruskin, "Afterword: Nicht blutbefleckt?" 274–84.

10. Potter, *The Art of Suppression*.

11. Willson, *Ligeti, Kurtág, and Hungarian Music During the Cold War*; Fosler-Lussier, *Music Divided*; Daughtry, "Sonic Samizdat," 27–65; Schmelz, *Such Freedom, If Only Musical*; Silverberg, "Between Dissonance and Dissidence," 44–84; Thomas, *Polish Music Since Szymanowski*.

12. A point strongly advocated in Schmelz, "Introduction: Music in the Cold War," 3–16. The nuanced, regional terms of various cultural Cold Wars are well demonstrated in the eight articles in the Winter 2009 and Spring 2009 issues of *Journal of Musicology*.

13. Three sensitive, multifaceted portraits of the *Stunde Null* moment in music are Beal, *New Music, New Allies*, 11–23; Mosch, "'Freiheit war es immer, die er meinte,'" 111–26; and Potter, *The Art of Suppression*, 123–29. For personal reflections, see Wapnewski, "1945: Wie der Anfang anfing," 13–27; and Cahn, "Zur Musikgeschichte der 40er und frühen 50er Jahre," 28–39.

14. Davidson and Hake, eds., *Framing the Fifties*; Fehrenbach, *Cinema: Democratizing Germany, Reconstructing National Identity*; Shandley, *Rubble Films*.

15. Herf, *Divided Memory*; Jarausch, *After Hitler*; Wolf, *The Undivided Sky*.

16. Fulcher, *Renegotiating French Identity*; Jacobsen, *Operation Paperclip*; Monod, *Settling Scores*; Potter, *Most German of the Arts*, 235–65; Potter, *The Art of Suppression*, 90–123; Thacker, *The End of the Third Reich*; Thacker, *Music After Hitler 1945–55*.

17. Calico, *Arnold Schoenberg's* A Survivor from Warsaw *in Post-War Europe*; Sprigge, "Abilities to Mourn"; Sprigge, "Tape Work and Memory Work"; Wlodarski, *Musical Witness and Holocaust Representation*. To acknowledge the Holocaust trauma and to memorialize victims in artworks was complicated and difficult. Recall Adorno's famous dictum that "to write poetry after Auschwitz is barbaric" ("Cultural Criticism and Society," 21); and likewise Elie Wiesel's suggestion that "just as no one could imagine Auschwitz before Auschwitz, no one could now retell Auschwitz after Auschwitz" (*From the Kingdom of Memory*, 166).

18. Bohlman, ed. *Jewish Musical Modernism, Old and New*; Frühauf and Hirsch, eds. *Dislocated Memories*; Young, *Writing and Rewriting the Holocaust*; Young, *The Texture of Memory*; Young, *At Memory's Edge*.

19. Beal, "Negotiating Cultural Allies," 105–39; Borio and Danuser, eds., *Im Zenit der Moderne*; Iddon, *New Music at Darmstadt*; Kordes, "Darmstadt, Postwar Experimentation, and the West German Search for a New Musical Identity," 205–17.

20. Berio, "Luciano Berio, Umberto Eco, and Roberto Leydi Remember," 226.

21. Badenoch, *Voices in Ruins*, 1.

22. Heinrich-Franke, "Airy Curtains," 158–79; Holt, *Radio Free Europe*; Paulu, *Radio and Television Broadcasting on the European Continent*; Schlosser, *Cold War on the Airwaves*.

23. Beal, "The Army, the Airwaves, and the Avant-Garde," 487–90; Dussel, "Radio Programming, Ideology, and Cultural Change," 80–94.

24. Gilfillan, *Pieces of Sound*; Badenoch, *Voices in Ruins*; Wolf, *The Undivided Sky*.

25. Otto Tomek, "Avantgarde in kulturellem Auftrag: Der Rundfunk und die Neue Musik," in *ARD Jahrbuch 1969*, 50; quoted in Handke, *Präsenz und Dynamik regionaler Musikkulturen*, 87.

26. *Am Puls der Zeit*, vol. 1; Custodis, *Die soziale Isolation der neuen Musik*, 53–75; Hilberg and Vogt, eds., *Musik der Zeit; Klangraum: 40 Jahre Neue Musik in Köln*; Schütte, *Die Westdeutsche Funkstunde*.

27. Short histories of the studio include Chadabe, *Electric Sound*, 35–42; Cross, "Electronic Music 1948–1953," 45–53; Hilberg and Vogt, eds., *Musik der Zeit*, 125–45; Holmes, *Electronic and Experimental Music*, 63–69; Manning, *Electronic and Computer Music*, 39–67; and Morawska-Büngeler, *Schwingede Elektronen*, 7–19.

28. My use of terms like network, node, and hub loosely references a growing body of sociological and cultural theory. For more, see Jagoda, *Network Aesthetics*. Similar research on the WDR network is underway: Romão, "After Mapping the Avant-Garde."

29. Aguila, *Le Domaine Musical*.

30. Most of the correspondence remains unpublished but can be consulted in composers' individual collections at archives such as the Paul Sacher Foundation, the Stockhausen Foundation, and the Akademie der Künste. Much of John Cage's correspondence, including that with Boulez and others, has been published. See Nattiez, ed., *The Boulez-Cage Correspondence*, and Kuhn, ed., *The Selected Letters of John Cage*.

31. Custodis, *Die soziale Isolation*, 54–55. I use WDR throughout this book for simplicity, as the electronic studio was always located in the Cologne station.

32. The names of Schaeffer's studio (and the Paris national radio) underwent several permutations—during wartime, the *Studio d'Essai*; in the immediate postwar era, *Club d'Essai*; and after 1951, *Groupe de Recherches Musicales*. Fulcher, "From 'The Voice of the Maréchal' to Musique Concrète," 381–402; Schaeffer, *In Search of a Concrete Music*.

33. Böhme-Mehner, "Berlin Was Home to the First Electronic Studio in the Eastern Bloc," 33–47; Böhme-Mehner, "Interview with Gerhard Steinke," 15–23; Böhme-Mehner, "Interview with Bernd Wefelmeyer," 49–52.

34. Stuckenschmidt, "Musikfest der Vergleiche und Sensation."

35. Manning, *Electronic and Computer Music*, 21; Chadabe, *Electronic Sound*, 31–32. For a sonic and intellectual introduction to the history of electronic music hear Gardner, *These Hopeful Machines*.

36. Respectively, G. Sch., "Komponisten ohne Publikum?"; K. H. R., "Elektronische Musik: Hart an der Grenze"; H. K. M., "Elektronische Musik auf neuen Wegen." For more on the transfer of electronic sounds from the concert stage to television advertisement, see Taylor, "The Avant-Garde in the Family Room," 387–408.

37. K. H. R., "Elektronische Musik: Hart an der Grenze."

38. Müller, "Entdeckung neuer Klangräume."

39. "Chaos oder Ordnung?"

40. "Die Spieldose der elektronischen Musik."

41. Neukirchen, "Und es raschten weiß die Sinus-Töne."

42. When we read Babbitt's famous 1958 polemic "The Composer as Specialist," we assume modernist composers wrote off audiences, but this kind of dismissal was the exception rather than the rule. European and American composers enjoyed substantial, unequivocal funding from the state and the university, respectively, but both groups cared about issues of audience perception and reception of their music.

43. For a particularly good instance that traces the history of electronic music all the way back to Ancient Greece, see Luening, "An Unfinished History of Electronic Music," 42–49, 135–42, and 145.

44. Eimert, "Was ist elektronische Musik?," 1–5; see also Eimert, "What is Electronic Music?," 1–10; Beyer, "Zur Geschichte der elektronischen Musik," 278–80.

45. Borio, "Kontinuität und Bruch," in *Im Zenit der Moderne*, vol. 1, 141–48.

46. Russolo, "The Art of Noises," 10–14; Schwitters, *Ursonate*.

47. Bijsterveld, "Servile Imitation," 121–35; see also Kahn, *Noise, Water, Meat*.

48. Patteson, *Instruments for New Music*, 157–63.

49. For instance, Beyer, "Die Klangwelt der elektronischen Musik," 74–79; Eimert, "Elektronische Musik—eine neue Klangwelt."

50. Brilmayer, "Das Trautonium"; Donhauser, *Elektrische Klangmaschinen*; Patteson, *Instruments for New Music,* 125–44.

51. Badge, *Oskar Sala*.

52. Patteson, *Instruments for New Music*, 136.

53. Sala Nachlass, Deutsches Museum, Munich.

54. Patteson, *Instruments for New Music*, 134–35.

55. Herf, *Reactionary Modernism*.

56. Fritzsche, "Nazi Modern," 4.

57. See for instance, Boulez, " . . . Near and Far," and "Schoenberg is Dead."

58. Böhlandt, " 'Kontakte'–Reflexionen naturwissenschaftlich-technischer Innovations-prozesse," 226–48; Hui, *The Psychophysical Ear*; Hui, Kursell, and Jackson, eds., "Music, Sound, and the Laboratory," 1–11; Wittje, *The Age of Electroacoustics*.

59. Betts, *The Authority of Everyday Objects*; Mesch, *Modern Art at the Berlin Wall*.

60. Galison, "Constructing Modernism," 17–44.

61. Heterogeneity in technoscientific scenarios is a theme in Callon, "Some Elements of a Sociology of Translation," 196–233; Callon, "Society in the Making," 83–103; Law, "Technology and Heterogeneous Engineering," 116–38; Star and Griesemer, "Institutional Ecology, 'Translations,' and Boundary Objects," 387–420; Fujimura, "Crafting Science," 168–211; Turner, *From Counterculture to Cyberculture*.

62. The names of people in these roles will come up throughout the chapters in the body of the book, but readers who wish to familiarize themselves now can consult the "Glossary of Actors" at the end of the book.

63. Bernstein, ed., *The San Francisco Tape Music Center*; Born, *Rationalizing Culture*; Gottstein, *Musik Als Ars Scientia*; Kuljuntausta, *First Wave*; Loubet, "The Beginnings of Electronic Music in Japan," 11–22; Nelson, *The Sound of Innovation*; Niebur, *Special Sound*; Novati and Dack, eds., *The Studio di Fonologia*; Spoerri, ed., *Musik aus dem Nichts*; Tazelaar, *On the Threshold of Beauty*.

64. Parolini, "Music Without Musicians . . . ," 286–96; Pigott, "Across Fields," 276–85; Pinch and Trocco, *Analog Days*; Théberge, *Any Sound You Can Imagine*; Wittje, "The Electrical Imagination," 40–63; Wittje, *The Age of Electroacoustics; Zauberhafte Klangmaschinen*.

65. On laboratory cultures, see Cetina, *The Manufacture of Knowledge*; Cetina, *Epistemic Cultures*; Galison, *How Experiments End*; Latour and Woolgar, *Laboratory Life*; Latour, *Science in Action*; Hacking, "The Self-Vindication of the Laboratory Sciences," 29–64; Gooding, "Putting Agency Back into Experiment," 65–112; Cetina, "The Couch, the Cathedral, and the Laboratory," 113–38.

66. Pickering, *The Mangle of Practice*.

67. Pickering, *The Mangle of Practice*, 17.

68. Pickering, *The Mangle of Practice*, 22.

69. Texts that sketch the disciplinary history and main claims of ANT include Latour, *Reassembling the Social*; Mol, "Actor-Network Theory: Sensitive Terms and Enduring Tensions," 253–99; Pickering, "From Science as Knowledge to Science as Practice," 1–26; Sayes, "Actor-Network Theory and Methodology," 134–49.

70. See Callon, "Some Elements of a Sociology of Translation," and Latour, "Where Are the Missing Masses?" For critiques, see the "epistemological chicken debate": Collins and Yearley, "Epistemological Chicken," 301–26; Woolgar, "Some Remarks About Positivism: A Reply to Collins and Yearley," 327–42; Callon and Latour, "Don't Throw the Baby Out With the Bath School! A Reply to Collins and Yearley," 343–68; Collins and Yearley, "Journey into Space," 369–89. See also the "anti-Latour" debate: Bloor, "Anti-Latour," 81–112; and Latour, "For David Bloor . . . and Beyond," 113–29.

71. In musicology, see Gallope, "Why Was This Music Desirable?," 199–230; Taruskin, "Agents and Causes and Ends, Oh My!," 272–93; Piekut, "Actor-Networks in Music History," 191–215; Stanyek and Piekut, "Deadness: Technologies of the Intermundane," 25–48.

72. Piekut, "Actor-Networks in Music History," 199.

73. More modest approaches to the question of machinic agency include Bijker and Pinch, "Preface to the Anniversary Edition," xi–xxxiv; Pinch and Kline, "Users as Agents of Technological Change," 763–95.

74. Callon, "Society in the Making," 108.

75. Manning, "The Significance of *Techné*," 81–90; Pennycook, "Who Will Turn the Knobs When I Die?" 199–208; Ungeheuer, "Imitative Instrumente und innovative Maschinen?" 45–60; Wierenga, "Searching for Sounds"; Williams, "Stockhausen Meets King Tubby's," 163–88; Zattra, "The Identity of the Work," 113–18.

76. Pickering, *The Mangle of Practice*, 26, 53.

77. For more on black boxes, see Latour, *Science in Action*, 1–17.

78. Mitch Miller quoted in Horning, *Chasing Sound*, 126, 101, respectively. For more on the producer's key role in popular music production, see Moorefield, *The Producer as Composer*; Zak, *Poetics of Rock*; and Savage, *Bytes & Backbeats*. For an analysis of the importance of collaboration for creation and innovation, see Sawyer, *Group Genius*.

79. Shapin, "The Invisible Technician," 554–63.

80. Born, *Rationalizing Culture*, 113, 204.

81. See for example Cornelius Cardew's comments on realizing and orchestrating Stockhausen's *Carré* based on Stockhausen's sketches. Cardew, "Report on Stockhausen's *Carré*," 619–22, and "Report on Stockhausen's *Carré*: Part 2," 698–700.

82. Law, "After ANT: Complexity, Naming, and Topology," 1–14; Latour, "On Recalling ANT," 15–25. Callon's "Some Elements of a Sociology of Translation" and Latour's *Science in Action* also show how power is accumulated by actors.

83. Wilson, "György Ligeti and the Rhetoric of Autonomy," 17. See also Danuser, "Die "Darmstädter Schule," 333–62; Fox, "Other Darmstadts," 1–3; Fox, "Darmstadt and the Institutionalization of Modernism," 115–23; Grant, *Serial Music, Serial Aesthetics*; Iddon, "Darmstadt Schools," 2–8; Osmond-Smith, "New Beginnings: The International Avant-Garde, 1945–62," 336–63; Trudu, *La "Scuola" di Darmstadt*.

84. Goldman, "Of Doubles, Groups, and Rhymes," 139–76.

85. Drott, "The End(s) of Genre"; Lewis, *A Power Stronger Than Itself*; Piekut, *Experimentalism Otherwise*; Piekut, "Indeterminacy, Free Improvisation, and the Mixed Avant-Garde"; Steinbeck, *Message to Our Folks*.

86. Kovács, "Frauen in Darmstadt," 94–9.

87. Abbate, *Recoding Gender*; Ensmenger, *The Computer Boys Take Over*, 14–20; Smith, *The Secrets of Station X*; Smith, *The Hidden History of Bletchley Park*; Holt, *Rise of the Rocket Girls*.

88. Hinkle-Turner, *Women Composers and Music Technology in the United States*; Hinkle-Turner, "Women and Music Technology," 31–47; Niebur, *Special Sound*; Rodgers, *Pink Noises*.

89. Turner, *The Democratic Surround*.

90. May, *Homeward Bound*.

91. Morgan, "Pioneer Spirits," 238–49; Rodgers, "Tinkering with Cultural Memory," 5–30; Vágnerová, "'Nimble Fingers' in Electronic Music," 250–58.

92. Rodgers, "Tinkering With Cultural Memory," 13, emphasis in original.

93. The gendered dimension of electronic studio work, especially at the BBC Radiophonic Workshop, is explored somewhat in Gardner, *These Hopeful Machines*, episode 3.

94. Morgan, "Pioneer Spirits," 238; Rodgers, "Tinkering with Cultural Memory," 9.

95. Vágnerová, "'Nimble Fingers' in Electronic Music"; Vágnerová, "Sirens/Cyborgs."

96. Rodà, "Evolution of the Technical Means," 33–81.

97. Pinch and Trocco, *Analog Days*, 13–14, 37, 75–76, 173, 280–85.

98. Kittler, *Gramophone, Film, Typewriter*, 96–97.

99. Kittler, *Gramophone*, 105–108; Kittler, "Rock Music," 152–64; Winthrop-Young, "Drill and Distraction," 825–54.

100. McMurray, "Once Upon a Time," 38; Braun, "Introduction," 9–32.

101. Kittler, *Gramophone*, 107.

102. Kane, "Relays," 66–75; and other articles in "Tape," a special issue of *twentieth-century music* 14, no. 1 (February 2017), Bohlman and McMurray, eds.; Gardner, *These Hopeful Machines*, episode 2.

103. Shannon and Weaver, *The Mathematical Theory of Communication*; Gertner, *The Idea Factory*.

104. Cohen, "Translator's Introduction"; Geoghegan, "From Information Theory to French Theory," 96–126.

105. Wiener, *Cybernetics*; Galison, "The Ontology of the Enemy," 228–66; Geoghegan and Peters, "Cybernetics," 109–13.

106. Wiener, *The Human Use of Human Beings*; Mills, "On Disability Cybernetics," 74–111.

107. Heims, *Constructing a Social Science for Postwar America*; Kline, *The Cybernetics Moment*; Pickering, *The Cybernetic Brain*.

108. For instance, Perle, "*Die Reihe* Vol. III," 102–104; Backus, "*Die Reihe*: A Scientific Evaluation," 160–71; Fokker, "Wherefore, and Why?," 68–79.

109. Gottfried Michael Koenig, private email communication with author, June 13, 2016; Both, "The Influence of Concepts of Information Theory on Electronic Music Composition"; Maconie, "Boulez, Information Science, and IRCAM"; Wilson, "György Ligeti and the Rhetoric of Autonomy."

110. Edwards, *The Closed World*; James Gleick, *The Information*; Martin, *The Organizational Complex*; Mendelsohn, Smith, and Weingart, eds., *Science, Technology, and the Military*; Turner, *From Counterculture to Cyberculture*.

111. Galison, "Physics Between War and Peace," 48.

112. Fulcher, "French Identity in Flux," 290–95; Galison, "Constructing Modernism"; Herf, *Reactionary Modernism*; Potter, *Most German of the Arts*, 200–34; Vincent, "Political Violence and Mass Society" 388–406.

Chapter 1

1. Cross, "Electronic Music," 50.

2. Thumbnail histories of the founding and early development of the studio include *Am Puls der Zeit: 50 Jahre WDR. Die Vorläufer 1924–1955*, 177–89; Chadabe, *Electric Sound*, 35–42; Cross, *Electronic Music 1948–1953*; Hilberg and Vogt, *Musik der Zeit*, 125–45; Holmes, *Electronic and Experimental Music*, 63–79; Manning, *Electronic and Computer Music*, 39–67; Morawska-Büngeler, *Schwingende Elektronen*, 7–19.

3. Eimert, *Atonale Musiklehre*; Weaver, "Theorizing Atonality," 9–12 and 83–124.

4. Kirchmeyer, *Kleine Monographie über Herbert Eimert*; Blüggel, *E. = Ethik + Aesthetic*.

5. Ungeheuer, *Wie die elektronische Musik "erfunden" wurde* . . . .

6. The full name of the research division was *Kriegsmarine Arbeitsgemeinschaft II bei der Schwingungsforschung für den Ubootskrieg*, led by Marineoberbaurat Dr. H. Rindfleisch. Correspondence between Rindfleisch and Meyer-Eppler. Meyer-Eppler 252.

7. Meyer-Eppler folders 243, 245, 246, 247, 251.

8. Jacobsen, *Operation Paperclip*.

9. Meyer-Eppler folders 244, 246, 249, 250, 251.

10. Stammerjohann et al., *Lexicon Grammaticorum*, 1016–17.

11. He does not appear in Fred K. Prieberg's *Handbuch Deutsche Musiker 1933–1945*, perhaps because he was primarily a scientist on the fringe of the musical community. Elena Ungeheuer's biography *Wie die elektronische Musik "erfunden" wurde* . . . passes lightly over the Nazi period, noting the ways that Meyer-Eppler's research was useful to the military without delving deeply into the scope of his collaboration (23–24). Dave Tompkins (*How to Wreck a Nice Beach*, 191–99) and James Gardner (*These Hopeful Machines*, episode 2) both sketch Meyer-Eppler's connections to the *Kriegsmarine* and *Luftwaffe*, drawing upon as-yet-unpublished research by Ian Pace (private email communication with this author, September 4, 2017).

12. For an excellent discussion of the question "What Makes it 'Nazi'?" see Potter, *The Art of Suppression*, 241–49. For more on such entanglements, see Donhauser, *Elektrische Klangmaschinen*; Herf, *Reactionary Modernism*; Fritzsche, "Nazi Modern"; Patteson, *Instruments for New Music*; Wiesen, *West German Industry*, 17–51.

13. Wittje, *The Age of Electroacoustics*.

14. At the very end of his life, Meyer-Eppler did work on two reports apparently commissioned by the West German government or military, perhaps for the BMVdg. [Bundesministerium für Verkehr]. One, dated May 6, 1960, is titled "Zur informationstheoretischen Systematik der geheimen Übermittlung von gesprochener Sprache" [An Information-Theoretic Classification for the Secret Transmission of Spoken Messages]. The second, which is undated but must have been authored in late 1959 or

early 1960, is titled "Verfahren zur Sprachverschlüsselung" [Techniques of Ciphering]. Meyer-Eppler 243.

15. For more on early electronic instruments, see Brilmayer, "Das Trautonium"; Donhauser, *Elektrische Klangmaschinen*; Holmes, *Electronic and Experimental Music*, 3–41; *Zauberhafte Klangmaschinen*.

16. Morawska-Büngeler, *Schwingende Elektronen*, 7.

17. Borio and Danuser, *Im Zenit der Moderne*, 68–89.

18. For more speculation on the fault lines among Eimert, Beyer, and Stockhausen as recollected by Stockhausen, see Custodis, *Die soziale Isolation der neuen Musik*, 62–63. The scenario is also discussed in Patteson, *Instruments for New Music*, 159–62.

19. Beyer, "Zur Geschichte der elektronischen Musik," 278.

20. Beyer, "Zur Geschichte der elektronischen Musik," 278.

21. Eimert, "Elektronische Musik—eine neue Klangwelt"; see also Eimert, "Was ist elektronische Musik?" and Eimert, "What is Electronic Music?" *Die Reihe*, 1.

22. For more, see Patteson, *Instruments for New Music*, 52–81 and 144–51.

23. Eimert, "Der Sinus-Ton," 171.

24. Many composers were likely to repeat their own version of such a lineage. For instance, see Luening, "An Unfinished History of Electronic Music," 43–49, 135–42, and 145; Berio, "Musica per Tape Recorder," 10–13; and discussion in de Benedictis, "Opera Prima," 26–54.

25. Beyer, "Das Problem der 'kommenden Musik.'"

26. Boulez, "At the Edge of Fertile Land," in *Stocktakings*, 169; similar comments in Adorno, "Music and Technique," 197–215; Boulez, "Tendencies in Recent Music," 173–81; Boulez, "Claude Debussy," 259–77; Boulez, "Arnold Schoenberg," 278–86; Stockhausen, "Arbeitsbericht 1952/53: Orientierung," 32–38.

27. Hui, *The Psychophysical Ear*; Kursell, "Experiments on Tone Color"; Kursell, "Klangfarbe um 1850."

28. Schoenberg, *Theory of Harmony*, 421.

29. Beyer, "Elektronische Musik," 39.

30. Patteson, *Instruments for New Music*, 114–67; also discussed in Donhauser, *Elektrische Klangmaschinen*; Brilmayer, "Das Trautonium."

31. Unpublished text and notes for Darmstadt lecture, August 1950. Akademie der Künste, Berlin, Meyer-Eppler Collection. "Unseren Musikinstrumenten, besteht ein verwickelter Zusammenhang zw[ischen] Instrumentenform und Klangfarbe, der es unmöglich macht, die Verbindung von einer KF [Klangfarben] zur anderen herzustellen. Was liegt z.B. [zum Beispiel] klanglich in der Mitte zwischen Klarinette und Oboe? Kein kontinuierlicher Übergang. Dies gelingt erst, wenn man die Elektrizität zu Hilfe nimmt. Analogie: Farbe in d.[ie] Malerei. Früher: Naturfarben, wenige Töne, Auswahl nicht dem Künstler überlassen, sondern zufallsbestimmt. Jetzt: Anilinfarben, freie Kompositionsmöglichkeit."

32. Meyer-Eppler, "Möglichkeiten der elektronischen Klangerzeugung [1951]," 102.

33. Beyer, "Die Klangwelt der elektronischen Musik," 76.

34. Eimert, "Elektronische Musik—eine neue Klangwelt," unpaginated.

35. Beyer, "Die Klangwelt," 75.

36. Beyer, "Die Klangwelt," 75, emphasis in original.

37. Horning, *Chasing Sound*.

38. Shapin, "The Invisible Technician."

39. Zattra, "Les Origines du Nom de RIM"; Zattra, "Collaborating on Composition"; Born, *Rationalizing Culture*.

40. Eimert, "The Place of Electronic Music." See also Eimert, "Was ist elektronische Musik?"

41. For more, see Sawyer, *Group Genius*. Similarly, see new research from Theel, "Governance von kreativen Praktiken in der Musikbranche." For a personal narrative about creative collaboration with Stockhausen, see Cardew, "Report on Stockhausen's *Carré*" and "Report on Stockhausen's *Carré*: Part 2."

42. Shapin, "The Invisible Technician," 560. For more on asymmetries and hierarchies within scientific laboratories, see Latour and Woolgar, *Laboratory Life*; Latour, *Science in Action*.

43. Moorefield, *The Producer as Composer*; Savage, *Bytes & Backbeats*; Stahl, *Unfree Masters*; Zak, *Poetics of Rock*.

44. Borio and Danuser, *Im Zenit der Moderne*, vol. 2, 63–89; Borio and Danuser, *Im Zenit der Moderne*, vol. 3, 540–57.

45. Maderna used this title for two very different pieces. *Musica su due dimensioni* (1952), discussed here, is for flute, tape, and cymbal. Maderna significantly rewrote the piece in 1958 for flute and tape. Aside from the flute, the two pieces—which share a title—bear little resemblance to one another. The original flute part and the tape part from the 1952 version are lost, but scholars have reconstructed the 1952 version from a recording of the Darmstadt premiere and various tape fragments and sketches. The 1952 version is available in score: *Musica su due dimensioni* (1952), edited and introduced by Nicola Scaldiferri, critical edition directed by Mario Baroni and Rossana Dalmonte (Milan: Editioni Suvini Zerboni, 2001). A recording of both the 1952 and 1958 versions of the piece appears on the CD *Bruno Maderna: Music in Two Dimensions. Works for Flute*, performed by Roberto Fabbriciani and Massimiliano Damerini (New York: Mode Records, 2013).

46. Eimert to Stockhausen, March 7, 1952, Stockhausen Foundation, Kürten: "Wir (Nono, Maderna, Eimert) waren jeden Tag zusammen, fuhren nach Bonn und ins Siebengebirge. In Bonn habe ich ihnen nicht nur das Beethovenhaus gezeigt, sondern auch in Meyer-Epplers Institut für Phonetik und Kommunikationsforschung unsere elektronischen Bänder vorführen lassen, über die sie fast aus dem Häuschen gerieten. Maderna fing an Ort und Stelle an, elektronisch zu komponieren und montierte auf Band drei auf dem Melochord produzierte Melodien übereinander. Kürzlich war Jelinek aus Wein hier, den ich zu einem Diskussionsvortrag von Prof. Mentzerath und Meyer-Eppler nach Bonn mitgenommen hatte und der schliesslich mit einer wahren Verve und scharmanten Verbindlichkeit die Diskussion an sich riß. Das alles zeigt mir doch, daß wir mit diesen Dingen auf dem rechten Weg sind."

47. Maderna to Nono, May 30, 1952; in Rizzardi and Scaldaferri, *"Musica su due Dimensioni,"* 433. For more on the serial schemes, see Neidhofer, "Bruno Maderna's Serial Arrays."

48. See Scaldaferri, Introduction to *Musica su due Dimensioni*.

49. Some Italian scholars think that Maderna continued to use "electronic material of German origin" in his radio-play scores from 1954 and 1955. See Rizzardi and de Benedictis, *Nuovo Musica Alla Radio*, 206, n.9.

50. Eimert to Stockhausen, April 15, 1952, Stockhausen Foundation, Kürten: "Ich werde jetzt auch mit solchen Experimenten anfangen. Meyer-Eppler stellt mir einen Katalog von Klangtypen zusammen, 12, 24 oder 48, damit muss man doch genau so komponieren können wie mit den 12 Tönen. Die Klänge muss man natürlich erst genau im Kopf haben; dann gilt der Satz aus der Zwölftontechnik: Komponieren heißt rhythmisieren, was praktisch auf eine mühselige Bandschneiderei hinausläuft. Nach langen Überlegungen glaube ich, daß es für den Anfang und bei dem jetzigen technischen Stand keine andere Möglichkeit gibt."

51. Sound sample titles, track numbers, and timings are from a CD of Meyer-Eppler's archival sound recordings included in Ungeheuer, *Wie die elektronische Musik "erfunden" wurde* . . . .

52. No sound or full transcript survives from the original October 18, 1951 *Nachtprogramm* broadcast, but these sound examples do appear in the October 19, 1961, rebroadcast, "Zehn Jahre *elektronische Musik*," WDR Historical Archive, Cologne.

53. Morawska-Büngeler, *Schwingende Elektronen*, 13; Ungeheuer, *Wie die elektronische Musik "erfunden" wurde* . . . , 90–91.

54. Bode, "Das Melochord des Studios," 27–29; Bode, "The Melochord of the Cologne Studio," 27–29.

55. *Studio für elektronische Musik des WDR Köln*, Musik in Deutschland 1950–2000 series, box 17, vol. 5 Deutscher Musikrat/RCA/Sony BMG, 2008.

56. Eimert, "The Place of Electronic Music," 42–46. Quote on translated p. 11.

57. Decroupet, "Timbre Diversification," 13–23; Ungeheuer, "From the Elements to the Continuum," 25–34; Grant, *Serial Music*, 76–102.

58. Iverson, "From Analog to Digital," 45.

59. Koenig, private email communication with the author, June 13, 2016.

60. Köhler, *Hörspiel und Hörbuch*, 11. For a historical definition from a composer of many *Hörspiel* scores, see Haentjes, "Über Hörspielmusik," 241–42.

61. Klippert, *Elemente des Hörspiels*, 50.

62. Verma, *Theatre of the Mind*; Gilfillan, *Pieces of Sound*.

63. Badenoch, *Voices in Ruins*, 14–16; Birdsall, *Nazi Soundscapes*; Lacey, *Feminine Frequencies*.

64. Cory and Haggh, "*Hörspiel* as Music and Music as *Hörspiel*"; Schlieper, "Vorwort," 7.

65. Schlieper et al., *Hörspiel 1954–55*, 642–54.

66. Helmut Kirchmeyer gives the year as 1948 in *Kleine Monographie*, 48. However, the only date of broadcast for Byron's *Kain* is given as December 9, 1946, in Schlieper et al., eds., *Hörspiel 1945–1949, 167*–68. Perhaps Eimert collaborated on that 1946 production, and then recomposed or expanded the music in 1948 for an additional broadcast or concert known to Kirchmeyer, in the way that film music is sometimes marketed as an album after the release of a film.

67. Klippert, *Elemente*, 66.

68. Klippert, *Elemente*, 80; de Benedictis, "Opera Prima"; de Benedictis, "A Conversation with Luciano Berio," 166; de Benedictis and Rizzardi, "Just Then I Heard a Voice . . . " 281–89; de Benedictis and Novati, "Introduction," in *Prix Italia*, 187–91; Kostelanetz, "John Cage as *Hörspielmacher*," 291–99.

69. De Benedictis, "A Conversation with Luciano Berio," 160–74.

70. Fearn, *Bruno Maderna*, 79–84; Buso, "A Portrait of *Ritratto*," 54–99.

71. De Benedictis, "Opera Prima," in *Nuova Musica Alla Radio*, 28.

72. Gardner, *These Hopeful Machines,* episode 3; Niebur, *Special Sound.*

73. Cox, " 'There Must Be a Poetry' "; Fulcher, "From 'The Voice of the Maréchal' "; Lautour, "Inaudible Visitors"; Stalarow, "Listening to a Liberated Paris."

74. Manning, *Electronic and Computer Music,* 37; Chadabe, *Electric Sound,* 26–28; Decroupet and Ungeheuer, "Karel Goeyvaerts und die serielle Tonbandmusik"; Kurtz, *Stockhausen: A Biography,* 45–57; Toop, "Stockhausen and the Sine-Wave."

75. Custodis, *Die soziale Isolation,* 64–71.

76. Stockhausen to Eimert, March 10, 1952, Stockhausen Foundation, Kürten: "Und ich fühle es mit, wie sie sich verrenken müssen, um ein Studio für M. Eppler oder eine Kammermusik-Reihe für die Jungen möglich zu machen. Und das ist die einzige Stelle in ganz Deutschland! Man weiß es sehr gut in Paris, daß nur in Köln was getan wird! Nur denken Sie nicht, daß es hier anders ist! [. . .] Aber die Jungen halten wenigstens zusammen. Es ist nahe daran, daß Boulez und Baraque [*sic*] den übergeschnappten Scheffer rausschmeissen und Fahrwasser kriegen. Boulez und Baraque [*sic*] haben es bald so weit, daß sie einigen Einfluß wenigsten auf den Funk haben, Sendungen über Rhythmik etc. machen können und Bandetüden konstruieren, die Scheffer [*sic*] völlig ausrangiert haben. Jedes Jahr gibt es eine Manifestation (öffentliches Konzert der Gruppe Scheffer [*sic*]) und in diesem stellen alle jungen Mitarbeiter ihre eingegangenen Experimente vor. In diesem Jahre werden die Leute wohl spüren, daß die "musique concrete" [*sic*] nichts mehr mit dem Unsinn gemein hat, den Scheffer [*sic*] bisher fabrizierte—und daß sie eben alles andere, als "musique concrete" [*sic*] zu sein hat."

77. Schaeffer, *In Search of a Concrete Music,* 85. Schaeffer says new colleagues will be interested "amateurs" who come to listen, "associates" who use *musique concrète* in their films and broadcasts, and "trainees" who will participate in "our work" depending on studio funds and their "gifts for concrete music." See also Toop, "Stockhausen and the Sine-Wave," 389; Custodis, *Die soziale Isolation,* 66.

78. Schaeffer, *In Search of a Concrete Music,* 4.

79. Kane, *Sound Unseen,* 15–41.

80. For a history of electronic music that focuses on technologies and techniques (*concrète,* synthesis, live electronics, etc.), see Supper, *Elektroakustiche Musik und Computer Musik.* See also Kane, "Relays"; Manning, "The Significance of *Techné*"; Zattra, "The Identity of the Work."

81. Schaeffer, *Treatise on Musical Objects.*

82. Cory and Haggh, "*Hörspiel* as Music," 265.

83. Cross, "Electronic Music 1948–1953," 49–50.

84. Eimert, "Elektronische Musik—eine neue Klangwelt," (pages unnumbered). For more on the animosity between French proponents of *musique concrète* and German proponents of *elektronische Musik* in this early era, see Holmes, *Electronic and Experimental Music,* 64–65; Fulcher, "From 'The Voice of the Maréchal' to Musique Concrète."

85. Schlieper et al., *Hörspiel 1954–55,* 576. A rebroadcast of the 1955 WDR production is available on YouTube: "Das Unternehmen der Wega—Friedrich Dürrenmatt," YouTube video, posted by "Hörspiel Fabrik," December 6, 2015, https://youtu.be/_I3tKdoa640.

86. Schütz's *Morgenröte* can be heard on *Studio für elektronische Musik des WDR Köln*; Eimert and Beyer's *Klangstudie II* and *Klang im unbegrenzten Raum* can be heard on *Cologne*

WDR: Early Electronic Music. The movements of *KuR* are separated by about ten seconds of silence. Movement I is 0:00–2:54; movement II is 3:00–6:03; movement III is 6:13–10:24.

87. Blueggel, *E. = Ethik + Aesthetic*. In pitching the studio idea to WDR administrators in 1951, Eimert and his collaborators headed off possible criticism by arguing that audiences just needed more time to get used to the new sounds. See Cross, "Electronic Music 1948–1953," 48.

88. Enkel and Schütz, "Magnetic Tape Technique."

89. Heinz Schütz in interview with Björn Gottstein in Hilberg and Vogt, eds., *Musik der Zeit*, 147.

90. Thanks to Jason Holt Mitchell and electronic music composers at CCRMA (Stanford University) for helping me develop this insight.

91. See for instance Holmes, *Electronic and Experimental Music*, 67–68.

92. Stockhausen to Pousseur, no date, probably October 21–27, 1953, Pousseur Collection, Paul Sacher Foundation, Basel: "Meine Situation wird schwer. Eimert "komponiert" wieder und hat meine Zeit auf 3 Stunden täglich beschränkt. Ich glaube, er hasst mich und meine Musik. [. . .] Ich brauche Musik und diese Arbeit und einen Techniker, der mich nicht auslacht, weil er Hörspielgeräusche reißend los wird."

93. Another invisible collaborator is the technical production manager [*technische Aufnahmeleiter*]. For *Klangstudie II* and *Klang im unbegrenzten Raum* this was Winfried Bierhals. WDR Archive and Morwaska-Büngeler, *Schwingende Elektronen*, 109.

94. Williams, "Technical Influence and Physical Constraint," particularly 22:00–22:30; Williams, "Interpretation and Performance Practice," 445–81.

95. Williams, "Technical Influence and Physical Constraint," 18:08–19:08.

96. See Stockhausen, "The Origins of Electronic Music," 649–50.

Chapter 2

1. Decroupet, "Aleatorik und Indetermination—Die Ferienkurse als Forum der europäischen Cage-Rezeption," in *Im Zenit der Moderne*, vol. 2, 231–40; Griffiths, *Cage*, 30–38; Gann, *There's No Such Thing as Silence*, 193; Shultis, "Cage and Europe," 20–40; Taruskin, *Oxford History of Western Music*, vol. 5, 55, 64–65.

2. The most detailed and nuanced account of the event, which I rely on here, is Iddon, *New Music at Darmstadt*, 196–303.

3. Cage, "Changes" (18–34), "Indeterminacy" (35–40), and "Communication" (41–56), in *Silence*.

4. Iddon, *New Music at Darmstadt*, 216–20.

5. Shultis, "Cage and Europe," 38.

6. Nattiez, "Introduction," *The Boulez-Cage Correspondence*, 3–26; Cage, *The Selected Letters of John Cage*, 103, 111; Haskins, *John Cage*, 51–70.

7. Boulez to Cage, May 7–21, 1951, *The Boulez-Cage Correspondence* #27, 91.

8. Cage to Boulez, May 22, 1951, *The Boulez-Cage Correspondence* #28, 94.

9. See Kostelanetz, *John Cage (ex)plain(ed)*, 7–24; Griffiths, *Cage*, 21–37; Revill, *The Roaring Silence*, 107–61; Richards, *John Cage As . . .* , 7–18 and 89–103; Nyman, *Experimental Music*, 50–71; Kahn, "John Cage: Silence and Silencing," 556–98.

10. Cage, "Composition," in *Silence*, 59.

11. Boulez, "Possibly . . . ," 112–13.

12. Beal, *New Music, New Allies*; Carroll, *Music and Ideology in Cold War Europe*; Fosler-Lussier, *Music Divided: Bartók's Legacy*; Fosler-Lussier, *Music in America's Cold War Diplomacy*; Shreffler, "'Music Left and Right,'" 67–87.

13. Taruskin, *Oxford History*, vol. 5, 17.

14. Boulez to Cage, December 1951, *The Boulez-Cage Correspondence* #35, 112.

15. Boulez to Cage, July 1954, *The Boulez-Cage Correspondence* #45, 150.

16. Boulez, "Alea," 26–38.

17. Beal, "Negotiating Cultural Allies," 121–23; Beal, "The Army, the Airwaves," 487–90; Beal, *New Music, New Allies*, 55–64.

18. Iddon, *New Music at Darmstadt*, 228.

19. Eimert's broadcast transcript from November 27, 1952 is held in WDR Historical Archives, folio 15198.

20. On Cage's early influences, see Bernstein, "John Cage, Arnold Schoenberg, and the Musical Idea," 15–45; Joseph, "'A Therapeutic Value for City Dwellers,'" 135–75; and Pritchett, *The Music of John Cage*.

21. Eimert to Stockhausen, September 23, 1952, Stockhausen Foundation, Kürten. "Die Sachen von Cage sind interessant und völlig unbelastet von herkömmlichen Begriffen, darunter eine 'Konstruktion in Metall' und Musik für Prepared Piano, die ich senden werde."

22. Boulez to Cage, October 1, 1952, *The Boulez-Cage Correspondence* #39, 134.

23. Boulez's introduction to Cage's *Sonatas and Interludes*, *The Boulez-Cage Correspondence*, 30.

24. My thanks to David Bernstein who helped me sort out likely corresponding pieces for Eimert's unclear titles and mistaken attributions.

25. Varèse and Wen-chung, "The Liberation of Sound," 11–19.

26. Eimert to Stockhausen, September 23, 1952, Stockhausen Foundation, Kürten. "Die elektronischen Bänder von ihm sind dagegen darg primitiv und geben nichts weiter als ein paar Rückkoppelungstöne."

27. Eimert, *Nachtprogramm* transcript, 7. In the transcript, Eimert also speaks of "eine Musik ohne Psychologie, und die Entwicklung der musikalischen Ideen soll dabei ähnlich vor sich gehen wie die Bildung von Kristallen . . . Und das ist nun wieder einer der jüngsten Begriffe: 'Authentische Musik.'"

28. Eimert, "Was ist elektronische Musik?," 5.

29. Eimert to Stockhausen, March 7, 1952, Stockhausen Foundation, Kürten.

30. Eimert to Stockhausen, March 7–10, 1952, Stockhausen Foundation, Kürten.

31. Eimert to Stockhausen, March 7, 1952, Stockhausen Foundation, Kürten.

32. Eimert to Stockhausen, April 15, 1952, Stockhausen Foundation, Kürten.

33. Schaeffer, *In Search of a Concrete Music*, 18.

34. Goeyvaerts, "Paris: Darmstadt 1947–56," 40.

35. Kurtz, *Stockhausen: A Biography*, 55.

36. Toop, "Stockhausen's Electronic Works," 151.

37. Boulez, "Possibly . . . ," 111–40; excerpted in *The Boulez-Cage Correspondence* #37, 128–29. Emphasis in original.

38. Cage, *Bacchanale*. For more on how and with what Cage prepared the piano, see Pritchett, *The Music of John Cage*, 23.

39. Cage, *Bacchanale*. In my discussion, the piano octaves are numbered from the bottom up, such that C4 is middle C.

40. Manning, *Electronic and Computer Music*, 55.

41. Kirchmeyer, *Kleine Monographie über Herbert Eimert*, 48; Manning, *Electronic and Computer Music*, 41.

42. Beal, "The Army, the Airwaves," 491.

43. On Strobel's musical and journalistic activities in wartime France, where he was an effective conduit between the Nazi and Vichy regimes, see Fulcher, *Renegotiating French Identity*, 43–44 and 113–14.

44. Cage to Eimert, February 13, 1954, WDR Historical Archive folio 10662.

45. Beal, "The Army, the Airwaves," 491–96.

46. Quoted in Beal, "The Army, the Airwaves," 493.

47. Cage to Kruttge, April 9, 1954, WDR Historical Archive folio 10662.

48. Cage to Kruttge, May 10, 1954, WDR Historical Archive folio 10662.

49. Kruttge to Cage, June 1, 1954, WDR Historical Archive folio 10662.

50. Beal, "The Army, the Airwaves," 494.

51. Peyser, *To Boulez and Beyond*, 178.

52. Beal, "The Army, the Airwaves," 497; see also Iddon, *New Music at Darmstadt*, 160–61; Shultis, "Cage and Europe," 31–33; Taruskin, *Oxford History*, vol. 5, 65.

53. Custodis, *Die soziale Isolation der neuen Musik*, 104–108; Hilberg and Vogt, eds., *Musik der Zeit 1951–2001*, 35.

54. E. R. T., "Klavier mit Papierstreifen und Büroklammern," WDR Historical Archive 02240.

55. Beal gives the figure of "several hundred dollars" in "The Army, the Airwaves," 499. She has confirmed in private correspondence that the SWF paid Cage and Tudor 2000 DM, which was the 1954 equivalent of several hundred dollars—about $476. For the conversion of historical Deutsche Marks to dollars, http://fxtop.com/en/currency-converter-past.php; for the conversion of 1954 dollars to 2017 dollars, http://usinflationcalculator.com (both accessed September 4, 2017).

56. Beal, "The Army, the Airwaves," 493–94.

57. Custodis, *Die soziale Isolation*, 9–27.

58. Beal, "The Army, the Airwaves," 497; Custodis, *Die soziale Isolation*, 104–107.

59. Beal, "An Interview with Earle Brown," 341.

60. Digitized recordings of the *Handapparat* library are available at the WDR Historisches Archiv in Cologne.

61. Unpublished portion of an interview between the author and Gottfried Michael Koenig, The Hague, Netherlands, May 10, 2015. It seems likely that the *Handapparat* library contained recordings used on the *Nachtprogramm*, including Cage's *Sonatas and Interludes, Bacchanale, Three Dances*, and *First Construction*, as well as a recording of the 23′ 56.176″ and related prepared-piano pieces from the 1954 concert.

62. Ligeti, "Auswirkungen der elektronischen Musik," 86.

63. Kane, "Relays," 66–75; McMurray, "Once Upon a Time," 25–48.

64. The last explanation is favored by Pritchett in *The Music of John Cage*, 102.

65. Pritchett, *The Music of John Cage*, 90–91; Holmes, *Electronic and Experimental Music*, 108.

66. Boulez, "Alea," 30.

67. *The Boulez-Cage Correspondence*, 31.

68. *The Boulez-Cage Correspondence*, 31.

69. Cage to Boulez, January 17, 1950, *The Boulez-Cage Correspondence* #7, 49–50.

70. Boulez to Cage, January 3, 11, 12, 1950, *The Boulez-Cage Correspondence* #6, 44.

71. Square-root form is explained most carefully in Bernstein, "In Order to Thicken the Plot," 7–40; see also Shultis, "No Ear for Music," 83–104; van Emmerik, "An Imaginary Grid," 217–37; Jenkins, "Structure vs. Form in the *Sonatas and Interludes for Prepared Piano*," 239–61; Pritchett, *The Music of John Cage*, 15–22.

72. Stockhausen to Goeyvaerts, December 3, 1952. Translated in Toop, "Stockhausen's Electronic Works," 151.

73. Stockhausen, "Arbeitsbericht 1952/53: Orientierung," 34. Boulez raises similar points in "Possibly . . . " (111–40) and "Tendencies in Recent Music" (173–79) in *Stocktakings*, respectively.

74. Stockhausen, "Arbeitsbericht 1952/53," 34.

75. 25th root of 5 can also be expressed as the fractional exponent $5^{1/25}$.

76. Beal, *New Music, New Allies*, 78–98; Holzaepfel, "Cage and Tudor," 169–85; Holzaepfel, "David Tudor and the *Solo for Piano*," 137–56; Holzaepfel, "David Tudor and the Performance of American Experimental Music 1950–59"; Nakai, "On the Instrumental Natures of David Tudor's Music"; and the special issue (*Composers Inside Electronics: Music After David Tudor*) of *Leonardo Music Journal* 14 (2004): 1–115.

77. Stockhausen to Pousseur, ca. October 18–19, 1954, Pousseur Collection, Paul Sacher Foundation. "Augenblicklich ist David Tudor hier, mit dem der Rest 'freie' Zeit verbracht wird. Er ist anregend, und die Vorstellungswelt der Cage-Gruppe ist ein ernst zu nehmendes Monstrum. [. . . .] Sie haben nichts zu verantworten, nichts zu beraten, keine Tradition. Das ist unheimlich, wenn man es so unmittelbar erkannt, betont, der Beleg benutzt antreffen kann, wie bei Tudor, der in Augenblich (in Namen der 'Cage-Gruppe' spricht) Brown, Wolff, Feldmann."

78. Stockhausen to Pousseur, December 5, 1954, Pousseur Collection, Paul Sacher Foundation. By his own account, Stockhausen gave the last *Klavierstück* manuscript (VI?) to Tudor on December 8 for the performance on December 16—an extraordinarily short lead time considering international mail. Tudor discusses this a bit in Holzaepfel, "Interview with David Tudor," 630.

79. Evidently, for administrators at Darmstadt, Tudor was the more desirable half of the Cage–Tudor pair from the start. See Iddon, *New Music at Darmstadt*, 196.

80. Data compiled from Borio and Danuser, eds., *Im Zenit der Moderne*, vol. 3, 577–613.

81. Data compiled from Holzaepfel, *David Tudor and the Performance*, Appendix D, 328–62.

82. Beal, "David Tudor in Darmstadt," 77–88; Beal, "An Interview with Earle Brown," 355; Nakai, "On the Instrumental Natures of David Tudor's Music"; Yaffé, "An Interview With Composer Earle Brown," 296.

83. Meehan makes a similar argument about Cathy Berberian in "Not Just a Pretty Voice."

84. Latour, *Science in Action*; Piekut, *Experimentalism Otherwise*; Piekut, "Indeterminacy, Free Improvisation, and the Mixed Avant-Garde," 769–824.

Chapter 3

1. Grant, *Serial Music, Serial Aesthetics*; Iddon, *New Music at Darmstadt*; Toop, "Messiaen-Goeyvaerts, Fano-Boulez, Stockhausen," 141–69; Whittall, *Serialism*.

2. For instance, note the thematic overlap in the articles in *Die Reihe,* vol. 1, "Electronic Music" (1955) and *Die Reihe,* vol. 2, "Anton Webern" (1955). For a nuanced critical perspective, see Grant, *Serial Music, Serial Aesthetics,* 75–128.

3. Borio and Danuser, eds., *Im Zenit der Moderne,* 68–89; Iddon, *New Music at Darmstadt,* xi–xii.

4. Goeyvaerts, "Paris-Darmstadt 1947–56," 45.

5. Hui, Kursell, and Jackson, "Music, Sound, and the Laboratory From 1750 to 1980," 1–11; Parolini, "Music Without Musicians," 286–96; Pigott, "Across Fields: Sound, Art and Technology," 276–85.

6. Cetina, *Epistemic Cultures*; Cetina, "The Couch, the Cathedral, and the Laboratory" 113–38; Galison, *How Experiments End*; Latour and Woolgar, *Laboratory Life*; Latour, *Science in Action*; Pickering, *The Mangle of Practice.*

7. Born, *Rationalizing Culture*; Horning, *Chasing Sound.*

8. Levy, "Shades of the Studio," 59–87; Iverson, "The Emergence of Timbre," 61–89.

9. Decroupet, "Timbre Diversification in Serial Tape Music," 13–23; Decroupet, "Komponieren im analogen Studio," 36–66.

10. Böhlandt, " 'Kontakte'–Reflexionen naturwissenschaftlich-technischer Innovationsprozesse," 226–48; Hui, *The Psychophysical Ear*; Klotz, "Tonpsychologie und Musikforschung als Katalysatoren," 195–210; Kursell, "Experiments on Tone Color in Music and Acoustics," 191–211; Kursell, "Klangfarbe um 1850," 21–40; Steege, *Helmholtz and the Modern Listener.*

11. Manning, *Electronic and Computer Music,* 48; Morawska-Büngeler, *Schwingende Elektronen,* 111–12; Stockhausen, "Two Lectures," 59–66.

12. Eimert, "Der Sinus Tone," 1–5; Helmholtz, *On the Sensations of Tone,* 23–25 and 49–65.

13. Volmar, "Listening to the Cold War," 80–102; Volmar, "Psychoakustik und Signalanalyse," 65–96; Wittje, "The Electrical Imagination," 40–63; Wittje, *The Age of Electroacoustics.*

14. Karlheinz Stockhausen, "Arbeitsbericht 1953," 42.

15. The idea that "musical" tones have harmonic spectra follows from Helmholtz, who, in *On the Sensations of Tone*, said that tones with inharmonic spectra "should not be reckoned as musical tones at all" (70). The dichotomy between harmonic and inharmonic sounds isn't entirely substantiated, as some "musical" sounds, like bells, have inharmonic spectra.

16. Williams, "Interpretation and Performance Practice," 445–81; Williams, "Stockhausen Meets King Tubby's," 163–88; Williams, "Technical Influence and Physical Constraint."

17. Iverson, "From Analog to Digital," 48.

18. Ungeheuer, "From the Elements to the Continuum," 25–34; Ungeheuer, "Die Geburt der Idee aus dem Geist der Technik?," 27–36.

19. Stockhausen to Goeyvaerts, July 1953, quoted in Toop, "Stockhausen and the Sine-Wave," 390. Translation by Toop. On Eimert's invitation, Stockhausen was the first *Mitarbeiter* [assistant] in the studio beginning in mid-1953, with a monthly stipend of 500–700 DM and creative autonomy to undertake individual experiments. Eimert to Stockhausen, November 26, 1952, Stockhausen Foundation, Kürten.

20. Eimert to Nono, September 17, 1953, Archivio Luigi Nono, Venice. © Luigi Nono heirs. "Karlheinz arbeitet jeden Tag 8 bis 10 Stunden und hat bisher—in einem

Vierteljahr!—etwa drei Minuten Musik fertig. Es ist das eine sehr umständliche und langwierige Arbeit."

21. Toop, "Messiaen-Goeyvaerts, Fano-Boulez, Stockhausen," 141–69; Toop, "Stockhausen and the Sine-Wave," 379–91; Sabbe, "Goeyvaerts and the Beginnings of 'Punctual' Serialism," 55–94; Delaere, "The Projection in Time and Space," 11–14; Decroupet and Ungeheuer, "Karel Goeyvaerts und die serielle Tonbandmusik," 95–118.

22. Sabbe, "Goeyvaerts and the Beginnings," 75.

23. Goeyvaerts, "Paris–Darmstadt 1947–56," 50–52.

24. Sabbe, "Goeyvaerts and the Beginnings," 77; Decroupet and Ungeheuer, "Karel Goeyvaerts und die serielle Tonbandmusik," 109.

25. Stockhausen's metaphor is "raindrops in the sun"; see Toop, "Stockhausen and the Sine-Wave," 391.

26. When Goeyvaerts and Stockhausen performed an excerpt from the *Sonata for Two Pianos* at Darmstadt in 1951 and suffered Adorno's disdain, Stockhausen consoled Goeyvaerts by saying that "whenever asked with whom he [Stockhausen] had studied, he would mention only my [Goeyvaerts's] name." See Goeyvaerts, "Paris–Darmstadt 1947–56," 45.

27. Stockhausen to Eimert, March 10, 1952, Stockhausen Foundation, Kürten. "In diesen beiden Stücken habe ich zu ersten male auf den Grund des menschlich begreifbaren sehen dürfen, in den reinen Niederschlag einer Musikalischen Idee." Stockhausen is speaking about Goeyvaerts's acoustic *Compositions No. 2* and *No. 3*, but the observation holds.

28. Toop, "Stockhausen and the Sine-Wave," 380–81; Decroupet and Ungeheuer, "Karel Goeyvaerts und die serielle Tonbandmusik," 112; Morawska-Büngeler, *Schwingende Elektronen*, 109; Hilberg and Vogt, eds., *Musik der Zeit*, 138.

29. For more on the modulo-6 permutations Stockhausen extensively worked with at this time, see Toop, "Stockhausen's Electronic Works," 149–97.

30. Stockhausen to Pousseur, no date, but probably late September or early October 1953. Pousseur Collection, Paul Sacher Foundation, Basel.

31. Goeyvaerts, "Paris–Darmstadt 1947–56," 51.

32. Posseur to Stockhausen, December 17, 1953, Stockhausen Foundation, Kürten.

33. Decroupet and Ungeheuer, "Karel Goeyvaerts und die serielle Tonbandmusik," 117.

34. Eimert, "Der Sinus-Ton," 170.

35. Houtsma, "Pitch Perception," 267–95; Vogel, "Sensation of Tone, Perception of Sound, and Empiricism," 263–73; Steege, *Helmholtz and the Modern Listener*, 46–57.

36. Rehding, "Of Sirens Old and New," 84–87; Houtsma, "Pitch Perception," 275–76.

37. Helmholtz, *On the Sensations of Tone*, 52–65.

38. Houtsma, "Pitch Perception," 275.

39. Steege, *Helmholtz and the Modern Listener*, 56; Rehding, "Of Sirens Old and New," 85.

40. Pousseur, "Formal Elements in a New Compositional Material," 32. Herbert Eimert makes similar remarks in his introduction to the piece on the WDR *Nachtprogramm* broadcast from December 12, 1954. For more, refer to Eimert, "Die Sieben Stücke," *Musikalisches Nachtprogramm Sendung*, 19:45–25:05. WDR Historical Archive.

41. Handel, "Timbre Perception," 425–61.

42. Gredinger, "Serial Technique," 38.

43. Stockhausen to Pousseur, no date, probably September 8–10, 1954, Pousseur Collection, Paul Sacher Foundation, Basel. "Ich denke, da ich alle die 'Akkordeonstöne' oder eher Orgeltöne von Gredinger im Ohr habe."

44. Pousseur to Stockhausen, December 17, 1953, Stockhausen Foundation, Kürten.

45. Maconie, *The Works of Karlheinz Stockhausen*, 51.

46. Pousseur to Stockhausen, December 17, 1953, Stockhausen Foundation, Kürten. " . . . sie produzieren einen gemeinsamen *hörbaren* Kontinuation-Grundton."

47. Hui, *The Psychophysical Ear*, 81–83; A good introduction to combination tones can be found in Campbell and Greated, *The Musician's Guide to Acoustics*, 64–67 or Moore, "Loudness, Pitch and Timbre," 423–28.

48. Pousseur to Stockhausen, December 17, 1953, Stockhausen Foundation, Kürten.

49. Meyer-Eppler, "Mathematisch-akustische Grundlagen," 33–34.

50. Stockhausen to Pousseur, no date, but before February 24, 1954. Pousseur Collection, Paul Sacher Foundation, Basel. "Ich studiere seit längeren Akustik bei M. Eppler, experimentiere viel und lerne."

51. Toop, "Stockhausen and the Sine-Wave," 383; Stockhausen to Eimert, March 10, 1952, Stockhausen Foundation, Kürten.

52. Klüppelholz, *Sprache als Musik*, 39–40.

53. Sirker, "W. Meyer-Epplers Untersuchungen zu elektronischen Musik," 111–22; Ungeheuer, *Wie die elektronische Musik "erfunden" wurde.* For a contemporary discussion of the many factors that contribute to and affect timbre, see Handel, "Timbre Perception," 425–61.

54. Meyer-Eppler, *Elektrische Klangerzeugung*; Ungeheuer, *Wie die elektronische Musik "erfunden" wurde*, 69–96.

55. Maconie, *Other Planets*, 125–38; Kurtz, *Stockhausen: A Biography*, 68–72.

56. Helmholtz, *On the Sensations of Tone*, 103–19; Stumpf, *Tonpsychologie*; Stumpf, *Die Sprachlaute.* On Helmholtz's, Stumpf's, and others' insights on the continuums among pulses, pitches, vowels, and timbre, see Klotz, "Tonpsychologie und Musikforschung," 199–206; Vogel, "Sensation of Tone," 274–77; Rehding, "Of Sirens Old and New," 87. On the extensive relationship between phonetics and music, the subject of Chapter 6, see Ungeheuer, "Sprache und Musik" 355–68.

57. Rehding, "Three Music Theory Lessons," 271–78.

58. Stockhausen to Pousseur, no date, presumably December 18–25, 1953. Pousseur Collection, Paul Sacher Foundation, Basel. " . . . beruht weiter auf der Tatsache, dass sich diese Spektren in jedem Zeitaugenblick *verändern*: Töne hinzutreten, wegbleiben, in der Lautstärke wechseln."

59. Meyer-Eppler, "Mathematisch-akustische Grundlagen," 34.

60. Stockhausen to Pousseur, no date, presumably December 18–25, 1953. Pousseur Collection, Paul Sacher Foundation, Basel. "Die ideale 'Tonform' von der Sie sprechen, ist das weiße bzw. farbige Rauschen, eben ein Bandspektrum (Denken Sie an die Konsonanten t s f p etc. unserer Sprache, Glocken, Metall, etc. Wasser). Die Kombinationstöne helfen Ihnen nicht weiter: Sie rechnen mit weiteren einzelnen verschiedenen Frequenzen, aber nach wie vor mit (mehr zwar) Einzelnen."

61. Stockhausen, "Arbeitsbericht 1952/53," 38.

62. Toop, "Stockhausen's Electronic Works," 170–71; Maconie, *The Works of Karlheinz Stockhausen*, 54–57.

63. Stockhausen discusses this process in Stockhausen to Pousseur, no date, presumably early May 1954. Pousseur Collection, Paul Sacher Foundation, Basel. For more, explore the contemporary reconstruction by Williams, "Interpretation and Performance Practice."

64. Stockhausen to Pousseur, no date, presumably December 18–25, 1953. Pousseur Collection, Paul Sacher Foundation, Basel. For more on how reverberation was added in the Cologne studio, see Manning, *Electronic and Computer Music*, 57–60.

65. Iverson, "Statistical Form Amongst the Darmstadt Composers," 341–87.

66. Boehmer, "Koenig—Sound Composition—*Essay*," 62–63; Decroupet and Ungeheuer, "Through the Sensory Looking Glass," 1–40; Williams, "Technical Influence and Physical Constraint."

67. Stockhausen to Pousseur, no date, presumably early May 1954. Pousseur Collection, Paul Sacher Foundation, Basel. "Die 'Verwischung' am Anfang der Klänge müssen Sie noch genauer präzisieren, da es tausend Möglichkeiten gibt der Spektralen Evolution (Einschwingvorgang) im Abhängigkeit von Zeitquanten."

68. Stockhausen to Pousseur, no date, presumably early May 1954. Pousseur Collection, Paul Sacher Foundation, Basel. "Es ist das erste Mal, dass ich mich frei fühle, ganze Komplexe auszuprobieren und komponieren zu können (*praktisch*)."

69. Decroupet and Ungeheuer, "Karel Goeyvaerts und die serielle Tonbandmusik," 117.

70. Pousseur to Stockhausen, June 2, 1954, Stockhausen Foundation, Kürten. "Wenn ich Ihnen etwas versichern kann, so ist es, daß es wirklich nichts in Ihrem vor-vorigen Briefe gab, was mir 'nicht behagte.' Wenn es doch so aussah, so bitte ich um Verziehung. Schuld ist nun mein doch nicht so perfekte Beherrschen der deutschen Sprache, das warscheinliche gebrauchen von einem Ausdrucke für ein anderes, so dazu es vielleicht scheint, ich hätte etwas hinter meinem Gedanken, was ich nun 'durch die Blume' sagen möchte, und in Wirklichkeit ist nichts. Ehrenwort. Was meine elektronische Arbeit angeht, so bin ich sehr ungeduldig zu hören, gerade weil ich über das Resultat unsicher bin."

71. Stockhausen to Pousseur, May 15, 1954, Pousseur Collection, Paul Sacher Foundation, Basel. "Daß wir Hüllkurven auch in Zukunft mehr als statistische Phänomene betrachten sollten—also als eine übergeordnete Gruppe von mikroskopischen Lautstärke-veränderungen in Abhängigkeit von einer kleinsten Zeiteinheit, und dass dann ebenso wenig stetige evolutionäre Bewegungen wie Schablonen vorkommen dürfen, wie in Tonhöhen und Zeitdauern, wo man ja auch niemals chromatische Leitern zu lassen würde ist klar."

72. Stockhausen to Pousseur, no date, presumably September 8–10, 1954. Pousseur Collection, Paul Sacher Foundation, Basel. "[. . .] die einzelner Töne werde ich in sehr dichten und raschen folgen (winzig Kurze) ineinander, lieben ('Konfettiwolke') und dann aber noch mit einer übergeordneten dynamischen kurve versehen."

73. Eimert's *Etüde über Tongemische* is commercially unavailable, but the piece is played in its entirety on the *Nachtprogramm* broadcast from December 9, 1954 (Eimert, "Die Sieben Stücke," 38:40–43:17, WDR Historical Archive). In a short introduction, Eimert explains that the piece is composed of sounds arranged in an inharmonic spectrum; each sound in this piece has nine partials [*neun Teiltöne*], which are synthesized into five sounds [*funf Klänge*], transposed at nine different levels [*neun verschiedene Stufen*], and grouped in nine different time fields [*Zeitfeldern*].

74. Nono to Maderna, November 5, 1953, Maderna Collection, Paul Sacher Foundation, Basel.

75. Eimert to Stockhausen, March 7, 1952, Stockhausen Foundation, Kürten.

76. Goeyvaerts, "Paris–Darmstadt 1947–56," 51–52.

77. Iverson, "From Analog to Digital," 55.

78. Stockhausen to Pousseur, December 5, 1954, Pousseur Collection, Paul Sacher Foundation, Basel.

79. Stockhausen to Pousseur, December 5, 1954, Pousseur Collection, Paul Sacher Foundation, Basel. "Eine zweite Neuigkeit: Schlee von der U.E. [Universal Edition] will mir eine Zeitschrift finanzieren. Mit Eimert mache ich dann nominell zusammen diese Zeitschrift, effektive werde ich doch die ganze Arbeit übernehmen müssen. Ich habe es so verlangt: Redaktion Eimert, Regie Stockh. Der Title ist noch nicht ganz endgültig. Kannst Du mir für das erste Heft einen Artikel (ca. 8 Druckseiten, möglichst nicht mehr) schreiben zum Sujet da elektronischen Musik? Das erste Heft ist ausschließlich der elektr. Musik gewidmet. Ich möchte gerne, dass Du 'von außen gesehen' in diesem Artikel unter anderen einmal deutlich und doch geschickt verborgen berichtest, was effektiv getan und neu gesehen, was Klischee und was aktive Erweiterung des Kompositionsmetiers, was dummes äußerliches Getue und effektive, prinzipielle Neufundierung ist, welche Dinge Kritisch stimmen, kurz: was Du als wirklichen Gewissen der ersten 1 ½ Jahre elektronischer Komposition siehst."

80. Grant, *Serial Music, Serial Aesthetics*, 2.

81. For instance, see the 1955–1956 correspondence between Berio and Stockhausen. Berio collection, Paul Sacher Foundation, Basel.

82. Priore, "The Origins of *Incontri Musicali*," 7–26. Unfortunately, Priore discusses only the print journal, when in fact the concert series was probably just as, if not more, impactful, especially in reaching the interested public.

83. See for instance, the correspondence between Pousseur and Berio in 1955–1957. Berio Collection and Pousseur Collection, Paul Sacher Foundation, Basel.

84. Samuel, liner notes to *Pierre Boulez: Le Domaine Musical*, 8–14; Aguila, *Le Domaine Musical*; Beal, "An Interview with Earle Brown," 349.

85. Beal, *New Music, New Allies*, 52–77; Iddon, *New Music at Darmstadt*, 156–64; Thacker, *Music After Hitler 1945–55*, 75–98.

86. Darmstadt is studied most comprehensively in Borio and Danuser, *Im Zenit der Moderne*, 3 vols; and Iddon, *New Music at Darmstadt*. On competition between *Die Reihe* and similar journals, see Custodis, *Die soziale Isolation*, 87.

87. Steinitz, *György Ligeti*, 72–95; Toop, *György Ligeti*, 45–72.

88. Private conversation with Lukas Ligeti, March 17, 2008; see also Taruskin, *Oxford History*, 49–53.

89. Steinitz, *György Ligeti*, 77.

90. Sallis, *An Introduction to the Early Works*, 204–17 and 226–61.

91. Ligeti, *Gesammelte Schriften*. See the genesis at the end of each essay.

92. "Decision and Automatism," 36–62; "The Third Piano Sonata by Boulez [1959]," 56–58; "Metamorphoses of Musical Form [1960]," 5–19. Ligeti lectured at Darmstadt in 1959 ("Form and Strukturprobleme bei Webern"); 1960 ("Entwicklung der elektronische Musik"); 1961 ("Theoretische Konsequenzen der Webernschen Musik"); 1962 ("Komposition mit Klangfarben"); 1964 ("Klangtechnik und Form"); and 1966 ("Kompositionstechnik und musikalische Form"); see Borio and Danuser, *Im Zenit der Moderne*, vol. 3, 583–638.

93. Ligeti, "Auswirkungen der elektronischen Musik," 86–94. See also "Mein Kölner Jahr 1957," 29–32; "Musik und Technik," 237–61.

94. Stockhausen, *Stockhausen on Music*, 71; Ligeti, *Ligeti in Conversation*, 34; Lobanova, *György Ligeti: Style, Ideas, and Poetics*, 29–31.

95. Ligeti, *"Träumen Sie im Farbe?,"* 84. "Koenig war der beste und hilfreichste Mensch, den man sich nur vorstellen kann." See also Koenig, "Ligeti und die elektronische Musik," 11–26.

96. *Glissandi* is available on Wergo 60161; *Artikulation* is available on this disc as well as Teldec 510998 and 88262. A "listening score" for *Artikulation*, which is an artistic rendering by Rainer Wehinger, is available from Schott (ED 6378-20). For critical analysis, see Levy, "Shades of the Studio," 59–87.

97. It was finally realized with digital technology in 1996 by Kees Tazelaar and Johan von Kreij of the Institute of Sonology: *His Masters Noise*, BVHAAST CD 06/0701, 1996, or *Anthology of Noise and Electronic Music*, vol. 4, SubRosa Records SR 250, 2007. The Paul Sacher Foundation holds Ligeti's original, hand-drawn score, Schott holds a facsimile of this score, and a facsimile appears in Ove Nordwall, ed., *Ligeti-dokument* (Stockholm: P.A. Norstedt & Söners, 1968).

98. Ligeti, "Auswirkungen der elektronischen Musik," 77. Seppo Heikinheimo quotes Stockhausen in 1958 expressing a similar sentiment, though of course Stockhausen did continue to compose electronic music; see *The Electronic Music of Karlheinz Stockhausen*, 50–51. "Ich befinde mich in den letzten Jahren in einem Zustand, in dem ich ein wenig unbefriedigt bin über die akustischen Ergebnisse dessen, was man im elektronischen Studio machen kann, unabhängig davon, welche Studioeinrichtung vorhanden ist, es geht nicht um die Perfektion der Studioeinrichtung."

99. Iverson, "Shared Compositional Techniques," 29–33; Iverson, "The Emergence of Timbre," 62–63; Levy, "The Electronic Works of György Ligeti."

100. See Dibelius, *György Ligeti*, 61; Koenig, "Ligeti und die elektronische Musik," 25; Ligeti, "Auswirkungen der elektronischen Musik," 86; Ligeti, "Musik und Technik," 246; Steinitz, *György Ligeti*, 111; Toop, *György Ligeti*, 61.

101. In producing Figure 3.13, I made the conversion from pitch to hertz with a chart that Stockhausen used, apparently for a similar purpose, in planning *Gesang der Jünglinge*, faksimilie ed., 19.

102. For more on Ligeti's micropolyphony and voice-leading techniques, see Bernard, "Inaudible Structures, Audible Music," 207–36; Bernard, "Voice Leading as a Spatial Function," 227–53; Clendinning, "Contrapuntal Techniques"; Clendinning, "Structural Factors in the Microcanonic Compositions," 229–58; Lobanova, *György Ligeti*, 3–38; Roig-Francoli, "Harmonic and Formal Processes," 242–77.

103. Ligeti, *Ligeti in Conversation*, 37.

104. Ligeti, "Auswirkungen der elektronischen Musik," 92.

105. Ligeti, "Auswirkungen der elektronischen Musik," 92.

106. For more, see Levy, "Shades of the Studio," 81–83.

107. Wilson, "György Ligeti and the Rhetoric of Autonomy," 5–28.

108. See for instance Stockhausen, "The Origins of Electronic Music," 649–50 and Eimert's counter narrative in "How Electronic Music Began," 347–49.

109. Shapin, "The Invisible Technician," 554–63.

110. Goeyvaerts, "Paris: Darmstadt 1947–56," 53–54.

111. http://www.horizont.net/agenturen/nachrichten/Verstorbener-GGK-Gruender-Nachruf-auf-Paul-Gredinger-117184 (accessed February 5, 2016).

112. Pickering, *The Mangle of Practice*, 21–27.

113. Pousseur's *Symphonies à quinze solistes* (1954–1955) is contemporaneous with his *Seismogrammes*; Koenig continued to compose acoustic music—such as *Diagonalen* (1955; orch.), *Zwei Klavierstücke* (1957) and Wind Quintet (1958–1959)—as he simultaneously became an expert in the WDR machinery and realized numerous electronic works including *Klangfiguren I* (1955), *Klangfiguren II* (1955–1956), and *Essay* (1957–1958).

Chapter 4

1. Eimert, "Werner Meyer-Eppler," 5–6.

2. Meyer-Eppler, "Statistic and Psychologic Problems of Sound," 57–58; Heike, "Informationstheorie und musikalische Komposition," 269–72; Heike, "Informationstheorie und serielle Musik," 35–45.

3. Koenig, private email communication with author, June 13, 2016. Also of interest is a letter from Stockhausen to Heike about compositional technique, followed by Heike's information-theoretic interpretation in Heike, *Musiksprache und Sprachmusik*, 119–24.

4. Stockhausen, "Von Webern zu Debussy: Bermerkungen zur statistischen Form," 75–85.

5. Koenig, "Commentary," 98; Stockhausen, " . . . how time passes . . . ," 10–40. Koenig's article "Music and Number" formulates similar concepts as Stockhausen's.

6. For more, see Nakai, "In Other Words," 63–78.

7. Fokker, "Wherefore, and Why?," 68–79.

8. Backus, "*Die Reihe:* A Scientific Evaluation," 160–71.

9. Backus, "*Die Reihe:* A Scientific Evaluation," 165.

10. Backus, "*Die Reihe:* A Scientific Evaluation," 165, 163, respectively.

11. Perle, "*Die Reihe* Vol. III: Musical Craftsmanship: A Review," 102–104; a good critical discussion of these exchanges and complaints is Grant, *Serial Music, Serial Aesthetics*, 1–7.

12. Gieryn, "Boundary-Work," 781–95; Kline, "What Is Information Theory a Theory Of?," 15–28.

13. Gieryn, "Boundary-Work," 791–92.

14. Gieryn, "Boundary-Work," 781.

15. Riesch, "Theorizing Boundary Work as Representation and Identity," 452–73.

16. Bertalanffy, *General System Theory*; von Neumann and Morgenstern, *Theory of Games and Economic Behavior*; Wiener, *Cybernetics, or Control and Communication in the Animal and the Machine*.

17. Heims, *John von Neumann and Norbert Wiener*; Rider, "Operations Research and Game Theory," 225–39.

18. Galison, "The Ontology of the Enemy," 228–66.

19. Edwards, *The Closed World*; Turner, *From Counterculture to Cyberculture*; Turner, *The Democratic Surround*.

20. Geoghegan and Peters, "Cybernetics," 109–13; Hayles, *How We Became Posthuman*, 50–112; Heims, *Constructing a Social Science for Postwar America*; Kline, *The Cybernetics Moment*; Pickering, *The Cybernetic Brain*; Wiener, *The Human Use of Human Beings*.

21. Edwards, *The Closed World*, 43–73.

22. Mailman, "Cybernetic Phenomenology of Music."

23. WDR *Musikalisches Nachtprogramm*, December 23, 1954. WDR Historical Archive, folio 15199.

24. Stockhausen to Pousseur, December 5, 1954, Pousseur collection, Paul Sacher Foundation. "Gerade hatte ich in der Woche vorher an der Arbeit für ein Debussy Nachtprogramm angefangen ('Jeux' in Hinsicht auf unsere neuen statischen Formprobleme analysiert). Was denkst Du: aus dem Zusammenhang ein kleines Stückchen Debussy, das Wort 'statistisch' dazwischen, ein Stückchen aus der Etüde f. Tongemische: voila— Debussy + die elektronische Musik."

25. Stockhausen, "Von Webern zu Debussy," 78; emphasis Stockhausen's. Vertical density probably referred to the thickness of the orchestration, whereas horizontal density probably referred to the number of attacks in a time frame, both concerns that Stockhausen explicitly addressed in sketching *Gruppen* (1955–1957), as we will see.

26. Stockhausen to Boulez, no date but probably beginning of November 1953, letter 35, transcribed by Robert Piencikowski, translation mine. Pierre Boulez Collection, Paul Sacher Foundation. All grammatical and spelling errors preserved from Stockhausen's orthography. "Je me trouve de plus en plus dans la composition statistique: 'improvisation' serielle entre limits des espaces serielles du temps, de l'hauteur, de l'intensité. Le propoportions [*sic*] logarithmic (fonctionnelle) des series de frequence et db [*sic*] sont liées au temps. Les groups serielles des intervalles (d'hauteur,—egalement d'intensité et durée) divisent les espaces statistiques. On se tient entre les limites travaillant sur les directions des intervalles. Permutations dans les groups silences et superpositions (aspect polyphon et egalement du timbre non stationär) sont resultat de cette rotation en valves."

27. Stockhausen, *Conversations With the Composer*, ed. Jonathan Cott, 73; Trochim, "Descriptive Statistics."

28. Boulez to Stockhausen, no date but probably mid-November 1953, letter 36, transcribed by Robert Piencikowski, translation mine. Pierre Boulez collection, Paul Sacher Foundation. "Votre dernière lettre est vraiment très ésotérique. Et j'avoue que malgré toute mon application, et malgré mon habitude à déchiffrer les ellipses, je n'ai pu résoudre toutes les énigmes que me proposait votre dernière lettre. [. . .] Qu'est-ce que vous appelez composition 'statistique'? Qu'est-ce que vous entendez exactement par 'improvisation' entre les différentes limites? Qu'est-ce que vous appelez 'espaces statistiques'? Qu'est-ce que vous entendez par 'travailler sur les directions des intervalles'? Qu'est-ce que vous appelez 'rotations en valves'?"

29. Pousseur, "Formal Elements in a New Compositional Material," 32–33.

30. Eimert, "What is Electronic Music?," 7.

31. Berio, "Aspetti di artigianato formale," 65–66. I am grateful to Matthew Schullman for pointing me toward this text and for sharing his draft of an English translation.

32. Iverson, "Statistical Form Amongst the Darmstadt Composers," 341–87; Ungeheuer, "Statistical Gestalts—Perceptible Features in Serial Music," 103–113; Cohen and Dubnov, "Gestalt Phenomena in Musical Texture," 386–405.

33. Shannon and Weaver, *The Mathematical Theory of Communication*. The work first appeared split into two technical articles in the *Bell System Technical Journal* 27, no. 3 (379–423) and no. 4 (623–56). In the 1949 book version, Weaver's summary comments are reprinted from his layperson gloss that first appeared in *Scientific American*.

34. Soni and Goodman, *Mind at Play*; Nahin, *The Logician and the Engineer*; Gleick, *The Information*, 168–268; and Gertner, *The Idea Factory*, 115–48.

35. The contributions of Nyquist and Hartley were especially consequential; see Gleick, *The Information*, 198–200; Kline, "What is Information Theory a Theory Of?," 16–17; Sterne, *MP3*, 80–87.

36. Pierce, *Introduction to Information Theory*, 8.

37. For more on this, see Sterne, *MP3*, 78–91.

38. For more on this, see Halsey and Swaffield, "Analysis-Synthesis Telephony," 391–406; Gertner, *The Idea Factory*, 20–21.

39. Mills, "Deaf Jam," 35–58; Mills, "The Dead Room."

40. Kittler, "Signal-to-Noise Ratio," 165–77; Sterne, *MP3*.

41. I refer to the 1966 translation by Joel Cohen: Moles, *Information Theory and Esthetic Perception*, 10–11.

42. http://monoskop.org/Abraham_Moles (accessed March 2, 2016).

43. Moles, *Information Theory*, 11. For more on the "domestication of noise," see Sterne, *MP3*, 92–127.

44. Gertner, *The Idea Factory*, 123–24; Kline, *The Cybernetics Moment*, 9–36; Kittler, "Signal-to-Noise Ratio," 165–77.

45. Quoted in Gleick, *The Information*, 188; see also Gertner, *The Idea Factory*, 161–62.

46. Shannon and Turing were acquaintances, but not direct collaborators. They met at Bell Labs during the war, and though they were prohibited from discussing their respective cryptography work by their high-level security clearances, they did discuss abstract, theoretical mathematics. Gleick, *The Information*, 212–15.

47. Hodges, *Alan Turing*; Kittler, "The Artificial Intelligence of World War," 178–94.

48. Kittler, "Unconditional Surrender," 123.

49. Kittler, *Grammophone, Film, Typewriter*, 97.

50. For more on the perceptual, acoustic, and physical-science considerations of radio broadcasting, see Nahin, *The Science of Radio*, 1–118.

51. Ungeheuer, *Wie die elektronische Musik*, 217.

52. Meyer-Eppler, *Grundlagen und Anwendungen der Informationstheorie*.

53. Shannon and Weaver, *The Mathematical Theory of Communication*, 25.

54. Sterne, *MP3*, 32–60; Mills, "Deaf Jam," 35–58; Mills, "Media and Prosthesis," 107–49; Mills, "On Disability Cybernetics," 74–111.

55. Meyer-Eppler, *Grundlagen und Anwendungen*, 175; emphasis in original. "Nach der *Abgrenzung* des Wahrnehmungsraumes kann dessen *empfindungsbezogene Struktur* erforscht werden." In the passage, Meyer-Eppler uses these terms, especially *Empfindung*, which usually connotes intuitive sensibility, in a rather idiosyncratic way. This is part of a twentieth-century German scientific tradition of reshaping and even inventing new terminology, as a counter to the more nineteenth-century Nietzschean practice of moving in between the layered and implicit meanings that accrue to words in order to exploit this multiplicity.

56. Klüppelholz, *Sprache als Musik*, 39–40.

57. Ligeti, *Ligeti in Conversation*, 10.

58. See Boulez, "Current Investigations," 15–19; Xenakis, "Wahrscheinlichkeitstheorie und Musik," 28–34; Pousseur, "Outline of a Method," 44–48.

59. Ligeti, *Ligeti in Conversation*, 10.

60. Grant, *Serial Music, Serial Aesthetics*, 131–64; Griffiths, *Modern Music and After*, 76–69; Osmond-Smith, "New Beginnings: The International Avant-Garde, 1945–62," 336–63.

61. In the United States, Milton Babbitt spoke about American serial music in these terms. Babbitt, "The Composer as Specialist," 48–54.

62. Iverson, "Statistical Form," 343, 365.

63. Maconie, *Other Planets*, 133.

64. Misch, "On the Serial Shaping of Stockhausen's *Gruppen für drei orchester*," 143–87; Misch, *Zur Kompositionstechnik Karlheinz Stockhausens*.

65. Koenig, *Essay*. Koenig explains a graphic notation system used by Bo Nilsson (and Stockhausen in *Studie II*) in Koenig, "Bo Nilsson," 85–88. For a more speculative article that grapples with the problem of notation in electronic music, see Eimert, Enkel, and Stockhausen, "Problems of Electronic Music Notation," 52–54.

66. Gertner, *The Idea Factory*, 129.

67. Sterne, *MP3*, 61–91.

68. Shannon and Weaver, *The Mathematical Theory of Communication*, 108.

69. Pierce, *Introduction to Information Theory*, 76.

70. For a thorough discussion of the many factors and debates around sampling and compression, including an illuminating discussion of the perceptual testing process for various musical codecs (MP3, MPEG, etc.), see Sterne, *MP3*, 138–83.

71. Ligeti, "Musik und Technik," 237; Ligeti, "Auswirkungen der elektronischen Musik," 86–94; *Ligeti in Conversation*, 39–40.

72. This is an insight that seemingly every generation rediscovers; see Rehding, "Of Sirens Old and New," 86–87; Rehding, "Three Music Theory Lessons," 271–79; Rehding, "Instruments of Music Theory."

73. Stockhausen, " . . . how time passes . . . ," 10.

74. Stockhausen, " . . . how time passes . . . ," 10.

75. This is all described in the score for *Essay*, in both German and English. Koenig explained to me, "The design of many little tape pieces was only used to produce a so-called material. This material (tape) was then multiplied with simple tape techniques to produce a couple of derivations; all derivations together, according to a time schedule, then form a section (section, e.g. consists of 7 such tapes). In this way I was able to produce the whole of *Essay* in 4 weeks time!" (private email communication with author, June 13, 2016).

76. Koenig, *Essay*, 13.

77. London, *Hearing in Time*, 27.

78. Studies summarized by London in *Hearing in Time*, 28–29.

79. London, *Hearing in Time*, 27.

80. In his analysis, Boehmer focuses much more on these statistical and textural aspects of *Essay*; Boehmer, "Koenig-Sound Composition-*Essay*," 64–70.

81. Koenig, private email communication with author, June 19, 2014. "Besonders interessant für mich waren 'Stauchung' und 'Dehnung' der Klangstruktur, vergleichbar der Betrachtung einer optisch wahrnehmbaren Struktur durch ein Opernglas, richtig bzw. verkehrt herum gehalten. Durch Verlängerung schaut man gewissermaßen 'ins Innere' der Struktur, während durch Verkürzung die Struktur zusammenschrumpft, zu einem Farbfleck sozusagen, wodurch wohl der Ausdruck 'Bewegungsfarbe' (d.h.

Farbwirkung durch einen Bewegungsvorgang) entstand. Ligeti, der mir bei Essay assistierte, bezeichnete diesen Effekt auch als 'Sukzessionsverwischung,' ein Ausdruck, der das Phänomen besser beschreibt als Bewegungsfarbe. Denn dieser 'Farbfleck' bewegt sich nicht, auch sein Zustandekommen durch Bewegung (Beschleunigung) wird nicht bemerkt, und das Wort 'Farbe' verdankt sich, mangels einer musikalischen Terminologie, nur der Assoziation an die reichhaltigere Begriffswelt des Sichtbaren."

82. "I learned from him [Koenig] not only the technique, but also a compositional way of thinking. Stockhausen and Koenig were the teachers in my 'second schooling' (I was at the time 33 years old, soon to be 34)." Ligeti, quoted in Hilberg and Vogt, eds., *Musik der Zeit*, 152.

83. Clendinning, "The Pattern-Meccanico Compositions of György Ligeti," 192–234.

84. Levy, "Shades of the Studio," 59–87; Iverson, "The Emergence of Timbre," 61–89.

85. Kaiser, "Listening to Recorded Voices in Modern Music," 184–237; Stockhausen, *Gesang der Jünglinge*, 3–4.

86. Boehmer, "Koenig—Sound Composition—*Essay*," 62–63. Boehmer represents the technique as Koenig's solution to a compositional problem in Stockhausen's *Gesang*; Koenig remembers this technique relating to glissandi production in his later piece *Terminus*. In any event, it remains possible that Koenig and Stockhausen experimented together with these kinds of approximations as early as 1954 or 1955; recall the discussion in Chapter 3 of the *Konfettiwolke* in a letter to Pousseur in September 1954.

87. Williams, "Technical Influence and Physical Constraint."

88. Stockhausen, *Conversations With the Composer*, 72.

89. A point also made strongly by Sean Williams. For more, see Williams, "Interpretation and Performance Practice," 445–81; Williams, "Stockhausen Meets King Tubby's," 163–88.

90. Koenig, "Studio Technique [1955]," 54.

91. Gleick, *The Information*, 224.

92. Smith, *The Secrets of Station X*; Smith, *The Hidden History of Bletchley Park*; for first-hand accounts, see Hinsley and Stripp, eds., *Codebreakers: The Inside Story of Bletchley Park*. The classic and thorough history of ciphering more generally is Kahn, *The Codebreakers*.

93. Good, "Enigma and Fish," 149–66; Haufler, *Codebreakers' Victory*, 22–34; Beckman, *Codebreakers*; Stripp, "The Enigma Machine," 83–88.

94. Beckman, *Codebreakers*, 75–76; Ratcliff, *Delusions of Intelligence*, 202–13.

95. Gleick, *The Information*, 216

96. Gleick, *The Information*, 225; Moles, *Information Theory*, 41; Shannon and Weaver, *The Mathematical Theory of Communication*, 39.

97. Shannon and Weaver, *The Mathematical Theory of Communication*, 43.

98. Eimert, "Debussy's *Jeux*"; Meyer-Eppler, "Statistic and Psychologic Problems," 57–58.

99. Lewin, "Some Applications of Communication Theory to the Study of Twelve-Tone Music," 50.

100. Xenakis's writings appear in *Gravesaner Blätter* nos. 11–12 and 18–24; they were later expanded into *Musiques formelles* and translated as *Formalized Music*. For more on the founding and mission of the *Gravesaner Blätter*, see Tazelaar, *On the Threshold of Beauty*, 59–61.

101. His electronic music comprises only ten percent of his oeuvre, but as for many of his peers, is transformational for his development in this period. For a complete list

of electroacoustic works, visit http://www.iannis-xenakis.org/xen/works/genres/genre_
10.html (accessed March 2, 2016).

102. Moles, "Informationstheorie und ästhetische Empfindung," and "Kolloquium: Informationstheorie und Musik."

103. Huron, *Sweet Anticipation.*

104. Moles, *Information Theory and Esthetic Perception,* 65–70.

105. Xenakis, "Wahrscheinlichkeitstheorie," 28–34.

106. Gibson, *The Instrumental Music of Iannis Xenakis,* 66–67.

107. Lovelace, "How Do You Draw a Sound," 35–94; Harley, *Iannis Xenakis*; Squibbs, "An Analytical Approach"; Tazelaar, *On the Threshold of Beauty,* 115 and 138.

108. The best account of this important interdisciplinary collaboration is Tazelaar, *On the Threshold of Beauty,* 101–71. Xenakis was an invisible collaborator behind the more famous Le Corbusier, who initially refused to acknowledge Xenakis's leading role; see also Xenakis, "Le Corbusier's 'Electronic Poem'—the Philips Pavilion," 51–54; Varga, *Conversations with Iannis Xenakis,* 24; Flašar, "Poème Électronique (1958)"; Squibbs, "An Analytical Approach," 4–6; Harley, *Iannis Xenakis,* 17–18; and Lovelace, "How Do You Draw a Sound," 53.

109. Varga, *Conversations with Iannis Xenakis,* 24.

110. This interlude resembles *Concret PH* but is not identical to it; see Tazelaar, *On the Threshold of Beauty,* 153.

111. Pierce, *An Introduction to Information Theory,* 80.

112. Varga, *Conversations With Iannis Xenakis,* 77.

113. Varga, *Conversations With Iannis Xenakis,* 77.

114. Childs, "*Achorripsis:* A Sonification of Probability Distributions"; Squibbs, "The Composer's Flair"; Wannamaker, "Mathematics and Design in the Music of Iannis Xenakis," 127–41.

115. Xenakis, *Formalized Music,* 22–38.

116. Rowe, "Iannis Xenakis and Algorithmic Composition," 42–44.

117. Meyer-Eppler, *Grundlagen und Anwendungen,* 33–38, 105–9, 162–72, 222–23, 247–48.

118. Koenig, "Music and Number," [1958].

119. Quoted in Iverson, "From Analog to Digital," 52.

120. Koenig, "My Experiences with Programmed Music" [1975], 3.

121. Koenig, "My Experiences," 4.

122. Koenig, "The Construction of Sound."

123. As Gibson wrote, "While avant-garde composers such as Boulez or Stockhausen developed their compositional methods on the basis of serial techniques, Xenakis followed criteria other than those stemming from any musical tradition" (*The Instrumental Music of Iannis Xenakis,* 65). See also Hewett, "A Music Beyond Time," 26–27. For a refreshingly more nuanced perspective that sees Boulez and Xenakis as approaching the same problems from different angles, see LeBlanc, "Xenakis's Aesthetic Project," 65–66.

124. Touloumi, "The Politics of Totality," 121–22.

125. Hewett, "A Music Beyond Time," 31.

126. Harley, *Iannis Xenakis,* 4–16; Varga, *Conversations with Iannis Xenakis,* 33–37.

127. For more, see Varga, *Conversations with Iannis Xenakis,* 110–22.

128. Varga, *Conversations with Iannis Xenakis,* 43.

129. Varga, *Conversations with Iannis Xenakis*, 35–36.

130. Ligeti, *"Träumen Sie im Farbe?"* "Meine Schwierigkeiten sind die Schwierigkeiten, die alle Leute mit ihm haben: Stockhausens unendliche Selbstbezogenheit. Das wurde mit dem Alter immer extremer. Er und Iannis Xenakis sind die zwei Komponisten, die absolut nichts von Kollegen wissen wollten" (95). "Für Stockhausen und Boulez existierte er nicht" (98).

131. Stockhausen to Christoph Both, quoted in "The Influence of Concepts of Information Theory on Electronic Music Composition," 275–76, emphasis Stockhausen's.

132. For more, see Turner, *From Counterculture to Cyberculture*, 11–40; Turner, *The Democratic Surround*, 259–93.

133. Benjamin, "Theses on the Philosophy of History," 257–58. Benjamin wrote, "His face is turned toward the past. Where we perceive a chain of events, he sees one single catastrophe which keeps piling wreckage upon wreckage and hurls it in front of his feet. The angel would like to stay, awaken the dead, and make whole what has been smashed. But a storm is blowing from Paradise; it has got caught in his wings with such violence that the angel can no longer close them. The storm irresistibly propels him into the future to which his back his turned, while the pile of debris before him grows skyward. The storm is what we call progress."

Chapter 5

1. Decroupet, "Aleatorik und Indetermination," in *Im Zenit der Moderne*, vol. 2, 231–40; Griffiths, *Cage*, 30–38; Gann, *There's No Such Thing as Silence*, 193; Iddon, *New Music at Darmstadt*, 196–303; Shultis, "Cage and Europe," 20–40; Taruskin, *Oxford History of Western Music*, vol. 5, 55, 64–65.

2. Two scholars that provide extremely nuanced accounts, and caution against this kind of reductionism, include Iddon, *New Music at Darmstadt*, 215; Shultis, "Cage in Europe," 34–35.

3. Data collated from programs included in Borio and Danuser, *Im Zenit der Moderne*, vol. 3, 583–601. Note that the performance date for Boulez's *Troisième Sonate* is erroneously given by Jameux as 1957 (*Pierre Boulez*, 87) and by Edwards as 1958 ("Unpublished Bouleziana," 4).

4. Cage, "Changes" (18–34), "Indeterminacy" (35–40), and "Communication" (41–56), in *Silence*.

5. Boehmer, *Zur Theorie der offenen Form*; Decroupet, "Aleatorik und Indetermination"; Schmidt, "Die offene Frage der offenen Form."

6. For more on how the pianist David Tudor realized the indeterminate and graphic scores of the Cage group, see Nakai, "On the Instrumental Natures of David Tudor's Music"; Holzaepfel, "David Tudor and the Performance of American Experimental Music 1950–59"; Iddon, *John Cage and David Tudor: Correspondence on Interpretation and Performance*, 56–94 and 138–87; Haskins, *John Cage*, 70–72.

7. Dibelius, *György Ligeti*, 9–18; Steinitz, *György Ligeti*, 79–82; Toop, *György Ligeti*, 56–61; Wehinger, *Ligeti-Artikulation*, 5–19.

8. Ligeti, "Bermerkungen zu *Artikulation*," 166–68.

9. Wehinger, *Ligeti-Artikulation*, 17–19; Levy, "The Electronic Works of György Ligeti," 100–102; Levy, *Metamorphosis in Music*, 63–76; Iverson, "Learning the Studio," 375–80.

10. Enkel, "The Technical Facilities," 8–15; Manning, *Electronic and Computer Music*, 43–57. For a similar sketch with more sound materials, see Wehinger, *Ligeti-Artikulation*, 12.

11. Weisstein, "Arithmetic Series."

12. Ligeti, "Pierre Boulez: Decision and Automatism," 39, 54. See also Levy, "The Electronic Works of György Ligeti," 96–97; Levy, "Shades of the Studio," 61–63.

13. Ligeti, "Bermerkungen zu *Artikulation*," 166.

14. John Cage to Pierre Boulez, May 22, 1951, *The Boulez–Cage Correspondence* #28, 94–95.

15. Wehinger, Ligeti-Artikulation, 17–18.

16. Ligeti, "Bermerkungen zu *Artikulation*," 168.

17. Levy, "The Electronic Works of György Ligeti," 105.

18. Jakobson and Halle, *Fundamentals of Language*, 8, 17. Jakobson's ideas were transmitted by Hans G. Helms, a Cologne intellectual who hosted a James Joyce reading group that Ligeti attended in 1957. Helms studied with Jakobson at Harvard in the mid-1950s. See Fricke, "Helms, Hans G."

19. Quoted in Kurtz, *Stockhausen: A Biography*, 70; see also Maconie, *Other Planets*, 160–61.

20. Berio to Pousseur, October 5, 1956, Pousseur Collection, Paul Sacher Foundation, Basel. For the conversion of historical Lire to dollars, http://fxtop.com/en/currency-converter-past.php; for the conversion of 1957 dollars to 2017 dollars, http://usinflationcalculator.com (both accessed September 9, 2017). Although the correspondence suggests Pousseur was invited for an intended stay of two or three months, Pascal Decroupet says he only had six weeks to compose *Scambi* ("Studio di Fonologia," 101). A condensed version of this analysis appears in Iverson, "Learning the Studio," 373–75.

21. Lietti, "The Technical Equipment of the Electronic Music Studio of Radio Milan," 116–21; see also John Cage's schematic diagrams and photographs of the actual equipment in *The Studio di Fonologia*, ed. Novati and Dack (color plates).

22. De Benedictis, "A Meeting of Music and the New Possibilities of Technology" (3–18); Vidolin, "The School of Fonologia" (19–31); Rodà, "Evolution of the Technical Means" (33–81); Belletti, "The Audio Laboratory and the Studio di Fonologia Musicale" (83–87) in *The Studio di Fonologia*, ed. Novati and Dack.

23. Berio to Pousseur, January 25, 1957, Pousseur Collection, Paul Sacher Foundation.

24. Manning, *Electronic and Computer Music*, 71–72. Forthcoming research on this machine and its related scientific, intellectual, and cultural discourses is Mara Mills and Jonathan Sterne, *Tuning Time: Histories of Sound and Speed* (forthcoming, University of Minnesota Press).

25. Rodà, "Evolution of the Technical Means," 35; Vidolin, "The School of Fonologia," 26.

26. Berio to Pousseur, January 25, 1957, Pousseur Collection, Paul Sacher Foundation, Basel.

27. Dack, "*Scambi* and the Studio di Fonologia," 129.

28. Pousseur, "*Scambi:* Description of a Work in Progress," 36–47 (German) and 48–54 (English, poorly translated). Christine North produced a second English translation from the original French, which is available at http://www.scambi.mdx.ac.uk/documents.html (accessed April 13, 2016). Quotation appears on p. 3 of North's translation.

29. Pousseur, "*Scambi*," 3.

30. Cohen and Dubnov "Gestalt Phenomena in Musical Texture," 386–405; Iverson, "Statistical Form," 341–87; Stockhausen, "Von Webern zu Debussy," 75–85; Ungeheuer, "Statistical Gestalts," 103–13.

31. Pousseur, "*Scambi*," 10.

32. Stockhausen to Pousseur, no date, probably December 18–25, 1953. Pousseur Collection, Paul Sacher Foundation.

33. Pousseur, "*Scambi*," 8.

34. Pousseur "*Scambi*," 10.

35. Pousseur "*Scambi*," 10.

36. For more, see Dack, "*Scambi* and the Studio di Fonologia," 123–39; Dack, "The Electroacoustic Music of Henri Pousseur and the 'Open Form,'" 177–89; Decroupet, "Studio di Fonologia," 99–104; and Decroupet, "Vers une théorie generale," 31–43.

37. Pousseur, "*Scambi*," 12.

38. Pousseur, "*Scambi*," 12; Wilkinson, "Two Months in the 'Studio di Fonologia,'" 41–48.

39. Pousseur, "*Scambi*," 12.

40. Earle Brown, Prefatory Note to *Folio and Four Systems* (1954), http://www.earle-brown.org/works/view/12 (accessed May 12, 2016).

41. Pousseur, "*Scambi*," 12.

42. Decroupet sees a political dimension to Pousseur's work with mobile and open forms; see Decroupet, "Henri Pousseur, Composition, Perception, Utopia," 182–92.

43. This further connects to Xenakis's probability techniques and prefigures the granular synthesis preoccupations of later computer music. See Roads, *Microsound*; Xenakis, "Wahrscheinlichkeitstheorie und Musik," 28–34; Xenakis, *Formalized Music*.

44. Iverson, "Learning the Studio," 380–81.

45. Maconie, *The Works of Karlheinz Stockhausen*, 76–80.

46. Cage, "Indeterminacy," in *Silence*, 36.

47. For much more, including reconstructions of Tudor's and other pianists' performance choices, see Krytska, *Karlheinz Stockhausens Klavierstück XI (1956)*. See also Maconie, *Other Planets*, 165; Vickery, "Mobile Scores and Click Tracks."

48. Tudor, "From Piano to Electronics," 25.

49. Stockhausen, *Conversations With the Composer*, 70.

50. See Maconie, *The Works of Karlheinz Stockhausen*, 76–93; Misch, *Zur Kompositionstechnik Karlheinz Stockhausens*; Decroupet, "Gravitationsfeld *Gruppen*," 37–51.

51. Truelove, "The Translation of Rhythm Into Pitch," 189–220; Stockhausen, " . . . how time passes . . . ," 10–40.

52. Truelove, "The Translation of Rhythm Into Pitch," 209; on the "Webern octave," see Pousseur, "Webern's Organic Chromaticism," 51–60.

53. Stockhausen, " . . . how time passes . . . ," 11.

54. Boulez, "Alea," 29.

55. Decroupet, "Pousseur: Theorie und Praxis," 223–31.

56. Mobile form is also explored in *Rimes* (1958–59) for tape and chamber orchestra and *Caractères* (1961) for piano.

57. This could have been a practical consideration. Once the pianist had selected one of the mobile notebooks—a loose leaf separate from the bound score—it made practical sense to use all three of its sections before setting it aside in favor of another leaf.

58. Decroupet, "Vers un théorie générale," 36.

59. Decroupet, "Vers un théorie générale," 35.

60. Pousseur, *Mobile pour deux pianos*, 8.

61. Boulez, "Alea," 28.

62. Boulez, "Alea," 31–32.

63. Boulez, "Alea," 32.

64. Boulez, "Sonate, que me veux-tu?," 143–54; Campbell, *Boulez, Music, and Philosophy*, 195–96; Harbison, "Performer Indeterminacy and Boulez's Third Sonata," 16–20; Jameux, *Pierre Boulez*, 299–309.

65. Boulez's propensity to leave works unfinished, returning to them again and again to add, subtract, mine, and rework, was by this time a well-known compositional trait. Edwards, "Unpublished Bouleziana," 4–15; Goldman, *The Musical Language of Pierre Boulez*, 10.

66. Boulez, *Troisième Sonate pour piano: Formant 2—Trope.*

67. Harbinson, "Performer Indeterminacy," 17.

68. Trenkamp, "The Concept of Alea in Boulez's *Constellation-Miroir*," 1–10.

69. Trenkamp, "The Concept of Alea in Boulez's *Constellation-Miroir*," 6.

70. Trenkamp, "The Concept of Alea in Boulez's *Constellation-Miroir*," 7–8.

71. Jameux, *Pierre Boulez*, 99–100.

72. Boulez, "Sonate, que me veux-tu?," 143–48. See also Black, "Boulez's Third Piano Sonata," 182–98; Campbell, *Boulez, Music, and Philosophy,* 193; Jameux, *Pierre Boulez*, 86–105.

73. Boulez, "Sonate, que me veux-tu?," 153–54.

74. Kim, ed., *Beyond Notation.*

75. Beal, "An Interview With Earle Brown," 341–356; Yaffé, "An Interview with Composer Earle Brown," 289–310; Nicholls and Potter, "Earle Brown"; Earle Brown Foundation, "Chronology," http://earle-brown.org/-life_in_music_chronology (accessed October 2017); Borio and Danuser, eds., *Im Zenit der Moderne*, vol. 3, 625–33.

76. Yaffé, "An Interview with Composer Earle Brown" 305; Beal, "An Interview With Earle Brown," 348.

77. Beal, "An Interview With Earle Brown," 341.

78. Beal, "An Interview With Earle Brown," 342–43.

79. Brown, Prefatory Note to *Folio* and *Four Systems* (1952–1954).

80. Brown, Program note to *Pentathis* (1958).

81. Holmes, *Electronic and Experimental Music*, 104–12; Cady, "An Overview of Earle Brown's Techniques," 1–20.

82. Earle Brown Foundation, "Chronology," http://earle-brown.org/-life_in_music_chronology (accessed October 11, 2017); Beal, "An Interview With Earle Brown," 342, 356, n. 3.

83. Yaffé, "An Interview With Composer Earle Brown," 295.

84. Gann, *American Music in the Twentieth Century*, 145.

85. Yaffé, "An Interview With Composer Earle Brown," 297.

86. Yaffé, "An Interview With Composer Earle Brown," 299.

87. Yaffé, "An Interview With Composer Earle Brown," 304. We might even speculate that the studio-like notation was an inside joke that refers back to Brown, Tudor, and Cage's long days in the Barron studio.

88. Blum, "Remarks Re: *Four Systems*," 367–69.

89. Yaffé, "An Interview With Composer Earle Brown," 299.

90. Yaffé, "An Interview With Composer Earle Brown," 302.

91. Wierenga, "Searching for Sounds."

92. Nicholls and Potter, "Earle Brown"; Gann, *American Music in the Twentieth Century*, 145; Yaffé, "An Interview With Composer Earle Brown," 295. Brown's friends and associates from the art world included Jackson Pollock, Robert Rauschenberg, Jasper Johns, Cy Twombly, Willem de Koonig, Mark Rothko, and Franz Kline. Brown also spoke on several occasions about his affinity for Calder's mobiles.

93. George Lewis, "Improvised Music After 1950"; Piekut, "Indeterminacy, Free Improvisation, and the Mixed Avant-Garde."

94. This a foundational insight of actor-network theory. See Callon, "Some Elements of a Sociology of Translation," 196–233; Latour and Woolgar, *Laboratory Life*; Latour, *Science in Action*; Piekut, *Experimentalism Otherwise*.

95. Berio to Pousseur, November 24, 1958 (Pousseur Collection, Paul Sacher Foundation, Basel). "Tout ca est merveilleux: Dans quelque arrivée nous errons le Palais des Nation Unies de la musique: à New York!" Berio's French is idiosyncratic, surely because he is a native Italian speaker writing to Pousseur in French.

96. Pousseur, "Erinnerungen an Luciano Berio," 1–11.

97. Beal, "An Interview With Earle Brown," 345.

98. Manning, "The Significance of *Techné*," 81–90; Pennycook, "Who Will Turn the Knobs When I Die?," 199–208; Pickering, *Mangle of Practice*; Stanyek and Piekut, "Deadness: Technologies of the Intermundane," 25–48.

99. Quoted in Holmes, *Electronic and Experimental Music*, 117.

Chapter 6

1. Stockhausen, "Music and Speech," 40–64; Stockhausen, "Musik und Sprache III," 58–68; Stockhausen, "Two Lectures," 59–82; Böhlandt, "'Kontakte'–Reflexionen naturwissenschaftlich-technischer Innovationsprozesse," 226–48; Kirchmeyer, "Stockhausens Elektronische Messe," 235–60; Metzer, "The Paths From and to Abstraction," 695–721; Decroupet and Ungeheuer, "Through the Sensory Looking Glass," 1–40; Williams, "Technical Influence and Physical Constraint."

2. Anhalt, *Alternative Voices*; Attinello, "The Interpretation of Chaos"; Budde, "Zum Verhältnis von Sprache, Sprachlaut und Komposition," 9–19; Klüppelholz, *Sprache als Musik*; Pollock, "Opera After *Stunde Null*"; Ungeheuer, "Sprache und Musik," 355–68.

3. Kaiser, "Listening to Recorded Voices in Modern Music"; Young, *Singing the Body Electric*.

4. Kohler, "Three Trends in Phonetics," 161–78. As Kohler explains, experimental phonetics is by nature an interdisciplinary field, which since its late nineteenth-century beginnings, involves "physiology, physics [acoustics], psychology, and linguistics" (176). My terminology in this chapter follows that of my sources. Contemporary linguists may well use terms in more circumscribed ways.

5. Ungeheuer, *Wie die elektronischen Musik "erfunden" werde*, 23–26.

6. Helmholtz, *On the Sensations of Tone* [1877] 1954; Miller, *The Science of Musical Sounds*, 244–70; Stumpf, *Die Sprachlaute*; Koch et al., "The Berlin Phonogramm-Archiv."

7. Kemp, "Phonetics: Precursors to Modern Approaches," 371–88. For interactive experimentation with a virtual vocal tract, see Thapen, "Pink Trombone" v1.1, https://dood.al/pinktrombone/.

8. Volmar, "Psychoakustik und Signalanalyse," 65–96; Wittje, "The Electrical Imagination," 40–63; Wittje, *The Age of Electroacoustics*.

9. Stewart, "An Electrical Analogue of the Vocal Organs," 311–12; Fletcher, *Speech and Hearing*; Gertner, *The Idea Factory*.

10. Mills, *On the Phone: Hearing Loss and Communication Engineering* (Durham, NC: Duke University Press, forthcoming); Mills, "Media and Prosthesis," 107–49; Mills, "Deaf Jam," 35–58; Mills, "The Dead Room."

11. Gethmann, *Klangmaschinen zwischen Experiment und Medientechnik*; Hui, *The Psychophysical Ear;* Hui, Kursell, and Jackson, "Music, Sound, and the Laboratory from 1750 to 1980," 1–11; Klotz, "Tonpsychologie und Musikforschung als Katalysatoren," 195–210; Kursell, "Experiments on Tone Color in Music and Acoustics," 191–211; Steege, *Helmholtz and the Modern Listener*; Sterne, *The Audible Past*.

12. See for example Luening, "An Unfinished History of Electronic Music," 43–49, 135–42, and 145; Winckel, "The Psycho-Acoustical Analysis of Structure," 194–246.

13. Brilmayer, "Das Trautonium"; Donhauser, *Elektrische Klangmaschinen*.

14. Slawson, *Sound Color*, following up in particular on Peterson and Barney, "Control Methods Used in a Study of the Vowels."

15. Ungeheuer, *Wie die elektronischen Musik "erfunden" werde*, 102–103; Luening, "An Unfinished History of Electronic Music," 46.

16. Ungeheuer, *Wie die elektronischen Musik "erfunden" werde*, 168–75.

17. Dudley, Riesz, and Watkins, "A Synthetic Speaker," 759; Dudley, "The Vocoder," 125–26; Scheuer, "Mr. Vocoder Adds Voice to Babel," C3; "A Perfect Back-Talker," X4.

18. Dudley, "The Vocoder," 126.

19. Ungeheuer, *Wie die elektronischen Musik "erfunden" werde*, 117–18.

20. Ungeheuer, *Wie die elektronischen Musik "erfunden" werde*, 61.

21. Klüppelholz, *Sprache als Musik*, 39–53; Kurtz, *Stockhausen: A Biography*; Maconie, *The Works of Karlheinz Stockhausen*; Maconie, *Other Planets*.

22. Karlheinz Stockhausen, "Musik und Sprache III," 60 (translation mine); this article forms the third part of "Music and Speech," esp. 57–64.

23. *Stimmung* also includes some literary and spiritual elements, including "magic names" for divine characters in multiple religions and cultures such as Islam, Buddhism, Hinduism, Christianity, Ancient Egypt, Indonesian Timor, Aztec, Ancient Greece, Native American, etc. For more, see Maconie, *The Works of Karlheinz Stockhausen*, 151–54. For an interesting discussion of the riot at the Amsterdam premiere, which revealed the growing chasm between the student-organized political left and the free-love hippie culture in the late 1960s, see Adlington, "Tuning In and Dropping Out."

24. Heile, *The Music of Mauricio Kagel*, 7–15; Richter-Ibáñez, *Mauricio Kagels Buenos Aires (1946–1957)*, 93–162; Heile and Iddon, eds., *Mauricio Kagel bei den Internationalen Ferienkursen*; Attinello, "Kagel, Mauricio."

25. Mauricio Kagel Collection (Paul Sacher Foundation, Basel).

26. See especially Latour and Woolgar, *Laboratory Life*.

27. Mauricio Kagel Collection, Paul Sacher Foundation, Basel. "die Sprache erhalt der caracter der Musik y la musica el caracter die Sprache. die Musik formanten sind moduliert IN sprache formanten." All capitalization and orthography reproduced from Kagel's original notes.

28. For another hint of how Meyer-Eppler worked with sound and electronic technologies in his research and teaching, see Meyer-Eppler, "Reversed Speech and Repetition Systems," 804–806.

29. Illustration from Dudley, "Synthesizing Speech," 100; the technology is also described in Dudley, "The Vocoder," 122–26; Dudley, "Remaking Speech," 169–77.

30. Ohala, "Speech Technology: Historical Antecedents," 419; Halsey and Swaffield, "Analysis-Synthesis Telephony," 391–406.

31. Mills, "Media and Prosthesis," 111; Scanlon, "Vocal Codes."

32. "Voice Transmission: Simultaneous Messages on One Line," 2.

33. "Post Office Telecommunications Research," *The Engineer*, May 17, 1946, 458. For more on the trans-Atlantic telephone network, see Starosielski, *The Undersea Network*.

34. "A Perfect Back-Talker," X4.

35. Voder is short for "voice operation demonstrator." For more, see Mills, "Media and Prosthesis," 107–49; Mills, "Medien und Prosthesen," 127–52.

36. Dudley, Riesz, and Watkins, "A Synthetic Speaker," 759–64; "Pedro the Voder: A Machine That Talks," 170–71.

37. Dudley, Riesz, and Watkins, "A Synthetic Speaker," 761–64.

38. Copeland, "Delilah—Encrypting Speech," 183–87; Hodges, *Alan Turing: The Enigma*, 274–89; Mills, "Media and Prosthesis," 133–34.

39. Bauer, "The Early History of Voice Encryption," 159–87.

40. Bauer, "The Early History of Voice Encryption," 172; Tompkins, *How to Wreck a Nice Beach,* 52–73 and 168–203.

41. Scheuer, "Mr. Vocoder Adds Voice to Babel," C3. One postwar British report hinted that wartime advances in communication and atomic fission were reclaimed for domestic progress; see "Voice Transmission: Simultaneous Messages on One Line."

42. Dudley, "The Vocoder," 126.

43. Meyer-Eppler 243, Akademie der Künste.

44. Geoghegan, "From Information Theory to French Theory," 96–126.

45. Jakobson and Halle, *Fundamentals of Language.*

46. See Kline, *The Cybernetics Moment*; Heims, *Constructing a Social Science for Postwar America.*

47. Jakobson and Halle, *Fundamentals*, 8.

48. A contemporary source that explains principles of acoustics as it relates to phonetics and speech is Ladefoged, *Elements of Acoustic Phonetics.*

49. Jakobson and Halle, *Fundamentals*, 17.

50. Jakobson and Halle, *Fundamentals*, 5, 9, 17.

51. Borio, "Vokalmusik als integrals Komponieren von Sprache," 41–58; Fricke, "Helms, Hans G."

52. Meyer-Eppler, *Grundlagen und Anwendungen*, 282–354; see also the famous and oft-cited Peterson and Barney, "Control Methods Used in a Study of the Vowels," 175–184.

53. It is Ligeti who likened the reading group to a "Talmud circle" or a "secret society" (*Ligeti in Conversation*, 57). Ligeti was quite influenced by Helms (Ligeti, "On *Aventures*," 423–424). See also Helms, "Lauter 'Originale,'" 130–39; Rebstock, *Komposition zwischen Musik und Theatre*, 95.

54. "Luciano Berio, Umberto Eco, and Roberto Leydi Remember," 216–32; Berio, *Two Interviews*, 142.

55. Saussure, *Course in General Linguistics*. Midcentury discussions on structural linguistics include Ruwet, "Contradictions Within the Serial Language," 65–76; Pousseur, "Music, Form, and Practice," 77–93. Secondary sources that relate structural linguistics and midcentury avant-garde music include Grant, *Serial Music, Serial Aesthetics*, 193–221; Goldman, *The Musical Language of Pierre Boulez*, 18–28; Campbell, *Boulez, Music, and Philosophy*, 112–37.

56. Scaldaferri, "'Bronze by Gold,' by Berio by Eco," 100–157. The radio documentary version of *Omaggio a Joyce* was not broadcast, as it was deemed too experimental, but it can be heard on CDs that accompany the *Nuova Musica* volume. For the RAI composers who frequently worked in both "functional" music (such as documentaries, radio plays, and overdubbing of American films) and "avant-garde" music, the radio plays are very often important works of art. See de Benedictis and Novati, "Introduction," in *Prix Italia*, 187–91; de Benedictis and Rizzardi, "Just then I heard a voice . . . ," 281–89; de Benedictis, "Opera Prima: *Ritratto di Città*," 26–53.

57. Ramazzotti, "Luciano Berio's *Sequenza III*," 82 n9.

58. Dalmonte, "Maderna, Bruno," §1; de Benedictis, "Opera Prima," 26–27.

59. *Musik der Zeit*, Cologne, March 25, 1958 included Ligeti's *Artikulation*, Stockhausen's *Gesang der Jünglinge*, Maderna's *Continuo*, and Berio's *Perspectives* (WDR Historical Archive, 11615). *Incontri Musicali*, Milan, June 14, 1958, included Maderna's *Continuo*, Berio's *Thema (Omaggio a Joyce)*, Eimert's *Fünf Stücke*, and Stockhausen's *Gesang der Jünglinge* (Decroupet, "Studio di Fonologia," 104).

60. Jonathan Sterne elaborates a similarly interdisciplinary nexus around the concept of hearing: Sterne, "Hearing," 68–71.

61. Mills, "Deaf Jam," 35–58; Mills, "The Dead Room," 29–143.

62. Hayles, *How We Became Posthuman*, 50–112 and 131–59; Heims, *Constructing a Social Science for Postwar America*; Pickering, *The Cybernetic Brain*.

63. Geoghegan, "From Information Theory to French Theory," 105.

64. Gertner, *The Idea Factory*.

65. Mills, "Do Signals Have Politics?" 320–46; Mills, "On Disability Cybernetics," 74–111; Ohala, "Speech Technology: Historical Antecedents," 416–19; Alexander Melville Bell's Visible Speech chart from 1867 can be seen at https://www.loc.gov/exhibits/treasures/images/at0123a_1s.jpg (accessed May 24, 2016).

Deaf is capitalized because it refers to a cultural identity. This is an important distinction that makes visible Deaf people's long struggle against the dominant hearing culture for recognition, agency, and linguistic and cultural autonomy. The prevalent attitude of the early to mid-twentieth century was that Deaf children should be normalized and integrated into hearing culture. Although Bell Labs researchers may have been well intentioned with their research and their adaptive technologies, they treated deafness as a "problem" that needed to be "fixed." More sadistically, in schools of this era, Deaf children were often physically prohibited from signing, punished for doing so, and forcibly subjected to hours and hours of speech therapy, all because it was believed that they needed to "function" in hearing culture. For more on this complex and politicized history of marginalization, see Davis, *Enforcing Normalcy*; Mills, "Deafness," 45–54; Jones,

"Imagined Hearing: Music-Making in Deaf Culture"; and Solomon, *Far From the Tree*, 49–114.

66. Brilmayer, "Das Trautonium"; Donhauser, *Elektrische Klangmaschinen*; Wittje, *The Age of Electroacoustics*.

67. Oskar Sala Nachlass, Deutsches Museum.

68. Glinsky, *Theremin*; Rutner, "The Art of the Theremin (Clara Rockmore, 1977)."

69. Kagel commonly worked simultaneously on two or more pieces. See Attinello, "Kagel, Mauricio."

70. Like many pieces of this era, *Anagrama* also has several integral serial dimensions, some of which seem to have also been conditioned by the electronic studio. For example, pitch and tempo ranges may correspond to the sum-and-difference functions of the ring modulator, and Kagel's collage and montage techniques may be a translation of tape-editing techniques. See Kassel, "Das Fundament in Turm zu Babel," 5–26; Rebstock, *Komposition zwischen Musik und Theatre*, 115–25; Holtsträter, *Mauricio Kagels musikalisches Werk*, 147–78; Heile, "Collage vs. Compositional Control," 287–99.

71. IPA (International Phonetic Alphabet) is a system for transcribing speech sounds that descended from Bell's and others' nineteenth-century systems for visible speech. It was codified as a stable system around the mid-twentieth century and used by specialists in phonetics and linguistics, as well as by singers in diction courses and foreign language learners. For more, see Kemp, "History of Phonetic Transcription," 388–401; Tillmann, "Early Modern Instrumental Phonetics," 401–16; Pullman and Ladusaw, *Phonetic Symbol Guide*, vii.

72. Klüppelholz, *Sprache als Musik*, 77–85.

73. Ungeheuer, *Wie die elektronischen Musik "erfunden" werde*, 249, CD track 22; Meyer-Eppler, *Elektrische Klangerzeugung*, 81–85.

74. Kagel, *Anagrama*, 25. "Jeder Gesangsolist wird bis Ende des Satzes die (und um die) gleichen Tonhöhe weitersingen; er soll kontinuierliche Übergänge von Vokalen (mit Ausnahme des 'A') in den verschiedensten Kombinationen und Nacheinanderfolge ausführen. Die Übergänge zwischen den Vokalen immer anders gestalten: schnell, verlangsamend, langsam beschleunigend usw. Kurze crescendi und diminuendi können durchgeführt werden; Mund- und Lippenbewegungen übertreiben."

75. Bosma, "*Thema: (Omaggio a Joyce)*: A Listening Experience," 97–120; Meehan, "Not Just a Pretty Voice," 33–42.

76. Berio, "Musik und Dichtung," 36–45; in English as "Poetry and Music," quote p. 252. Translation by Petrina, italics in original.

77. Categories and descriptions of consonants in Figure 6.8 are necessarily schematic, as phonetics is too complex to fully encapsulate in a figure of this type. For more information, see Ladefoged and Maddieson, *The Sounds of the World's Languages*.

78. Berio, "Poetry and Music," 238. Translation by Petrina, italics in original. On this point, see also p. 248 in the same article and Berio, *Two Interviews*, 141.

79. Berberian quoted in Scaldaferri, "'Bronze by Gold,'" 124.

80. Berio, "Poetry and Music," 240.

81. Berio, "Poetry and Music," 246.

82. Kagel analyzes *Anagrama* in a 1960 Darmstadt lecture: "Behandlung von Wort und Stimme," 354–67; see also the secondary analytical literature cited in n.70 of this chapter.

83. Kassel, "Das Fundament in Turm zu Babel," 7–8.

84. *Anagrama* Mappe 3, Mauricio Kagel Collection, Paul Sacher Foundation, Basel. "The Phoneme hacer del anagrama una EVOLUCION Fonction. Estructuras Fonética de desarrolla y Forma la forma de estructuras fonética del italiano, frances, etc." My transcription; orthography, spelling, and capitalization preserved from Kagel's original sketch.

85. Attinello, "Imploding the System," 263–85.

86. Although the work is now little discussed, David Osmond-Smith says that at Darmstadt 1960, *Dimensioni II* made a "profound impression." Osmond-Smith, "The Tenth Oscillator," 7; Maderna later incorporated the *Dimensioni II* material into the staged version of *Hyperion*, where it was associated with the "Machine" in scenes 5 and 6 and reused it in the electronic work *Tempo Libero* (1970–1971) and the radio drama *Ages* (1972); see Vincis, "Totus mundus agit histrionem," 261–68. Berberian disputed with Maderna over his unwillingness to credit her as the voice in these works and his unwillingness to pay her royalties accordingly; see Meehan, "Not Just a Pretty Voice," 45–49.

87. The text is reproduced in Borio, "Vokalmusik als integrals Komponieren von Sprache," 41–58; Fearn, *Bruno Maderna*, 89.

88. The piece is available on the CD *Acousmatrix*, vol. 7: Luciano Berio and Bruno Maderna, BVHaast 9109. For an example of an *elektronische Musik* excerpt, listen to 9:50–9:54; for a *musique concrète* layered polyphony, listen to 10:05–10:09.

89. Helms, *Fa:m' Ahniesgwow*. Text + LP record; some sections were not recorded presumably for reasons of space on the record. Helms is the speaker on the LP and Koenig handled the recording and montage (Koenig, private email correspondence, June 9, 2016). The Cologne-based spoken-word performance group *Sprechbohrer* has since recorded the entire work on Wergo WER63142 (2011). Analyses of *Fa:m* include Attinello, "The Interpretation of Chaos," 37–38; Borio, "Vokalmusik," 43–48; Klüppelholz, *Sprache als Musik*, 54–67.

90. On the provocations of *Visage*, see Berio, "*Visage*: Author's Note"; Causton, "Berio's *Visage* and the Theatre of Electroacoustic Music," 15–21; Cox, "Embodying Music," §58; Cremaschi and Giomi, "*Parrrole*: Berio's Words on Music Technology," 26–36; Flynn, "Listening to Berio's Music," 388–421; Ramazzotti, "Luciano Berio's *Sequenza III*," 84–89.

91. For more on the emotional affects produced by damaged voices, see Stras, "The Organ of the Soul," 173–84. For discussion of the misogynist undertones of modernist electroacoustic music more generally, see McClary, "Terminal Prestige," 57–81.

92. Neukirchen, "Und es raschten weiß die Sinus-Töne."

93. Ligeti, "On *Aventures*," Darmstadt 1964 lecture, transcribed and translated by Lee in "György Ligeti's *Aventures* and *Nouvelles Aventures*," 426.

94. In addition to the works discussed and mentioned in this chapter, see Blacher's *Abstrakte Oper* (1953); Pousseur's *Phonemes pour Cathy* (1966) and *Votre Faust* (1960–69); Bussotti's "Voix de femme" in *Pièces de chair II* (1958–60); Berio's *Circles* (1960), *Epifanie* (1961), *Folk Songs* (1964), *Sequenza III* (1965), and *Recital I (For Cathy)* (1972). For more on Berberian's life and works, see Meehan, "Not Just a Pretty Voice" and the essays in Karantonis, et al., eds., *Cathy Berberian*.

95. Rodgers, "Tinkering with Cultural Memory," 9.

96. De Benedictis, " . . . *at the Time of the Tubes*," 184; Osmond-Smith, "The Tenth Oscillator," 4.

97. Lietti, "The Technical Equipment," 116–21.

98. Reville, *The Roaring Silence,* 193–94; Nicholls, *John Cage,* 75–76.

99. Zuccheri quoted in de Benedictis, " . . . at the Time of the Tubes," 192–94.

100. Pritchett, *The Music of John Cage,* 128–37.

101. Like the technicians in the WDR studio, Zuccheri, the RAI studio's main technician, was an invaluable technical and creative consultant whose contributions, in Umberto Eco's opinion, even approached authorship. See Eco's comments in "Luciano Berio, Umberto Eco, and Roberto Leydi Remember," 222; see also a producer's comments in de Benedictis and Rizzardi's interview "Just then I heard a voice . . . ," 281–89. About *Fontana Mix,* Zuccheri said that Cage became more independent in the sound editing and montage phases, depending less on him as he learned more about the equipment (" . . . at the Time of the Tubes," 192–94).

102. For more on Cage and colleagues in the Barron studio, see Holmes, *Electronic and Experimental Music,* 106–112. For more on the centrality of montage techniques for Maderna and Berio, see Scaldaferri, "Montage und Synchronisation," 72–77.

103. As Judy Lochhead points out, indeterminate works like *Variations I* often become "fixed" by recorded performances, which is even more true for fixed-media electroacoustic pieces like *Fontana Mix.* The piece can technically be re-created, but Cage's version, realized at the RAI studio, is often considered "the work." See Lochhead, "Performance Practice," 233–41. For a recording of Cathy Berberian singing *Aria* with *Fontana Mix,* hear *Earle Brown Contemporary Sound Series,* vol. 6: *The Voice of Cathy Berberian* (Wergo 6934, 2010); for a solo performance of *Aria,* hear Linda Hirst, *Songs Cathy Sang* (Virgin Classics, 1988).

104. Pritchett, *The Music of John Cage,* 132; Nicholls, *John Cage,* 75.

105. Cage, *Aria,* score preface (New York: Henmar Press, 1960).

106. Meehan, "Not Just a Pretty Voice," 66–82; Verstraete, "Cathy Berberian's *Stripsody,*" 64–75.

107. Rodgers, "On the Process and Aesthetics of Sampling," 313–20; Meehan, "Not Just a Pretty Voice," 66.

108. Osmond-Smith, "The Tenth Oscillator," 5–6; Wierenga, "Searching for Sounds."

109. Young, *Singing the Body Electric*; Vágnerová, "Sirens/Cyborgs."

110. Kittler, *Gramophone,* 94–105; see also Kittler, "Rock Music," 152–64, "Signal-to-Noise Ratio," 165–77, and "Unconditional Surrender," 195–208; Winthrop-Young, "Drill and Distraction in the Yellow Submarine," 825–54. Peter Galison asks similar questions in "The Ontology of the Enemy," 228–66.

111. Sprigge, "Tape Work and Memory Work in Post-War Germany," 49–63.

Epilogue

1. Turner, *From Counterculture to Cyberculture,* 4.

2. Turner, *From Counterculture to Cyberculture,* 4.

3. Gertner, *The Idea Factory*; Kahn, "James Tenney at Bell Labs," 131–46; Born, *Rationalizing Culture*; Maconie, "Boulez, Information Science, and IRCAM," 38–50; Nelson, *The Sound of Innovation.*

4. Oliveros initially objected to the "coolness" of the Buchla's transistor-generated sound, but later created two seminal pieces (*Beautiful Soop* {1966} and *Alien Bog* {1967})

with the Buchla. For more, see Bernstein, ed., *The San Francisco Tape Music Center*; Gordon, " 'The Composer's Black-Box' "; Gordon's dissertation, "Bay Area Experimentalism: Music & Technology in the Long 1960s" provides more detail.

5. Pinch and Trocco, *Analog Days*.

6. Heike, *Musiksprache und Sprachmusik*.

7. Kröger, Riek, and Sachse, eds. *Festschrift Georg Heike*.

8. Fox, "Where the River Bends," 27–42; Barlow is now a professor at University of California Santa Barbara, http://music.ucsb.edu/people/clarence-barlow (accessed 10 June 2016).

9. Barlow, "On the Spectral Analysis of Speech for Subsequent Resynthesis," 183–190; Poller, "Clarence Barlow's Technique of 'Synthrumentation,' " 7–23.

10. Ablinger, *Annäherung: Texte-Werke-Textwerke*; Nonnenmann, "Mit der Wahrnehmung die Warhnehmung widerlegen," 63–66; Berlin-based Ablinger is now a professor at University of Huddersfield, https://research.hud.ac.uk/institutes-centres/cerenem/peterablinger/ (accessed 20 November 2017).

11. For instance, the sine-wave speech and "perceptual insight" studied in MRC Cognition and Brain Sciences Unit of the University of Cambridge, http://www.mrc-cbu.cam.ac.uk/people/matt.davis/sine-wave-speech/#lightbox/0/ (accessed November 20, 2017), and the musical and sonic illusions explored by the psychologist Diana Deutsch, http://deutsch.ucsd.edu/psychology/pages.php?i=201 (accessed November 20, 2017).

12. Fleischhauer and Janssen, "Project for 200,000 Inhabitants," 72–75; Janssen, "Initial Project: Designed for Gottfried Michael Koenig," 76–85. Private email communication with Gottfried Michael Koenig, June 9, 2016. On architecture and music, see also Joseph, *Expermentations: John Cage in Music, Art, and Architecture*.

13. Fleischhauer and Janssen, "Project for 200,000 Inhabitants," 72.

14. Janssen, "Initial Project," 85.

15. Martin, *The Organizational Complex*, 4.

16. Adlington, *Sound Commitments*; Gottschalk, *Experimental Music Since 1970*; Kahn, *Noise, Water, Meat*; Kutsche and Norton, eds. *Music and Protest in 1968*; Mesch, *Art and Politics*; Nyman, *Experimental Music*; Piekut, *Experimentalism Otherwise*; Piekut, ed. *Tomorrow is the Question*; Turner, *The Democratic Surround*.

17. Custodis, *Die soziale Isolation*, 117–47; Beal, *New Music, New Allies*, 114–22; Herzogenrath and Lueg, eds., *Die 60er Jahre: Kölns Weg zur Kunstmetropole*.

18. Gendron, *Between Montmartre and the Mudd Club*; Goldman, "Of Doubles, Groups, and Rhymes," 139–76; Grubbs, *Records Ruin the Landscape*; Piekut, "Indeterminacy, Free Improvisation, and the Mixed Avant-Garde," 769–824.

19. Everett, *The Beatles as Musicians: Revolver Through the Anthology*, 32, 119, 178; Holmes, "Electronic Music and the Beatles," *Noise and Notations Blog*, November 29, 2008, http://www.thomholmes.com/Noise_and_Notations/Noise_and_Notations_Blog/Entries/2008/11/29_Electronic_Music_and_The_Beatles.html (accessed November 21, 2017); Gardner, "These Hopeful Machines," episode 3; Prendergast, *The Ambient Century*, 51–57; Ross, "Beethoven Was Wrong," *The Rest Is Noise*, 515–18; Spitz, *The Beatles: The Biography*, 597–601.

20. Pinch and Trocco, *Analog Days*; Prendergast, *The Ambient Century*.

21. Taylor, *Strange Sounds*; Taylor, *Sounds of Capitalism*; Taylor, "The Avant-Garde in the Living Room."

22. See Brodsky, *From 1989*; Bohlman and McMurray, "Tape: Or, Rewinding the Phonographic Regime," 3–24; Sprigge, "Tape Work and Memory Work," 49–63.

23. Rodgers, "Synthesis," 216–17.

The WDR studio is a complex network filled with heterogeneous professionals. Several lesser-known figures made key contributions to the studio's and the composers' success. The following bio-sketches may help readers manage the human actors who travel in and out of the studio scene.

Artists and Architects

BAUERMEISTER, Mary (b. 1934) German visual artist whose Cologne apartment became a gathering place for the Fluxus artists' collective in the early 1960s. Involved with experimental and electronic music, especially through her collaboration with Stockhausen. In the mid-to-late 1960s and early 1970s, the partner and later wife of Stockhausen.

FLEISCHHAUER, Rainer (dates unknown) German architect in Cologne area who, with Jörn Janssen, visited the WDR studio. He developed plans, based on the proportions and aspirations of electronic music, for a new Karlsruhe, which were published in the seventh volume of *Die Reihe*.

JANSSEN, Jörn (dates unknown) German architect of Marxist persuasion who, with Rainer Fleischhauer, visited the WDR studio. He developed plans, based on the proportions and aspirations of electronic music, for a new Karlsruhe, which were published in the seventh volume of *Die Reihe*.

Composers

BARLOW, Clarence (b. 1945) Composer of international heritage and training, currently teaching at University of California in Santa Barbara. For some time in the late 1980s and 1990s, a major player in electronic music scenes in Cologne and the Netherlands.

Works widely in multimedia, including electronics, video, computer programming, and acoustic music. Uses phonetics and timbral analysis in "synthrumentation" (synthesis + instrumentation), an experimental technique in which the orchestra appears to "speak" words and phrases.

BARRAQUÉ, Jean (1928–1973) French composer who brushed shoulders with Boulez, Stockhausen, and others in Pierre Schaeffer's studio between 1951–1954. A committed serialist, scholar of Debussy, and ambitious humanist composer, he nevertheless remained somewhat more distant from the European avant-garde scene after the initial encounters in 1950s.

BERIO, Luciano (1925–2003) Italian composer famous for his work in both electronic and acoustic spheres. Major player in founding and developing the Italian national radio electronic studio (RAI), along with collaborators such as Alfredo Lietti, Veniero Rizzardi, Bruno Maderna, and Umberto Eco. For some time in the 1950s through early 1960s, the husband of mezzo-soprano Cathy Berberian, who was his muse. His early electronic works are frequently preoccupied with and informed by her voice. In this era he was also a composer of radio plays and documentaries.

BOULEZ, Pierre (1925–2016) French composer and conductor of extraordinary influence. Composed *musique concrète* in Paris in 1952 but stepped away from the studio until the late 1970s in favor of composing acoustic music and conducting. Nevertheless, his acoustic music shows deep engagement with techniques and ideas of the electronic studio; a frequent correspondent with the WDR composers as well as with John Cage. In the 1950s he was influential for his polemical articles as well as his new-music concert series and conducting activities.

BROWN, Earle (1926–2002) American experimental composer associated with the Cage–Tudor group in the 1950s and 1960s. Influential in dialogue with the younger European composers for his innovations with indeterminacy, especially in the use of graphic notation.

BUSONI, Ferruccio (1866–1924) Italian composer and pianist active in Germany, who was most well known as a keyboard virtuoso and arranger. He worked simultaneously as an avant-garde composer and writer, whose *Entwurf einer neuen Ästhetik der Tonkunst* [Concepts of a New Aesthetic for Musical Art, 1907] embraced sonic exploration.

BUSSOTTI, Sylvano (b. 1931) Italian composer of esoteric, experimental, and beautiful graphic scores. After compositional studies with Dallapiccola, in the 1950s he was a frequent attendee of the Darmstadt Summer Courses and a collaborator of pianist David Tudor. For several years in the late 1950s and early 1960s, he had a visible partnership with German scholar Heinz-Klaus Metzger.

CAGE, John (1912–1992) American composer of extraordinary influence who shaped midcentury music in particular with the use of prepared piano, chance, and indeterminacy. His European visits in 1949, 1954, and 1958 were provocative and memorable; he was a central interlocutor for the European composers throughout the 1950s and 1960s.

FELDMAN, Morton (1926–1987) American composer associated with the Cage–Tudor group in the 1950s and 1960s. Influential in dialogue with the younger European composers for his innovations with indeterminacy, especially in the use of graphic notation, liminal musical states (such as very long durations and very quiet sounds) and slow-changing sounds.

GOEYVAERTS, Karel (1923–1993) Belgian composer who was, in the early 1950s, one of the first proponents of pointillist integral serialism. After studies with Milhaud and Messiaen, he was a close friend of Stockhausen from 1951 to 1954. He was the first to compose a serial electronic work at the WDR studio, where the sine tones and durations were determined based on an integrated serial scheme. He left the field of music composition in 1957 after an emotional crisis and restarted his career with a Belgian airline in 1958. He later returned to music composition and teaching in the 1970s.

GREDINGER, Paul (1927–2013) German polymath who worked as an architect, electronic music composer, and influential advertising magnate. In 1954 composed *Formanten I and II* at the WDR studio, after the proportional principles of the architect Le Corbusier, but did not return to music composition after this experience.

KAGEL, Mauricio (1931–2008) Argentinian-born composer and filmmaker who resettled in Cologne, Germany after 1957. After a cosmopolitan childhood and education in Buenos Aires, he began composing electronic music at the WDR, writing radio broadcasts and Darmstadt lectures and teaching experimental music and theatre. He is known for his provocative tone, and his works are often absurdist, theatrical, and dramatic.

KOENIG, Gottfried Michael (b. 1926) German composer who first performed crucial work as the technician for a number of WDR pieces of the 1950s, including Stockhausen's *Gesang der Jünglinge* (1955–1956), Bengt Hambraeus's *Doppelrohr II* (1956), Giselher Klebe's *Interferenzen* (1955), and Franco Evangelisti's *Incontri di fasce sonore* (1957), among many others. He is a composer of both electronic and acoustic works, a prolific theorist and writer, and one of the first to experiment with using computers and algorithms for music composition. After leaving the WDR in 1964 he directed the Institute for Sonology in the Netherlands until 1986. He continues to write and compose computer music.

LIGETI, György (1923–2006) Hungarian composer who emigrated to Austria and later Germany in late 1956. One of his first experiences in the West was working at the WDR studio in early 1957, where he composed two pieces and left a third unfinished. Although he purported his independence from the Cologne–Darmstadt composers, he was ingratiated into the network, producing radio broadcasts on Webern's music, composing electronic and acoustic music, and frequently attending and teaching at the Darmstadt summer courses. He is well known for his development of acoustic sound-mass music, which uses a large orchestra to produce changing timbres with relatively little melody or harmony. There is strong evidence that this development is a direct continuation of the work he left unfinished in the electronic studio.

LUENING, Otto (1900–1996) American–German composer of early tape music in the United States. Together with collaborator Vladimir Ussachevsky, founded the Columbia–Princeton electronic music studio in 1959. Maintained an interest in the development of European electronic music, especially through his relationship with Meyer-Eppler, and wrote early histories of these developments. Berio, Stockhausen, and others occasionally mentioned him in passing in their correspondence, but seemed to regard his work with disdain perhaps because his early tape pieces explored film-like sound effects.

MADERNA, Bruno (1920–1973) Italian composer with strong connections to Darmstadt, Germany, in the postwar era. He was a child prodigy whose talents were exploited for Fascists' gain during the war; in the postwar era, he grew to much prominence as a conductor, especially of new music scores. Although he never held a permanent or salaried position at the Italian RAI studio, he was active with Berio and other collaborators in its founding, and composed radio plays and electronic music there (using Cathy Berberian's voice) in the 1950s.

MESSIAEN, Olivier (1908–1992) French composer, organist, and scholar who was an important teacher of many composers in the postwar generation. At the Paris Conservatoire, he ran an influential composition class attended by Boulez, Goeyvaerts, Xenakis, and Stockhausen, among others. His *Mode de valuers et d'intensitiés* (1951) experiments with extending systematic processes to register, dynamics, and rhythms, and is often cited as an inspiration for the development of integral serialism among the Darmstadt circle in the early 1950s. In this era, Messiaen also composed *musique concrète* at Schaeffer's Paris studio. His incorporation of Indian and other non-Western elements, as well as his deep engagement with symmetry, modality, rhythm, and musical timbre, were also influential in postwar new music.

MILHAUD, Darius (1892–1974) French composer who was associated with the avant-garde of the 1920s and continued to advocate for experimental, avant-garde, and electronic music in the Cold War era. Under pressure from the Nazis, he emigrated to California in 1940. Between 1947–1971, he taught at both Mills College and the Paris Conservatoire. In the 1950s he experimented with scoring for film, producing radio plays, and composing *musique concrète*.

NONO, Luigi (1924–1990) Italian composer associated with the development of serialism around Darmstadt in the 1950s. Works of this era, such as *Il canto sospeso* [*Interrupted Song*], are often texted and are explicitly anti-Fascist; Nono was openly Communist, and his music was often politically charged. In the early 1950s he was a proponent of the idea of a Darmstadt "school" of composers, actively cultivating relationships with Boulez, Maderna, Berio, and Stockhausen. In the mid-to-late 1950s, Nono's camaraderie with these friends wavered over a series of disagreements. Although he expressed only a little interest in electronic music in the 1950s, he later composed electronic and live electronic music.

POUSSEUR, Henri (1929–2009) Belgian (French-speaking) composer active in the midcentury electronic and acoustic scenes. In the 1950s, best friends with Karlheinz Stockhausen, with whom he corresponded frequently. Like Koenig, a very intelligent thinker and prolific writer who wrote frequently about his and others' music. He was especially influential for his use of open and mobile forms in electronic and acoustic music in the late 1950s.

SCHAEFFER, Pierre (1910–1995) French composer and broadcast engineer, founder of electronic music studio at the Paris radio in the mid-1940s. From 1949 to 1959 he composed *musique concrète* as part of a research group with collaborators including Pierre Henry, which extensively explored recorded sound, sampling, and tape manipulations. He is also well known for his theoretical writings that aimed to develop a multifaceted classification scheme for (recorded) sounds based on their acoustical properties.

SCHNEBEL, Dieter (1930–2018) German composer and theologian who associated some with the Cologne–Darmstadt group. Like his friends Helms and Metzger, he was a left-leaning intellectual well versed in the sociological critiques of the Frankfurt school. He is known as a composer especially of experimental vocal scores, many that deconstruct religious texts into their constituent phonemes.

STOCKHAUSEN, Karlheinz (1928–2007) German composer of exceptional renown. One of the intellectual leaders of the Cologne–Darmstadt group, in part because of his early and extended experience in the WDR electronic music studio, where he worked continuously in the 1950s and 1960s. Productive throughout the second half of the twentieth century, he wrote many influential pieces of both electronic and acoustic music in many different genres and styles. He was also a prolific writer about his and others' music and contemporary compositional technique.

USSACHEVSKY, Vladimir (1911–1990) Russian–American composer of early electronic music in the United States. Together with collaborator Otto Luening, founded the Columbia–Princeton electronic music studio in 1959. Kept abreast of the developments in European electronic music in the 1950s, but because of the sound effects aesthetic of his early works, seems to have been regarded with disdain by Stockhausen and the younger generation of European composers.

WOLFF, Christian (b. 1934) American composer of French birth, associated with the Cage–Tudor group in the 1950s and 1960s. Influential in dialogue with the younger European composers for his use of indeterminacy, especially for rule-based group improvisation. Wolff helped link American and European scenes, as he was fluent in German as well as French and English.

XENAKIS, Iannis (1922–2001) Greek–French composer and mathematician. Trained as a civil engineer, fought as part of the Greek Resistance movement during World War II, and fled to France in 1947. In the immediate postwar decade he worked as an apprentice in the architectural studio of Le Corbusier and designed the parabolic arches of the Philips Pavilion for the World's Fair in Brussels in 1958, where electronic music by Varèse and images by Le Corbusier were played for the world. Le Corbusier refused to credit Xenakis for his design, and he left the studio for a career in composition. Highly capable with advanced mathematics, his scores for large orchestra often used formulas from physics to model the behavior of musical instruments. Although his music of the 1950s and 1960s sounded similar to Ligeti's, he remained on the fringes of the Cologne–Darmstadt group, claiming that he was never welcomed or in some cases actively discouraged from joining the discourse. He did compose *musique concrète* extensively, especially at Scherchen's electronic music studio in Gravesano, Switzerland, and wrote numerous articles on information theory, probability, and music in the associated journal *Gravesano Blätter*.

Impresarios

BEYER, Robert (1901–1989) German sound engineer and composer who was one of the founders of the WDR electronic music studio in Cologne with Meyer-Eppler and Eimert. In the late 1920s and early 1930s he worked as a sound engineer [*Tonmeister*] for the German film company Tobis and in the postwar era as a sound engineer for the NWDR. As a result of his early experience with recorded sound and magnetic tape, he was an early and enthusiastic proponent of electronic music. Coauthored several of the earliest German electronic musical works with Eimert but left the WDR studio for unknown reasons, probably related to aesthetic disagreements, in 1953.

EIMERT, Herbert (1897–1972) German musicologist and composer. Together with Meyer-Eppler and Beyer, one of the founders of the WDR studio. His early writing advocated for atonal music and was controversial in the mid-1920s. Throughout the 1920s and into the postwar era, he worked as a music critic for several newspapers. He was a strong advocate for new music by means of his regular radio broadcast *Musikalisches Nachtprogramm* and a powerful administrator, who shaped the direction of new music by his leadership of the WDR studio in the 1950s, his founding (with Stockhausen) of the journal *Die Reihe*, and his mentoring of younger composers.

HARTMANN, Hans (1901–1972) served as the *Intendant* [Director] of the Cologne radio between 1947 and 1961. Known as a man of letters, he supported the electronic music studio and channeled funding toward new music, among other initiatives.

SCHERCHEN, Hermann (1891–1966) German conductor, impresario, and champion of new music. Influential for his affiliation with the new music journal *Melos* and the Donaueschingen and Musica Viva new music festivals, as well as his promotion and conducting of new works. As an impresario, used his home as the site of an experimental electronic music studio in Gravesano, Switzerland. Here, he brought together numerous collaborators such as instrument builders, technicians, composers, and scholars, who met for summits and contributed articles to the associated journal *Gravesano Blätter* [*Gravesano Review*].

STEINECKE, Wolfgang (1910–1961) German impresario and the first director of the Darmstadt Summer Courses (1946–1961). A champion of new music, he connected many of the composers and performers in the new music scene. His unexpected death after a car accident in 1961 sent shockwaves through the new music community.

STROBEL, Heinrich (1898–1970) German impresario and music critic. In the postwar years, an influential champion of new music by means of positions such as editor of the journal *Melos*, organizer of the Donaueschingen music festival, and administrator who supported various new music activities through the SWF [Southwest German Radio].

TÉZENAS, Suzanne (1898–1991) French patron and supporter of new music who hosted Cage, performing prepared-piano works, in her Paris salon during his first visit to Europe in 1949. She was a reliable advocate of new music, who provided support to composers like Boulez in establishing interested audiences, funding for concert series, and so on.

Instrument Builders

BODE, Harald (1909–1987) German engineer and builder of electronic music instruments. His Melochord was incorporated into the original WDR studio equipment and the earliest pieces of German electronic music through the advocacy of Meyer-Eppler and Eimert.

MAGER, Jörg (1880–1939) German inventor and pioneer of electronic music instruments. Esoteric figure whose one-of-a-kind instruments explored quarter-tones and other microtonal sounds. Mager's inventions were not embraced by the Nazis; he was ostracized, impoverished, and chronically ill at the time of his death.

TRAUTWEIN, Friedrich (1888–1956) German instrument builder and pioneer of electronic music. Builder of the electronic organ called the Trautonium, embraced by the Nazis in the late 1930s and 1940s and used occasionally in the early 1950s by Meyer-Eppler and Eimert.

Intellectuals Part I—Social Scientists and Humanists

ADORNO, Theodor (1903–1969) Philosopher, critical theorist, and sociologist with a strong expertise in music. Along with colleagues in the Frankfurt school, he advanced strong critiques of postwar society and art based on the thoughts of Freud, Hegel, Husserl, Heidegger, and Marx. A champion of the music of Schoenberg and Mahler and sometime attendee of the Darmstadt Summer Courses, he was an important interlocutor for the younger generation of avant-garde composers. He was sometimes supportive of certain strands of midcentury serial music, but was also fiercely critical of it, especially in the widely read essay "The Aging of the New Music [1955]."

ECO, Umberto (1932–2016) Italian scholar, philosopher, linguist, and novelist. In his early career, he was a medieval literary scholar and a cultural producer at RAI in Milan, where he was good friends with Berio, Maderna, and Berberian. Later, he became influential as a semiotician, literary critic, and novelist.

HALLE, Morris (1923–2018) Latvian-American linguist who trained under Roman Jakobson and served as co-author for their *The Fundamentals of Language* (1956). He continued a career in generative phonology, working closely with Noam Chomsky and working at the Massachusetts Institute of Technology throughout his career.

HELMS, Hans G. (1932–2012) German intellectual who frequently attended Darmstadt, translated Cage's 1958 Darmstadt lectures, and mingled with composers on the fringes of the WDR studio circle. After studying comparative linguistics with Roman Jakobson as well as philosophy and Marxist thought with Adorno, among others, he worked for the German radio, producing broadcasts and films on new music topics. In 1957, he hosted a reading group in Cologne where friends gathered to read James Joyce's *Finnegans Wake*. His experimental sound-poetry pieces were important in the phonetics works of Ligeti, Kagel, Berio, Maderna, and others.

HORNBOSTEL, Erich Moritz von (1877–1935) Austrian ethnomusicologist, music psychologist, and scholar who is remembered for his work classifying instruments and collecting folk songs in various locales, including World War I prisoner-of-war camps. With Carl Stumpf, he studied music perception and psychology, and transcribed much non-Western music as performed by prisoners of war. The recordings he and Stumpf collected formed the foundation of the Berliner Phonogramm-Archiv, for which he was the first director between 1905–1933.

JAKOBSON, Roman (1896–1982) Russian linguist who emigrated to the United States via Scandinavia in the early 1940s. Expert in phonology and an influential promoter of the structuralist approach of Saussure. During his association with Harvard University beginning in 1949, he interacted with an interdisciplinary network of intellectuals, including Wiener and Shannon. His writings drew out many connections between acoustics, phonetics, linguistic structure, and speech synthesis technology such as the Vocoder. His teachings were probably transmitted to the Cologne and WDR circle by Hans G. Helms, who apparently studied with him in the early 1950s.

METZGER, Heinz-Klaus (1932–2009) Studied musicology at the University of Tübingen. An adherent to the dialectical Marxist–Hegelian critical style of the Frankfurt school, he became something of an in-house intellectual among the Cologne–Darmstadt avant-garde. He was one of the translators for the Cage lectures in 1958 and wrote a famous rebuttal to Adorno's "The Aging of the New Music" in *Die Reihe*, as well as a number of concert reviews and scholarly texts about his friends' music. For several years in the late 1950s and early 1960s, had a visible gay partnership with Italian composer Sylvano Bussotti.

STUMPF, Carl (1848–1936) German scientist and philosopher with wide-ranging expertise in psychology, acoustics, musical aesthetics, and phenomenology. Read by Meyer-Eppler and the WDR composers for insights into the psychology of music listening and spoken language, as well as experimental phonetics.

Intellectuals Part II—Scientists and Engineers

BELL, Alexander Melville (1819–1905) Father of Alexander Graham Bell, phonetics expert and creator of Visible Speech, a graphic system for transcribing phonemes intended to help the deaf speak. In the early twentieth century, Visible Speech insights were used in Vocoder research and electronic music.

DUDLEY, Homer (1896–1980) American electrical engineer who worked primarily on speech synthesis. He developed the Vocoder at Bell Labs in the 1920s and 1930s and transmitted his work to the WDR studio by means of Meyer-Eppler, whom he met on a European tour in the late 1940s.

FLETCHER, Harvey (1884–1981) American physicist and engineer employed by Bell Labs. In the 1920s and 1930s, contributed essential research on topics of speech, hearing, and speech synthesis used in the Voder and Vocoder, among other communication technologies. His book *Speech and Hearing* was cited by Meyer-Eppler.

HELMHOLTZ, Hermann von (1821–1894) German scientist with important and wide-ranging contributions, including to the physics of light and sound, thermodynamics, geometry, and philosophy of science. His widely read *On the Sensations of Tone as a Physiological Basis for the Theory of Music* (1863) was extremely important in both the nineteenth and twentieth centuries, especially to the WDR composers as they sought to integrate acoustics and perception.

MEYER-EPPLER, Werner (1913–1960) PhD scientist and WDR studio founder with Beyer and Eimert. He was extraordinarily well versed in a number of areas, including acoustics, psychoacoustics, phonetics, electronic equipment, and information theory. His dissertation research concerned radio-broadcasting technologies, periodicity, and distortion. During World War II he continued to work at the University of Bonn and, between 1943–45, in an interdisciplinary research group for the U-boat division of the Nazi military. After denazification, he turned his research toward the related fields of experimental phonetics, electronic sound production, and information theory. He worked in his later career at the Phonetics Institute in Bonn until an early death from kidney disease. He was an extremely important conduit for technical, scientific, and information-theoretic ideas, and connected engineers, instrument builders, intellectuals, and composers.

MILLER, Dayton (1866–1941) American physicist and acoustician whose research broadly concerned wave propagation, including X-rays, cathode ray tubes, and the visual reproduction of sound waves. His *Science of Musical Sounds* (1916) was cited by Meyer-Eppler.

MOLES, Abraham André (1920–1992) French intellectual polymath, whose expertise included electrical engineering, acoustics, information theory, sociology, and psychology. In the late 1940s and early 1950s, he was a frequent correspondent in Pierre Schaeffer's studio at the French Radio. From 1954–1960 he was a frequent correspondent in Hermann Scherchen's electronic studio in Gravesano, Switzerland. In these roles, he encountered many of the European avant-garde composers and conveyed scientific insights to them. His *Information Theory and Esthetic Perception*, published in French in 1958 and translated into English in 1966, was one of the first texts to relate information theory to music and other arts.

SHANNON, Claude (1916–2001) American engineer and PhD mathematician employed by Bell Labs. During the war, he did important work on cryptography and code-breaking. He published an influential treatise on information theory, in which equations described the information density, predictability, and interference in messages of any kind.

TURING, Alan (1912–1954) British cryptographer and PhD mathematician. His wartime work in code-breaking for the Allies at Bletchley Park was essential to the success of the war effort; the Turing machines he developed there are widely regarded as protocomputers. Tragically, he was persecuted for homosexuality and committed suicide by cyanide poisoning.

WIENER, Norbert (1894–1964) PhD mathematician and philosopher widely regarded as the founder of cybernetics. A child prodigy, during World War II he worked on antiaircraft missile defense research groups at MIT, where he used statistical prediction and probability to shoot down planes and missiles with more accuracy. From this wartime experience, he evolved an entire theory about feedback mechanisms, dubbed cybernetics, which had implications in biology, psychology, computer science, philosophy, and other fields. He was one of the key participants in the interdisciplinary, postwar Macy Conferences, where he became much more interested in applying cybernetic insights to social and psychological problems than to military and communications research.

Performers

BERBERIAN, Cathy (1925–1983) American mezzo-soprano and composer who performed many of the experimental and avant-garde works of the midcentury composers. Between 1950 and 1964 she was married to Luciano Berio and continued to be based in Italy after the marriage ended. She was extremely important as a performer in the mid-1950s and 1960s, and also began to compose experimental vocal works in the late 1960s.

TUDOR, David (1926–1996) American pianist and composer of exceptional ability with contemporary, experimental, and avant-garde scores. Because he was nearly the only pianist in the 1950s who would or could play much of the new music, which often included graphic notation, indeterminacy, and exceptionally difficult extended techniques, he gave much exposure to composers and music that otherwise would have fallen into the shadows. Throughout his career, he was a close collaborator of John Cage and other composers and dancers in the New York scene. Later, beginning in the late 1960s, he became a composer of electronic music and multimedia works.

Studio Technicians

LIETTI, Alfredo (1919–1998) Technical director of the RAI studio in Milan in the early 1950s. Having worked as a broadcasting technician during World War II, he engineered and built many of the RAI's one-of-a-kind oscillators and filters from discarded wartime equipment.

SCHÜTZ, Heinz (dates unknown) Technician at the WDR studio from 1951 to 1958. In addition to working with composers such as Eimert, Beyer, Brün, Stockhausen, and Krenek, he also worked in sound production for *Hörspiel*.

ZUCCHERI, Marino (b. 1923) Recording technician at the RAI studio in Milan during the 1950s and later. Like Koenig at the WDR, he was an extremely important and talented collaborator, an essential mediator who helped composers such as Berio, Maderna, Pousseur, Cage, and Nono find technical solutions for their ideas in an unfamiliar medium.

Archives

Akademie der Künste (Berlin, Germany)
New York Public Library (New York World's Fair 1939–1940: http://archives.nypl.org/
    mss/2233)
Paul Sacher Foundation (Basel, Switzerland)
Stockhausen Foundation (Kürten, Germany)
WDR Historical Archive (Cologne, Germany)

Scores

Boulez, Pierre. *Troisième Sonate pour piano: Formant 2—Trope.* Universal Edition 13 292.
    London: Universal Edition, 1961.
Brown, Earle. *Pentathis* for nine solo instruments. New York: C.F. Peters, 1958.
———. *Folio and Four Systems.* New York: Associated Music Publishers, 1961.
———. *Available Forms I.* New York: Associated Music Publishers, 1962.
Cage, John. *31'57.9864" for a Pianist.* New York: Henmar Press, 1960.
———. *Aria.* New York: Henmar Press, 1960.
———. *Bacchanale.* 67886a. New York: Edition C. F. Peters, 1960.
———. *Fontana Mix.* New York: Edition C. F. Peters, 1965.
Helms, Hans G. *Fa:m' Ahniesgwow.* Cologne: DuMont Schauberg, 1959.
Kagel, Mauricio. *Anagrama für vier Gesangsoli, Sprechchor, und Kammerensemble.*
    Vienna: Universal Edition, 1965.
Koenig, Gottfried Michael. *Essay: Komposition für elektronische Klänge.* Vienna: Universal
    Edition, 1960.
Ligeti, György. *Atmosphères.* UE 11418. Vienna: Universal Edition, 1961.
———. *Aventures* and *Nouvelles Aventures.* Study Score 5913. New York: C.
    F. Peters, 1966.
Maderna, Bruno. *Musica su due Dimensioni* (1952). Critical edition. Edited by Maroni
    Baroni and Rossana Dalmonte. Milan: Edition Suvini Zerboni, 2001.

Pousseur, Henri. *Mobile pour deux pianos*. Milan: Edition Suvini Zerboni, 1961.

———. *Phonemes pour Cathy*. Milan: Edizione Suvini Zerboni, 1966.

Schnebel, Dieter. *für Stimmen (. . . missa est): dt 31,6 für 12 Vokalgruppen*. Schott Partitur 6458. Mainz: Schott, 1973.

———. *Glossolalie 61*. Schott Partitur 6414. Mainz: Schott, 1974.

Stockhausen, Karlheinz. *Gruppen für drei Orchester*. London: Universal Edition, 1963.

———. *Stimmung für 6 Vokalisten*. UE 14805. Vienna: Universal Edition, 1969.

———. *Studie II: Work No. 3*. Kürten: Stockhausen-Verlag, 2000.

———. *Gesang der Jünglinge: Faksimile-Edition*. Kürten: Stockhausen-Verlag, 2001.

Discography

Anthology of Noise and Electronic Music. Vol. 1. SubRosa SR190, 2001.

Atelier Schola Cantorum 1. Directed by Clytus Gottwald. Cadenza 800891, Bayer-Records, 1993.

Berio/Maderna. Acousmatrix series. Vol. 7. BVHaast 9109, n.d.

Cologne WDR: Early Electronic Music. Acousmatrix series. No. 6. BVHaast 9106, 2005.

Gottfried Michael Koenig. Acousmatrix series. Nos. 1–2. BVHaast 9001/2, n.d.

Hans G. Helms: Fa:m' Ahniesgwow. Performed by Sprechbohrer. Wergo 63142, 2011.

Karel Goeyvaerts. The Serial Works. Nos. 1–7. MDC 7845, Megadisc Classics, 1998.

Karlheinz Stockhausen: CD No. 3. Kürten: Stockhausen Verlag, 1991.

Kurt Schwitters: Ursonate. Wergo 6304-2, 1993.

Songs Cathy Sang. Performed by Linda Hirst. Virgin Classics, 1988.

Studio für elektronische Musik des WDR Köln. Musik in Deutschland 1950–2000 Series. Box 17. Vol. 5. Deutscher Musikrat/RCA/Sony BMG, 2008.

The Voice of Cathy Berberian. Earle Brown Contemporary Sound Series. Vol. 6. Wergo 6934, 2010.

Published Correspondence

The Boulez–Cage Correspondence. Edited by Jean-Jacques Nattiez. Translated by Robert Samuels. Cambridge: Cambridge University Press, 1993.

Bruno Maderna and Wolfgang Steinecke: Carteggio Briefwechsel. Edited by Rossana Dalmonte. Lucca, Italy: Libreria Musicale Italiana, 2001.

John Cage and David Tudor: Correspondence on Interpretation and Performance. Edited by Martin Iddon. Cambridge: Cambridge University Press, 2015.

The Selected Letters of John Cage. Edited by Laura Kuhn. Middletown, CT: Wesleyan University Press, 2016.

Primary Sources

Ablinger, Peter. *Annäherung: Texte-Werke-Textwerke*. Cologne: MusikTexte, 2016.

Adorno, Theodor. "Cultural Criticism and Society." In *The Adorno Reader*, 195–210. Edited by Brian O'Connor. London: Blackwell, [1951] 2000.

———. "The Aging of the New Music." In *Essays on Music*, 181–202. Edited by Richard Leppert. New translation by Susan H. Gillespie. Berkeley: University of California Press, [1955] 2002.

————. "The Curves of the Needle." In *Essays on Music*, 271–76. Edited by Richard
Leppert. New translation by Susan H. Gillespie. Berkeley: University of California
Press, [1927/1965] 2002.

————. "Music and Technique." In *Sound Figures*, 197–214. Translated by Rodney
Livingstone. Stanford, CA: Stanford University Press, [1958] 2012.

Babbitt, Milton. "The Composer as Specialist." In *The Collected Essays of Milton Babbitt*,
48–54. Edited by Stephen Peles. Princeton, NJ: Princeton University Press,
[1958] 2003.

Barlow, Clarence. "On the Spectral Analysis of Speech for Subsequent Resynthesis
by Acoustic Instruments." In *Festschrift Georg Heike*, 183–90. Edited by Bernd
J. Kröger, Christine Riek, and Georg Sachse. Frankfurt: Wissenschaftliche
Buchhandlung Theo Hector & Co., 1998.

Benjamin, Walter. "Theses on the Philosophy of History." In *Illuminations*, 253–59.
Edited by Hannah Arendt. Translated by Harry Zohn. New York: Schocken
Books, 1968.

————. "The Work of Art in the Age of Mechanical Reproduction." In
Illuminations, 217–51. Edited by Hannah Arendt. Translated by Harry Zohn.
New York: Schocken Books, 1968.

Berio, Luciano. "Musica per Tape Recorder." *Il Diapason* IV/3–4 (1953): 10–13.

————. "Aspetti di artigianato formale." *Incontri musicali* 1 (1956): 65–66.

————. "Musik und Dichtung: Eine Erfahrung." *Darmstädter Beiträge* 2 (1959): 36–45.
Available in English as "Poetry and Music: An Experience," in *Nuova Musica Alla
Radio/New Music on the Radio*, 236–56. Translated by Alessandra Petrina. Edited by
Veniero Rizzardi and Angela Ida de Benedictis. Milan: RAI/Eri, 2000.

————. *Luciano Berio: Two Interviews*. With Rossana Dalmonte and Bálint András Varga.
Translated and Edited by David Osmond-Smith. New York: Marion Boyars, 1985.

————. *Scritti sulla musica*. Edited by Angela Ida De Benedictis. Turin: Giulio
Einaudi, 2013.

————. "*Visage:* Author's Note," Centro Studio Luciano Berio. http://www.
lucianoberio.org/node/1505?2019623839=1 (accessed June 10, 2016).

Bertalanffy, Ludwig von. *General System Theory: Foundations, Development, Applications*.
Revised edition. New York: George Braziller, 1969.

Beyer, Robert. "Das Problem der 'kommenden Musik.'" *Die Musik* 20/12
(1928): 861–66.

————. "Die Klangwelt der elektronischen Musik." *Zeitschrift für Musik* (February
1952): 74–79.

————. "Zur Geschichte der elektronischen Musik." *Melos* 20 (October 1953): 278–80.

————. "Elektronische Musik." *Melos* 21 (January 1954): 35–39.

————. "Zur Situation der elektronische Musik." *Zeitschrift für Musik* (August/
September 1955): 452–56.

Bode, Harald. "Das Melochord des Studios für elektronische Musik im Funkhaus Köln."
In *Technische Hausmitteilungen der NWDR 1954*, 27–29. Cologne: Westdeutsche
Rundfunk, 1954.

————. "The Melochord of the Cologne Studio for Electronic Music." In *Papers on
Electronic Music: Technical Translation TT607* of *Technical Hausmitteilungen des NWDR*

1954, vol. 6, 27–29. Translated by D. A. Sinclair. Ottawa: National Research
    Council of Canada.

———. "History of Electronic Sound Modification." *Journal of the Audio Engineering
    Society* 32/10 (October 1984): 730–39.

Boulez, Pierre. "Debussy: Jeux (Poème de danse)." *Gravesaner Blätter* 2–3 (1956): 5.

———. "At the Ends of Fruitful Land . . . " In *Die Reihe* 1, 19–29. English edition.
    Uncredited translator. Bryn Mawr, PA: Theodore Presser, [1955] 1958. Also avail-
    able as "At the Edge of Fertile Land," in *Stocktakings From an Apprenticeship*, 158–72.
    Translated by Stephen Walsh. Oxford: Clarendon, 1991.

———. "Sonate, que me veux-tu?" In *Orientations*, 143–54. Edited by Jean-Jacques
    Nattiez. Translated by Martin Cooper. London: Faber and Faber, [1963] 1986.

———. "Alea." In *Stocktakings From an Apprenticeship*, 26–38. Translated by Stephen
    Walsh. Edited by Paule Thévenin. Oxford: Clarendon, [1957] 1991.

———. "Arnold Schoenberg." In *Stocktakings From an Apprenticeship*, 278–86.
    Translated by Stephen Walsh. Edited by Paule Thévenin. Oxford: Clarendon,
    [1961] 1991.

———. "Claude Debussy." In *Stocktakings From an Apprenticeship*, 259–77. Translated
    by Stephen Walsh. Edited by Paule Thévenin. Oxford: Clarendon, [1958] 1991.

———. " . . . Near and Far." In *Stocktakings From an Apprenticeship*, 141–57. Translated
    by Stephen Walsh. Edited by Paule Thévenin. Oxford: Clarendon, [1954] 1991.

———. "Possibly." In *Stocktakings From an Apprenticeship*, 111–40. Translated by
    Stephen Walsh. Edited by Paule Thévenin. Oxford: Clarendon, [1952] 1991.

———. "Schoenberg is Dead." In *Stocktakings From an Apprenticeship*, 209–214.
    Translated by Stephen Walsh. Edited by Paule Thévenin. Oxford: Clarendon,
    [1952] 1991.

———. "Tendencies in Recent Music." In *Stocktakings From an Apprenticeship,* 173–
    79. Translated by Stephen Walsh. Edited by Paule Thévenin. Oxford: Clarendon,
    [1954] 1991.

Brown, Earle. Prefatory Note to *Folio and Four Systems* (1954). Available at http://www.
    earle-brown.org/works/view/12 (accessed May 12, 2016).

———. Program note to *Pentathis* (1958). Available at http://www.earle-brown.org/
    works/view/23 (accessed May 11, 2016).

Cage, John. *Silence*. Middletown, CT: Wesleyan University Press, 1973.

Cardew, Cornelius. "Report on Stockhausen's *Carré*." *The Musical Times* 102/1424
    (October 1961): 619–22.

———. "Report on Stockhausen's *Carré*: Part 2." *The Musical Times* 102/1425
    (November 1961): 698–700.

"Chaos oder Ordnung?" *Kölner Stadt-Anzieger*, June 2, 1956.

Dahlhaus, Carl and Rudolph Stephan. "Eine 'dritte Epoch' der Musik? Kritische
    Bermerkungen zur elektronischen Musik." *Deutsche Universitäts Zeitung: das
    Hochschulmagazin* 10/17 (1955): 14–17.

Dudley, Homer. "Synthesizing Speech." *Bell Laboratories Record* 15 (December
    1936): 98–102.

———. "Remaking Speech." *Journal of the Acoustical Society of America* 11/2 (October
    1939): 169–77.

———. "The Vocoder." *Bell Laboratories Record* 18 (December 1939): 122–26.

Dudley, Homer, R. R. Riesz, and S. S. A. Watkins. "A Synthetic Speaker." *Journal of The Franklin Institute* 227/6 (June 1939): 739–64.

Eimert, Herbert. *Atonale Musiklehre*. Leipzig: Breitkopf and Härtel, 1924.

———. "Der Sinus-Ton." *Melos* 21 (1954): 168–72.

———. "Die Sieben Stücke." *Musikalisches Nachtprogramm Sendung*. Cologne: WDR Historical Audio Archives, December 12, 1954.

———. "The Place of Electronic Music in the Musical Situation." In *Papers on Electronic Music: Technical Translation TT610 of Technical Hausmitteilungen des NWDR 1954*, Vol. 6, 42–46. Translated by D. A. Sinclair. Ottawa: National Research Council of Canada, [1954] 1956.

———. "Was ist elektronische Musik?" *Melos* 20, (1953): 1–5. Translated as "What is Electronic Music?," in *Die Reihe* 1, 1–10. Uncredited translator. English edition. Bryn Mawr, PA: Theodore Presser, [1955] 1958.

———. "Debussy's *Jeux*." In *Die Reihe* 5, 3–20. Translated by Leo Black. English edition. Bryn Mawr, PA: Theodore Presser, [1959] 1961.

———. "Werner Meyer-Eppler." In *Die Reihe* 8, 5–6. Translated by Ruth Koenig. English edition. Bryn Mawr, PA: Theodore Presser, [1962] 1968.

———. "How Electronic Music Began." *Musical Times* 113/1550 (April 1972): 347–49.

———. "Elektronische Musik—eine neue Klangwelt." Printed in *Darmstadt Ferienkurse 1952* program book, Meyer-Eppler Collection, Akademie der Künste, Berlin. Reprinted in *New Music Darmstadt 1950–1960: Text and Picture Book*. Edited by Hommel and Schülter. Darmstadt: Internationales Musikinstitut Darmstadt, [1952] 1987.

Eimert, Herbert, Fritz Enkel, and Karlheinz Stockhausen. "Problems of Electronic Music Notation." In *Papers on Electronic Music: Technical Translation TT612 of Technical Hausmitteilungen des NWDR 1954*, vol. 6, 52–54. Translated by D. A. Sinclair. Ottawa: National Research Council of Canada, [1954] 1956.

Enkel, Fritz. "The Technical Facilities of the Electronic Music Studio." In *Technische Hausmitteilungen der NWDR 1954*, vol. 6, 8–15. Translated by D. A. Sinclair. Ottawa: National Research Council of Canada, [1954] 1956.

Enkel, Fritz, and Heinz Schütz. "Magnetic Tape Technique." In *Technische Hausmitteilungen der NWDR 1954*, vol. 6, 16–18. Translated by D. A. Sinclair. Ottawa: National Research Council of Canada, [1954] 1956.

E. R. T., "Klavier mit Papierstreifen und Büroklammern: Musik der Zeit im Nordwestdeutschen Rundfunk Köln," *Westfalen Zeitung*, September 24, 1954.

Fleischhauer, Rainer and Jörn Janssen. "Project for 200,000 Inhabitants." In *Die Reihe* 7, 72–75. Translated by Cornelius Cardew. English edition. Bryn Mawr, PA: Theodor Presser, [1960] 1965.

Fletcher, Harvey. *Speech and Hearing*. New York: D. Van Nostrand Company, 1929.

Fokker, Adriaan. "Wherefore, and Why? Questions Relating to New Music." In *Die Reihe* 8, 68–79. Uncredited translator. English edition. Bryn Mawr, PA: Theodor Presser, [1962] 1968.

G. Sch., "Komponisten ohne Publikum?" *Die Welt* Nr. 127, June 1, 1956, 9.

Goeyvaerts, Karel. "The Sound Material of Electronic Music." In *Die Reihe* 1, 35–37. Uncredited translator. Bryn Mawr, PA: Theodore Presser, [1955] 1958.

———. "Paris: Darmstadt 1947–56. Excerpt From the Autobiographical Portrait."
Revue Belge de Musicologie 48 (1994): 35–54.

Gredinger, Paul. "Serial Technique." In *Die Reihe* 1, 38–44. Uncredited translator.
English edition. Bryn Mawr, PA: Theodore Presser, [1955] 1958.

Haentjes, Werner. "Über Hörspielmusik," *Melos* 20/9 (September 1953): 241–42.

Halsey, R. J. and J. Swaffield. "Analysis-Synthesis Telephony, With Special Reference
to the Vocoder." *Journal of the Institution of Electrical and Electronics Engineers* 95/37
(September 1948): 391–406.

Heike, Georg. "Informationstheorie und musikalische Komposition." *Melos* 28
(1961): 269–72.

———. "Informationstheorie und serielle Musik: Komposition als Rechenprogramm."
In *Musiksprache und Sprachmusik: Texte zur Musik, 1956–1998*, 35–45. Edited by
Stefan Fricke. Saarbrücken, Germany: PFAU-Verlag, 1999.

Helmholtz, Hermann von. *On the Sensations of Tone as a Physiological Basis for the Theory
of Music*, 4th German ed. Translated by Alexander J. Ellis. 2nd English edition.
New York: Dover, [1885] 1954.

Helms, Hans G. "Gedanken eines progressive Musikers über die beschädigte
Gesellschaft." In *Musik-Konzepte Sonderband John Cage*, 18–40. Edited by Heinz-
Klaus Metzger and Rainer Riehn. Munich: edition text + kritik, 1978.

———. "Lauter 'Originale.'" In *Die 60er Jahre. Kölns Weg zur Kunstmetropole: vom
Happening zur Kunstmarkt*, 130–39. Edited by Wulf Herzogenrath and Gabriele
Lueg. Cologne: Kölnische Kunstverein, 1986.

H. K. M., "Elektronische Musik auf neuen Wegen," *Kölnische Rundschau*, June 2, 1956.

Jakobson, Roman, and Morris Halle. *Fundamentals of Language*. The Hague: Mouton &
Co., 1956.

Janssen, Jörn. "Initial Project: Designed for Gottfried Michael Koenig." In *Die Reihe* 7,
76–85. Translated by Cornelius Cardew. English edition. Bryn Mawr, PA: Theodor
Presser, [1960] 1965.

Kagel, Mauricio. "Behandlung von Wort und Stimme: Über ANAGRAMA für vier
Sänger, Sprechchor und Kammerensemble, 1957–58." In *Im Zenit der Moderne*,
vol. 3, 354–67. Edited by Gianmario Borio and Hermann Danuser. Freiburg im
Breisgau: Rombach, [1960] 1997.

K. H. R., "Elektronische Musik: Hart an der Grenze: Das Ereignis der Kölner
Musikfestes 1953." *Die Welt*, 28 May 1953.

Koch, Gerhard, Winrich Hopp, and Johannes Fritsch. *Feedback Studio*.
Cologne: Dumont, 2006.

Koenig, Gottfried Michael. "Studio Technique." In *Die Reihe* 1, 52–54. Uncredited
translator. English edition. Bryn Mawr, PA: Theodor Presser, [1955] 1958.

———. "Commentary: On Stockhausen's . . . *how time passes* . . . , on Fokker's
'Wherefore, and Why?' and on present musical practice as seen by the author."
In *Die Reihe* 8, 80–98. Translated by Ruth Koenig. English edition. Bryn Mawr,
PA: Theodor Presser, 1968.

———. "Ligeti und die elektronische Musik." In *György Ligeti: Personalstil-
Avantgardismus-Popularität*, 11–26. Edited by Otto Kolleritsch. Vienna:
Graz, 1987.

———. "Music and Number." Translated by Koenig. Available at http://www.
koenigproject.nl/indexe.htm (accessed March 14, 2016). German version in

Aesthetische Praxis: Texte zur Musik, vol. 1: 1954–61. Saarbrücken, Germany: PFAU, [1958] 1991.

———. "The Construction of Sound." Translated by Koenig. Available at http://
www.koenigproject.nl/indexe.htm (accessed March 14, 2016). German version in
Aesthetische Praxis: Texte zur Musik, vol. 2: 1962–67. Saarbrücken, Germany: PFAU
[1963] 1992.

———. "My Experiences With Programmed Music." Translated by Koenig. http://
www.koenigproject.nl/indexe.htm (accessed March 14, 2016). German version in
Aesthetische Praxis: Texte zur Musik, vol. 3: 1968–91. Saarbrücken, Germany: PFAU
[1975] 1993.

Lietti, Alfredo. "The Technical Equipment of the Electronic Music Studio of Radio
Milan." In *Elettronica* 5/3, 116–21. Translated by D. A. Sinclair. Ottawa: National
Research Council of Canada, [1956] 1960.

Ligeti, György. "Pierre Boulez: Decision and Automatism in *Structures Ia*." In *Die Reihe*
4, 36–62. Translated by Leo Black. English edition. Bryn Mawr, PA: Theodor
Presser, [1958] 1960.

———. "Some Remarks on Boulez's 3rd Piano Sonata." In *Die Reihe* 5, 56–58.
Translated by Leo Black. English edition. Bryn Mawr, PA: Theodor Presser,
[1958] 1961.

———. "Metamorphoses of Musical Form." In *Die Reihe* 7, 5–19. Translated by
Cornelius Cardew. English edition. Bryn Mawr, PA: Theodor Presser, [1960] 1965.

———. *Ligeti in Conversation with Peter Varnai, Josef Hausler, Claude Samuel, and Himself.*
London: Eulenberg, 1983.

———. "On *Aventures*" (Darmstadt 1964 lecture). Transcribed and translated by
Joanna Ching-Yun Lee in "György Ligeti's *Aventures* and *Nouvelles Aventures*: A
Documentary History," 387–444. PhD dissertation, Columbia University, 1993.

———. "On the Possibilities of Staging *Aventures*." Transcribed and translated by
Joanna Ching-Yun Lee in "György Ligeti's *Aventures* and *Nouvelles Aventures*: A
Documentary History," 469–87. PhD dissertation, Columbia University, 1993.

———. *Träumen Sie im Farbe? György Ligeti im Gesprach mit Eckhard Roelcke.*
Vienna: Paul Zsolnay, 2003.

———. *Gesammelte Schriften*. 2 Vols. Edited by Monika Lichtenfeld. Mainz,
Germany: Schott, 2007.

———. "Auswirkungen der elektronischen Musik auf mein kompositorisches
Schaffen." In *Gesammelte Schriften*, vol. 2, 86–94. Edited by Monika Lichtenfeld.
Mainz: Schott, 2007.

———. "*Aventures* und *Nouvelles Aventures*." In *Gesammelte Schriften*, vol. 2, 197–98.
Edited by Monika Lichtenfeld. Mainz, Germany: Schott, 2007.

———. "Bermerkungen zu *Artikulation*." In *Gesammelte Schriften*, vol. 2, 166–67.
Edited by Monika Lichtenfeld. Mainz Germany: Schott, 2007.

———. "Libretto zu *Aventures* und *Nouvelles Aventures*." In *Gesammelte Schriften*, vol. 2,
201–25. Edited by Monika Lichtenfeld. Mainz, Germany: Schott, 2007.

———. "Mein Kölner Jahr 1957." In *Gesammelte Schriften*, vol. 2, 29–32. Edited by
Monika Lichtenfield. Mainz, Germany: Schott, 2007.

———. "Musik und Technik: Eigene Erfahrungen und subjektive Betrachtungen."
In *Gesammelte Schriften*, vol. 1, 237–61. Edited by Monika Lichtenfeld.
Mainz: Schott, 2007.

————. "Über *Aventures.*" In *Gesammelte Schriften*, vol. 2, 196–97. Edited by Monika Lichtenfeld. Mainz, Germany: Schott, 2007.

————. "Über szenische Möglichkeiten von *Aventures.*" In *Gesammelte Schriften*, vol. 2, 198–201. Edited by Monika Lichtenfeld. Mainz, Germany: Schott, 2007.

"Luciano Berio, Umberto Eco, and Roberto Leydi Remember the Studio di Fonologia Forty Years after its Birth." In *Nuova Musica Alla Radio: Experiences at the Studio di Fonologia of the RAI, Milan 1954–59*, 216–32. Edited by Veniero Rizzardi and Angela Ida de Benedictis. Translated by Alessandra Petrina. Milan: Rai/Eri, 2000.

Luening, Otto. "Some Random Remarks About Electronic Music." *Journal of Music Theory* 8/1 (Spring 1964): 89–98.

————. "An Unfinished History of Electronic Music." *Music Educators Journal* 55/3 (November 1968): 43–49, 135–42, and 145.

Metzger, Heinz-Klaus. "Intermezzo I: Just Who is Growing Old? and Intermezzo II." In *Die Reihe* 4, 63–84. Translated by Leo Black. English edition. Bryn Mawr, PA: Theodor Presser, [1958] 1960.

Metzger, Heinz-Klaus. "'das neue werk' wagt sich hervor: zur Hamburger Aufführung von Dieter Schnebels *dt* 31,6." In *Dieter Schnebel: Beiträge, Meinungen und Analysen zur neuen Musik*, 15–17. Edited by Stefan Fricke. Saarbrücken, Germany: Pfau, 2000.

Meyer-Eppler, Werner. *Elektrische Klangerzeugung: elektronische Musik und synthetische Sprache.* Bonn: Dümmler, 1949.

————. "Reversed Speech and Repetition Systems as a Means of Phonetic Research." *Journal of the Acoustical Society of America* 22/6 (November 1950): 804–06.

————. "Mathematisch-akustische Grundlagen der elektrischen Klang-Komposition." In *NWDR Technische Hausmitteilungen* Vol. 6 (1954): 29–39.

————. "Statistic and psychologic problems of sound." In *Die Reihe* 1, 57–58. Uncredited translator. English edition. Bryn Mawr, PA: Theodore Presser, [1955] 1958.

————. *Grundlagen und Anwendungen der Informationstheorie.* Berlin: Springer, 1959.

————. "Möglichkeiten der elektronischen Klangerzeugung." In *Im Zenit der Moderne*, vol. 3, 102–104. Edited by Gianmario Borio and Hermann Danuser. Freiburg im Breisgau: Rombach, [1951] 1997.

Miller, Dayton Clarence. *The Science of Musical Sounds.* New York: Macmillan, 1922.

Moles, Abraham André. "Informationstheorie und ästhetische Empfindung." *Gravesaner Blätter* 6 (December 1956): 3–9.

————. "Kolloquium: Informationstheorie und Musik." *Gravesaner Blätter* 6 (December 1956): 16–18.

————. *Information Theory and Esthetic Perception.* Translated by Joel E. Cohen. Urbana and London: University of Illinois Press, 1966.

Müller, Paul. "Entdeckung neuer Klangräume." *Rheinische Post*, May 28, 1953.

Neukirchen, Alfons. "Und es raschten weiß die Sinus-Töne." *Düsseldorfer Nachrichten*, June 2, 1956.

Neumann, John von and Oskar Morgenstern. *Theory of Games and Economic Behavior.* Princeton, NJ: Princeton University Press, 1944.

"Pedro the Voder: A Machine That Talks." *Bell Laboratories Record* 17/6 (February 1939): 170–71.

"A Perfect Back-Talker." *New York Times*. July 2, 1939, X4.

Peterson, Gordon E. and Harold L. Barney. "Control Methods Used in a Study of the Vowels." *Journal of the Acoustical Society of America* 24/2 (March 1952): 175–84.

"Post Office Telecommunications Research." *The Engineer* (May 17, 1946): 458.

Pousseur, Henri. "Formal Elements in a New Compositional Material." In *Die Reihe* 1, 32–33. Uncredited translator. English edition. Bryn Mawr, PA: Theodore Presser, [1955] 1958.

———. "Webern's Organic Chromaticism." In *Die Reihe* 2, 51–60. Translated by Leo Black. English edition. Bryn Mawr, PA: Theodor Presser, [1955] 1958.

———. "*Scambi:* Description of a Work in Progress." *Gravesaner Blätter* 1, (1959): 36–47 (German) and 48–54 (English). In *Écrits Théoriques* 1954–1967, 147–59 (French). Sprimont, Belgium: Mardaga, 2004. Much improved English translation by Christine North available at http://www.scambi.mdx.ac.uk/documents.html (accessed April 13, 2016).

———. "Music, Form, and Practice (an attempt to reconcile some contradictions)." In *Die Reihe* 6, 77–93. Translated by Margaret Shenfield. English edition. Bryn Mawr, PA: Theodor Presser, [1960] 1964.

———. "Erinnerungen an Luciano Berio." In *Topographien der Kompositionsgeschichte seit 1950*, 1–11. Edited by Tobias Hünermann and Christoph von Blumröder. Vienna and Cologne: Verlag der Apfel and Signale, 2011.

Russolo, Luigi. "The Art of Noises: A Futurist Manifesto." In *Audio Culture: Readings in Modern Music*, 10–14. Edited by Christoph Cox and Daniel Warner. New York: Continuum, [1913] 2008.

Ruwet, Nicholas. "Contradictions Within the Serial Language." In *Die Reihe* 6, 65–76. Translated by Margaret Shenfield. English edition. Bryn Mawr, PA: Theodor Presser, [1960] 1964.

Saussure, Ferdinand de. *Course in General Linguistics*. Edited by Charles Ballay, Albert Sechehaye, and Albert Riedlinger. Translated by Wade Baskin. New York: McGraw-Hill, [1915] 1966.

Schaeffer, Pierre. *In Search of a Concrete Music*. Translated by Christine North and John Dack. Berkeley: University of California Press, [1952] 2012.

———. *Treatise on Musical Objects: An Essay Across Disciplines*. Translated by Christine North and John Dack. Berkeley: University of California Press, [1966] 2017.

Scheuer, Philip K. "Mr. Vocoder Adds Voice to Babel: Future Possibilities of Vocoder Seen." *Los Angeles Times*. July 2, 1939, C3.

Schnebel, Dieter. *Denkbare Musik: Schriften 1952–1972*. Edited by Hans Rudolf Zeller. Cologne: DuMont Schauberg, 1972.

Schoenberg, Arnold. *Theory of Harmony*. Translated by Roy E. Carter. Berkeley and Los Angeles: University of California Press, 1978.

Shannon, Claude. "A Mathematical Theory of Communication," 2 parts. *Bell System Technical Journal* 27/3 (July 1948): 379–423, and 27/4 (October 1948): 623–56.

Shannon, Claude E. and Warren Weaver. *The Mathematical Theory of Communication*. Urbana: University of Illinois Press, [1949] 1964.

Sinclair, D.A., trans. *Papers on Electronic Music: Technical Translation TT610 of Technical Hausmitteliungen des NWDR 1954*, vol. 6. Ottawa: National Research Council of Canada, 1956.

"Die Spieldose der elektronischen Musik," *Süddeutsche Zeitung*, June 13, 1953.

Stewart, John Q. "An Electrical Analogue of the Vocal Organs." *Nature* (London) 2757/110 (September 2, 1922): 311–12.

Stockhausen, Karlheinz. "Electronic Musical Composition No. 2, 1953." In *Papers on Electronic Music: Technical Translation TT611 of Technical Hausmitteliungen des NWDR 1954*, vol. 6, 46–51. Translated by D. A. Sinclair. Ottawa: National Research Council of Canada, [1954] 1956.

———. "Aktuelles." In *Texte*, vol. 2, 51–58. Cologne: M. DuMont Schauberg, [1957] 1963. Translated as "Actualia." In *Die Reihe* 1, 45–51. Uncredited translator. English edition. Bryn Mawr, PA: Theodor Presser, [1955] 1958.

———. " . . . *how time passes* . . . " In *Die Reihe* 3, 10–40. Translated by Cornelius Cardew. English edition. Bryn Mawr, PA: Theodor Presser, [1957] 1959.

———. "Two Lectures: Electronic and Instrumental Music." In *Die Reihe* 5, 59–82. Translated by Ruth Koenig. English edition. Bryn Mawr, PA: Theodore Presser, [1958] 1961.

———. "Arbeitsbericht 1952/53: Orientierung." In *Texte*, vol. 1, 32–38. Cologne: DuMont Schauberg, [1953] 1963.

———. "Arbeitsbericht 1953: Die Entstehung der Elektronischen Musik." In *Texte*, vol. 1, 39–44. Cologne: Du Mont Schauberg, [1953] 1963.

———. "Musik und Sprache III." In *Texte*, vol. 2, 58–68. Cologne: M. DuMont Schauberg, [1957] 1963.

———. "Situation des Handwerks." In *Texte*, vol. 1, 17–23. Cologne: Du Mont Schauberg, [1952] 1963.

———. "Von Webern zu Debussy: Bermerkungen zur statistischen Form." In *Texte*, vol. 1, 75–85. Cologne: DuMont Schauberg, [1954] 1963.

———. "Music and Speech." In *Die Reihe* 6, 40–64. Translated by Ruth Koenig. English edition. Bryn Mawr, PA: Theodor Presser, [1960] 1964.

———. "The Origins of Electronic Music." *Musical Times* 112/1541 (July 1971): 649–50.

———. *Conversations With the Composer*. Edited by Jonathan Cott. New York: Simon & Schuster, 1973.

———. *Stockhausen on Music*. Edited by Robin Maconie. London: Marion Boyars, 1989.

———. *Karlheinz Stockhausen bei den Internationalen Ferienkursen für Neue Musik in Darmstadt 1951–1996, Dokumente und Briefe*. Edited by Imke Misch and Markus Bandur. Kürten, Germany: Stockhausen-Stiftung für Musik, 2001.

———. "Programmtext (3. Seite) for *Gesang der Jünglinge*." In *Gesang der Jünglinge*, Faksimilie-edition, 72–74. Kürten, Germany: Stockhausen Verlag, 2001.

Stuckenschmidt, H. H. "Musikfest der Vergleiche und Sensation." *Die Neue Zeitung*, 28 May 1953.

Stumpf, Carl. *Tonpsychologie*. 2 vols. Leipzig: Hirzell, 1883–1890.

———. *Die Sprachlaute: Experimentell-Phonetische Untersuchungen nebst einem Anhang über Instrumentalklänge*. Berlin: Julius Springer, 1926.

Ussachevsky, Vladimir. "La 'Tape Music' aux Etats-Unis." In *Vers une musique expérimentale*, special issue of *La Revue musicale* 236 (1957): 50–55.

Varèse, Edgard and Chou Wen-chung. "The Liberation of Sound." *Perspectives of New Music* 5/1 (Autumn/Winter 1966): 11–19.

"Voice Transmission: Simultaneous Messages on One Line." *The Times* (London). Friday January 3, 1947, 2.

Wiener, Norbert. *The Human Use of Human Beings: Cybernetics and Society.* 2nd edition. Boston: Da Capo Press, [1950] 1954.

———. *Cybernetics. Or, Control and Communication in the Animal and the Machine.* 2nd edition. Cambridge, MA: MIT Press, [1948, 1961] 1965.

Wilkinson, Marc. "Two Months in the 'Studio di Fonologia.'" *The Score* 22 (1958): 41–48.

Winckel, Fritz. "The Psycho-Acoustical Analysis of Structure as Applied to Electronic Music." Translated by Louise Eitel Peake. *Journal of Music Theory* 7/2 (Winter 1963): 194–246.

Xenakis, Iannis. "Wahrscheinlichkeitstheorie und Musik," *Gravesaner Blätter* 6 (December 1956): 28–34.

———. "Le Corbusier's 'Electronic Poem'—The Philips Pavilion." *Gravesaner Blätter* 9 (1957): 51–54.

———. *Art/Sciences: Alloys.* Translated by Sharon Kanach. No. 2A of *Aesthetics in Music.* New York: Pendragon Press, 1985.

———. *Formalized Music: Thought and Mathematics in Music.* Revised edition. No. 6 of Harmonologia Series. New York: Pendragon Press, 1992.

Zwanzig Jahre Musik im Westdeutschen Rundfunk: Eine Dokumentation der Hauptabteilung Musik 1948–1968. Edited by Westdeutschen Rundfunk Köln. Cologne: Westdeutscher Rundfunk, 1969.

Secondary Sources

Abbate, Carolyn. "Sound Object Lessons." *Journal of the American Musicological Society* 69/3 (Fall 2016): 793–829.

Abbate, Janet. *Recoding Gender: Women's Changing Participation in Computing.* Cambridge, MA: MIT Press, 2012.

Adlington, Robert. "Tuning In and Dropping Out: The Disturbance of the Dutch Premiere of Stockhausen's *Stimmung*." *Music and Letters* 90/1 (February 2009): 94–112.

Adlington, Robert, ed. *Sound Commitments: Avant-Garde Music and the Sixties.* New York: Oxford University Press, 2009.

Aguila, Jésus. *Le Domaine musical: Pierre Boulez et vingt and de creation contemporaine.* Paris: Librairie Arthème Fayard, 1992.

Amichai, Yehuda. "An Appendix to the Vision of Peace." In *Great Tranquility: Questions and Answers*, 18. Translated by Glenda Abramson and Tudor Parfitt. Riverdale-on-Hudson, NY: Sheep Meadow Press, 1997.

Am Puls der Zeit: 50 Jahre WDR. Band 1: Die Vorläufer: 1924–1955. Cologne: Kiepenheuer & Witsch, 2006.

Anhalt, Istvan. *Alternative Voices: Essays on Contemporary Vocal and Choral Composition.* Toronto: University of Toronto Press, 1984.

Attinello, Paul. "The Interpretation of Chaos: A Critical Analysis of Meaning in European Avant-Garde Vocal Music 1958–1968." PhD dissertation, University of California Los Angeles, 1997.

———. "Imploding the System: Kagel and the Deconstruction of Modernism." In *Postmodern Music/Postmodern Thought*, 263–85. Edited by Joseph Auner and Judy Lochhead. New York: Routledge, 2002.

———. "Dialectics of Serialism: Abstraction and Deconstruction in Schnebel's *für Stimmen (. . . missa est)*." *Contemporary Music Review* 26/1 (February 2007): 39–52.

———. "Kagel, Mauricio." *Grove Music Online. Oxford Music Online.* Oxford University Press. http://www.oxfordmusiconline.com.proxy.lib.uiowa.edu/subscriber/article/grove/music/14594 (accessed May 26, 2016).

———. "Schnebel, Dieter." *Grove Music Online. Oxford Music Online.* Oxford University Press. http://www.oxfordmusiconline.com.proxy.lib.uiowa.edu/subscriber/article/grove/music/24978 (accessed June 1, 2016).

Baade, Christina. *Victory Through Harmony: The BBC and Popular Music in World War II.* New York: Oxford University Press, 2012.

Backus, John. "*Die Reihe*: A Scientific Evaluation." *Perspectives of New Music* 1/1 (Autumn 1962): 160–71.

Badenoch, Alexander. *Voices in Ruins: West German Radio Across the 1945 Divide.* New York: Palgrave Macmillan, 2008.

Badge, Peter. *Oskar Sala: Pionier der elektronische Musik.* Edited by Peter Frieß and Deutsches Museum Bonn. Göttingen, Germany: Satzwerk, 2000.

Baroni, Mario and Rossana Dalmonte, eds. *Studi su Bruno Maderna.* Milan: Edition Suvini Zerboni, 1989.

Bauer, Amy. *Ligeti's Laments: Nostalgia, Exoticism, and the Absolute.* Surrey, UK: Ashgate, 2011.

Bauer, Craig. "The Early History of Voice Encryption." In *Philosophical Explorations of the Legacy of Alan Turing*, 159–87. Edited by Juliet Floyd and Alisa Bokulich. Boston Studies in the Philosophy and History of Science. Cham, Switzerland: Springer International, 2017.

Bauermeister, Mary. *Ich hänge im Triolengitter: Mein Leben mit Karlheinz Stockhausen.* Munich: Elke Heidenreich bei C. Bertelsmann, 2011.

Beal, Amy. "Negotiating Cultural Allies: American Music in Darmstadt, 1946–1956." *Journal of the American Musicology Society* 53/1 (Spring 2000): 105–139.

———. "The Army, the Airwaves, and the Avant-Garde: American Classical Music in Postwar West Germany." *American Music* 21/4 (Winter 2003): 474–513.

———. *New Music, New Allies: American Experimental Music in West Germany from the Zero Hour to Reunification.* Berkeley: University of California Press, 2006.

———. "David Tudor in Darmstadt." *Contemporary Music Review* 26/1 (February 2007): 77–88.

———. "An Interview with Earle Brown." *Contemporary Music Review* 26/3–4 (June–August 2007): 341–56.

Beckles Willson, Rachel. *Ligeti, Kurtág, and Hungarian Music During the Cold War.* Cambridge: Cambridge University Press, 2007.

Beckman, Bengt. *Codebreakers: Arne Beurling and the Swedish Crypto Program during World War II.* Translated by Kjell-Ove Widman. Providence, RI: American Mathematical Society, 2002.

Belletti, Giovanni. "The Audio Laboratory and the Studio di Fonologia Musicale." In *Nuovo Musica Alla Radio/New Music on the Radio*, 83–87. Edited by Veniero Rizzardi and Angela Ida de Benedictis. Milan: RAI/Eri, 2000.

Bernard, Jonathan. "Inaudible Structures, Audible Music: Ligeti's Problem, and His Solution." *Music Analysis* 6/3 (October 1987): 207–36.

———. "Voice Leading as a Spatial Function in the Music of Ligeti." *Music Analysis* 13/2–3 (July–October 1994): 227–53.

Bernstein, David W. "In Order to Thicken the Plot." In *Writings Through John Cage's Music, Poetry, and Art*, 7–40. Edited by Bernstein and Christopher Hatch. Chicago: University of Chicago Press, 2001.

———. "John Cage, Arnold Schoenberg, and the Musical Idea." In *John Cage: Music, Philosophy, and Intention 1933–1950*, 15–45. Edited by David W. Patterson. New York: Routledge, 2002.

Bernstein, David W., ed. *The San Francisco Tape Music Center: 1960s Counterculture and the Avant-Garde*. Berkeley: University of California Press, 2008.

Betts, Paul. *The Authority of Everyday Objects: A Cultural History of West German Industrial Design*. Berkeley: University of California Press, 2004.

Bijker, Wiebe and Trevor Pinch. "Preface to the Anniversary Edition." In *The Social Construction of Technological Systems: New Directions in the Sociology and History of Technology*, xi–xxxiv. Edited by Wiebe E. Bijker, Thomas P. Hughes, and Trevor Pinch. Anniversary edition. Cambridge, MA: MIT Press, [1987] 2012.

Bijsterveld, Karin. "Servile Imitation: Disputes About Machines in Music, 1910–1930." In *Music and Technology in the Twentieth Century*, 121–35. Edited by Hans-Joachim Braun. Baltimore, MD: Johns Hopkins University Press, 2002.

———. *Mechanical Sound: Technology, Culture, and Public Problems of Noise in the Twentieth Century*. Cambridge, MA: MIT Press, 2008.

Birdsall, Carolyn. *Nazi Soundscapes: Sound, Technology, and Urban Space in Germany, 1933–1945*. Amsterdam: Amsterdam University Press, 2012.

Black, Robert. "Boulez's Third Piano Sonata: Surface and Sensibility." *Perspectives of New Music* 20/1–2 (Autumn 1981–Summer 1982): 182–98.

Bloor, David. "Anti-Latour." *Studies in the History and Philosophy of Science* 30/1 (March 1999): 81–112.

Blüggel, Christian. *E. = Ethik + Aesthetic: Zur Musikkritik Herbert Eimerts*. Saarbrücken, Germany: Pfau, 2002.

Blum, Eberhard. "Remarks Re: *Four Systems*." *Contemporary Music Review* 26/3–4 (June–August 2007): 367–69.

Blumröder, Christoph von. "Karlheinz Stockhausen: 40 Jahre Elektronische Musik." *Archiv für Musikwissenschaft* 50/4 (1993): 309–23.

Böhlandt, Marco. "'Kontakte'–Reflexionen naturwissenschaftlich-technischer Innovationsprozesse in der frühen Elektronischen Musik Karlheinz Stockhausens (1952–1960)." *Berichte zur Wissenschaftsgeschichte* 31 (September 2008): 226–48.

Böhme-Mehner, Tatjana. "Berlin Was Home to the First Electronic Studio in the Eastern Bloc: The Forgotten Years of the Research Lab for Interdisciplinary Problems in Musical Acoustics." *Contemporary Music Review*, 30/1 (February 2011): 33–47.

———. "Interview With Gerhard Steinke, 12 October 2010, Steinke's apartment, Berlin." *Contemporary Music Review*, 30/1 (February 2011): 15–23.

———. "Interview With Bernd Wefelmeyer, by email between 9 and 14 February 2009." *Contemporary Music Review*, 30/1 (February 2011): 49–52.

Boehmer, Konrad. *Zur Theorie der Offenen Form in der neuen Musik*. Inaugural dissertation, Philosophischen Fakultät der Universität Cologne, 1966.

———. "Koenig—Sound Composition—*Essay*," In *Electroacoustic Music: Analytical Perspectives*, 59–71. Edited by Thomas Licata. Westport, CT: Greenwood, 2002.

Bohlman, Andrea F. and Peter McMurray. "Tape: Or, Rewinding the Phonographic Regime." *twentieth-century music* 14/1 (February 2017): 3–24.

Bohlman, Philip V. *Jewish Music and Modernity*. New York: Oxford University Press, 2008.

Bohlman, Philip V., ed. *Jewish Musical Modernism, Old and New*. Chicago: University of Chicago Press, 2008.

Borges, Jorge Luis. "The Library of Babel." In *Collected Fictions*, 112–18. Translated by Andrew Hurley. New York: Penguin, [1941] 1998.

Borio, Gianmario. "New Technology, New Techniques: The Aesthetics of Electronic Music in the 1950s." *Interface* 22 (1993): 77–87.

———. "Vokalmusik als integrals Komponieren von Sprache." In *Autoren-Musik: Sprache im Grenzbereich der Künste. Musik-Konzepte* 81, 41–58. Edited by Günter Peters. Munich: edition text + kritik, 1993.

Borio, Gianmario, ed. *Musical Listening in the Age of Technological Reproduction*. Surrey, UK: Ashgate, 2015.

Borio, Gianmario and Hermann Danuser, eds., *Im Zenit der Moderne: die Internationalen Ferienkurse für Neue Musik Darmstadt 1946–1966*. 4 Vols. Freiburg im Breisgau: Rombach, 1997.

Born, Georgina. *Rationalizing Culture: IRCAM, Boulez, and the Institutionalization of the Musical Avant-Garde*. Berkeley: University of California Press, 1995.

———. *Uncertain Vision: Birt, Dyke and the Reinvention of the BBC*. London: Secker & Warburg, 2004.

Born, Georgina, ed. *Music, Sound, and Space: Transformations of Public and Private Experience*. Cambridge: Cambridge University Press, 2015.

Bosma, Hannah. "*Thema: (Omaggio a Joyce)*: A Listening Experience as Homage to Cathy Berberian." In *Cathy Berberian: Pioneer of Contemporary Vocality*, 97–120. Edited by Pamela Karantonis, Francesca Placanica, Anne Sivuoja-Kauppala, and Pieter Verstraete. Burlington, VT: Ashgate, 2014.

Both, Christopher. "The Influence of Concepts of Information Theory on Electronic Music Composition: Lejaren A. Hiller and Karlheinz Stockhausen 1953–1960." PhD dissertation, University of Victoria, British Columbia, 1995.

Braun, Hans-Joachim, ed. *Music and Technology in the Twentieth Century*. Baltimore, MD: Johns Hopkins University Press, 2002.

Brilmayer, Benedikt. "Das Trautonium: Prozesse des Technologietransfers im Musikinstrumentenbau." PhD dissertation, University of Augsburg, 2014.

Brodsky, Seth. *From 1989, or European Music and the Modernist Unconscious*. Berkeley: University of California Press, 2017.

Budde, Elmar. "Zum Verhältnis von Sprache, Sprachlaut und Komposition in der Neuen Musik." In *Über Musik und Sprache*, 9–19. Edited by Rudolf Stefan. Mainz: B. Schott's Söhne, 1974.

Buso, Nicola. "A Portrait of *Ritratto*." In *Nuova Musica Alla Radio/New Music on the Radio*, 54–99. Edited by Veniero Rizzardi and Angela Ida de Benedictis. Milan: RAI/Eri, 2000.

Bürger, Peter. *Theory of the Avant-Garde*. Translated by Michael Shaw. Minneapolis: University of Minnesota Press, 1984.

Cady, Jason. "An Overview of Earle Brown's Techniques and Media." In *Beyond Notation: The Music of Earle Brown*, 1–20. Edited by Rebecca Kim. Ann Arbor: University of Michigan Press, 2017.

Cahn, Peter. "Zur Musikgeschichte der 40er und frühen 50er Jahre: Erfahrungen, Erlebnisse, und persönliche Anmerkungen." In *Stunde Null—zur Musik um 1945*, 28–39. Edited by Volker Scherliess. Kassel, Germany: Bärenreiter, 2014.

Calico, Joy H. "'Für eine neue deutsche Nationaloper': Opera in the Discourses of Unification and Legitimation in the German Democratic Republic." In *Music and German National Identity*, 190–204. Edited by Celia Applegate and Pamela Potter. Chicago: University of Chicago Press, 2002.

———. *Arnold Schoneberg's* A Survivor from Warsaw *in Postwar Europe*. Berkeley: University of California Press, 2014.

Callon, Michel. "Some Elements of a Sociology of Translation: Domestication of the Scallops and the Fishermen of St Brieuc Bay." In *Power, Action and Belief: A New Sociology of Knowledge*, 196–233. Edited by John Law. London: Routledge & Kegan Paul, 1986.

———. "Society in the Making: The Study of Technology as a Tool for Sociological Analysis." In *The Social Construction of Technological Systems: New Directions in the Sociology and History of Technology*, 83–103. Edited by Wiebe E. Bijker, Thomas P. Hughes, and Trevor Pinch. Anniversary edition. Cambridge, MA: MIT Press, [1987] 2012.

Callon, Michael and Bruno Latour. "Don't Throw the Baby Out With the Bath School! A Reply to Collins and Yearley." In *Science as Practice and Culture,* 343–68. Edited by Andrew Pickering. Chicago and London: University of Chicago Press, 1992.

Campbell, Edward. *Boulez, Music and Philosophy*. Cambridge: Cambridge University Press, 2010.

Campbell, Murray and Clive Greated. *The Musician's Guide to Acoustics*. New York: Schirmer, 1988.

Carroll, Mark. *Music and Ideology in Cold War Europe*. Cambridge: Cambridge University Press, 2003.

Causton, Richard. "Berio's *Visage* and the Theatre of Electroacoustic Music." *Tempo* 194 Italian series (October 1995): 15–21.

Cetina, Karin Knorr. *The Manufacture of Knowledge: An Essay on the Constructivist and Contextual Nature of Science*. Oxford: Pergamon, 1981.

———. "The Couch, the Cathedral, and the Laboratory: On the Relationship Between Experiment and Laboratory in Science." In *Science as Practice and Culture*, 113–38. Edited by Andrew Pickering. Chicago and London: University of Chicago Press, 1992.

———. *Epistemic Cultures: How the Sciences Make Knowledge*. Cambridge, MA: Harvard University Press, 1999.

Chadabe, Joel. *Electric Sound: The Past and Promise of Electronic Music*. Upper Saddle River, NJ: Prentice Hall, 1997.

Childs, Edward. "*Achorripsis*: A Sonification of Probability Distributions." In *Proceedings of the International Conference on Auditory Display*, 2002, https://smartech.gatech.edu/handle/1853/51332 (accessed March 14, 2016).

Clendinning, Jane Piper. "Contrapuntal Techniques in the Music of György Ligeti."
PhD dissertation, Yale University, 1989.

———. "The Pattern-Meccanico Compositions of György Ligeti." *Perspectives of New
Music* 13/1 (Winter 1993): 192–234.

———. "Structural Factors in the Microcanonic Compositions of György Ligeti."
In *Concert Music, Rock, and Jazz Since 1945: Essays and Analytical Studies*, 229–58.
Edited by Elizabeth W. Marvin and Richard Hermann. Rochester, NY: University
of Rochester Press, 1995.

Cohen, Dalia and Shlomo Dubnov. "Gestalt Phenomena in Musical Texture." In *Music,
Gestalt and Computing*, 386–405. Edited by Marc Leman. Series of Lecture Notes in
Artificial Intelligence. Berlin: Springer Verlag, 1997.

Cohen, Joel E. "Translator's Introduction." In *Information Theory and Esthetic Perception*,
1–6. Translated by Joel E. Cohen. Urbana and London: University of Illinois
Press, 1966.

Collins, H. M. and Steven Yearley. "Epistemological Chicken." In *Science as Practice and
Culture*, 301–26. Edited by Andrew Pickering. Chicago and London: University of
Chicago Press, 1992.

———. "Journey Into Space." In *Science as Practice and Culture*, 369–89. Edited by
Andrew Pickering. Chicago and London: University of Chicago Press, 1992.

Copeland, Jack. "Delilah—Encrypting Speech." In *The Turing Guide*, 183–87. Edited by
Jack Copeland, Jonathan Bowen, Mark Sprevak, and Robin Wilson. Oxford: Oxford
University Press, 2017.

Cory, Mark and Barbara Haggh. "*Hörspiel* as Music and Music as *Hörspiel*: The Creative
Dialogue Between Experimental Radio Drama and Avant-Garde Music." *German
Studies Review* 4/2 (May 1991): 257–79.

Cox, Arnie. "Embodying Music: Principles of the Mimetic Hypothesis." *Music Theory
Online* 17/2 http://www.mtosmt.org/issues/mto.11.17.2/mto.11.17.2.cox.html
(accessed June 10, 2016).

Cox, Geoffrey. "'There Must Be a Poetry of Sound That None of Us Knows . . . ': Early
British Documentary Film and the Prefiguring of *Musique Concrète*." *Organised Sound*
22/2 (August 2017): 172–86.

Cremaschi, Andrea and Francesco Giomi. "*Parrrole*: Berio's Words on Music
Technology." *Computer Music Journal* 28/1 (Spring 2004): 26–36.

Cross, Lowell. "Electronic Music 1948–1953." *Perspectives of New Music* 7/1 (Fall/Winter
1968): 32–65.

Currid, Brian. *A National Acoustics: Music and Mass Publicity in Weimar and Nazi
Germany*. Minneapolis: University of Minnesota Press, 2006.

Custodis, Michael. *Die soziale Isolation der neuen Musik: Zum Kölner Musikleben nach 1945*.
Stuttgart: Franz Steiner Verlag, 2004.

Dack, John. "The Electroacoustic Music of Henri Pousseur and the 'Open' Form." In
The Modernist Legacy: Essays on New Music, 177–89. Edited by Björn Heile. Farnham,
UK: Ashgate, 2009.

———. "*Scambi* and the Studio di Fonologia." In *The Studio di Fonologia: A Musical
Journey 1954–1983. Update 2008–2012*, 123–39. Edited by Maria Maddalena
Novati and John Dack. English edition. Milan: Ricordi, 2012.

Dalmonte, Rossana. "Maderna, Bruno." *Grove Music Online. Oxford Music Online.* Oxford
  University Press, http://www.oxfordmusiconline.com.proxy.uchicago.edu/sub-
  scriber/article/grove/music/17392 (accessed October 25, 2017).
Danius, Sara. *The Senses of Modernism: Technology, Perception, and Aesthetics.* Ithaca, NY and
  London: Cornell University Press, 2002.
Danuser, Hermann. "Die "Darmstädter Schule"—Faktizität und Mythos." In *Im Zenit
  der Moderne*, vol. 2, 333–62. Edited by Gianmario Borio and Hermann Danuser.
  Freiburg im Breisgau: Rombach, 1997.
Daughtry, J. Martin. "Sonic Samizdat: Situating Unofficial Recording in the Post-
  Stalinist Soviet Union." *Poetics Today* 30/1 (Spring 2009): 27–65.
Davidson, John and Sabine Hake, eds. *Framing the Fifties: Cinema in a Divided Germany.*
  New York: Berghahn Books, 2007.
Davis, Lennard. *Enforcing Normalcy: Disability, Deafness, and the Body.* London:
  Verso, 1995.
De Benedictis, Angela Ida. " . . . *at the Time of the Tubes*: A Conversation with Marino
  Zuccheri." In *Nuovo Musica Alla Radio/New Music on the Radio*, 176–212. Edited by
  Veniero Rizzardi and Angela Ida de Benedictis. Milan: RAI/Eri, 2000.
———. "A Conversation with Luciano Berio." In *Nuovo Musica Alla Radio/New Music
  on the Radio*, 160–75. Edited by Veniero Rizzardi and Angela Ida de Benedictis.
  Milan: RAI/Eri, 2000.
———. "Opera Prima: *Ritratto di Città* and the Beginning of Electroacoustic Music in
  Italy." In *Nuovo Musica Alla Radio/New Music on the Radio*, 26–53. Edited by Veniero
  Rizzardi and Angela Ida de Benedictis. Milan: RAI/Eri, 2000.
———. "A Meeting of Music and the New Possibilities of Technology: The
  Beginnings of the Studio di Fonologia Musicale di Milano della Rai." In *The Studio
  di Fonologia: A Musical Journey 1954–1983. Update 2008–2012*, 3–18. Edited by
  Maria Maddalena Novati and John Dack. English edition. Milan: Ricordi, 2012.
———. "'Live is Dead?': Some Remarks About Live Electronics Practice and
  Listening." In *Musical Listening in the Age of Technological Reproduction*, 301–21.
  Edited by Gianmario Borio. Surrey, UK and Burlington, VT: Ashgate, 2015.
De Benedictis, Angela Ida and Maria Maddalena Novati. "Introduction." In *Prix
  Italia*, 187–91. Edited by Angela Ida de Benedictis and Maria Maddalena Novati.
  Milan: die Schachtel and Rai Trade, 2012.
De Benedictis, Angela Ida and Veniero Rizzardi. "Just then I heard a
  voice . . . : Conversation With Vittorio Sermonti." In *Prix Italia*, 281–89. Edited
  by Angela Ida de Benedictis and Maria Maddalena Novati. Milan: die Schachtel and
  Rai Trade, 2012.
Decroupet, Pascal. "Timbre Diversification in Serial Tape Music and its Consequence on
  Form." *Contemporary Music Review* 10/2 (1994): 13–23.
———. "Henri Pousseur: Composition, Perception, Utopia." In *New Music, Aesthetics
  and Ideology*. 182–92. Edited by Mark Delaere. Wilhelmshaven, Germany: Florian
  Noetzel GmbH, 1995.
———. "Aleatorik und Indetermination—Die Ferienkurse als Forum der europäischen
  Cage-Rezeption." In *Im Zenit der Moderne*, vol. 2,189–98. Edited by Gianmario
  Borio and Hermann Danuser. Freiburg im Breisgau: Rombach Verlag, 1997.

———. "Gravitationsfeld *Gruppen*: Zur Verschränkung der Werke *Gesang der Jünglinge, Gruppen* und *Zeitmasze* und deren Auswirkung auf Stockhausens Musikdenken in der zweiten Hälfte der fünfziger Jahre." *Musiktheorie* 12/1 (1997): 37–51.

———. "Pousseur: Theorie und Praxis." In *Im Zenit der Moderne*, vol.2, 223–31. Edited by Gianmario Borio and Hermann Danuser. Freiburg im Breisgau: Rombach Verlag, 1997.

———. "Studio di Fonologia Musicale della RAI Milano." In *Im Zenit der Moderne*, vol. 2, 99–104. Edited by Gianmario Borio and Hermann Danuser. Freiburg im Breisgau: Rombach Verlag, 1997.

———. "Archaeology of a Phoenix: Electronic/Electroacoustic Music: A Category Consigned to the Past?" In *Nuovo Musica Alla Radio/New Music on the Radio*, 2–25. Edited by Veniero Rizzardi and Angela Ida de Benedictis. Milan: RAI/Eri, 2000.

———. "Komponieren im analogen Studio—eine historisch-systematische Betrachtung." In *Elecktroakustische Musik*, 36–66. Edited by Elena Ungeheuer. Laaber, Germany: Laaber Verlag, 2002.

———. "Vers une théorie generale—Henri Pousseurs 'Allgemeine Periodik' in Theorie und Praxis." *MusikTexte* 98 (August 2003): 31–43.

———. "Floating Hierarchies: Organization and Composition in Works by Pierre Boulez and Karlheinz Stockhausen During the 1950s." In *A Handbook to Twentieth-Century Musical Sketches*, 146–60. Edited by Patricia Hall and Friedemann Sallis. Cambridge: Cambridge University Press, 2004.

Decroupet, Pascal and Elena Ungeheuer. "Karel Goeyvaerts und die serielle Tonbandmusik." *Revue belge de Musicologie* 48 (1994): 94–118.

———. "Through the Sensory Looking Glass: The Aesthetic and Serial Foundations of *Gesang der Jünglinge*." In *Electroacoustic Music: Analytical Perspectives*, 1–40. Edited by Thomas Licata. Westport, CT: Greenwood, 2002.

Delaere, Mark. "The Projection in Time and Space of a Basic Idea Generating Structure: The Music of Karel Goeyvaerts." *Revue belge de Musicologie* 48 (1994): 11–14.

Delaere, Mark, ed. *Rewriting Recent Music History: The Development of Early Serialism 1947–1957*. Leuven, Belgium: Peeters, 2011.

de Lautour, Reuben. "Inaudible Visitors: Theories of Sound Reproduction in the Studio Practice of Pierre Schaeffer." *Organised Sound* 22/2 (August 2017): 161–71.

Demers, Joanna. *Listening through the Noise: The Aesthetics of Experimental Electronic Music*. Oxford: Oxford University Press, 2010.

Dibelius, Ulrich. *Moderne Musik I, 1945–1965*. Mainz: Schott, 1984.

———. "*Abfälle—Ausfälle*: Notizen zum Musikbegriff bei Dieter Schnebel." In *Dieter Schnebel, Musik-Konzepte* 16, 3–11. Edited by Heinz-Klaus Metzger and Rainer Riehn. Munich: edition text + kritik, 1980.

———. *György Ligeti: Eine Monographie in Essays*. Mainz: Schott, 1994.

Donhauser, Peter. *Elektrische Klangmaschinen: Die Pionierzeit in Deutschland und Österreich*. Vienna: Böhlau, 2007.

Drott, Eric. "Ligeti in Fluxus." *Journal of Musicology* 21/2 (Spring 2004): 201–40.

———. "The Politics of *Presque Rien*." In *Sound Commitments: Avant-Garde Music and the Sixties*, 145–66. Edited by Robert Adlington. Oxford: Oxford University Press, 2009.

———. "Lines, Masses, Micropolyphony: Ligeti's Kyrie and the Crisis of the Figure." *Perspectives of New Music* 49/1 (Winter 2011): 4–46.

———. *Music and the Elusive Revolution: Cultural Politics and Political Culture in France, 1968–1981*. Berkeley: University of California Press, 2011.

———. "The End(s) of Genre." *Journal of Music Theory* 57/1 (Spring 2013): 1–45.

Dussel, Konrad. "Radio Programming, Ideology, and Cultural Change: Fascism, Communism and Liberal Democracy, 1920s–1950s." In *Mass Media, Culture, and Society in Twentieth-Century Germany*, 80–94. Edited by Karl Christian Führer and Corey Ross. Houndmills, Basingstoke, Hampshire, and New York: Palgrave Macmillan, 2006.

Eco, Umberto. *The Open Work*. Translated by Anna Cancogni. Cambridge, MA: Harvard University Press, 1989.

Edwards, Allen. "Unpublished Bouleziana at the Paul Sacher Foundation." *Tempo* 169 (June 1989): 4–15.

Edwards, Paul N. *The Closed World: Computers and the Politics of Discourse in Cold War America*. Cambridge, MA: MIT Press, 1996.

Ensmenger, Nathan. *The Computer Boys Take Over: Computers, Programmers, and the Politics of Technical Expertise*. Cambridge, MA: MIT Press, 2010.

Everett, Walter. *The Beatles as Musicians: Revolver Through the Anthology*. New York: Oxford University Press, 1999.

Fauser, Annegret. *Sounds of War: Music in the United States During World War II*. New York: Oxford University Press, 2013.

Fearn, Raymond. *Bruno Maderna*. Chur, Switzerland and London: Harwood Academic, 1990.

Fehrenbach, Heide. *Cinema: Democratizing Germany, Reconstructing National Identity After Hitler*. Chapel Hill: University of North Carolina Press, 1995.

Flašar, Martin. "*Poème Électronique* (1958): Le Corbusier—E. Varèse—I. Xenakis." PhD dissertation, Masarykova University, Brno, Czech Republic, 2012.

Flynn, George W. "Listening to Berio's Music." *The Musical Quarterly* 61/3 (July 1975): 388–421.

Fosler-Lussier, Danielle. *Music Divided: Bartók's Legacy in Cold War Culture*. Berkeley: University of California Press, 2007.

———. *Music in America's Cold War Diplomacy*. Berkeley: University of California Press, 2015.

Fox, Christopher. "Other Darmstadts: An Introduction." *Contemporary Music Review* 26/1 (February 2007): 1–3.

———. "Music After Zero Hour." *Contemporary Music Review* 26/1 (February 2007): 5–24.

———. "Darmstadt and the Institutionalization of Modernism." *Contemporary Music Review* 26/1 (February 2007): 115–23.

———. "Where the River Bends: The Cologne School in Retrospect." *The Musical Times* 148/1901 (Winter 2007): 27–42.

Fricke, Stefan. "Helms, Hans G." *Grove Music Online. Oxford Music Online*. Oxford University Press, http://www.oxfordmusiconline.com.proxy.lib.uiowa.edu/subscriber/article/grove/music/12753 (accessed June 1, 2016).

Fricke, Stefan, ed. *Dieter Schnebel: Beiträge, Meinungen und Analysen zur neuen Musik*. Saarbrücken, Germany: Pfau, 2000.

Fritzsche, Peter. "Nazi Modern." *Modernism/Modernity* 3/1 (January 1996): 1–22.

Frühauf, Tina, and Lily E. Hirsch, eds. *Dislocated Memories: Jews, Music, and Postwar German Culture*. New York: Oxford University Press, 2014.

Fulcher, Jane. *The Composer as Intellectual: Music and Ideology in France, 1914–1940*. New York: Oxford University Press, 2005.

———. "French Identity in Flux: Vichy's Collaboration and Antigone's Operatic Triumph." *Proceedings of the American Philosophical Society* 150/2 (June 2006): 261–95.

———. "From 'The Voice of the Maréchal' to Musique Concrète: Pierre Schaeffer and the Case for Cultural History." In *Oxford Handbook of the New Cultural History of Music*, 381–402. Edited by Jane Fulcher. New York: Oxford University Press, 2011.

———. *Renegotiating French Identity: Musical Culture and Creativity in France during Vichy and the German Occupation*. New York: Oxford University Press, 2018.

Fujimura, Joan H. "Crafting Science: Standardized Packages, Boundary Objects, and 'Translation.'" In *Science as Practice and Culture*, 168–211. Edited by Andrew Pickering. Chicago and London: University of Chicago Press, 1992.

Galison, Peter. *How Experiments End*. Chicago and London: University of Chicago Press, 1987.

———. "Physics Between War and Peace." In *Science, Technology, and the Military*, 47–86. Edited by Everett Mendelsohn, Merrit Roe Smith, and Peter Weingart. Dordecht, The Netherlands: Kluwer Academic, 1988.

———. "The Ontology of the Enemy: Norbert Wiener and the Cybernetic Vision." *Critical Inquiry* 21/1 (Autumn 1994): 228–66.

———. "Constructing Modernism: The Cultural Locations of *Aufbau*." In *The Origins of Logical Empiricism*, vol. 16, 17–44. Edited by Ronald N. Giere and Alan W. Richardson. Minneapolis: University of Minnesota Press, 1996.

Gallope, Michael. "Why Was This Music Desirable? On a Critical Explanation of the Avant-Garde." *Journal of Musicology* 31/2 (Spring 2014): 199–230.

———. "Michael Gallope Responds." *Journal of Musicology* 31/2 (Spring 2014): 297–98.

Gann, Kyle. *American Music in the Twentieth Century*. New York: Schirmer, 1997.

———. *No Such Thing as Silence: John Cage's 4´33˝*. New Haven, CT: Yale University Press, 2010.

Gardner, James. *These Hopeful Machines*. Six-part radio series plus outtakes. New Zealand Radio, July–August 2013, http://www.radionz.co.nz/concert/programmes/hopefulmachines (accessed July 21, 2017).

———. "Even Orpheus Needs a Synthi." *Tempo* 70/276 (April 2016): 56–70.

———. "Don Banks Music Box to the Putney: The Genesis and Development of the VCS3 Synthesizer." *Organised Sound* 22/2 (August 2017): 217–27.

Gendron, Bernard. *Between Montmartre and the Mudd Club: Popular Music and the Avant-Garde*. Chicago: University of Chicago Press, 2002.

Geoghegan, Bernard Dionysius. "From Information Theory to French Theory: Jakobson, Lévi-Strauss, and the Cybernetic Appartus." *Critical Inquiry* 38/1 (Autumn 2011): 96–126.

———. "After Kittler: On the Cultural Techniques of Recent German Media Theory." *Theory, Culture, and Society* 30/6 (August 2013): 66–82.

Geoghegan, Bernard, and Benjamin Peters. "Cybernetics." In *Johns Hopkins Guide to Digital Media*, 109–113. Edited by Marie-Laure Ryan, Lori Emerson, and Benjamin J. Robertson. Baltimore, MD: Johns Hopkins University Press, 2014.

Gertner, Jon. *The Idea Factory: Bell Labs and the Great Age of American Innovation.* New York: Penguin Books, 2012.

Gethmann, Daniel. *Klangmaschinen zwischen Experiment und Medientechnik.* Bielefeld, Germany: transcript, 2010.

Gibson, Benoît. *The Instrumental Music of Iannis Xenakis: Theory, Practice, Self-Borrowing.* Hillsdale, NY: Pendragon Press, 2011.

Gieryn, Thomas F. "Boundary-Work and the Demarcation of Science from Non-Science: Strains and Interests in Professional Ideologies of Scientists." *American Sociological Review* 48/6 (December 1983): 781–95.

Gilfillan, Daniel. *Pieces of Sound: German Experimental Radio.* Minneapolis: University of Minnesota Press, 2009.

Gleick, James, *The Information: A History, A Theory, A Flood.* New York: Vintage Books, 2011.

Glinsky, Albert. *Theremin: Ether Music and Espionage.* Urbana: University of Illinois Press, 2000.

Goldman, Jonathan. *The Musical Language of Pierre Boulez: Writings and Compositions.* Vol. 3 of the Contemporary Music Series. Cambridge: Cambridge University Press, 2011.

———. "Of Doubles, Groups, and Rhymes: A Seriation of Works for Spatialized Orchestral Groups (1958–60)." In *The Dawn of Music Semiology: Essays in Honor of Jean-Jacques Nattiez*, 139–76. Edited by Jonathan Dunsby and Jonathan Goldman. Rochester, NY: University of Rochester Press, 2017.

Good, Jack. "Enigma and Fish." In *Codebreakers: The Inside Story of Bletchley Park*, 149–66. Edited by F. H. Hinsley and Alan Stripp. Oxford: Oxford University Press, 1993.

Gooding, David. "Putting Agency Back Into Experiment." In *Science as Practice and Culture*, 65–112. Edited by Andrew Pickering. Chicago and London: University of Chicago Press, 1992.

Gordon, Ted. " 'The Composer's Black-Box': Cybernetics, Creativity, and Technology at the San Francisco Tape Music Center." Paper presented at the Society for American Music Conference, Montreal, Quebec, March 2017.

———. "Bay Area Experimentalism: Music & Technology in the Long 1960s." PhD dissertation, University of Chicago, 2018.

Gottschalk, Jennie. *Experimental Music Since 1970.* New York: Bloomsbury, 2016.

Gottstein, Björn. "Das Studio für elektronische Musik des WDR." In *Musik der Zeit 1951–2001: 50 Jahre Neue Musik im WDR*, 125–54. Edited by Frank Hilberg and Harry Vogt. Hofheim, Germany: Wolke, 2002.

———. *Musik als Ars Scientia: Die Edgard-Varèse-Gastprofessoren des DAAD an der TU Berlin 2000–2006.* Saarbrücken, Germany: Pfau, 2006.

Goslich, Siegfried. *Musik im Rundfunk.* Tutzing, Germany: Hans Schneider, 1971.

Grant, M. J. *Serial Music, Serial Aesthetics: Compositional Theory in Post-War Europe.* Cambridge: Cambridge University Press, 2001.

Griffiths, Paul. *Cage.* London: Oxford University Press, 1981.

————. *Modern Music: The Avant-Garde Since 1945*. London: J. M. Dent and Sons, 1981.

Grubbs, David. *Records Ruin the Landscape: John Cage, the Sixties, and Sound Recording*. Durham, NC and London: Duke University Press, 2014.

Hacking, Ian. "The Self-Vindication of the Laboratory Sciences." In *Science as Practice and Culture*, 29–64. Edited by Andrew Pickering. Chicago and London: University of Chicago Press, 1992.

Handel, Stephen. "Timbre Perception and Auditory Object Identification." In *Hearing*, 425–61. Edited by Brian C. J. Moore. San Diego: Academic, 1995.

Handke, Silvia. *Präsenz und Dynamik regionaler Musikkulturen in den Sendekonzepten des WDR-Hörfunks*. Kassel, Germany: Merseburger, 1997.

Harbison, William G. "Performer Indeterminacy and Boulez's Third Sonata." *Tempo* 169 (June 1989): 16–20.

Harley, James. *Xenakis: His Life in Music*. New York: Routledge, 2004.

————. *Iannis Xenakis: Kraanerg*. Surrey, UK and Burlington, VT: Ashgate, 2015.

Hartmann, William Morris. "The Physical Description of Signals." In *Hearing*, 1–40. Edited by Brian C. J. Moore. San Diego: Academic, 1995.

Haskins, Rob. *John Cage*. London: Reaktion Books, 2012.

Haufler, Hervie. *Codebreakers' Victory: How the Allied Cryptographers Won World War II*. New York: New American Library, 2003.

Hayles, N. Katherine. *How We Became Posthuman: Virtual Bodies in Cybernetics, Literature, and Informatics*. Chicago: University of Chicago Press, 1999.

Heile, Björn. "Collage vs. Compositional Control: The Interdependency of Modernist and Postmodernist Approaches in the Work of Mauricio Kagel." In *Postmodern Music/Postmodern Thought*, 287–99. Edited by Joseph Auner and Judy Lochhead. New York: Routledge, 2002.

————. *The Music of Mauricio Kagel*. Burlington, VT: Ashgate, 2006.

Heile, Björn and Martin Iddon, eds. *Mauricio Kagel bei den Internationalen Ferienkursen für Neue Musik in Darmstadt*. Holheim, Germany: Wolke Verlag, 2009.

Heims, Steve J. *John von Neumann and Norbert Wiener: From Mathematics to the Technologies of Life and Death*. Cambridge, MA: MIT Press, 1980.

————. *Constructing a Social Science for Postwar America: The Cybernetics Group, 1946–1953*. Cambridge, MA: MIT Press, 1993.

Heinrich-Franke, Christian. "Airy Curtains: Demarcating Cold War Europe in the Ether." *East Central Europe* 41 (2014): 158–79.

Herf, Jeffrey. *Reactionary Modernism: Technology, Culture, and Politics in Weimar and the Third Reich*. Cambridge: Cambridge University Press, 1984.

————. *Divided Memory: The Nazi Past in the Two Germanys*. Cambridge, MA: Harvard University Press, 1999.

Herzogenrath, Wulf and Gabriele Lueg, eds. *Die 60er Jahre: Kölns Weg zur Kunstmetropole: vom Happening zum Kunstmarkt*. Kölnischer Kunstverein. Cologne: Druckeri Henke, 1986.

Hilberg, Frank and Harry Vogt, eds. *Musik der Zeit: 50 Jahre neue Musik im WDR*. Hofheim, Germany: Wolke, 2002.

Hinkle-Turner, Elizabeth. "Women and Music Technology: Pioneers, Precedents and Issues in the United States." *Organised Sound* 8/1 (April 2003): 31–47.

————. *Women Composers and Music Technology in the United States: Crossing the Line.* Aldershot, UK: Ashgate, 2006.

Hinsley, F. H. "An Introduction to Fish." In *Codebreakers: The Inside Story of Bletchley Park*, 141–48. Edited by F. H. Hinsley and Alan Stripp. Oxford: Oxford University Press, 1993.

Hinsley, F. H. and Alan Stripp. *Codebreakers: The Inside Story of Bletchley Park.* New York: Oxford University Press, 1993.

Hirsch, Michael. "*dt 31,6*: das frühe Meisterwerk." In *Dieter Schnebel: Querdenken der musikalischen Avantgarde*, 66–78. Edited by Theda Weber-Lucks. Munich: edition text + kritik, 2015.

Hodges, Andrew. *Alan Turing: The Enigma.* Centenary edition. Princeton, NJ: Princeton University Press, 2012.

Holmes, Thom. *Electronic and Experimental Music: Technology, Music, and Culture.* 5th edition. New York: Routledge, 2016.

Holt, Nathalia. *Rise of the Rocket Girls: The Women Who Propelled Us, from Missiles to the Moon to Mars.* New York: Little, Brown, 2016.

Holt, Robert T. *Radio Free Europe.* Minneapolis: University of Minnesota Press, 1958.

Holtsträter, Knut. *Mauricio Kagels musikalisches Werk: Der Komponist als Erzähler, Medienarrangeur und Sammler.* Cologne: Böhlau, 2010.

Holzaepfel, John. "Der Tudor Faktor." In *John Cage: Anarchic Harmony*, 43–56. Edited by Stefan Schädler and Walter Zimmerman. Mainz: Schott, 1993.

————. "David Tudor and the Performance of American Experimental Music 1950–59." PhD dissertation, City University of New York, 1994.

————. "Interview with David Tudor." *The Musical Quarterly* 78/3 (Autumn 1994): 626–36.

————. "David Tudor and the *Solo for Piano*." In *Writings Through John Cage's Music, Poetry, and Art*, 137–56. Edited by David Bernstein and Christopher Hatch. Chicago: University of Chicago Press, 2000.

————. "Cage and Tudor." In *Cambridge Companion to John Cage*, 169–85. Edited by David Nicholls. Cambridge: Cambridge University Press, 2002.

Hommel, Friedrich and Wilhelm Schlüter eds., *New Music Darmstadt 1950–1960: Text and Picture Book.* Darmstadt: Internationales Musikinstitut Darmstadt, 1987.

Horning, Susan Schmidt. *Chasing Sound: Technology, Culture, and the Art of Studio Recording from Edison to the LP.* Baltimore: Johns Hopkins University Press, 2013.

Houtsma, Adrianus J. M. "Pitch Perception." In *Hearing*, 267–95. Edited by Brian C. J. Moore. San Diego: Academic, 1995.

Hui, Alexandra. *The Psychophysical Ear: Musical Experiments, Experimental Sounds, 1840–1910.* Cambridge, MA: MIT Press, 2013.

Hui, Alexandra, Julia Kursell, and Myles W. Jackson. "Music, Sound, and the Laboratory from 1750 to 1980." *Osiris* 28/1 (January 2013): 1–11.

Humpert, Hans Ulrich. *Elektronische Musik: Geschichte—Technik—Kompositionen.* Mainz: Schott, 1987.

————. "So begann die elektronische Musik in Köln." In *Neue Musik im Rheinland*, 67–72. Edited by Heinz Bremer. Kassel, Germany: Merseberger, 1996.

Huron, David. *Sweet Anticipation: Music and the Psychology of Expectation.* Cambridge, MA: MIT Press, 2006.

Iddon, Martin. "Gained in Translation: Words About Cage in Late 1950s Germany."
Contemporary Music Review 26/1 (February 2007): 89–104.

———. "Darmstadt Schools: Darmstadt as Plural Phenomenon." Tempo 65/256 (April 2011): 2–8.

———. New Music at Darmstadt: Nono, Stockhausen, Cage, and Boulez. Cambridge: Cambridge University Press, 2013.

———. "Spectres of Darmstadt." Tempo 67/263 (January 2013): 60–67

Iverson, Jennifer. "Shared Compositional Techniques Between György Ligeti's Pièce électronique No. 3 and Atmosphères." Mitteilungen der Paul Sacher Stiftung 22 (April 2009): 29–33.

———. "The Emergence of Timbre: Ligeti's Synthesis of Electronic and Acoustic Music in Atmosphères." twentieth-century music 7/1 (March 2010): 61–89.

———. "Statistical Form Amongst the Darmstadt Composers." Music Analysis 33/3 (October 2014): 341–87.

———. "From Analog to Digital: An Interview with Gottfried Michael Koenig." Tempo 70/276 (April 2016): 43–55.

———. "Invisible Collaboration: The Dawn and Evolution of Electronic Music." Music Theory Spectrum 39/2 (Fall 2017): 1–23.

———. "Learning the Studio: Sketches for Mid-Century Electronic Music." Contemporary Music Review 36/5 (2017): 362–87.

Jacobsen, Annie. Operation Paperclip. New York: Little, Brown, 2014.

Jagoda, Patrick. Network Aesthetics. Chicago: University of Chicago Press, 2016.

Jameux, Dominique. Pierre Boulez. Translated by Susan Bradshaw. Cambridge, MA: Harvard University Press, 1991.

Jarausch, Konrad. After Hitler: Recivilizing Germans 1945–1995. New York: Oxford University Press, 2006.

Jenkins, Chadwick. "Structure vs. Form in the Sonatas and Interludes for Prepared Piano." In John Cage: Music, Philosophy, and Intention 1933–1950, 239–61. Edited by David Patterson. New York: Routledge, 2002.

Jones, Jeannette DiBernardo. "Imagined Hearing: Music-Making in Deaf Culture." In Oxford Handbook of Music and Disability Studies, 54–72. Edited by Blake Howe, Stephanie Jensen-Moulton, Neil Lerner, and Joseph Straus. New York: Oxford University Press, 2015.

Joseph, Branden W. "'A Therapeutic Value for City Dwellers': The Development of John Cage's Early Avant-Garde Aesthetic Position." In John Cage: Music, Philosophy, and Intention 1933–1950, 135–75. Edited by David Patterson. New York: Routledge, 2002.

———. Experimentations: John Cage in Music, Art, and Architecture. New York: Bloomsbury, 2016.

Jurkowski, Nicholas. "The Electronic Avant-Garde and the Genesis of Music as Collaborative Research." Paper presented at AMS/SMT Conference, Milwaukee, WI, November 7, 2014.

Kahn, David. Hitler's Spies: German Military Intelligence in World War II. New York: Macmillan, 1978.

———. The Codebreakers: The Story of Secret Writing. 2nd edition. New York: Scribner, 1996.

Kahn, Douglas. "John Cage: Silence and Silencing." *The Musical Quarterly* 81/4 (Winter 1997): 556–98.

—. *Noise, Water, Meat: A History of Sound in the Arts.* Cambridge, MA: MIT Press, 2001.

—. "James Tenney at Bell Labs." In *Mainframe Experimentalism: Early Computing and the Foundations of the Digital Arts,* 131–46. Edited by Hannah B. Higgins and Douglas Kahn. Berkeley: University of California Press, 2012.

Kaiser, Katherine. "Listening to Recorded Voices in Modern Music." PhD dissertation, Stony Brook University, 2015.

Kakavelakis, Konstantinos. *György Ligetis* Aventures *und* Nouvelles Aventures: *Studien zur Sprachkomposition und Ästhetik der Avantgarde.* Frankfurt: Peter Lang, 2001.

Kane, Brian. *Sound Unseen: Acousmatic Sound in Theory and Practice.* Oxford: Oxford University Press, 2014.

—. "Relays: Audiotape, Material Affordances, and Cultural Practice." *twentieth-century music* 14/1 (February 2017): 66–75.

Karantonis, Pamela, Francesca Placanica, Anne Sivuoja-Kauppala, and Pieter Verstraete, eds. *Cathy Berberian: Pioneer of Contemporary Vocality.* Burlington, VT: Ashgate, 2014.

Kassel, Matthias. "Das Fundament in Turm zu Babel: Ein weiterer Versuch, *Anagrama* zu lesen." In *Mauricio Kagel,* 5–26. *Musik-konzepte* 124. Edited by Ulrich Tadday. Munich: edition text + kritik, 2004.

Kater, Michael H. *The Twisted Muse: Musicians and Their Music in Nazi Germany.* New York: Oxford University Press, 1997.

Katz, Mark. *Capturing Sound: How Technology Has Changed Music.* Revised edition. Berkeley: University of California Press, 2010.

Kelly, Elaine. *Composing the Canon in the German Democratic Republic: Narratives of Nineteenth-Century Music.* New York: Oxford University Press, 2014.

Kemp, J. A. "Phonetics: Precursors to Modern Approaches." In *Concise History of the Language Sciences: From the Sumerians to the Cognitivists,* 371–88. Edited by E. F. K. Koerner and R. E. Asher. New York: Pergamon, 1995.

Kim, Rebecca, ed. *Beyond Notation: The Music of Earle Brown.* Ann Arbor: University of Michigan Press, 2017.

Kirchmeyer, Helmut. *Kleine Monographie über Herbert Eimert.* Abhandlung der Sächscischen Akademie der Wissenschaften Leipzig, Band 75 Heft 6. Leipzig: Herzel, 1998.

—. "Stockhausens Elektronische Messe nebst einem Vorspann unveröffentlicher Briefe aus seiner Pariser Zeit an Herbert Eimert." *Archiv für Musikwissenschaft* 66/3 (2009): 234–59.

Kittler, Friedrich A. *Gramophone, Film, Typewriter.* Translated by Geoffrey Winthrop-Young and Michael Wutz. Stanford, CA: Stanford University Press, 1999.

—. "The Artificial Intelligence of World War: Alan Turing." In *The Truth of the Technological World: Essays on the Genealogy of Presence,* 178–94. Translated by Erik Butler. Stanford, CA: Stanford University Press, 2013.

—. "Rock Music: A Misuse of Military Equipment." In *The Truth of the Technological World: Essays on the Genealogy of Presence,* 152–64. Translated by Erik Butler. Stanford, CA: Stanford University Press, 2013.

—. "Signal-to-Noise Ratio." In *The Truth of the Technological World: Essays on the Genealogy of Presence,* 165–77. Translated by Erik Butler. Stanford, CA: Stanford University Press, 2013.

———. "Unconditional Surrender." In *The Truth of the Technological World: Essays on the Genealogy of Presence*, 195–208. Translated by Erik Butler. Stanford, CA: Stanford University Press, 2013.

Klangraum: 40 Jahre Neue Musik in Köln 1945–1985. Edited by Kölner Gesellschaft für Neue Musik. Cologne: Wienand, 1991.

Kline, Ronald R. "What is Information Theory a Theory Of? Boundary Work Among Information Theorists and Information Scientists in United States and Britain During the Cold War." In *Conference on the History and Heritage of Scientific and Technological Information Systems*, 15–28. Proceedings of the 2002 Conference. Edited by W. Boyd Rayward and Mary Ellen Bowden. Medford, NJ: Information Today, 2004.

———. *The Cybernetics Moment: Or Why We Call Our Age the Information Age*. Baltimore, MD: Johns Hopkins University Press, 2015.

Klippert, Werner. *Elemente des Hörspiels*. Saarbrücken, Germany: Verlag für Politik & Cultur, 2012.

Klotz, Sebastian. "Tonpsychologie und Musikforschung als Katalysatoren wissenschaftlich-experimenteller Praxis und der Methodenlehre im Kreis von Carl Stumpf." *Berichte zur Wissenschaftsgeschichte* 31/3 (September 2008): 195–210.

Klüppelholz, Werner. *Sprache als Musik: Studien zur Vokalkomposition bei Karlheinz Stockhausen, Hans G Helms, Mauricio Kagel, Dieter Schnebel und György Ligeti*. Saarbrücken, Germany: Pfau, 1995.

———. "Mauricio Kagel und die Literatur." In *Über Mauricio Kagel*. Saarbrücken, Germany: Pfau-Verlag, 2003.

Koch, Lars-Christian, Albrecht Wiedmann, and Susanne Ziegler. "The Berlin Phonogramm-Archiv: A Treasury of Sound Recordings." *Acoustical Science and Technology* 25/4 (2004): 227–31.

Kohler, K. "Three Trends in Phonetics: The Development of Phonetics as a Discipline in Germany since the Nineteenth Century." In *Towards a History of Phonetics*, 161–78. Edited by R. E. Asher and Eugénie J. A. Anderson. Edinburgh: Edinburgh University Press, 1981.

Köhler, Stefan. *Hörspiel und Hörbuch: Mediale Entwicklung von der Weimarer Republik bis zur Gegenwart*. Marburg, Germany: Tectum, 2005.

Kordes, Gesa. "Darmstadt, Postwar Experimentation, and the West German Search for a New Musical Identity." In *Music and German National Identity*, 205–17. Edited by Celia Applegate and Pamela Potter. Chicago: University of Chicago Press, 2002.

Kostelanetz, Richard. "John Cage as a *Hörspielmacher*." *Journal of Musicology* 8/2 (Spring 1990): 291–99.

Kostelanetz, Richard. *John Cage (ex)plain(ed)*. New York: Schirmer, 1996.

Kovács, Inge. "Frauen in Darmstadt." In *Im Zenit der Moderne*, vol. 1, 94–99. Edited by Gianmario Borio and Hermann Danuser. Freiburg im Breisgau: Rombach, 1997.

Krellmann, Hanspeter. "Metzger, Heinz-Klaus." *Grove Music Online. Oxford Music Online*. Oxford University Press, http://www.oxfordmusiconline.com.proxy.lib.uiowa.edu/subscriber/article/grove/music/18530. (accessed June 1, 2016).

Kröger, Bernd J., Christine Riek, and Georg Sachse, eds. *Festschrift Georg Heike*. Frankfurt: Wissenschaftliche Buchhandlung Theo Hector, 1998.

Krytska, Iryna. *Karlheinz Stockhausens Klavierstück XI (1956): Interpretationsanalysen*. Kassel, Germany: Gustav Bosse Verlag, 2005.

Kuljuntausta, Petri. *First Wave: A Microhistory of Early Finnish Electronic Music.* Helsinki: Like, 2008.

Kursell, Julia. "Experiments on Tone Color in Music and Acoustics: Helmholtz, Schoenberg, and *Klangfarbenmelodie.*" *Osiris* 28/1 (January 2013): 191–211.

———. "Klangfarbe um 1850—ein epistemischer Raum." In *Wissensgeschichte des Hörens in der Moderne*, 21–40. Edited by Netzwerk Hör-Wissen im Wandel. Berlin: de Gruyter, 2017.

Kurtz, Michael. *Stockhausen: A Biography.* Translated by Richard Toop. London: Faber and Faber, 1992.

Kutsche, Beate and Barley Norton, eds. *Music and Protest in 1968.* Cambridge: University of Cambridge Press, 2013.

Lacey, Kate. *Feminine Frequencies: Gender, German Radio, and the Public Sphere, 1923– 1945.* Ann Arbor: University of Michigan Press, 1996.

Ladefoged, Peter. *Elements of Acoustic Phonetics.* 2nd edition. Chicago: University of Chicago Press, 1996.

Ladefoged, Peter and Ian Maddieson. *The Sounds of the World's Languages.* Oxford: Blackwell, 1996.

Latour, Bruno. *Science in Action: How to Follow Scientists and Engineers Through Society.* Cambridge, MA: Harvard University Press, 1987.

———. "On Recalling ANT." In *Actor Network Theory and After*, 15–25. Edited by John Law and John Hassard. Oxford: Blackwell, 1999.

———. "For David Bloor . . . and Beyond: A Reply to David Bloor's 'Anti-Latour.'" *Studies in the History and Philosophy of Science* 30/1 (March 1999): 113–129.

———. *Reassembling the Social: An Introduction to Actor-Network-Theory.* Oxford: Oxford University Press, 2005.

———. "Where Are the Missing Masses? The Sociology of a Few Mundane Artifacts." In *Shaping Technology/Building Society: Studies in Sociotechnical Change*, 225–59. Edited by Wiebe Bijker and John Law. Cambridge, MA: MIT Press, 1992. Republished in *Technology and Society, Building Our Sociotechnical Future*, 151–80. Edited by Deborah J. Johnson and Jameson M Wetmore. Cambridge, MA: MIT Press, 2008.

Latour, Bruno and Steve Woolgar. *Laboratory Life: The Construction of Scientific Facts.* 2nd edition. Princeton, NJ: Princeton University Press, [1979] 1986.

Lavey, Nate, and Jay Kang, producers. "Object of Interest: The Vocoder." *The New Yorker*, August 19, 2014, http://www.newyorker.com/tech/elements/object-interest-vocoder (accessed February 9, 2016).

Law, John. "After ANT: Complexity, Naming, and Topology." In *Actor Network Theory and After*, 1–14. Edited by John Law and John Hassard. Oxford: Blackwell, 1999.

———. "Technology and Heterogeneous Engineering: The Case of Portuguese Expansion." In *The Social Construction of Technological Systems: New Directions in the Sociology and History of Technology*, 116–38. Edited by Wiebe E. Bijker, Thomas P. Hughes, and Trevor Pinch. Anniversary edition. Cambridge, MA: MIT Press, [1987] 2012.

LeBlanc, Jimmie. "Xenakis's Aesthetic Project: The Paradoxes of a Formalist Intuition." In *Xenakis Matters: Contexts, Processes, Applications*, 59–80. Edited by Sharon Kanach. Hillsdale, NY: Pendragon Press, 2012.

Lee, Joanna Ching-Yun. "György Ligeti's *Aventures* and *Nouvelles Aventures*: A Documentary History." PhD dissertation, Columbia University, 1993.

Levine Packer, Renée. *This Life of Sounds: Evenings for New Music in Buffalo.* New York: Oxford University Press, 2010.

Levy, Benjamin R. "The Electronic Works of György Ligeti and Their Influence on His Later Style." PhD dissertation, University of Maryland, 2006.

———. "Shades of the Studio: Electronic Influences on Ligeti's *Apparations*." *Perspectives of New Music* 47/2 (Summer 2009): 59–87.

———. *Metamorphosis in Music: The Compositions of György Ligeti in the 1950s and 1960s.* New York: Oxford University Press, 2017.

Lewin, David. "Some Applications of Communication Theory to the Study of Twelve-Tone Music." *Journal of Music Theory* 12/1 (Spring 1968): 50–84.

Lewis, George E. "Improvised Music After 1950: Afrological and Eurological Perspectives." *Black Music Research Journal* 16/1 (Spring 1996): 91–122.

———. *A Power Stronger Than Itself: The AACM and American Experimental Music.* Chicago: University of Chicago Press, 2008.

Lobanova, Marina. *György Ligeti: Style, Ideas, and Poetics.* Translated by Mark Shuttleworth. Berlin: Verlag Ernst Kuhn, 2002.

Lochhead, Judy. "Performance Practice in the Indeterminate Works of John Cage." *Performance Practice Review* 7/2 (Fall 1994): 233–41.

———. *Reconceiving Structure in Contemporary Music: New Tools in Music Theory and Analysis.* Routledge Studies in Music Theory. New York: Routledge, 2016.

London, Justin. *Hearing in Time: Psychological Aspects of Musical Meter.* 2nd edition. New York: Oxford University Press, 2012.

Loubet, Emmanuelle. "The Beginnings of Electronic Music in Japan, With a Focus on the NHK Studio: The 1950s and 1960s." Translated by Curtis Roads and Brigitte Robindoré. *Computer Music Journal* 21/4 (Winter 1997): 11–22.

Lovelace, Carey. "How Do You Draw a Sound?" In *Iannis Xenakis: Composer, Architecht, Visionary*, 35–94. Edited by Sharon Kanach and Carey Lovelace, *Drawing Papers 88.* New York: The Drawing Center, 2010.

Löw, Bernd. *Hörspiel 1945–1949: Veröffentlichungen des Deutschen Rundfunkarchivs.* Band 12. Potsdam, Germany: Verlag für Berlin-Brandenburg, 1997.

Maconie, Robin. *The Works of Karlheinz Stockhausen*, 2nd edition. Oxford: Clarendon, [1976] 1999.

———. *Other Planets: The Music of Karlheinz Stockhausen.* Lanham, MD: Scarecrow Press, 2005.

———. "Boulez, Information Science, and IRCAM." *Tempo* 71/279 (January 2017): 38–50.

Mailman, Joshua Banks. "Cybernetic Phenomenology of Music, Embodied Speculative Realism, and Aesthetics-Driven Techné for Spontaneous Audio-Visual Expression." *Perspectives of New Music* 54/1 (Summer 2016): 5–95.

Manning, Peter. "The Significance of *Techné* in Understanding the Art and Practice of Electroacoustic Composition." *Organised Sound* 11/1 (April 2006): 81–90.

———. *Electronic and Computer Music*, 4th edition. Oxford: Oxford University Press, 2013.

Martin, Reinhold. *The Organizational Complex: Architecture, Media, and Corporate Space.* Cambridge, MA: MIT Press, 2003.

Masani, P. R. *Norbert Wiener 1884–1964.* Basel, Switzerland: Birkhäuser, 1990.

Mathon, Geneviève, Laurent Feneyrou and Giordano Ferrari, eds. *Bruno Maderna*. Vol. 2. Paris: Basalte, 2009.

May, Elaine Tyler. *Homeward Bound: American Families in the Cold War Era*. New York: Basic Books, 2008.

McClary, Susan. "Terminal Prestige: The Case of Avant-Garde Music Composition." *Cultural Critique* 12 (1989): 57–81.

McMurray, Peter. "Once Upon a Time: A Superficial History of Early Tape." *Twentieth-Century Music* 14/1 (February 2017): 25–48.

Meehan, Kate. "Not Just a Pretty Voice: Cathy Berberian as Collaborator, Composer, and Creator." PhD dissertation, Washington University, 2011.

Mendelsohn, Everett, Merrit Roe Smith, and Peter Weingart, eds. *Science, Technology, and the Military*. Dordecht, The Netherlands: Kluwer Academic, 1988.

Mendelsohn, Everett, Merrit Roe Smith, and Peter Weingart. "Science and the Military: Setting the Problem." In *Science, Technology, and the Military*, xi–xxix. Edited by Everett Mendelsohn, Merrit Roe Smith, and Peter Weingart. Dordecht, The Netherlands: Kluwer Academic, 1988.

Mesch, Claudia. *Modern Art at the Berlin Wall: Demarcating Culture in the Cold War Germanys*. London: Tauris, 2009.

———. *Art and Politics: A Small History of Art for Social Change Since 1945*. London: Tauris, 2013.

Metzer, David. "The Paths From and to Abstraction in Stockhausen's *Gesang der Jünglinge*." *Modernism/Modernity* 11/4 (November 2004): 695–721.

Metzger, Heinz-Klaus and Rainer Riehn, eds., *Dieter Schnebel. Musik-Konzepte* 16. Munich: edition text + kritik, 1980.

Mills, Mara. "The Dead Room: Deafness and Communication Engineering." PhD dissertation, Harvard University, 2008.

———. "Deaf Jam: From Inscription to Reproduction to Information." *Social Text* 28/1: 102 (Spring 2010): 35–58.

———. "Medien und Prosthesen: Über den künstlichen Kehlkopf und den Vocoder." In *Klangmaschinen zwischen Experiment und Medientechnik*, 127–52. Edited by Daniel Gethmann. Bielefeld, Germany: Transcript, 2010.

———. "On Disability Cybernetics: Helen Keller, Norbert Wiener, and the Hearing Glove." *differences* 22/2–3 (2011): 74–111.

———. "Do Signals Have Politics? Inscribing Abilities in Cochlear Implants." In *Oxford Handbook of Sound Studies*, 320–46. Edited by Trevor Pinch and Karin Bijsterveld. New York: Oxford University Press, 2012.

———. "Media and Prosthesis: The Vocoder, the Artificial Larynx, and the History of Signal Processing." *Qui Parle: Critical Humanities and Social Sciences* 21/1 (Fall/Winter 2012): 107–49.

———. "Deafness." *Keywords in Sound*, 45–54. Edited by David Novak and Matt Sakakeeny. Durham, NC: Duke University Press, 2015.

———. *On the Phone: Hearing Loss and Communication Engineering*. Durham, NC: Duke University Press, forthcoming.

Misch, Imke. "On the Serial Shaping of Stockhausen's *Gruppen für drei orchester*." Translated by Frank Hentschel and Jerome Kohl. *Perspectives of New Music* 36/1 (1998): 143–87.

———. *Zur Kompositionstechnik Karlheinz Stockhausens:* Gruppen für drei Orchester (1955–57). Saarbrücken, Germay: PFAU-Verlag, 1999.

Mol, Annemarie. "Actor-Network Theory: Sensitive Terms and Enduring Tensions." *Kölner Zeitschrift für Soziologie und Sozialpsychologie* 5/1 (2010): 253–69.

Monod, David. *Settling Scores: German Music, Denazification, and the Americans, 1945–1953.* Chapel Hill: University of North Carolina Press, 2005.

Mooney, James, Dorien Schampaert, and Tim Boon, eds. *Alternative Histories of Electronic Music.* Special issue of *Organised Sound* 22/2 (August 2017).

Moore, Brian C. J. "Loudness, Pitch and Timbre." In *Blackwell Handbook of Sensation and Perception,* 423–28. Edited by Goldstein. Malden, MA: Blackwell, 2005.

Moore, Brian C. J., ed. *Hearing.* San Diego: Academic, 1995.

Moorefield, Virgil. *The Producer as Composer: Shaping the Sounds of Popular Music.* Cambridge, MA: MIT Press, 2005.

Morawska-Büngeler, Marietta. *Schwingende Elektronen: Eine Dokumentation über das Studio für Elektronische Musik des Westdeutschen Rundfunks in Köln 1951–1986.* Cologne: P. J. Tonger, 1987.

Morgan, Frances. "Pioneer Spirits: New Media Representations of Women in Electronic Music History," *Organised Sound* 22/2 (August 2017): 238–49.

Mosch, Ulrich. "'Freiheit war es immer, die er meinte'—Karl Amadeus Hartmann und die 'Stunde Null.'" In *"Stunde Null"—zur Musik um 1945,* 111–26. Edited by Volker Scherliess. Kassel, Germany: Bärenreiter, 2014.

Nahin, Paul J. *The Science of Radio.* 2nd edition. New York: Springer, 2001.

———. *The Logician and the Engineer: How George Boole and Claude Shannon Created the Information Age.* Princeton, NJ: Princeton University Press, 2013.

Nakai, You. "In Other Words: How Stockhausen Stopped Writing Theory (and Resumed Ten Years Later)." In *The Musical Legacy of Karlheinz Stockhausen: Looking Back and Forward,* 63–78. Edited by M. J. Grant and Imke Misch. Hofheim, Germany: Wolke Verlag, 2016.

———. "On the Instrumental Natures of David Tudor's Music." PhD dissertation, New York University, 2016.

Nauck, Gisela. "Elektronische Musik: die ersten Jahre." In *Von Kranichstein zur Gegenwart: 50 Jahre Darmstädter Ferienkurse 1946–1996,* 265–72. Stuttgart: DACO Verlag, 1996.

———. *Dieter Schnebel: Lesegänge durch Leben und Werk.* Mainz: Schott, 2001.

Neidhofer, Christoph. "Bruno Maderna's Serial Arrays." *Music Theory Online* 13/1 (2007), http://www.mtosmt.org/issues/mto.07.13.1/mto.07.13.1.neidhofer.html (accessed February 15, 2016).

Nelson, Andrew J. *The Sound of Innovation: Stanford and the Computer Music Revolution.* Cambridge, MA: MIT Press, 2015.

Neumeyer, David and Nathan Platte. *Franz Waxman's* Rebecca: *A Film Score Guide.* Lanham, MD: Scarecrow Press, 2012.

Nicholls, David. *John Cage.* Urbana and Chicago: University of Illinois Press, 2007.

Nicholls, David, and Keith Potter. "Brown, Earle." *Grove Music Online. Oxford Music Online.* Oxford University Press, http://www.oxfordmusiconline.com.proxy.uchicago.edu/subscriber/article/grove/music/04098 (accessed October 10, 2017).

Niebur, Louis. *Special Sound: The Creation and Legacy of the BBC Radiophonic Workshop.* New York: Oxford University Press, 2012.

Nonnenmann, Rainer. "Mit der Wahrnehmung die Wahrnehmung widerlegen: Der Komponist und Klangkünstler Peter Ablinger im Gespräch mit Rainer Nonnenmann." *Österreichische Musikzeitschrift* 70/5 (2015): 63–66.

Novati, Maria Maddalena and John Dack, eds. *The Studio di Fonologia: A Musical Journey 1954–1983, Update 2008–2012.* Milan: Ricordi, 2012.

Novati, Maria Maddalena. "The Archive of the *Studio di Fonologia Musicale di Milano della Rai.*" In *The Studio di Fonologia: A Musical Journey 1954–1983 Update 2008–2012,* 143–298. Edited by Maria Maddalena Novati and John Dack. Milan: Ricordi, 2012.

Nyman, Michael. *Experimental Music: Cage and Beyond.* 2nd edition. Cambridge: Cambridge University Press, 1999.

Ohala, John J. "Speech Technology: Historical Antecedents." In *Concise History of the Language Sciences: From the Sumerians to the Cognitivists,* 416–19. Edited by E. F. K. Koerner and R. E. Asher. New York: Pergamon, 1995.

Orledge, Robert. *Debussy and the Theatre.* Cambridge: Cambridge University Press, 1982.

Osmond-Smith, David. "New Beginnings: The International Avant-Garde, 1945–62." In *Cambridge History of Twentieth-Century Music,* 336–63. Edited by Nicholas Cook and Anthony Pople. Cambridge: Cambridge University Press, 2004.

———. "The Tenth Oscillator: The Work of Cathy Berberian 1958–1966." *Tempo* 58/227 (January 2004): 2–13.

———. "Bussotti, Sylvano." *Grove Music Online. Oxford Music Online.* Oxford University Press, http://www.oxfordmusiconline.com.proxy.uchicago.edu/subscriber/article/grove/music/04446 (accessed July 27, 2017).

Parolini, Giuditta. "Music Without Musicians . . . but with Scientists, Technicians and Computer Companies." *Organised Sound* 22/2 (August 2017): 286–96.

Paulu, Burton. *Radio and Television Broadcasting on the European Continent.* Minneapolis: University of Minnesota Press, 1967.

Patteson, Thomas. *Instruments for New Music: Sound, Technology, and Modernism.* Oakland: University of California Press, 2016.

Pennycook, Bruce. "Who Will Turn the Knobs When I Die?" *Organised Sound* 13/3 (2008): 199–208.

Perle, George. "*Die Reihe* Vol. III: Musical Craftsmanship: A Review." *Journal of Music Theory* 4/1 (April 1960): 102–104; reprinted as "The 'Simple Truth,'" in *The Right Notes: Twenty-Three Selected Essays by George Perle on Twentieth-Century Music,* 257–60. Stuyvesant, NY: Pendragon Press, 1995.

Peyser, Joan. *Boulez.* New York: Schirmer Books, 1976.

———. *To Boulez and Beyond.* Revised edition. Lanham, MD: Scarecrow Press, 2008.

Pickering, Andrew. "From Science as Knowledge to Science as Practice." In *Science as Practice and Culture,* 1–26. Edited by Andrew Pickering. Chicago and London: University of Chicago Press, 1992.

———. *The Mangle of Practice: Time, Agency, and Science.* Chicago: University of Chicago Press, 1995.

————. *The Cybernetic Brain: Sketches of Another Future.* Chicago: University of Chicago Press, 2010.

Piekut, Benjamin. *Experimentalism Otherwise: The New York Avant-Garde and Its Limits.* Berkeley: University of California Press, 2011.

————. "Actor-Networks in Music History: Clarifications and Critiques." *twentieth-century music* 11/2 (September 2014): 191–215.

————. "Indeterminacy, Free Improvisation, and the Mixed Avant-Garde: Experimental Music in London, 1965–75." *Journal of the American Musicological Society* 67/3 (Fall 2014): 769–824.

Piekut, Benjamin, ed. *Tomorrow is the Question: New Directions in Experimental Music Studies.* Ann Arbor: University of Michigan Press, 2014.

Pierce, John. *An Introduction to Information Theory.* 2nd edition. New York: Dover, 1980.

Pigott, Jon. "Across Fields: Sound, Art and Technology from an Electromechanical Perspective." *Alternative Histories of Electronic Music.* Special issue of *Organised Sound* 22/2 (August 2017): 276–85.

Pinch, Trevor and Karin Bijsterveld, eds. *The Oxford Handbook of Sound Studies.* New York: Oxford University Press, 2012.

Pinch, Trevor and Ronald Kline. "Users as Agents of Technological Change: The Social Construction of the Automobile in the Rural United States." *Technology and Culture* 37/4 (October 1996): 763–95.

Pinch, Trevor and Frank Trocco. *Analog Days: The Invention and Impact of the Moog Synthesizer.* Cambridge, MA: Harvard University Press, 2002.

Poller, Tom Rojo. "Clarence Barlow's Technique of 'Synthrumentation' and Its Use in *Im Januar am Nil.*" *Tempo* 69/271 (January 2015): 7–23.

Pollock, Emily Richmond. "Opera After *Stunde Null.*" PhD dissertation, University of California Berkeley, 2012.

Potter, Pamela M. *Most German of the Arts: Musicology and Society From the Weimar Republic to the End of Hitler's Reich.* New Haven, CT: Yale University Press, 1998.

————. *Art of Suppression: Confronting the Nazi Past in Histories of the Visual and Performing Arts.* Oakland, CA: University of California Press, 2016.

Prendergast, Mark. *The Ambient Century: From Mahler to Trance—The Evolution of Sound in the Electronic Age.* New York: Bloomsbury, 2000.

Prieberg, Fred K. *Handbuch Deutsche Musiker 1933–1945.* Self-published. Keil, Germany: Prieberg, 2004. Downloadable at https://miami.uni-muenster.de/Record/d1055068-e473-4431-ac71-1021d2b0cc81 (accessed June 13, 2017).

Priore, Irna. "The Origins of *Incontri Musicali.*" *Theoria* 21 (2014): 7–26.

Pritchett, James. *The Music of John Cage.* Cambridge: Cambridge University Press, 1993.

Pullum, Geoffrey K. and William A. Ladusaw. *Phonetic Symbol Guide.* 2nd edition. Chicago: University of Chicago Press, [1986] 1996.

Pustijanac, Ingrid. *György Ligeti: Il maestro dello spazio immaginario.* Lucca, Italy: Libreria Musicale Italiana, 2013.

Ramazzotti, Marinella. "Luciano Berio's *Sequenza III*: From Electronic Modulation to Extended Vocal Technique." *Ex Tempore* 15/1 (Spring/Summer 2010): 81–96.

Ratcliff, R. A. *Delusions of Intelligence: Enigma, Ultra, and the End of Secure Ciphers.* Cambridge: Cambridge University Press, 2006.

Rebstock, Matthias. *Komposition zwischen Musik und Theatre: Das instrumentale Theater von Mauricio Kagel zwischen 1959 und 1965*. Hofheim, Germany: Wolke, 2007.

Rehding, Alexander. "Magic Boxes and *Volksempfänger*: Music on the Radio in Weimar Germany." *Music, Theatre, and Politics in Germany*, 255–71. Edited by Nikolaus Bacht. Aldershot, UK: Ashgate, 2006.

———. "Of Sirens Old and New." In *Oxford Handbook of Mobile Music Studies*, vol. 2, 77–106. Edited by Sumanth Gopinath and Jason Stanyek. New York: Oxford University Press, 2014.

———. "Three Music-Theory Lessons." *Journal of the Royal Music Association* 141/2 (November 2016): 251–82.

———. "Instruments of Music Theory." *Music Theory Online* 22/4 (December 2016), http://mtosmt.org/issues/mto.16.22.4/mto.16.22.4.rehding.html

Revill, David. *The Roaring Silence: John Cage: A Life*. New York: Arcade, 1992.

Richards, Sam. *John Cage As . . . .* Oxford: Amber Lane Press, 1996.

Richter-Ibáñez, Christina. *Mauricio Kagels Buenos Aires (1946–1957): Kulturpolitik, Künstlernetzwrek, Kompositionen*. Bielefeld, Germany: transcript Verlag, 2014.

Rider, Robin E. "Operations Research and Game Theory: Early Connections." In *Toward a History of Game Theory*, 225–39. Edited by E. Roy Weintraub. Durham, NC: Duke University Press, 1992.

Riesch, Hauke. "Theorizing Boundary Work as Representation and Identity." *Journal for the Theory of Social Behaviour* 40/4 (December 2010): 452–73.

Rizzardi, Veniero and Nicola Scaldaferri. "*Musica su due Dimensioni (1952)*: Histoire, Vicissitudes et Importance d'une Oeuvre (Presque) Absente." In *à Bruno Maderna*, vol. 2, 423–48. Edited by Geneviève Mathon, Laurent Feneryolu, and Giordano Ferrari. Paris: Basalte, 2009.

Rizzardi, Veniero and Angela Ida De Benedictis, eds. *Nuovo Musica Alla Radio/New Music on the Radio*. Milan: RAI/Eri, 2000.

Roads, Curtis. *Microsound*. Cambridge, MA: MIT Press, 2001.

Rodà, Antonio. "Evolution of the Technical Means of the Studio di Fonologia Musicale." In *The Studio di Fonologia: A Musical Journey 1954–1983, Update 2008–2012*, 33–81. Edited by Maria Maddalena Novati and John Dack. English edition. Milan: Ricordi, 2012.

Rodgers, Tara. "On the Process and Aesthetics of Sampling in Electronic Music Production." *Organised Sound* 8/3 (December 2003): 313–20.

———. *Pink Noises: Women on Electronic Music and Sound*. Durham, NC: Duke University Press, 2010.

———. "Synthesis." In *Keywords on Sound*, 208–21. Edited by David Novak and Matt Sakakeeny. Durham, NC: Duke University Press, 2015.

———. "Tinkering with Cultural Memory: Gender and the Politics of Synthesizer Historiography." *Feminist Media Histories* 1/4 (Fall 2015): 5–30.

Roig-Francoli, Miguel. "Harmonic and Formal Processes in Ligeti's Net-Structure Compositions." *Music Theory Spectrum* 17/2 (Autumn 1995): 242–77.

Romão, João. "After Mapping the Avant-Garde: Music, Experimentalism, Technology, Science." PhD dissertation, Humboldt Universität Berlin, forthcoming, https://www.mpiwg-berlin.mpg.de/research/projects/after-mapping-avant-garde-music-experimentalism-technology-science (accessed July 4, 2018).

Romito, Maurizio, ed. "Lettere e Scritti." In *Studi su Bruno Maderna,* 52–73. Edited by Mario Baroni and Rossana Dalmonte. Milan: Suvini Zerboni, 1989.

Rosen, Charles. "Music and the Cold War." *New York Review of Books*, April 7, 2011, http://www.nybooks.com/articles/2011/04/07/music-and-cold-war/#fn-1 (accessed July 30, 2017).

Ross, Alex. *The Rest is Noise: Listening to the Twentieth Century.* New York: Farrar, Straus, and Giroux, 2007.

Rothenbuhler, Eric W. and John Durham Peters. "Defining Phonography: An Experiment in Theory." *The Musical Quarterly* 81/2 (Summer 1997): 242–64.

Rowe, Robert. "Iannis Xenakis and Algorithmic Composition: Precursors, Co-Cursors, Post-Cursors." In *Xenakis Matters*, 39–51. Edited by Sharon Kanach. No. 4 of The Iannis Xenakis Series. New York: Pendragon Press, 2012.

Rubin, Andrew N. *Archives of Authority: Empire, Culture, and the Cold War.* Princeton, NJ and Oxford: Princeton University Press, 2012.

Rutner, Josh. "The Art of the Theremin (Clara Rockmore, 1977)." Album of the Week podcast #38, http://www.joshrutner.com/aotw/2016/9/28/episode-38-the-art-of-the-theremin-clara-rockmore-1977 (accessed September 14, 2017).

Rutsky, R. L. *High Techné: Art and Technology From the Machine Aesthetic to the Posthuman.* Minneapolis and London: University of Minnesota Press, 1999.

Sabbe, Heerman. "Goeyvaerts and the Beginnings of 'Punctual' Serialism and Electronic Music." *Revue belge de Musicologie* 48 (1994): 55–94.

Sallis, Friedemann. *An Introduction to the Early Works of György Ligeti.* Cologne: Studio, 1996.

Samuel, Claude. Liner notes to *Pierre Boulez: Le Domaine Musical*, vol. 1, 1956–1967, 8–14. Translated by John Tyler Tuttle. Accord [476–9209.

Saunders, Frances Stonor. *The Cultural Cold War: The CIA and the World of Arts and Letters.* New York: New Press, [1999] 2013.

Savage, Steve. *Bytes & Backbeats: Repurposing Music in the Digital Age.* Ann Arbor: University of Michigan Press, 2011.

Sawyer, Keith. *Group Genius: The Creative Power of Collaboration.* New York: Basic Books, 2007.

Sayes, Edwin. "Actor-Network Theory and Methodology: Just What Does It Mean to say That Nonhumans Have Agency?" *Social Studies of Science* 44/1 (February 2014): 134–49.

Scaldaferri, Nicola. *Musica nel laboratorio elettroacustico: Lo Studio di Fonologia di Milano e la ricerca musicale negli anni Cinquanta.* Lucca, Italy: Libereria Musicale Italiana, 1997.

———. "'Bronze by Gold,' by Berio by Eco: A Journey Through the Sirensong." In *Nuova Musica Alla Radio/New Music on the Radio*, 100–157. Edited by Veniero Rizzardi and Angela Ida De Benedictis. Milan: RAI/Eri, 2000.

———. Introduction to *Musica su due Dimensioni* (1952), Critical edition. Edited by Maroni Baroni and Rossana Dalmonte. Milan: Edition Suvini Zerboni, 2001.

———. "Montage und Synchronization: Ein neues musikalisches Denken in der Musik von Luciano Berio und Bruno Maderna." In *Elecktroakustische Musik*, 66–82. Edited by Elena Ungeheuer. Laaber, Germany: Laaber Verlag, 2002.

Scanlon, Lisa. "Vocal Codes." In *The Technology Review*. November 1, 2003, https://www.technologyreview.com/s/402263/vocal-codes/ (accessed May 25, 2016).

Schlieper, Ulrike. "Einführung." In *Hörspiel 1954–1955: Eine Dokumentation*, 9–19. Berlin: Verlag für Berlin-Brandenburg, 1997.

Schlieper, Ulrike, ed. *Hörspiel 1950–1951: Veröffentlichungen des Deutschen Rundfunkarchivs*. Band 35. Potsdam, Germany: Verlag für Berlin-Brandenburg, 2003.

———. *Hörspiel 1952–1953: Veröffentlichungen des Deutschen Rundfunkarchivs*. Band 39. Potsdam, Germany: Verlag für Berlin-Brandenburg, 2004.

———. *Hörspiel 1954–1955: Veröffentlichungen des Deutschen Rundrunkarchiv*. Band 21. Berlin: Verlag für Berlin-Brandenburg, 2007.

Schlosser, Nicholas J. *Cold War on the Airwaves: The Radio Propaganda War Against East Germany*. Urbana: University of Illinois Press, 2015.

Schmelz, Peter. "From Scriabin to Pink Floyd: The ANS Synthesizer and the Politics of Soviet Music between Thaw and Stagnation." In *Sound Commitments: Avant-Garde Music and the Sixties*, 254–78. Edited by Robert Adlington. Oxford: Oxford University Press, 2009.

———. "Introduction: Music in the Cold War." *Journal of Musicology* 26/1 (Winter 2009): 3–16.

———. *Such Freedom, If Only Musical: Unofficial Soviet Music During the Thaw*. New York: Oxford University Press, 2009.

Schmidt, Christian Martin. "Die offene Frage der offenen Form." In *Form in der Neuen Musik*, 9–15. Edited by Ekkehard Jost. Mainz: Schott, 1992.

Schnebel, Dieter. *Mauricio Kagel: Musik, Theatre, Film*. Cologne: M. DuMont Schauberg, 1970.

Schütte, Wolfgang. *Die Westdeutsche Funkstunde: Frühgeschichte des WDR in Dokumenten*. Cologne and Berlin: Grote, 1973.

Shandley, Robert R. *Rubble Films: German Cinema in the Shadow of the Third Reich*. Philadelphia: Temple University Press, 2001.

Shapin, Steven. "The Invisible Technician." *American Scientist* 77/6 (November/December 1989): 554–63.

Shreffler, Anne. "Berlin Walls: Dahlhaus, Knepler, and Ideologies of Music History." *Journal of Musicology* 20/4 (Fall 2003): 498–525.

———. "'Music Left and Right': A Tale of Two Histories of Progressive Music." *Proceedings of the British Academy* 185 (2013): 67–87.

———. "Cold War Dissonance: Dahlhaus, Taruskin, and the Critique of the Politically Engaged Avant-Garde." In *Kultur und Musik nach 1945: Ästhetik im Zeichen des Kalten Krieges*, 40–60. Edited by Ulrich Blomann. Saarbrüchen, Germany: Pfau-Verlag, 2015.

Shultis, Cristopher. "No Ear for Music: Timbre in the Early Percussion Music of John Cage." In *John Cage: Music, Philosophy, and Intention 1933–1950*, 83–104. Edited by David Patterson. New York: Routledge, 2002.

———. "Cage and Europe." In *Cambridge Companion to John Cage*, 20–40. Edited by David Nicholls. Cambridge: Cambridge University Press, 2002.

Silverberg, Laura. "Between Dissonance and Dissidence: Socialist Modernism in the German Democratic Republic." *Journal of Musicology* 26/1 (Winter 2009): 44–84.

Sirker, Udo. "W. Meyer-Epplers Untersuchungen zu elektronischen Musik und seine akustisch-experimentellen Forschungen." In *Studien zur Musikgeschichte des*

Rheinlandes IV, 111–21. Edited by Klaus Wolfgang Niemöller. Cologne: Arno Folk, 1975.

Slawson, Wayne. *Sound Color*. Berkeley: University of California Press, 1985.

Smith, Christopher. *The Hidden History of Bletchley Park: A Social and Organisational History, 1939–1945*. New York: Palgrave Macmillan, 2015.

Smith, Michael. *The Secrets of Station X: How the Bletchley Park Codebreakers Helped Win the War*. London: Biteback Publishing, 2011.

Soni, Jimmy and Rob Goodman. *Mind at Play: How Claude Shannon Invented the Information Age*. New York: Simon & Schuster, 2017.

Spitz, Bob. *The Beatles: The Biography*. New York: Little, Brown, 2005.

Spoerri, Bruno, ed. *Musik aus dem Nichts: Die Geschichte der elektroakustischen Musik in der Schweiz*. Zurich: Chronos, 2010.

Sprigge, Martha. "Abilities to Mourn: Musical Commemoration in the German Democratic Republic 1945–1989." PhD dissertation, University of Chicago, 2013.

———. "Tape Work and Memory Work in Post-War Germany." *twentieth-century music* 14/1 (February 2017): 49–63.

Sprout, Leslie. *The Musical Legacy of Wartime France*. Berkeley: University of California Press, 2013.

Squibbs, Ronald. "An Analytical Approach to the Music of Iannis Xenakis: Studies of Recent Works." PhD dissertation, Yale University, 1996.

———. "The Composer's Flair: *Achorripsis* as Music," in *Definitive Proceedings of the International Symposium Iannis Xenakis*, 258–64. Edited by Makis Solomos, Anastasia Georgaki, and Giorgos Zervos. Athens, 2005. Available at http://cicm.mshparisnord.org/ColloqueXenakis/papers/Squibbs.pdf (accessed March 15, 2016).

Stahl, Matt. *Unfree Masters: Recording Artists and the Politics of Work*. Durham, NC and London: Duke University Press, 2013.

Stalarow, Alexander. "Listening to a Liberated Paris: Pierre Schaeffer Experiments with Radio." PhD dissertation, University of California Davis, 2017.

Stammerjohn, Harro, Sylvain Auroux, Lois Grossman, and Mark DeVoto, eds. *Lexicon Grammaticorum: A Bio-Bibliographical Companion to the History of Linguistics*. 2nd edition. Tübingen, Germany: Niemeyer, 2009.

Stanyek, Jason and Benjamin Piekut. "Deadness: Technologies of the Intermundane." *The Drama Review* 54/1 (Spring 2010): 25–48. Reprinted in *The Sound Studies Reader*, 304–24. Edited by Jonathan Sterne. New York: Routledge, 2012.

Star, Susan Leigh and James R. Griesemer. "Institutional Ecology, 'Translations,' and Boundary Objects: Amateurs and Professionals in Berkeley's Museum of Vertebrate Zoology 1907–39." *Social Studies of Science* 19/3 (August 1989): 387–420.

Starosielski, Nicole. *The Undersea Network*. Durham, NC: Duke University Press, 2015.

Steege, Benjamin. *Helmholtz and the Modern Listener*. Cambridge: Cambridge University Press, 2012.

Steinbeck, Paul. *Message to Our Folks: The Art Ensemble of Chicago*. Chicago: University of Chicago Press, 2017.

Steinitz, Richard. *György Ligeti: Music of the Imagination*. Boston: Northeastern University Press, 2003.

Sterne, Jonathan. *The Audible Past: The Cultural Origins of Sound Reproduction*. Durham, NC: Duke University Press, 2003.

———. *MP3: The Meaning of a Format*. Durham, NC: Duke University Press, 2012.

———. "Hearing." *Keywords in Sound*, 63–77. Edited by David Novak and Matt Sakakeeny. Durham, NC: Duke University Press, 2015.

Stras, Laurie. "The Organ of the Soul: Voice, Damage, and Affect." In *Sounding Off: Theorizing Disability in Music*, 173–84. Edited by Neil Lerner and Joseph N. Straus. New York: Routledge, 2006.

Stripp, Alan. "The Enigma Machine: Its Mechanism and Use." In *Codebreakers: The Inside Story of Bletchley Park*, 83–88. Edited by F. H. Hinsley and Alan Stripp. Oxford: Oxford University Press, 1993.

Stroh, Wolfgang Martin. *Zur Soziologie der elektronischen Musik*. Zurich: Amadeus, 1975.

Supper, Martin. *Elektroakustische Musik und Computermusik*. Darmstadt: Wissenschaftliche Buchgesellschaft, 1997.

Taruskin, Richard. *The Oxford History of Western Music*. Vol. 5: *The Late Twentieth Century*. Oxford: Oxford University Press, 2005.

———. "Afterword: *Nicht blutbefleckt?*" *Journal of Musicology* 26/2 (Spring 2009): 274–84.

———. "Agents and Causes and Ends, Oh My!" *Journal of Musicology* 31/2 (Spring 2014): 272–93.

Taylor, Timothy D. *Strange Sounds: Music, Technology & Culture*. New York: Routledge, 2001.

———. "The Avant-Garde in the Family Room: American Advertising and the Domestication of Electronic Music in the 1960s and 1970s." In *Oxford Handbook of Sound Studies*, 387–408. Edited by Trevor Pinch and Karin Bijsterveld. New York: Oxford University Press, 2012.

———. *The Sounds of Capitalism: Advertising, Music, and the Conquest of Culture*. Chicago: University of Chicago Press, 2012.

Taylor, Timothy D., Mark Katz, and Tony Grajeda, eds. *Music, Sound, and Technology in America: A Documentary History of Early Phonograph, Cinema, and Radio*. Durham, NC: Duke University Press, 2012.

Tazelaar, Kees. *On the Threshold of Beauty: Philips and the Origins of Electronic Music in the Netherlands 1925–1965*. Rotterdam: V2_Publishing, 2013.

Thacker, Toby. *The End of the Third Reich: Defeat, Denazification, and Nuremburg, January 1944–November 1946*. Stroud, England: Tempus, 2006.

———. *Music After Hitler 1945–55*. Aldershot, UK and Burlington, VT: Ashgate, 2007.

Thapen, Neil. "Pink Trombone." V1.1 Computer-based vocal synthesizer, https://dood.al/pinktrombone/ (accessed September 12, 2017).

Théberge, Paul. *Any Sound You Can Imagine: Making Music/Consuming Technology*. Hanover, NH: Wesleyan University Press, 1997.

Theel, Tobias. "Governance von Kreativität in der Musikbranche. Über die Bedeutung und Verteilung von Unsicherheit in kreativen Kollaborationen." PhD dissertation, Freie Universität Berlin, forthcoming. Part of research group "Organized Creativity," June 2016–May 2019, http://www.wiwiss.fu-berlin.de/forschung/organized-creativity/index.html (accessed July 4, 2018).

Thomas, Adrian. *Polish Music Since Szymanowski*. Cambridge: Cambridge University Press, 2005.

Tillmann, Hans Günter. "Early Modern Instrumental Phonetics." In *Concise History of the Language Sciences: From the Sumerians to the Cognitivists*, 401–16. Edited by E. F. K. Koerner and R. E. Asher. New York: Pergamon, 1995.

Tompkins, Dave. *How to Wreck a Nice Beach: The Vocoder From World War II to Hip-Hop, The Machine Speaks*. Brooklyn, NY: Melville House, 2011.

Toop, Richard. "Messian-Goeyvaerts, Fano-Boulez, Stockhausen." *Perspectives of New Music* 13/1 (Autumn, Winter 1974): 141–69.

———. "Stockhausen and the Sine-Wave: The Story of an Ambiguous Relationship." *The Musical Quarterly* 65/3 (July 1979): 379–91.

———. "Stockhausen's Electronic Works: Sketches and Work-Sheets from 1952–1967." *Interface* 10 (1981): 149–97.

———. *György Ligeti*. London: Phaidon, 1999.

Touloumi, Olga. "The Politics of Totality: Iannis Xenakis' *Polytope de Mycènes*." In *Xenakis Matters: Contexts, Processes, Applications*, 101–25. Edited by Sharon Kanach. Hillsdale, NY: Pendragon Press, 2012.

Trenkamp, Anne. "The Concept of Alea in Boulez's *Constellation-Miroir*." *Music and Letters* 57/1 (January 1976): 1–10.

Trochim, William M. "Descriptive Statistics." *The Research Methods Knowledge Base*, 2nd edition, www.socialresearchmethods.net/kb/statdesc.php (accessed August 10, 2011).

Trudu, Antonio. *La "Scuola" di Darmstadt: i Ferienkurse dal 1946 a oggia*. Milan: Ricordi, 1992.

Truelove, Stephen. "The Translation of Rhythm into Pitch in Stockhausen's *Klavierstück XI*." *Perspectives of New Music* 36/1 (Winter 1998): 189–220.

Tsing, Anna. "Worlding the Matsutake Diaspora: Or, Can Actor-Network Theory Experiment with Holism?" In *Experiments in Holism: Theory and Practice in Contemporary Anthropology*, 47–66. Edited by Ton Otto and Nils Bubandt. West Sussex, UK: Wiley-Blackwell, 2010.

Tudor, David. "From Piano to Electronics." Interview with Victor Schonfield in *Music and Musicians* 20/12 (August 1972): 24–26.

Turner, Fred. *From Counterculture to Cyberculture: Stewart Brand, the Whole Earth Network, and the Rise of Digital Utopianism*. Chicago: University of Chicago Press, 2006.

———. *The Democratic Surround: Multimedia & American Liberalism From World War II to the Psychedelic Sixties*. Chicago: University of Chicago Press, 2013.

Ungeheuer, Elena. *Wie die elektronische Musik "erfunden" wurde . . . Quellenstudie zu Werner Meyer-Epplers Entwurf zwischen 1949 und 1953*. Mainz: Schott, 1992.

———. "From the Elements to the Continuum: Timbre Composition in Early Electronic Music." *Contemporary Music Review* 10/2 (1994): 25–34.

———. "Parallelen und Antiparallelen: Meyer-Eppler und die elektronische Musik." In *Neue Musik im Rheinland*, 73–86. Edited by Heinz Bremer. Kassel, Germany: Merseberger, 1996.

———. "Die Geburt der Idee aus dem Geist der Technik? Anmerkungen zum Klangkontinuum in der elektronischen Musik." *Musiktheorie* 12/1 (1997): 27–36.

———. "Statistical Gestalts—Perceptible Features in Serial Music." In *Music, Gestalt and Computing*, 103–13. Edited by Marc Leman. Series of Lecture Notes in Artificial Intelligence. Berlin: Springer Verlag, 1997.

————. "Einleitung: Diskurse zu elektroakustischer Musik." In *Elecktroakustische Musik*, 11–17. Edited by Elena Ungeheuer. Laaber, Germany: Laaber Verlag, 2002.

————. "Sprache und Musik—Sprache mit Musik—Sprache oder Musik. Aspekte und Anwendungen einer funktionellen Klangwissenschaft." In *Systemische Musikwissenschaft. Festschrift für Jobst Peter Fricke zum 65. Geburtstag*, 355–68. Edited by Wolfgang Auhagen, Bram Gätjen, and Klaus Wolfgang Niemöller. Cologne, 2003.

————. "Imitative Instrumente und innovative Maschinen? Musikästhetische Orientierungen der elektrischen Klangerzeugung." In *Zauberhafte Klangmaschinen: Von der Sprechmaschine bis zur Soundkarte*, 45–60. Edited by IMA Institut für Medienarchäologie. Mainz: Schott, 2008.

Ungeheuer, Elena, ed. *Elektroakustische Musik*. Laaber, Germany: Laaber Verlag, 2002.

Ungeheuer, Elena and Pascal Decroupet. "Technik und Ästhetik der elektronischen Musik." In *Musik und Technik: Fünf Kongreßbeiträge und vier Seminarberichte*, 123–42. Edited by Helga de la Motte-Haber and Rudolf Frisius. Mainz: Schott Musik International, 1996.

Vágnerová, Lucie. "Sirens/Cyborgs: Sound Technologies and the Musical Body." PhD dissertatin, Columbia University, 2016.

————. "'Nimble Fingers' in Electronic Music: Rethinking Sound through Neo-Colonial Labour." *Organised Sound* 22/2 (August 2017): 250–58.

Valiquet, Patrick. "The Spatialisation of Stereophony: Taking Positions in Post-War Electronic Music." In *Proceedings of the International Computer Music Conference 2011*, 41–48. San Francisco: Computer Music Association, 2011.

Van Emmerik, Paul. "An Imaginary Grid: Rhythmic Structure in Cage's Music Up to Circa 1950." In *John Cage: Music, Philosophy, and Intention 1933–1950*, 217–37. Edited by David Patterson. New York: Routledge, 2002.

Varga, Bálint András. *Conversations with Iannis Xenakis*. London: Farber and Farber, 1996.

Verdú, Sergei. "50 Years of Shannon Theory." In *Information Theory: 50 Years of Discovery*, n.p. Edited by Verdú and McLaughlin. Ebook. Wiley-IEEE Press, 2000, http://ieeexplore.ieee.org/servlet/opac?bknumber=5273551 (accessed March 20, 2016).

Verma, Neil. *Theatre of the Mind: Imagination, Aesthetics, and American Radio Drama*. Chicago: University of Chicago Press, 2012.

Verstraete, Pieter. "Cathy Berberian's *Stripsody*—An Excess of Vocal Personas in Score and Performance." In *Cathy Berberian: Pioneer of Contemporary Vocality*, 64–75. Edited by Pamela Karantonis, Francesca Placanica, Anne Sivuoja-Kauppala, and Pieter Verstraete. Burlington, VT: Ashgate, 2014.

Vickery, Lindsay. "Mobile Scores and Click Tracks: Teaching Old Dogs." Unpublished paper presented at ACMC 2010 in Canberra, Australia, http://www.lindsayvickery.com/research-2008-10.html (accessed May 12, 2016).

Vidolin, Alvise. "The School of Fonologia." In *The Studio di Fonologia: A Musical Journey 1954–1983, Update 2008–2012*, 19–31. Edited by Maria Maddalena Novati and John Dack. Milan: Ricordi, 2012.

Vincent, Mary. "Political Violence and Mass Society: A European Civil War?" In *The Oxford Handbook of European History, 1914–1945*, 388–406. Edited by Nicholas Doumanis. New York: Oxford University Press, 2016.

Vincis, Claudia. "Totus mundus agit histrionem: *Ages*, an Invention for Radio by Bruno Maderna and Giorgio Pressburger." In *Prix Italia*, 261–68. Edited by Angela Ida de Benedictis and Maria Maddalena Novati. Milan: die Schachtel and Rai Trade, 2012.

Vogel, Stephen. "Sensation of Tone, Perception of Sound, and Empiricism: Helmholtz's Physiological Acoustics." In *Hermann von Helmholtz and the Foundations of Nineteenth Century Science*, 259–87. Edited by David Cahan. Berkeley: University of California Press, 1993.

Volmar, Axel. "Listening to the Cold War: The Nuclear Test Ban Negotiations, Seismology, and Psychoacoustics, 1958–1963." *Osiris* 28/1 (January 2013): 80–102.

———. "Psychoakustik und Signalanalyse: Zur Ökologisierung und Metaphorisierung des Hörens seit dem Zweiten Weltkrieg." In *Wissensgeschichte des Hörens in der Moderne*, 65–96. Edited by Netzwerk *Hör-Wissen im Wandel*. Berlin: de Gruyter, 2017.

Wannamaker, Robert. "Mathematics and Design in the Music of Iannis Xenakis." In *Xenakis Matters*, 127–41. Edited by Sharon Kanach. No. 4 of The Iannis Xenakis Series. New York: Pendragon Press, 2012.

Wapnewski, Peter. "1945: Wie die Anfang anfing." In *"Stunde Null"—zur Musik um 1945*, 13–27. Edited by Volker Scherliess. Kassel, Germany: Bärenreiter, 2014.

Weaver, Jennifer. "Theorizing Atonality: Herbert Eimert's and Jefim Golyscheff's Contributions to Composing with Twelve Tones." PhD dissertation, University of North Texas, 2014.

Wehinger, Rainer. *Ligeti-Artikulation: An Aural Score*. Mainz: Schott, 1994.

Weisstein, E. W. "Arithmetic Series." *MathWorld*—A Wolfram Web Resource, http://mathworld.wolfram.com/ArithmeticSeries.html (accessed October 9, 2017).

Whittall, Arnold. *Serialism*. Cambridge: Cambridge University Press, 2001.

Wierenga, Stephen Red. "Searching for Sounds: Instrumental Agency and Modularity in Electroacoustic Improvisation." PhD dissertation, City University of New York, 2016.

Wiesel, Elie. *From the Kingdom of Memory: Reminiscences*. New York: Summit Books, 1990.

Wiesen, Jonathan S. *West German Industry and the Challenge of the Nazi Past, 1945–1955*. Chapel Hill, NC: University of North Caroline Press, 2001.

Williams, Sean. "Stockhausen Meets King Tubby's: The Stepped Filter and Its Influence as a Musical Instrument on Two Different Styles of Music." In *Material Culture and Electronic Sound*, 163–88. Edited by Frode Weium and Tim Boon. Artefacts: Studies in the History of Science and Technology, vol. 8. Washington DC: Smithsonian Institution Scholarly Press, 2013.

———. "Interpretation and Performance Practice in Realizing Stockhausen's *Studie II*." *Journal of the Royal Music Association* 141/2 (2016): 445–81.

———. "Technical Influence and Physical Constraint in the Realization of *Gesang der Jünglinge*." Paper presented at Tracking the Creative Process in Music, IRCAM, October 9, 2015. Video of lecture available at http://medias.ircam.fr/xe7eafe (accessed July 19, 2017).

Wilson, Charles. "György Ligeti and the Rhetoric of Autonomy." *twentieth-century music* 1/1 (March 2004): 5–28.

Winthrop-Young, Geoffrey. "Drill and Distraction in the Yellow Submarine: On the Dominance of War in Friedrich Kittler's Media Theory." *Critical Inquiry* 28/4 (Summer 2002): 825–54.

Wittje, Roland. "The Electrical Imagination: Sound Analogies, Equivalent Circuits, and the Rise of Electroacoustics, 1863–1939." *Osiris* 28/1 (January 2013): 40–63.

———. *The Age of Electroacoustics: Transforming Science and Sound.* Cambridge, MA: MIT Press, 2016.

Wlodarski, Amy Lynn. *Musical Witness and Holocaust Representation.* Cambridge: Cambridge University Press, 2015.

Wolf, René. *The Undivided Sky: The Holocaust on East and West German Radio in the 1960s.* New York: Palgrave Macmillan, 2010.

Woolgar, Steven. "Some Remarks About Positivism: A Reply to Collins and Yearley." In *Science as Practice and Culture,* 327–42. Edited by Andrew Pickering. Chicago and London: University of Chicago Press, 1992.

Yaffé, John. "An Interview With Composer Earle Brown." *Contemporary Music Review* 26/3–4 (June-August 2007): 289–310.

Young, James E. *Writing and Rewriting the Holocaust: Narrative and the Consequences of Interpretation.* Bloomington: Indiana University Press, 1988.

———. *The Texture of Memory: Holocaust Memorials and Meaning.* Revised edition. New Haven, CT: Yale University Press, 1994.

———. *At Memory's Edge: After-Images of the Holocaust in Contemporary Art and Architecture.* New Haven, CT: Yale University Press, 2002.

Young, Miriama. *Singing the Body Electric: The Human Voice and Sound Technology.* New York: Ashgate and Routledge, 2015.

Zak, Albin. *Poetics of Rock: Cutting Tracks, Making Records.* Berkeley: University of California Press, 2001.

Zattra, Laura. "The Identity of the Work: Agents and Processes of Elecroacoustic Music." *Organised Sound* 11/2 (August 2006): 113–18.

———. "Les Origines du Nom de RIM (Realisateur en Informatique Musicale)." Actes des *Journées d'Informatique Musicale* (JIM 2013), Saint-Denis (2013): 113–20.

———. "Collaboration in Computer Music. An Analysis of the Role Played by Musical Assistants Obtained Through Semi-Structured Interviews." Paper presented at Tracking the Creative Process in Music, IRCAM, October 9, 2015. Video of lecture available at http://medias.ircam.fr/xb2f81c (accessed 26 September 2017).

———. "Collaborating on Composition: The Role of the Musical Assistant at IRCAM, CCRMA and CSC." In *Live Electronic Music: Composition, Performance, Study,* 59–80. Edited by Friedmann Sallis, Valentina Bartolani, Jan Burle, and Laura Zattra. New York: Routledge, 2017.

Zattra, Laura and Nicholas Donin. "A Questionnaire-Based Investigation of the Skills and Roles of Computer Music Designers." *Musicae Scientiae* 20/3 (September 2016): 436–56.

Zauberhafte Klangmaschinen: Von Sprechmaschine bis zur Soundkarte. Edited by IMA Institut für Medienarchäologie. Mainz: Schott, 2008.

INDEX

Figures are indicated by an italic *f* following the page number

Beatles, The: *Revolver,* 198; *Sgt. Pepper's Lonely Hearts Club Band,* 198

Beethoven, Ludwig van: *Moonlight Sonata,* 11

Bell Lab(oratorie)s, 168, 196; and code-breaking, 128; and deafness, 180, 236n65; and encryption, 175; and information theory, 20, 110; and Jakobson, 179; and Meyer-Eppler, 25, 114; and phonetics, 169; and Stockhausen, 87; and the Vocoder, 12, 21, 25, 169–70, 173, 179

Benjamin, Walter: on Klee's *Angelus Novus,* 138, 228n133

Berberian, Cathy, 16–18, 187–93; and *Aria* (Cage), 189–91; and Cage, 189–91; and *Dimensioni II* (Maderna), 187, 237n86; as "domesticator," 192; and Eco, 178; on the electronic studio, 185; and *Fontana Mix* (Cage), 189–90, 238n101; and Joyce's work, 178; *Stripsody,* 191; and *Thema (Omaggio a Joyce)* (Berio/Berberian), 184–89; *Visage,* 187; "vocal mimesis," 191

Berio, Luciano: and The Beatles, 198; and Berberian, 178, 184–85, 189; on the Darmstadt Summer Courses, 5; and Eco, 178; on the electronic studio, 185; and *Hörspiel,* 37; *Incontri Musicali,* 95; and Joyce's work, 178; and montaging, 189; "Palace of United Nations of Music," 164f; and Pousseur, 145, 149; on the RAI and its quirky equipment, 146, 147f; on statistical and probabilistic techniques, 110; on Stockhausen's excitement about Lietti's amplitude selector, 147; *Thema (Omaggio a Joyce)* (Berio/Berberian), 168, 184–89; on the use of electronic music to explore acoustic structures, 185; and the WDR, 7

Beyer, Robert, 25–26; aesthetic differences with Eimert, 25–26; borrowing from Schütz, 16; on the history of electronic music, 26; and Meyer-Eppler, 25; *Klang im unbegrenzten Raum,* 32, 40–46; *Klangstudie II,* 32, 40–46; sound effects and radio plays, 25–26; on technical knowledge, 29; and timbre, 27–29

Bijsterveld, Karin: on the sounds of the Futurist and Bruitist movements, 11

Bletchley Park: and "Delilah," 175; and the "domestic army," 128; and Turing, 113

Bode, Harald, 169; and Meyer-Eppler, 25, 32. *See also* Melochord

Boehmer, Konrad: on Koenig's quasi-aleatoric process, 126, 226n86

Borges, Jorge Luis: and Kagel, 171

Born, Georgina: on the value of studio technicians, 16

Boulez, Pierre, 30: on aesthetic freedom, 50; "Alea," 51, 65, 156–57; and Brown, 157; on Cage's aleatory durations, 65; on Cage's prepared piano, 55–56; on chance operation, 51; *Domaine Musical,* 95; and Eimert, 53; and Kagel, 171; on mobile complexity, 152; on performer-centered indeterminacy, 155–56; relationship with Cage, 49–51; and Schaeffer's Paris studio, 38; on Stockhausen's esotericism (in describing statistical form), 109; *Structures,* 115, 143; as target for Cage, 49; *Troisième Sonate,* 70, 150, 155–58; unfinished works, 231n65

boundary work, 106–7

British Broadcasting Corporation (BBC), 6, 13, 17, 37–38, 63; Radiophonic Workshop, 13, 37–38

Brown, Earle, 157–65; and the Barron (Louis and Bebe) studio, 158, 161; and Capital Records, 158; on collaboration and friendship, 163–65; on *Finnegans Wake* (Joyce), 163; and graphic scores, 159–62; on his own music (as mosaic), 161; at *Musiktage,* 1954, 60; on non-musician/composer connections, 63. Works: *Folio and Four Systems,* 149, 158, 159–62; *Octet I,* 158–59; *Pentathis,* 158; *Twenty-Five Pages,* 158, 160

Buchla, Don, 19, 196, 239n4

Busoni, Ferruccio, 26, 28

Bussotti, Sylvano: and Brown, 158; relationship with Metzger, 17

Byron, Lord: *Kain,* 37

Cage, John: 1958 lectures in Darmstadt, 49, 139, 150; and the Barron (Louis and Bebe) studio, 64, 158, 189; and Berberian, 189–91; and Brown, 158–59; as (underground) celebrity, 58–63; on chance operations, 50; and duration,

Emerson, Lake & Palmer, 198
entropy, 132

Feldman, Morton: *Intersections,* 151, 158–59;
 at *Musiktage,* 1954, 60
filters: Berio and, 184; Lietti and, 19,
 145–47, 189; Ligeti and, 143; and
 the Melochord, 32, 46, 58; mouths as,
 181–82, 188; Pousseur and, 147–48;
 Stockhausen and, 85, 126; and the
 Trautonium, 169, 180; and the Vocoder/
 Voder, 175, 184–85, 188. *See also*
 Atmosphères (Ligeti); subtractive synthesis
First Construction (in Metal) (Cage), 53,
 65–67, 69
fixity: of recorded indeterminate works, 149,
 238n103
Fleischhauer, Rainer: "Project for 200,000
 Inhabitants," 197–98
Fletcher, Harvey (Bell Labs), 169
Fluxus, 198
Fokker, Adriaan: and boundary work,
 107; on Stockhausen's ". . . how time
 passes . . . ," 106
Folio and Four Systems (Brown), 149,
 158, 159–62
Fontana Mix (Cage), 168, 189–90, 238n101
Fourier, Joseph: Fourier analysis, 172; on
 sound perception, 81
freedom: aesthetic (Boulez), 50; and
 Feldman, 151; from "freedom" (Cage),
 50; and the performer, 151, 155–56, 161
Fritzsche, Peter: on the Nazis as
 "modernists," 11–12
Futurists, 10–11

Galerie 22, 198
Galison, Peter: on the postwar
 construction, 13; on postwar physics and
 collaboration, 21
Gaussian distribution functions, 130,
 132, 172
Genzmer, Harald: and the Trautonium, 11
Gesang der Jünglinge (Stockhausen), 9, 85,
 90–91, 121, 125–27, 132–33, 136,
 141, 150, 152, 167, 170, 172, 184,
 187–88, 193
Gibson, Benoît: on Xenakis's compositional
 method, 227n123
Gieryn, Thomas: on boundary work, 106

Glock, William: and Brown, 63
Glockenspiel (Eimert), 56–58
Goebbels, Joseph, 4; and the
 Trautonium, 11
Goeyvaerts, Karel: on Cage's prepared
 piano, 55; on collaboration at the
 Darmstadt Summer Courses, 75;
 Composition No. 4, 78–79; *Composition
 No. 5,* 79–80; departure from music,
 103; and Schaeffer's Paris studio, 38;
 and serialism/structure, 78–79; stipends
 paid to, 61–62; and Stockhausen, 78–80,
 87, 217n26
Goldman, Jonathan: on midcentury avant-
 garde composers, 16
Goléa, Antoine, 30; and Xenakis, 135
Gombrowicz, Witold: and Kagel, 171
graphic scores, 141; Boulez on, 155; of
 Brown, 157, 159–62
Grateful Dead, The, 198
Gredinger, Paul: departure from music,
 103; *Formanten I and II,* 82–83; and
 the *Handapparat* library, 63; and
 Stockhausen, 87
Grunert, Ernst, 30
Gruppen (Stockhausen), 117–18, 130,
 150, 152

Hafner, Erhard, 36
Halle, Morris, 145, 176–78. *See also*
 Jakobson, Roman
Hambraeus, Bengt: and the *Handapparat*
 library, 63
Harbison, William: on *Troisième Sonate*
 (Boulez), 155
Harrison, Lou: and Tudor, 70
Hartmann, Hans: and Herbert
 Eimert, 23–24
Hartmann, Karl: *Musica Viva,* 95
Heike, Georg: research post-1960, 196–97;
 on information theory and music, 105
Helffer, Claude: on performing *Constellation-
 Miroir* (Boulez), 157
Helión, Jean: and Cage, 50
Helmholtz, Hermann von, 77–78, 82, 85,
 101–2, 168–69, 216n15
Helms, Hans G.: *Fa:m' Ahniesgwow,* 187;
 Joyce reading group, 178, 187, 198,
 229n18; and Maderna's *Dimensioni II,*
 187, 178

Minimalism, 199

Mobile (Pousseur), 150, 153–56

mobile/open form, 141–42, 150–165; literary, 157

modernism, aesthetic: of the Nazis, 11–12; re-exposure to, 5–6; as signaling political progressiveness, 3

Modulor, the (Le Courbusier): for Gredinger, 82

Moles, Abraham André, 111, 130; communication channel, 112; on predictability, 130; *Théorie de l'information et perception esthétique*, 111

Moog, Robert, 19, 196

Morgenröte (WDR's "piece zero") (Schütz), 16, 40–47

Morse code, 119, 128

mouth: as a filter, 181–82, 188

Musik der Zeit, 6–7, 94–95; 1954 concert, 52, 56, 57*f*, 59–62, 76, 92; 1956 concert, 10*f*, 93*f*, 125

musique concrète, 9, 38–39, 48, 55–58, 67; and *Dimensioni II* (Maderna), 187; and Kagel, 171; and "Project of Music for Magnetic Tape," 158; as "ungraspable and abstract" but "compelling in effect" (Stuckenschmidt), 8, and Xenakis, 130, 132, 135

Muzak corporation: and the Vocoder, 176

Nazis: embrace of some early electronic instruments, 11–12; and encryption, 175; and *Hörspiel*, 37; musical tastes of, 3–4; and weakness/laziness in code-sending protocol, 128. *See also* denazification

Neues Musikfest Köln (Cologne New Music Festival), 8–9

New Complexity, 199

Nicholls, David: on Cage's graphic notation in *Fontana Mix*, 190

Nilsson, Bo: and Tudor, 70

Nono, Luigi, 78; early electronic experiments with Meyer-Eppler, 30; on Eimert's leadership style, 92; *Incontri Musicali*, 95

Nuremburg trials, 4

NWDR (*Nordwestdeutsche Rundfunk*), 8, 23, 32–33, 37, 170. *See also* WDR (*Westdeutscher Rundfunk*)

Ohm, Georg Simon: on sound perception, 81–82, 101–2

Oliveros, Pauline, 196; on Buchla, 238n4

Ondes Martenot, 181

open form. *See* mobile/open form

Orff, Carl: and Nazi musical taste, 3

Osmond-Smith, David: on Berberian (as the RAI's "tenth oscillator"), 188; on the reception of *Dimensioni II* (Maderna) at Darmstadt 1960, 237n86

Paik, Nam Jun, 17

Patteson, Thomas: on "steel romanticism," 11

perception, 114–15, 116; vs. cognition, 114

Perle, George: on the content of *Die Reihe* Vol. III, 106

Peyser, Joan: on Cage and Tudor as treated like "a couple of clowns," 60

Philips Pavilion, 131–32

phonetics, 179, 191–93; and Bell Labs, 87, 169, 179; experimental, 20–21, 24, 113, 179, 195–96, 232n4; and Helms, 187; Kagel and, 172, 181–87; Maderna and, 178; Meyer-Eppler and, 24–25, 85, 87, 103–4, 107, 113, 116, 139, 142, 144–45, 148, 167–72, 181; phonology, 116*t*, 176–79; in Schwitters's *Ursonate*, 144; and Stockhausen, 85–87, 167, 170. *See also* International Phonetic Alphabet (IPA); Jakobson, Roman; speech synthesis

Pickering, Andrew: "mangle of practice," 13–15, 104

Pièce électronique No. 3 (Ligeti), 96–104, 132

Piekut, Benjamin, 16: on agency, 15

Pierce, John (Bell Labs), 196: on information theory, 110

pitch-residue theory, 82, 84, 90. *See also* combination tones

Pithoprakta (Xenakis), 129–31, 135

Poisson's formula, 133

Pousseur, Henri, 47; "ideal tone form" of complex sounds, 148; on inner partials as "statistic phenomena," 110; and Meyer-Eppler, 84–85; *Mobile*, 150, 153–56; and mobile form, 149; and the public as potential musicians, 149; *Scambi*, 145–54; as a schoolteacher, 83, 103; *Seismogramme I*, 90–91, 148; stipends paid to, 61–62; on Stockhausen's work, 81; temporal proportions as a desirable escape from serial music's interest in periodicity, 155; "Theory and Practice in the Newest Music" (1958 Darmstadt presentation), 152; and the WDR, 7

pragmatism: in the compositions of Koenig and Stockhausen, 90; in labor division, 30, 47; in the compositions of Pousseur, 149

prediction, 113–14, 128–32; of bombshell trajectory, 113, 133; and cryptography, 128–29; in music, 129–30, 134, 147

prepared piano, 55–58; and Boulez, 55–56; and Cage, 50, 52–54; and Eimert, 56, 72; and Schaeffer, 55–56, 72; and Stockhausen, 55

Pritchett, James: on Cage's graphic notation in *Fontana Mix*, 190

probability: 105; and code-breaking, 113, 128–29; and Berio, 110; and Koenig, 133–34; and Ligeti, 144; and Pousseur, 110; and Xenakis, 129–35, 230n43

Protschka, Josef: as boy soprano in *Gesang der Jünglinge*, 125, 167

radio: and Cage, 51–52; as the key medium for cultural offerings in West Germany, 6; and Ligeti, 96; objective of (Tomek), 6; *Radiodiffusion Française*, 8, 38, 54; Radio Free Europe (RFE), 6; Radio in the American Sector (RIAS), 6; *Südwestfunk* (SWF), 51; Voice of America (VOA), 6. *See also* British Broadcasting Corporation (BBC); *Hörspiel* (radio play); NWDR (*Nordwestdeutsche Rundfunk*); RAI (*Radio Audizioni Italiane*); WDR (*Westdeutscher Rundfunk*)

Rad Lab (MIT), 113, 196

RAI (*Radio Audizioni Italiane*), 168, 195; Berberian and, 16, 178, 188–89; Berio on, 146, 147f; *Cage* and, 163, 189–90; as heterogeneous, 13; and *Hörspiel*, 37; and Pousseur, 145, 149; and subtractive synthesis, 146. *See also* Lietti, Alfredo

Rebner, Wolfgang, 51

reclamation, 2–3, 13, 19, 105–38; cultural, 19–22, 107; imperfect, 193; and Meyer-Eppler, 25, 113–15, 176; and the narrative history of electronic music, 28

repetition: and audience reception, 44; in *Klangstudie II*, 46; and predictability, 128–29, 133

Risset, Jean Claude, 196

Rogers, Tara: on deep-seated heteronormativity in the figure of composer or technological innovator, 18; on "synthesis," 199

Rosbaud, Hans: and Brown, 63; and Xenakis, 135

"rubble films," 4

Russolo, Luigi, 10

Sala, Oskar: and Meyer-Eppler, 25; and the Trautonium, 11

sampling theorem, the, 119–20, 132–33, 135. *See also* information theory; Shannon, Claude

San Francisco Tape Music Center: as heterogeneous, 13, 17

Saussure, Ferdinand de: *Cours de linguistique générale*, 178

Scambi (Pousseur), 145–54

Schaeffer, Pierre: *Concert de bruits*, 9, 38; leadership style of, 92; *musique concrète*, 38–39, 55, 211n77; on prepared piano, 55; reception of *Orphée 53*, 9; and Stockhausen, 38; and the WDR, 8, 13, 30. *See also musique concrète*

Scherchen, Hermann, 95, 130; and Schaeffer's Paris studio, 38; and Xenakis, 135

Schnebel, Dieter: *für Stimmen*, 167; and *Hörspiel*, 37

Schoenberg, Arnold, 51–52: *Klangfarbenmelodie*, 27–28, 83; and Nazi musical taste, 3; and the path to electronic music, 26–28; *A Survivor From Warsaw*, 5; and timbre, 27–28

Schouten, J. A., 82

Schütz, Heinz, 1, 29, 36f; and *Hörspiel*, 40; *Morgenröte* (WDR's "piece zero"), 16, 40–47

Schwitters, Kurt, 10; *Ursonate*, 144

Scratch Orchestra, 198

Seebeck, August: on sound perception, 81–82, 101–2

Sender, Ramon, 196

serialism, 75–76, 78, 116: and Eimert, 35; and the electronic music studio,

Wiener, Norbert, 176; and cybernetics, 20, 107–8, 176; *The Human Use of Human Beings,* 107; and predictability, 113, 130. *See also* cybernetics

Wiesel, Elie, 202n17

Wilkinson, Marc: and Pousseur's *Scambi,* 149

Williams, Sean: reconstructive work of, 126

Wilson, Charles: on midcentury avant-garde composers, 16

Wolpe, Stefan: and Tudor, 70

women: body of, 191–92; code-breakers, 128; composers and technicians, 17–19; and the domestication of technology, 191–92; "Voderettes," 173–75, 188, 191–92

Wonder, Stevie, 198

World's Fair: 1939, 173–75; 1958, 131

Xenakis, Iannis, 129–36; *Achorripsis,* 133; compositional method of (Gibson), 227n123; on continuity–discontinuity, 132; and Le Courbusier: 131–32, 227n108; *Metastasis,* 129, 131–32, 135; as an outsider to the WDR-Cologne scene, 135–36; *Pithoprakta,* 129–31, 135; probability theory and music, 130–31, 133–35; on serial music, 132; stochastic music, 129–30; and Stockhausen, 136

Zappa, Frank, 198

Zhdanov, Andrei: Socialist Realist doctrines of, 3

Zoff, Otto, 51

Zuccheri, Marino: and authorship (Eco), 238n101; on Berberian (as the RAI's "tenth oscillator"), 188; and *Fontana Mix* (Cage), 189, 238n101; and *Thema (Omaggio a Joyce)* (Berio), 189

CPSIA information can be obtained
at www.ICGtesting.com
Printed in the USA
BVHW080252051219
565684BV00003B/13/P